Public Characters

Public Characters

THE POLITICS OF REPUTATION AND BLAME

**JAMES M. JASPER, MICHAEL P. YOUNG,
AND ELKE ZUERN**

OXFORD
UNIVERSITY PRESS

OXFORD
UNIVERSITY PRESS

Oxford University Press is a department of the University of Oxford. It furthers
the University's objective of excellence in research, scholarship, and education
by publishing worldwide. Oxford is a registered trade mark of Oxford University
Press in the UK and certain other countries.

Published in the United States of America by Oxford University Press
198 Madison Avenue, New York, NY 10016, United States of America.

CIP data is on file at the Library of Congress
ISBN 978–0–19–005004–7

9 8 7 6 5 4 3 2 1

Printed by Sheridan Books, Inc., United States of America

For Christine Williams, Suzette Hanser, and Sumedha Senanayake

CONTENTS

Conclusion: The Politics of Blame

SOURCES FOR FIGURES

If not otherwise credited, photos are by James M. Jasper.

PREFACE

Donald J. Trump won the U.S. presidency in 2016 because he was a master of character work, able to sum up opponents in a pithy epithet that made them appear weak or immoral. Zeroing in on competitors' flaws, he captured them in labels that tapped into widespread misgivings among voters. He both enhanced existing doubts and created further ones. He continued his ceaseless character work as president. Twitter diplomacy led "Little Rocket Man" to meet with a "mentally deranged U.S. dotard" to discuss the denuclearization of the Korean peninsula. This kind of character work is a regular part of politics, even if it did not denuclearize the Koreas.

Trump attracted 63 million votes by tapping into venerable themes in his country's history: foreigners threatening Americans with violence; a swamp of professional politicians and bureaucrats in control of D.C.; losers at the bottom of the social hierarchy feeding off a corrupt federal government; hardworking white men scorned by their own elected representatives. Heroic outsiders—especially generals and business leaders—who can ride in to set things right, are the classic heroes of American populism. The idle rich at the top, the idle poor at the bottom: these are the classic villains of American populism.

They are also traditional tropes of what we call character work: villains and their minions, the victims they prey upon, the heroes we hope will save them and us. These simplified protagonists have faded from serious literature, but they are alive and well in politics, popular culture, the visual arts, and international relations. Trump succeeded primarily because he mastered a new medium—Twitter—for conveying ancient rhetorical symbols. In a single phrase each, he summed up common doubts about his rivals' public characters: Little Rubio was too weak; Jeb was too passive; Hillary was corrupt. His caricatures were extreme: Obama was the worst president in history, Hillary the worst secretary of state. Amazingly, a label or two can define a person more effectively than a long biography of service, arguments, and actions. We need to understand how Trump's evil genius for epithets made him president.

My own interest in character rhetoric began under the presidency of George W. Bush, who at the time I considered the worst president in U.S. history. During the buildup to Bush's invasion of Iraq, I was doing occasional standup comedy. On the evening of February 15, 2003, the day of large protests around the world, and only a month before the attack, my routine at the Gotham Comedy Club was about "good enough" policies. Part of it went like this:

"Do we really have to INVADE Iraq? Saddam is in his seventies: how much longer will he be around? It's like going to war against your own grandfather. Are we really gonna run up a record federal deficit, ruin our economy, bankrupt social security, just to get rid of him?

"Wouldn't it be good enough just to confuse him a little bit: we could all go and take out magazine subscriptions in his name. Sign him up for *Playboy, Good Housekeeping, Field and Stream*. Distract him with a hobby.

"Then we could send in some spies to run around the palace and hide his reading glasses. See if he's really reading the articles in *Playboy*.

"While they're at it, they could saw half an inch off one of the legs on his walker."

"The good-enough standard could save a lot of lives."

Saddam Hussein was not powerful enough to take seriously as a real villain. He was a buffoon, a goofy old man who was no longer worth the bother. A joke, not a threat; a minion, not a villain. Character work like this occurs in many venues, comedy clubs ranking among the least influential. Impressions are formed out of news reports, jokes, gossip, personal conversations, books, and photographs. On February 15, 2003, the audience at the Gotham, in the middle of liberal Manhattan, did not wish to hear that Saddam was no threat. The war drums were beating. (My snide comments about the U.S. military did not help.) A few months later I gave up comedy and went back to sociology. Nothing funny there.

Character work is a tool that can be used, like all tools, for bad as well as good purposes. People can be inspired to great feats of courage and morality by their heroes; they can show exquisite compassion for victims, even remote victims. They can also harm those who have been portrayed as villains. Public characters—the tropes and reputations created by character work—are powerful because they tell us what emotions we are supposed to feel: admiration for heroes, pity for victims, fear and loathing of villains, ridicule and contempt for minions.

Ever since democracy was invented in ancient Greece, people have worried that emotions might crowd out rational decisions, that the anger and fear of the moment might lead to choices that the demos might later regret. We call this the great rhetorical anxiety: that rhetoric can be used to arouse audiences to bad acts as easily as to good ones. Plato hated rhetoric as a result. Aristotle had a more complex response: we need to study rhetoric in order to understand how it works, whether or not we always like the way it is used. Only if we understand it can we distinguish proper from wretched uses of oratory, including one of its central products, characters. Characters are as inevitable as they are entertaining.

One possible implication of character work is that, as Heraclitus put it, character is destiny: all actions and outcomes can be attributed to character traits. In politics, this amounts to a great-person theory of history, in which a few heroic leaders inspire their followers and make decisions that by themselves carry a country to greatness or failure. The ultimate form of this essentialism was fascist ideology, in which one man embodied the will of a people so completely that democratic elections and accountability were no longer needed.

In other words, the construction of characters is usually intended to persuade audiences to grant more power to those portrayed as heroes, less to those portrayed as villains or minions. We can trust heroes to do the right thing, which is typically to protect some weaker group of victims or potential victims. This can be dangerous stuff. As Aristotle argued, we need to understand it in order to combat its perils. Like all tools, character work can be put to good or bad uses, applied fairly or unfairly.

We have written this book on characters precisely because they can be so dangerous, because democracies need to understand where characters come from in order to keep their influence within proper bounds. We need to preserve public characters for the good effects they can have, and save ourselves from the bad. We need them for love and admiration, not contempt and hate. But the same elements go into both kinds of characters. Human life is complex and tragic, with good and bad tightly entwined.

Trump and I share a delight in ridicule, perhaps the most powerful tool in the arsenal of character work. He was running for president and I was trying to make a bunch of drunk people laugh, but we were both doing character assassination, revealing those who would present themselves as powerful, moral heroes as in fact weak, silly, petty.

My efforts to make people laugh using nothing but a microphone reignited my interest in rhetoric, which I have always perceived as a useful way to think about the role of culture in politics. It involves persuasion, audiences, interpretation, and the construction of characters. Rhetoric is a 2500-year-old tradition of studying how we actively construct our cultural meanings, often for strategic purposes.

I was able to persuade Michael Young to join me in a paper on characters. We decided that a simple table of two dimensions—strong versus weak and good versus bad—generates the main characters in political dramas: heroes, villains, victims, and minions. Not all characters fit this scheme, but a great many do. We also began to encounter complications. We discovered a third dimension in reading affect control theory, which posits strength, morality, and *activity* levels as three main dimensions that people use to evaluate situations and actors. We also puzzled over what to do about characters who mock the whole system of characters, namely clowns, who turn up in a variety of guises. We had to acknowledge that victims are not the only weak, good characters. And so on.

Once we began looking for character work, we saw it everywhere. Plenty of sociologists and political scientists describe character work without quite labeling it that. That is why we asked one of them, Elke Zuern, to join us on this project, for her expertise on the recent nations of southern Africa, where traditional hero tropes are still widely deployed in statues and museums. Nicole Doerr was also a member of the project for a while, using her knowledge of recent European movements to remind us that protestors can use humor to undermine characters as well as to build them. I took primary responsibility for crafting this text, with plentiful additions and edits from Michael and Elke. Michael also took on the task of collecting and compiling the images.

A number of people gave us helpful comments and encouragement, including Kelly Bergstrand, Roni Dorot, Gary Alan Fine, David Heise, Doug Husak, Mark Jacobs, Tod Jones, Eldad Levy, Ali Mozaffari, and Robert Zussman. At Oxford University Press James Cook was always loyal and encouraging, Emily Mackenzie cheerful and efficient, and Christina Nisha organized and professional. Katherine Eirene Ulrich was an extraordinary copy editor, suggesting numerous useful changes and no bad ones, diligently tracking down obscure grammatical distinctions, as well as offering entertaining commentary on the substance of our text. We also thank Tim McGovern for his excellent index.

James M. Jasper
Harris Park Guest House, Austin, Texas
January 20, 2018

Introduction

POLITICS AS CHARACTER WORK

You know, you have to brand people a certain way when they're your
opponents.

—*Donald Trump*

O
N DECEMBER 7, 2011, A local lawyer sent an email to Occupy
Nashville, which said in part: "I represent an elderly lady on social security who purchased a home with her two daughters back
in the 90s. Long story short, the daughters left their mom high and dry,
moved out and do not pay their share of the mortgage. Neither of them
have any money and are currently working part time jobs. My client's only
income is social security disability, which is not nearly enough to pay her
mortgage. Her lender is Chase, notorious for its foreclosure behavior. The
home is in foreclosure and the bank is set to sell the home in two weeks."
The lawyer went on to ask if Occupy Nashville were interested in helping,
and they agreed to launch an effort to negotiate with Chase.

In this pithy plea we have an elderly, female victim, whose problems
began with her daughters' irresponsibility rather than with her purchase of
a house that she could not afford on her own income (which was Chase's
alternative story). The daughters are minions: mildly culpable but not the
main villain, for which Chase—a big, bad bank—is firmly cast. To complete the cast of public characters, the lawyer is asking for Occupy's heroic aid in saving the victim from the villain. These are public characters,
constructed to arouse moral feelings of pride, pity, and anger.

Sometimes it seems as if heroes and villains are dead, as if the modern
world has ceased to view politics—or life itself—as a series of conflicts
between good and evil. We seem to be left only with victims, and victims

Public Characters. James M. Jasper, Michael P. Young, and Elke Zuern, Oxford University
Press (2020) © Oxford University Press.
DOI: 10.1093/oso/9780190050047.001.0001

of disaster or neglect rather than victims of outright evil. The politics of what is normal or abnormal seems to have displaced what is good or bad, who is strong and who is weak. A generation of researchers into the cultural dimensions of politics—what politics actually means to people—have ignored the great characters of the past in favor of frames, heuristics, codes, and identities. They even study narratives without noticing the characters in them.

We think they are making a mistake. Politics involves the deployment of material resources, but also the mobilization of favorable impressions, emotions, and moral sentiments. Politics is about the pursuit of power, but one central way to get power is to persuade others that you are competent, courageous, and benevolent while your opponents are none of these. Persuasion is the heart of both protest movements and electoral politics, with impression management as its goal. Perhaps more than ever in politics—in the era of television, Twitter, and Facebook—groups and individuals battle over their reputations, over what others will think and feel about them.

Gary Alan Fine defines reputation as "a socially recognized persona: an organizing principle by which the actions of a person (or an organization that is thought of as a person) can be linked together."[1] Characters are a salient subset of reputations. Societies build their solidarity—and policies—out of admiration for heroes but also outrage over villains. But "societies" never fully agree about basic moral values. Fine discusses the "character contests" found in a variety of strategic arenas, especially when public decisions are personalized: an individual embodies a policy or belief, so that support for policies rises and falls with that person's reputation. Character work consists of more than simple claims of fact; it is designed to accomplish various actions in political arenas.

One of the surest ways to solidify a player's reputation—whether for good or bad, for strength or weakness—is to form it into a familiar character: *a recurrent, simplified package of intentions, capacities, and actions that we expect to fit together.* In public characters our imaginations fuse cognitive understandings, moral judgments, emotional responses, and expectations for behavior. We perceive characters in individuals, primarily, but also in our anthropomorphic projections onto animals, deities, groups, formal organizations, and nations. We "personify" all of these, treating them as if they were individual people. Characters are familiar tropes because they are conveyed by diverse media, both fictional and nonfictional.

Characters are irresistible. We like to imagine them—and easily do imagine them—doing things in the world, having intentions, reacting emotionally, adjusting, scheming, and making decisions. This is why generations of readers have thrown themselves into novels, often with a passion rare in other spheres of life. Characters are close approximations of real human beings, only more compelling and more familiar. Narratives, rhetoric, ideologies, frames, and the like shape our understandings largely through the characters they create. When we see photos, caricatures, and other visual images, we can sum up a character in a split second. One or two words in a tweet can transform a person into a character.

The philosopher Alasdair MacIntyre recognizes that characters embody morals, as "those social roles which provide a culture with its moral definitions." He contrasts them with other roles that are tied more closely to occupations and organizations, such as dentists and garbage collectors. As contemporary examples of characters, he suggests the Rich Aesthete, the Manager, and the Therapist. These characters provide moral ideals— whether we embrace or denounce them. Characters represent something that people *are*, in contrast to other roles that they simply *do*. "The character morally legitimates a mode of existence."[2] By telling audiences who and what to admire or pity, fear or reject, characters help us lead our moral, emotional, and cognitive lives.

The characters that interest us are more general than MacIntyre's. We distinguish them along two basic dimensions (Table 1.1). The first is moral quality as shown through good or bad intentions and impulses. Not only friends and foes are created in this way, so are threats to public safety and morality. The second dimension concerns power, separating those who are relatively weak or ineffectual from those who can get things done (through bodily strength, intelligence, resources, sheer numbers, or other forms of strength). We will consider other dimensions later, but these two remain primary.

These two dimensions, continua in fact, generate the most familiar characters. Heroes are strong and well intentioned, even when it takes some time to find or motivate them. Villains are malevolent and strong enough to menace others, lending some urgency to a situation. We feel warmly enough toward victims to want to aid them, since they are too

TABLE 1.1 Main Characters

	STRONG	WEAK
GOOD	Heroes	Victims
BAD	Villains	Minions

weak to save themselves. We are contemptuous of minions, who are malevolent but too weak to be much of a threat until they hook up with a villain; they remain a cowardly mob until a demagogue whips them up. Martyrs and saints, each a special combination of victim and hero, remind us that heroes often suffer to save us, even to the point of death (see Table 1.2). And especially in the modern world we admire many heroes of endurance, often women, whose triumph is simply to survive.

Just as villains attract assistants in the form of minions, so heroes attract their own helpers: sidekicks who accompany them, supporters who fund them and cheer them on. They are not strong enough to be heroes themselves, but some of the hero's virtues rub off on them. They can feel her pride, exalt in her power, and embrace her confidence. They could be in the same table cell as victims, but they are not passive objects of other players' actions; they could also be in the upper left space with heroes, as they participate in the hero's active projects to protect others. They have a greater degree of agency than victims do.[3]

This intriguing third dimension, activity level, helps distinguish some interesting character subtypes in addition to sidekicks and victims. If morality is about a player's ends and strength is about her ability to achieve them, activity is related to whether or not she follows through on her intentions. Part of this dimension is simply how busy a character is, and part is about whether she *initiates* action or *responds* to the initiatives of others. Good characters rarely initiate strategic engagements; they mind

TABLE 1.2 Main Characters with Related Minor Characters

	STRONG	WEAK
BENEVOLENT	Heroes	Victims
	Martyrs and Saints (start in the cell across as victims)	Good Clowns
		Sympathetic Bystanders
	Judges, Donors	Followers, Supporters
	Converts (start in the cell below as villains)	Sidekicks
	Friends and Allies	
MALEVOLENT	Villains	Minions
	Outside Agitators	Scoundrels
	Traitors (start in the cell above as heroes)	Bad Clowns
		Losers
	Foes	Cowardly Bystanders

their own business. The best heroes are sleeping giants who must be roused—often reluctantly—to action.

Characters are caricatures, oversimplifications that exaggerate certain features of a player and disregard many of its complexities. They offer essences. We adopt them as schemas because they are familiar, because we have used them successfully in the past. Those in the business of characterization exaggerate their heroes' goodness, their opponents' viciousness. Victims become more pure and innocent, minions even more ridiculous and ineffectual. There are exceptions and limitations, of course: the hero with a flaw is often more admirable, or at least more likable, than one who is perfect. Today's human heroes are not as awe inspiring as the semi-divine heroes of myth once were. But in strategic arenas, we need to exaggerate their essential traits, even today.

We can identify with human characters. Real people can become heroes, villains, victims, and minions at different times and to different degrees. We all shape the world around us, do regrettable things to others, have vulnerabilities, and exhibit petty weaknesses such as cowardice. These are existential parts of being human. Character work hides—and is meant to hide—these complex combinations, teasing out one action or dimension to associate with an individual, making streamlined symbols out of messy flesh and blood.

We are especially prone to read intention into the actions of prominent figures: once we decided Bernie Madoff was a villain, we assumed he had always intended to bilk his investors, rather than being a schlemiel who made some mistakes and then covered them up in a cowardly way. We could not allow him to be a feckless minion or—as he insisted—a victim of circumstance. We want our characters to make moral or immoral choices, not simply reflect circumstances outside their control.

We can distinguish between *categorical characters*, who necessarily belong to one of the categories because of their essential nature, and characters whose *circumstances* have led to actions that fit one of the character types.[4] In reality, a coward can occasionally do something brave, a good person can do something monstrous. Most of the time, political rhetoric ignores circumstantial characters, or makes them appear categorical, in its effort to fix characters' "true" selves. We will see some exceptions, which threaten to disrupt the system of characters, usually through humor.

The ancient Greeks recognized that orators construct not one but two characters at the same time: that of the person they are describing and their own. If you are generous in praising others, you also appear stronger and more moral; if you ridicule someone too sharply or accuse them of a scandal, you may also be tarnished. Our own words are actions that convey our character. This authorship is sometimes hidden: we don't know who painted graffiti on a wall; we don't have a clear image of the cartoonist who lampoons a world leader. But when a politician attacks a rival, that attack can change the reputations of both. This is clearest in the case of jokes, which can rub off on the teller as well as the butt. Many comedians appear to be jerks.

Humor assaults the complacencies of character types, as it does of all cognitive systems. We considered including clowns as one of the basic public characters. But, while they play a role in assessing other characters, they are not really subject to character work themselves in the way the other characters are. When someone portrays other players as clownish, she is typically trying to make them appear to be ridiculous minions.

Nonetheless humor can be deployed rhetorically to mock another character's claims to power or goodness, challenging just how strong or how good the heroes are, finding the ridiculous in the most powerful villain, or suggesting that victims are not as innocent as they appear. Comedy can undermine the entire system of good versus bad, strong versus weak, questioning whether such essentializing characterizations are not in reality a fiction. (Of course they are, but a necessary fiction in politics.)[5] Satire in politics is as old as politics. Humor can weaken its creators or weaken their targets, and often it does both at the same time. Comedy always threatens to get out of hand and bring down an entire system of thought.

Like humor, dramatic tension can undercut the fixity of characters. Stories, especially in fiction but sometimes also in the news media, thrive on the uncertainties of suspense. Conversions, in which characters change their type, are gripping stories. Heroes who remain stolidly heroic, villains who remain predictably evil, grab less attention. We must be made to wonder if the hero will indeed act heroically, if the villain can find salvation. A plot's need for suspense is frequently at war with the establishment of dependable, predictable characters, one reason that sophisticated novelists often shun them, and narrative theorists often overlook them.

Many political players do not rate especially high or low on either dimension of our chart: they lie in the middle, neither good nor bad, strong nor weak. They are average people, or at least they see themselves—and others may see them—that way. For stigmatized groups, it is often a triumph to be seen as normal (this may require them to eradicate images of immorality or of weakness). This is often a way to avoid victimhood. American Muslims after 9/11 tried to be inconspicuous, "typical" citizens going about their business. Neither strong nor weak, and moral but not conspicuously so, they worked hard to occupy the middle of our chart, the position that most people, most of time, inhabit, avoiding the risks of character work. Character work is usually directed at public figures, not average folks, although it can also be deployed to shape group stereotypes.

Ordinary people are often the primary *audiences* for characterization efforts, the aim of which is sometimes to persuade these audiences that they belong firmly in one of the character boxes. They can be a bit heroic by contributing money to a just cause; they must join the hero, not tolerate the villain. They are under threat, or have been victimized in the past, and deserve justice. Trump won the presidency partly by appealing to white working-class men's sense of victimhood.

Most audiences are not called upon to leap into the character chart, but instead merely to identify properly the players around them. Some leaders are too good for us to identify with, or too powerful: this is why we need them, for the ways in which they are different from us. Our political choices and affiliations are shaped by our feelings about who is good or bad, strong or weak: these labels shape our actions.

The power of public characters is that we know immediately *how we are supposed to feel about them*. We admire heroes and fear villains. This is not the same as love and hate: there are unlovable heroes and lovable villains ("scoundrels"). In either case, they arouse strong emotions, just like our pity for victims or contempt for minions. The expression of these emotions gives power to morality plays, commedia dell'arte, professional wrestling, and political spectacles. We hiss and jeer, clap and cheer, playing a part in the unfolding drama. We also derive pride from the power and autonomy we associate with heroes. Compassion tends to focus on victims, although in a way that can encourage us to help transform them into heroes, or at least survivors. It is because of these feelings that simplified characters, or types, are powerful political resources, one of the "munitions of the mind," as Philip Taylor calls propaganda.[6] Professionals are well paid for the character work they perform.

Table 1.3 shows that there are always tradeoffs with characters. Each public character has both benefits and risks for the player involved. Often the characterization that helps in one strategic arena hurts in another: minions may defend themselves successfully in court proceedings but destroy their credibility as political players outside the courtroom. What this table does not show is the effects of characters on *other* players: how we can pull our group together by demonizing outsiders, or by stoking compassion for victims.

TABLE 1.3 Potential Impacts of Character Claims

	HELPFUL TO PLAYER CHARACTERIZED	DETRIMENTAL TO PLAYER CHARACTERIZED
HEROES	Admiration, confidence, pride; Others want to be on winning side	Others fear strength; Titan's Hubris (overconfidence)
VILLAINS	Can intimidate others who fear villain's strength; Less constrained by social norms	Dislike, distrust, hated by others; Internal distrust
VICTIMS	Sympathy, aid, indignation	Contempt for weakness; no reason to make an alliance
MINIONS	Escape some blame, which mostly attaches to villain	Ridicule, contempt, and dislike

Characters also display emotions themselves, and we recognize them partly through what they feel. Weak characters express fear, grief, and often shame. They weep and tremble. They are full of doubt. Strong characters are more likely to appear calm and confident, proud of their capacities and prospects. Strong and good characters are hopeful, able to see a better future that they will help create. Villains laugh cruelly, minions laugh nervously. Heroes rarely laugh.

Characters are not restricted to politics, obviously, since they first arose in myth and epic. Ever since traditional folktales and epic poems, there have been immediately recognizable characters. Such types remain central to the political stories of modern society, through which citizens try to understand the structures and events going on around them, and through which they are mobilized or frozen out of political action. These characterizations are often subtle and implicit, created through a photograph or an adjective in a supposedly "objective" news report (a "story"), but they are a central part of how we understand and act in the world around us. Narratives interest us primarily because of the characters they contain.

Not all struggles over characterization occur in narratives. It is possible to shape reputations outside of stories, for instance through direct arguments and evidence or visually through caricatures and cartoons. Characters are created out of tiny raw materials such as dress, nicknames, facial expressions, social standing in a group, manners, habits, comportment, lineage—very little of which is narrative. Whether we are reading a novel, sizing up a stranger, glancing at a political cartoon, or watching a paid advertisement on television, we look for the same signs of character in all of them. Character work imposes meaning on the world.

The neglect of characters in recent political analysis has really been the neglect of heroes, villains, and minions. In contrast, victim studies have flourished. Scholars have examined numerous social movements (especially for women's and children's rights) that have struggled to overcome the passivity of victimhood without losing broad public sympathy or legal protections. Victims demand action *because of* their weakness. Arguments calling for intervention in genocides focus on the victims to mobilize outsiders. In the aftermath of genocide and other gross human rights violations, victims work to regain their sense of agency by becoming "survivors." When scholars of the "risk society" attribute harmful events to complex technological, legal, and social systems, there are still victims, but they seem to suffer from trauma, not from evil. There are no villains who menace them or heroes to save them.[7]

Characters matter in politics because they help mobilize people and their passions. Your impressions of others are predictions of how they will treat you. You would like to find allies who are both good (well-intentioned toward you, supportive of your projects, willing to keep their promises) and strong (capable of fulfilling those promises). But you probably prefer them to be good. Jasper describes the powerful-allies dilemma: you welcome the power of strong allies (such as celebrities or politicians), but the risk is that they will use you for their own purposes rather than respecting and advancing yours.[8] Our negative characterizations also constrain our actions. If you have demonized your opponents as malevolent and unreliable, it may be hard for you to justify negotiations with them, an act of some trust. Initial diplomatic contacts between combatants are often kept secret for this reason.

We concentrate on the construction of political characters, which sometimes differ from other characters, for instance in literature or medical diagnoses (which often moralize illness and demonize the sick). Political villains must be a little more evil, victims a little more pure, in order to mobilize outrage and sympathy. In other arenas, villains can be more sympathetic, victims a bit less so. We sometimes even like villains and despise victims, ruining their potential rhetorical impact on politics.

Political players often try hard to simplify the public characters in a strategic arena, and we see this not only in contemporary conflict but also in battles over how to remember history. A country's leaders may try to stoke national pride by reducing the narrative of liberation to a few heroes, or to a heroic liberation movement, pitted against the (usually foreign) villains whom they eventually vanquished. More complicated stories—even if more accurate—dull the emotions that current leaders desire from their audiences.

Some simplification may occur over time even without active efforts, as those who actually endured a period of war or protest die off. That leaves the arena of public understandings open to those with a special interest in promoting certain characters. In France, for instance, commemorations of the liberation of Paris in 1944 have been streamlined over time, centering on the heroic General de Gaulle, with less attention to the British and American armies who carried him home. In the interest of European unity, the obvious villains of the story have also disappeared.[9] Collective memory usually highlights a small number of characters.

Although media reports of players' actions help build their reputations, the opposite causal effect may be just as strong: journalists' perceptions about a political leader constrain what they consider news. If a politician does something that reveals his "real" traits, or what we think they are, that is news. If Gary Hart, widely seen as a philanderer, sneaks off to be with Donna Rice, the media can wallow in the story for months. Once reporters had labeled Dan Quayle stupid, every little gaffe became an occasion for mockery: it was news when Quayle spelled potato with an e at the end; it was not news that an orthographically challenged aide had written "potatoe" on his cue card. Once a character trait becomes a hook for stories (a "heuristic" for reporters and the public to understand the world), it is difficult to dislodge it from media discourse. Journalists are as lazy, cognitively, as the rest of us.

Characters still matter in the modern world, but they have changed over time. Different cultures admire different aspects of character. As Nietzsche famously complained, Christian teachings tend to emphasize the moral dimension, in contrast to the ancient Greeks for whom strength was foremost. For the Greeks there were heroes at one end of the spectrum and slaves at the other, anchored by a carefully defended status system. Because the Christians moved the primary human struggle inside each individual, taking it out of the social realm, they featured heroic saints who could resist temptations and villainous sinners who could not. As the philosopher Hubert Dreyfus comments, "There could not have been saints in ancient Greece. At best there could only have been weak people who let everybody walk all over them. Likewise, there could not have been Greek-style heroes in the Middle Ages. Such people would have been regarded as pagan—prideful sinners who disrupted society by denying their dependence on God."[10] Even so, the moral dimension does not entirely displace strength: Christian saints are powerful because they can resist the temptations. The building blocks of character remain intact.

Cultures differ not only in what they admire, detest, and pity, but also in the ways they think about characters. Notably, Europe in the late eighteenth century began to psychologize its perceptions of individuals, in the Romantic (and Christian) quest for the interior, emotional self. Intentions became more important to moral judgments than actions, and intentions and actions were seen to diverge from time to time. As characters became more complicated and opaque, and more circumstantial, they eclipsed plots in importance.[11] But they became harder to see as heroes and villains.[12]

The emergence of complex characters in novels of the eighteenth and nineteenth centuries contributed to greater gender segregation among cultural audiences. Women embraced the inner psychological turn more than men, who found alternative entertainments. Literary critic Jane Tompkins shows how the American Western, with its exaggerated heroes and villains, is the macho retort to women's favorite genre of the nineteenth century, the domestic novel. "The Western *answers* the domestic novel," she says. "It is the antithesis of the cult of domesticity that dominated American Victorian culture. The Western hero, who seems to ride in out of nowhere, in fact comes riding in out of the nineteenth century. And every piece of baggage he doesn't have, every word he doesn't say, every creed in which he doesn't believe is absent for a reason. What isn't there in the Western hasn't disappeared by accident; it's been deliberately jettisoned. The surface cleanness and simplicity of the landscape, the story line, and the characters derive from the genre's will to sweep the board clear of encumbrances."[13] Those encumbrances include evangelical religiosity and the cult of domesticity. Men's culture continued to rely on traditional characters even while women's culture tended to transcend their simplifications. The hero makes the town safe for women, but he does not stay to live with them.

In the therapeutic culture of the twentieth century, women's complex culture came to have more and more influence. As we have come to understand the social and structural factors that shape our desires and actions, we are less likely to hold individuals responsible for their destinies. As blame becomes diffused, it is harder to identify credible villains or heroes. No one is strong enough to carry out all her intentions, and as the strength dimension of character shrinks it takes the moral dimension with it. We cannot be blamed for lacking the means to carry out our intentions. Passivity erodes all the characters, who become the tools of circumstance. Political players have to work harder to create believable characters.

Women's increased participation in politics—and war—has also changed modern characters. Strength and activity level have almost universally been associated with men, weakness and passivity with women. To play a greater role in politics, women have had to do two things. They have had to assert their own strength, for instance through feminists' efforts to allow women to display their anger in public in extremely unladylike ways. This sign of strength allowed them to be more heroic, although also—in the eyes of gender traditionalists—more villainous. In addition to changing images of gender, women have also challenged definitions of heroism to include endurance and survival as paths to heroism. Battered women and abused children are survivors, not victims. The *definition* of public characters and the *eligibility* of various social groups to be acknowledged as different characters are distinct processes.

The democratization of politics and war has also transformed characters, especially along the strength dimension. Great warriors and grand kings could place themselves in a line reaching back to the heroes of myth, doing prodigious deeds and creating new empires. In the nineteenth century mass parties and mass armies shifted strength to the group, notably with the virulent nationalism of Europe from the French Revolution to 1945. Yet even with different institutional underpinnings, politicians and armed forces still turn to traditional characters and their signs to mobilize passions. Democracy added *mass* heroes and villains, but still conducted the character work necessary to mobilize audiences. The hero on the white horse became more important symbolically because he embodied the nation, even as he became less important on the battlefield.

Characters have always existed independently of plots, and there have always been more direct, usually visual, means of constructing them. Sculptures, frescoes, and other forms have always celebrated heroes, just as graffiti have always mocked them, but visual media have flourished in the modern era, for example with the birth of the caricature in renaissance Italy or lithographic posters in the nineteenth century. Unfortunately, scholars deal in words and have been generally inept at acknowledging the ways in which visual information shapes our understandings—even though we speak of our moral "visions." Writers are more comfortable talking about texts and narratives and discourses than showing the icons of visual media.

We hope this book will redress some of this imbalance. We present ways of analyzing the characterological messages not only of words, but of posters and photos, statues and paintings. Cognitive psychologists in recent years have demonstrated just how much information we handle through subconscious and nonverbal pathways, and how we take a person's measure through a quick glance. Why else would political ads be effective?

The chapters that follow elaborate on these themes. Part I gleans insights into character work from across the human sciences. Chapter 1 examines the key role that characters play in narratives, but also surveys the rhetorical tradition that has always highlighted character. In chapter 2 we look at some ways that character is expressed visually, ranging from sculpture in renaissance Florence to modern magazine advertisements. We also briefly consider what characters sound like in music. Contributions from social psychology help us see, in chapter 3, how the human mind sums up the people we encounter in media and daily life, creating personalities and characters for them whether we wish to or not. Chapter 4 draws on sociology and political science to address some of the institutional underpinnings through which characters are accomplished, from Twitter to law courts.

Part II turns to the specific characters, drawing out subtypes and giving examples from politics and other strategic arenas. Many moral dramas start with the villains we are expected to fear and hate, so that is where we start in chapter 5. Then we turn to their sidekicks, the minions (chapter 6), before we address heroes and victims in chapters 7 and 8.

Part III complicates the characters. We devote chapter 9 to an important transformation, when victims manage to become heroes. Chapter 10 addresses a number of ways that traditional public characters have evolved in recent centuries to correspond with the way that moderns understand blame and causality. The public characters may have changed in some ways, but they are not—yet—obsolete. Our conclusion does the usual things, but also incorporates a reply to one of our kind reviewers, Robert Zussman. An appendix addresses the role of humor in creating characters, ridiculing them, but also in undermining the entire system of character work.

I | How We Imagine Characters

1 | The Art of the Word

S HAKESPEARE INVENTED RICHLY HUMAN PROTAGONISTS: earthy, bold, greedy, confused, mistaken, and brave. They seem "natural" to us. But he did not give up on great public characters in order to do this. He offered us delightful villains like Macbeth and Richard III, heroes like Henry V and Othello, victims like the little princes, and minions such as Roderigo. Many of his protagonists were complicated and ambivalent, especially compared to the stock figures in earlier drama, but much of his purpose was character work, often intended to demonstrate the legitimacy of the Tudor line.

Even in a complicated play like *King John*, we see the halting emergence of a hero in the person of Philip Faulconbridge, an earthy, funny fellow who plays with different kinds of language and social roles during the play. In the first act, he is revealed to be the bastard son of Richard the Lionhearted, and from then on is labeled simply as the Bastard. He gives up his claim to the Faulconbridge estate in order to embrace his new lineage, teasing his younger half-brother for his spindly arms and legs that look like the elder Faulconbridge's.[1]

Shakespeare largely invented the genre of the history play, and in this one he invented the Faulconbridge figure in order to explore a variety of themes about loyalty and legal inheritance. John was unsuitable as a hero, except for his conflict with the villain of the piece, the Pope's representative, a neat foreshadowing of the sixteenth century. John was also battling the French, who wished to install his nephew Arthur on the throne in his place. (Arthur was the first son of the first son of Henry II, giving him a claim at least as strong as John's, even if it followed primogeniture laws rather than Henry's written will: this pitted Norman against Angevin law.) Young and innocent, Arthur would prove a perfect victim, most likely killed on John's orders. King John also battled his own barons, a more

Public Characters. James M. Jasper, Michael P. Young, and Elke Zuern, Oxford University Press (2020) © Oxford University Press.
DOI: 10.1093/oso/9780190050047.001.0001

famous conflict thanks to the Magna Carta that temporarily ended the hostilities (ignored by Shakespeare).

The Bastard has the genetics of a hero-king (much burnished by Robin Hood legends that pitted the villainous John against the crusading hero Richard), but it takes war to make him into a full hero. As is usual in Shakespeare the combat takes place offstage, but the Bastard is different when we see him afterward. His dialogue is more confident (most of the time), and in most stagings he puts on the lion-skin mantle of his father. He has also absorbed the downside of many heroes, a righteous anger and fondness for violence, as well as that of kings, a cynical or strategic concern with gain (in the sense of personal advantage, although we never see him pursue it). He gains strength while King John loses it.

Yet the Bastard remains faithful to his king, vowing "true subjection everlasting." In a remarkable scene in act 4, he comes upon the dead body of Arthur, whom John has had murdered. Shaken and sympathetic, he nonetheless distances himself from Arthur with "Bear away that child." He energetically rushes to the king, since "A thousand businesses are brief in hand." There is work to be done. He is charged with "the ordering of this present time," like other heroes called upon to chart the course of history by creating institutions. He has the play's final lines, arguing for English unity in the face of foreign threats:

> This England never did nor never shall
> Lie at the proud foot of a conqueror
> But when it first did help wound itself . . .
>> Naught shall make us rue,
> If England to itself do rest but true.

Philip Faulconbridge has become a more heroic version of himself, acknowledged as the illegitimate son of Richard the Lionhearted. He is a bit darker and less entertaining, but stronger, than before. He speaks for England, which has united in the face of the French threat, legitimacy squabbles, threats from the Pope, and struggles between king and nobles. In a play written only two years after the defeat of the Spanish Armada, the Bastard (a fictional creation set four hundred years earlier) could heroically embody the imagined nation.[2]

Literature has given us the most memorable characters, drawn from all the world's cultures. Some are gods, like Vishnu in his many incarnations; others are half-god and half-human, like Achilles and Jesus Christ. Some are humans, simply more lovable, more clever, more powerful, or just more lucky than others, like Hikaru Genji or Luke Skywalker. Some are not special at all, but have interesting things happen to them, like Joseph Andrews or Harry "Rabbit" Angstrom. Others, such as Snow White or Tess of the D'Urbervilles, are victims of curses or violence. A few have sold themselves into evil, like Faust. Some are just plain bad, like the Wicked Witch of the West—although even she has been given a sympathetic makeover in a popular Broadway musical. Many characters defy easy labels.

Literary critics have examined the mechanisms that produce characters. In his study of the American Western, where character tropes are usually presented in stripped-down versions, Will Wright finds four contrasts that help generate them: good/bad, strong/weak, inside/outside, and wilderness/civilization. Heroes are strong and good, of course, villains strong and bad. Society is weak, and so needs protection. Sometimes at the end of the tale the town can incorporate heroes, but more often their potentially dangerous potency requires that they ride off alone to their next adventure. Indians and most cowboys partake of the strength of the wilderness; townspeople, women, and effete Easterners are part of debilitating civilization.

Insider/outsider is also a common rhetorical binary, especially in public arguments over collective identities, but it is less a character distinction than a form of political alliance or a reflection of social structures. The distinction tells us little about the content of character, except that outsiders are generally bad. Outsiders are often portrayed as villains, insiders as heroes or victims, but that merely shows a strategic use of character types, not their definition. This trait usually becomes salient as a way of amplifying someone's goodness or badness, as in an amusing study of children's animated television in the United States, which found many villains to have foreign accents (British, most often, but also German, Slavic, and generically "foreign" accents). Outsiders are threatening.[3]

Wright's other binary, wilderness/civilization, is a widespread contrast in industrial societies, but it is more salient in Westerns than in other narratives: wilderness is what "the West" symbolizes. It fuses the two main components of character: good (nature) versus bad (civilization), and strong (real men) versus weak (women and the men who are like them).[4]

A distinctly American form, Westerns have evolved in the same way that many other genres have, blurring public characters. Traditional Westerns presented simplified characters; the good guys wore white hats, the bad guys black. The contrast between good and evil in more recent films is often less stark, and often complicated by humor, but the basic typology of heroes and villains remains. Strength and benevolence are still the core attributes of a (now more diverse) set of heroes, from a fallible but still hypermasculine James Bond to an exceptionally strong girl in *Hunger Games*.

This chapter examines the two main traditions that have studied how basic characters are constructed through words, in narratives and in rhetoric. We then look at public relations, a version of rhetoric, before broadening our lens to performances linking words with images.

Narrative

One of the most fashionable terms in recent cultural analysis, narrative is the representation of an event or a sequence of events, real or fictitious, through thematically connected (as opposed to merely chronologically listed) words or images. The words can be oral, as in traditional folktales, or written, as in the modern novel. The images of movies or comic strips also convey sequenced events. Thinking and feeling are events as important as doing, and encompass a great deal of what happens to characters in modern novels (less so in movies, for obvious reasons). Narratives have beginnings, ends, and—in the form of setbacks and complicating action—middles.

Since the time of the ancient Greeks, narrative has been contrasted with other uses of language: with lyrical poetry that aims to capture facets of the world directly without recourse to a story, and with "discourse," which is also thought to consist of simple direct descriptions of the world such as those of scientific facts or personal expression. In this view, narrative differs from rhetoric, which emphasizes the relationship between speaker and audience. A traditional narrative was expected to stand by itself, to be accepted as fact without causing us to ask too much about the speaker or the context.[5]

The twentieth century saw an explosion of awareness, in literature and literary criticism, of the many tricks used to create narratives. A traditional literary narrative has a surface simplicity, as though it were a straightforward description of events. But this is always an illusion. In order to understand any story, readers and listeners make many assumptions drawn from common sense and from the discursive worlds of psychology and science. This is true even when we read writers like Ernest Hemingway, who assiduously avoided any obvious psychological references in his texts: the reader nonetheless adds them. We also infer connections (mostly causal) between events that appear in the narrative.[6]

Structuralists, who dominated narrative theory in the twentieth century, took inspiration from Aristotle's suggestion in the *Poetics* that plot is more important than character, and they proceeded to reduce characters to "functions" of the text or signs on a page.[7] Vladímir Propp, one the founders of this tradition, studied simple narratives such as folktales and crime novels, in which little work was needed to identify the stock characters, who were in his view only important for their contribution to moving the plot along. A function, said Propp, "is understood as an act of a character, defined from the point of view of its significance for the course of the action." The same functions could be performed by various characters, or even by non-characters. These are items like "The hero and the villain join in direct combat," or "The villain is defeated," with variations on each.[8]

Even while referring to them as "spheres of action," Propp could not ignore villains and heroes, with the latter group additionally divided into seekers and victims. There is also the donor (an appropriate word for our purposes, given the importance of fundraising in contemporary politics), who provides some kind of aid, often a magical substance that bestows special powers on the hero (just as money provides power today). Both villains and heroes have assistants who are given supporting tasks; we use the traditional term minions when they assist villains, sidekicks or supporters when they aid heroes.

There are also false heroes who claim to have done the deeds accomplished by the true hero (both politicians and protestors today claim credit for popular outcomes, whatever their real role may have been). There may also be a dispatcher who sends the hero on his search or a princess whom the hero aids, although these play tiny roles in Propp's analysis of events. (Princesses, more prominent in other folktale traditions, seem to be either prizes for the heroes or victims whom the heroes must help—or both.)[9] Much as he tried, even Propp could not avoid characters.

French structuralists transformed these ideas into binary oppositions within autonomous, rule-governed systems (such as language, kinship, or fashion). Greimas reduced Propp's thirty-one functions to twenty and pushed structuralism even further so that characters became mere "actants" with no life outside of their actions in the plot. An underlying binary code generates a variety of plots, much as *langue* generates *parole*: subject versus object of an action, sender versus receiver of a message, and helper versus opponents of the hero. Characters are defined purely in terms of their interactions with others, with no independent traits of their own.[10] There is no room to understand character work.

As we showed in the Introduction, binary codes can be used to understand characters rather than to reduce them to plots. In many rhetorical settings the goal is character definition, to which even the almighty plot becomes subordinated. But every story contains an unavoidable tension between stable characters and unexpected plot twists, a version of the constant tension in human life between actor and situation, between agency and constraint. Humans act, but in circumstances not entirely of their choosing.

Literary Characters

Structuralists never managed to banish characters entirely from their analyses, and in recent years the pendulum has swung against their extreme anti-humanism. Several literary theorists have called for the reversal of Propp's priority of plot over character. Rather, says Cesare Segre, "an action interests in the measure in which it reflects the intentions and will of a character: indeed a character who for the most part has a name and surname, is enrolled in however fictitious a parish register, and constitutes a cluster of aptitudes and character traits (hence the appropriateness of the English term 'character')." The character takes priority, according to Segre, since it "effects a unification of the functions, since these make sense because they are carried out by him, fanning out from him."[11]

Recognizing that humans populate their mental worlds with characters, Deidre Lynch offers an out-with-the-bathwater critique of structuralism's rejection of character for "dismissing the plenitude it should explain. It does not account for how characters' excesses—the residue left over after the structuralist analysis of narrative roles, the augmented vitality that humanist accounts ascribe to characters who seem to lead lives off the page—have been effective in history."[12] Characters matter because we believe in them. We expect to find them. And we enjoy them. We also learn from them, as they embody moral lessons that transcend their time and place.

Literary theorist Seymour Chatman calls character a "paradigm of traits," a combination of ways of thinking and feeling that transcend any given situation.[13] Like other elements of a narrative, character traits imply indirectly more than they say directly, conveying extra information beyond the literal text. Actions and routines are succinct hints of underlying character traits. We read into a subtle habit a wealth of information about the person. We learn that a protester has been jailed for her beliefs: we assume she is strong, good, and active (an "activist"), with abiding affective commitments to the cause. We form expectations about her future behavior.

Character is a paradigm because our minds put information together; it is a powerful schema for understanding individuals. Percy Lubbock concludes, "Nothing is simpler than to create for oneself the idea of a human being, a figure and a character, from a series of glimpses and anecdotes. Creation of this kind we practice every day; we are continually piecing together our fragmentary evidence about the people around us and molding their images in thought. It is the way in which we make our world."[14] Cognitive psychologists, we'll see in chapter 3, have generalized these mechanisms into a theory of how humans impose meaning through the use of schemas that fill in the gaps when information is sparse.

The cognitive power of characterization is often wrongly attributed to narratives. An amusing example comes from psychologists Fritz Heider and Marianne Simmel, who in 1944 made a small film of two triangles and a circle, moving around a blank background so that they are apparently interacting with each other. It is difficult for the viewer not to perceive the large triangle as menacing the others, and the small triangle as protecting the circle from its pursuer. Although this response is usually taken as proof of humans' tendency to see stories everywhere, it is also good evidence for our attribution of characters, in this case a threatening villain (larger than the others, and following them around the screen), a threatened victim (possibly female), and a plucky protective hero. It's conceivable that the power of narratives comes from the characters they contain, not the reverse. We have more rigid expectations about characters than we do about plots, suggesting that they often dominate our meaning-making.[15]

Some characters achieve a shorthand condensation of meaning more succinctly and completely than others. E. M. Forster famously distinguished "round" from "flat" characters.[16] Round, richly drawn characters reflect a number of sometimes-conflicting qualities that make their behavior more interesting precisely because it is harder to predict; they surprise us. They are appropriate for psychological narratives. Flat characters have a single trait (or a cluster of related traits) that defines them and leads them to act in predictable ways reflecting that characteristic. They do not surprise us. They are appropriate for comedy but too simple for tragedy. In Forster's eyes, flat characters are dead.

Recently James Wood (like Forster both a novelist and a critic) has challenged Forster's distinction. For one thing, flat characters can be both interesting and emotionally satisfying. Think of Falstaff. For another, even sophisticated novels typically have round central characters but also a number of minor flat characters who appear briefly. This fits with our real lives: we interact with many people only sporadically or only once, and we must craft simple ways of summing them up in order to avoid being surprised. For people we know well, we have more complex models, and they are still forever surprising us. True roundness, Wood insists, "is impossible in fiction, because fictional characters, while very alive in their way, are not the same as real people."[17] In the same way, political characterizations are fictions, whose creators are not especially interested in the opaque subtleties of roundness.

The literary theorist Robert Alter similarly remarks, "At first thought, stereotypes may seem intrinsically unrealistic, but a little reflection will suggest that they are often approximations rather than misrepresentations of reality and that no one can get along without them . . . . A fiction with no dependable stereotypes would be radically disorienting." Alter savages the French structuralist analysis of narrative as a system of formal relations and functions. It is "most conspicuously inadequate in its treatment of character," he observes, "because with its conception of narrative as a system of structural mechanisms, character can be little more than a function of plot."[18]

By linking them to flat and round characters, Tzvetan Todorov contrasts traditional plot-driven narratives with complicated psychological ones.[19] In the former, a character trait automatically leads to an action (a gluttonous person sits down to eat, a treacherous one betrays somebody), whereas in the latter, actions express character in more complex ways that allow protagonists greater choice. People have mixed motives, they make mistakes, they deceive even themselves. The potential of character may or may not always be fulfilled; character is open-ended, capable of development and transformation. Fictional protagonists are no longer characters in our sense; they no longer project essences.[20]

As we'll see, traditional drama was "stocked" with known characters, familiar from their dress or their masks. Audiences knew what to expect from Arlecchino, Pantalone, and Pulcinella. These were frequently allegorical arts, in which people and events stand in for qualities or ideas not directly present. Traditional allegories were often political and satirical, as authors could describe or comment upon current events without taking full responsibility or triggering repression. Arbitrary, nondemocratic regimes—once universal and even now all too common—imposed this kind of subterfuge on their subjects. Flat characters in political narratives today continue to allow a political figure to convey an idea without explicitly saying it (thus

Ronald Reagan attacked stereotyped "Cadillac welfare queens" without mentioning their race).

A few literary theorists have recognized that the power of characters lies in our emotional reactions to them, rather than simply in their ability to condense cognitive information. We pity or hate them, trust and admire them. They frighten us, outrage us, paralyze us, disgust us, amuse us. "In most works of any significance," insists Wayne Booth, "we are made to admire or detest, to love or hate, or simply to approve or disapprove of at least one central character, and our interest in reading from page to page, like our judgment upon the book after reconsideration, is inseparable from this emotional involvement . . . . We cannot avoid judging the characters we know as morally admirable or contemptible."[21] The best novels, he observes, contain characters facing important moral choices that resonate with readers. *Emotions are the motor propelling narrative through characters.*

Round characters have more complex emotions than flat ones, and we in turn have more complex emotional reactions *to* them. Narrators in modern novels, for instance, are rarely to be trusted. We may be tempted to admire them at times, but we also frequently see craven motives that have led them accidentally to heroic actions. We may even expect them to exaggerate their deeds boastfully. The deceitful narrator predates Freud, but he gave us a way to understand deeper layers of deceit: the narrator is often unconsciously fooling herself as well as consciously trying to dupe us.

Today, the central characters of highbrow novels and movies are mostly round. Our notions of character have grown more complex in the modern world, roughly in proportion to the rise of psychology as a way of understanding the complex social life around us. We believe in a deep interior self that drives our actions, we think in terms of personality types, we believe in an Unconscious that even its holder cannot understand (or rather, we think that observers can sometimes understand a person's unconscious better than the person herself can).

But flat characters are alive and well, especially in more melodramatic media, from soap operas to country and western songs, where they remain central protagonists. There is still something satisfying in watching people play out their predictable character traits. In the United States professional wrestling, a carefully crafted battle between good and evil, contains a number of delicious villains. World Wrestling's own website describes the Boogeyman (Figure 1.1), known for eating handfuls of live worms, as "hailing from a mysterious abyss known as the Bottomless Pit," and the aptly named Kane as demented, sadistic, and "consumed with a desire

FIGURE 1.1 Insanity is often associated with strength, producing a villain who will do anything, such as eating worms, signature of the Boogeyman.

to bring absolute anarchy to the lives of his fellow superstars." They are pitted against the (less popular) nice guys, "babyfaces" like Rey Mysterio, who sports a cross on his white and grey mask. Even Goldberg, a good guy as a former NFL player, is described as "an incendiary mix of raw power and wild intensity." For the supposed heroes as much as for the villains in wrestling, strength is the dimension that matters most in this arena.

The television comedy *GLOW* (gorgeous ladies of wrestling) parodies the creation of characters and their pairings in matches in a fictitious women's wrestling show. All are grossly stereotyped: the all-American blonde battles the Black Welfare Queen; two Black wrestlers rip the hoods and robes off two women billed as KKK members. As Welfare Queen apologizes to her Stanford-educated son, "I'm not the only offensive character, they're all offensive." The actress assigned to play a terrorist named "Beirut" complains, "But I'm Indian." Viking is good, Fortune Cookie is bad. Most evil is Zoya the Soviet Destroyer (the series is set in the 1980s), apparently modeled on Nikolai Volkoff, a Croatian weightlifter who played a Soviet villain in the ring in the 1970s.[22]

Children's literature and film contain plenty of stereotyped characters. The villains are particularly flamboyant. In *One Hundred and One Dalmatians* Cruella de Ville (a pun on cruel devil) wears a coat made of puppies. The Grinch who attempts to steal Christmas is green and ghastly, and *Peter Pan's* Captain Hook sports a hook instead of a hand. Even sophisticated examples like Rocky and Bullwinkle, despite plenty of jokes aimed at adults, feature unabashed villains such as Boris and Natasha and Snidely Whiplash—although they are reassuringly transformed into minions by looking ridiculous.

Classic heroes such as Huckleberry Finn and Pippi Longstocking demonstrate a simple morality along with unconventional behavior and sufficient cunning to observe and survive the foibles of adults. (Pippi also has superhuman strength, although it is not obvious why.) Harry Potter, a reluctant hero with special powers at first unknown to him but known to others, faces an entertaining series of villains linked to Lord Voldemort, even though—here's the suspenseful twist—he sometimes has trouble distinguishing friends from foes. In the world of magic appearances can deceive.

We often view politics as melodrama. Forster's complaint about flat characters was that they are a kind of caricature or cartoon, a stick figure instead of a fleshed-out one. Caricatures are uninteresting in literature, perhaps, *but have their purposes in politics*. Flat characters make for better political narratives, precisely because they display simple emotions and their audiences feel simple emotions about them. Flat characters are stereotypes that condense a lot of information and feelings. When we use people as symbols, we think we know them: what motivates them, whether we can trust them or not, how they will behave under normal or crisis situations, even whom they will choose as allies.

Exaggeration and distortion are inevitable. We don't expect flat characters to change, except perhaps via dramatic (and stereotyped) crises—but crises appropriate to their characters. People themselves are rarely so simple (even politicians!), but our images of them can be. In an age of supposedly casual attention to politics, of mediation by journalists, and of the reduction of news to sound bites, characters in the political dramas we watch unfold around us will be flat indeed. Especially when they are practiced entertainers, like Reagan and Trump.

In recent years the study of narrative has evolved into the study of stories: from content to context, from structured codes to the rhetorical milieu in which stories are told. Thus Francesca Polletta and her coauthors complain that sociologists "have treated stories more as texts to be analyzed for the meanings they express than as social performances that are interactively constructed."[23] Once we accept storytelling as a social interaction, we are in the realm of rhetoric, which always asks who is allowed to speak in an arena, what they can say, who listens, and to what effect.

Character Rhetoric

For 2500 years, theorists of rhetoric have described the tricks by which the creator of a speech attempts to have effects on her audiences, whether these are feelings, beliefs, or actions. Rhetoric flourished with democracy in the Greek city-states of the fifth century BCE, especially Athens, after political reforms made it possible for all citizens to participate in assemblies and—a darker side of democracy—to sue one another in front of juries. To speak cogently was a political advantage but also a necessary safeguard against predators.

Rhetoric has a number of benefits as an analytic framework. In contrast to narratology's obsession with content, or plot, the three parts of the oratorical process receive equal attention in rhetoric: the orator, what she says, and her audience.[24] There is balanced attention to the creator's context and intentions, to the form and the content embodied in the message, and to the perspectives and reactions of the audiences: all three are crucial for understanding cultural meanings.

In addition, rhetoric is our oldest body of theory about human meaning, continuously if unevenly accumulating knowledge about how people communicate with each other. Other traditions, especially Judaism and Christianity, have interpreted sacred texts in order to decipher the intent of God.[25] But such hermeneutic endeavors were hardly capable of recognizing the extent to which humans also create their own truths. Rhetoricians— both practitioners and theorists—acknowledge that orators may refer to the gods (or to science), but they do not assume that the gods exist.

Rhetoric is thoroughly social constructionist and, in this way, extremely modern. (The original Greek term *kharakter* was an engraving or stamping tool that left a distinctive mark, thus acknowledging the active process of constructing characters.) From the start, rhetoric has been controversial for its recognition that its tools are equally capable of constructing true arguments or false ones.

Socrates was not the first thinker to condemn rhetoric, only the most famous. His view that rhetoric is "mere" words, in contrast to the underlying truth, has come down to us in the pejorative sense that the word "rhetoric" still often has. "That's just empty campaign rhetoric," we say: verbal trickery that impresses at the moment but leaves no lasting impression. It can dangerously lead to poor political decisions. Across the millennia, those who sought some bedrock truth, from Plato to the empiricist and positivist philosophers of science, have condemned rhetoric as misleading and superficial, merely "literary." (Aristotle's distinction between direct evidence and esthetic style did not help, as the latter came to be associated with rhetoric.) Wrote Richard Braithwait in 1615:

> Heere is no substance, but a simple peece
> Of gaudy Rhetoricke.

This uneasiness about the uses to which rhetoric can be put—the great "rhetorical anxiety"—has led to various defenses. Aristotle said sensibly that we cannot blame rhetoric itself for those who misuse it. Quintilian's solution was to insist, nervously, that a good orator had to be a man of good character—apparently the only way to guarantee that he would not misuse his art. Rhetoricians both acknowledged and feared cultural constructionism, believing it led to moral relativism.[26]

There are still those whose instincts tell them that we can know some objective truth beneath all the words, but their philosophical position has largely collapsed in the last fifty years. The great debate over the meretriciousness of rhetoric has basically been solved. We cannot hope, on the one hand, to get at bedrock truths, no matter what our methods or languages for doing so. And yet we are not left with the arbitrary play of language, either. For what gets us closer to truths, or at least eliminates weaker notions, is precisely the clash of viewpoints that originally inspired rhetoric. It is by testing claims against each other, by patient (and sometimes not-so-patient) engagement between perspectives, that we can reach whatever kind of (always provisional) consensus is possible. Anthropologists don't learn about communities through observation alone; they interrogate their informants, test their own hunches, consider their own "positionality," and work to see if they have it right. Scientists too criticize and test each other's claims and findings; only when disagreements settle down do new "facts" enter the textbooks.[27] Rhetoric's constructionism reigns.

The rhetorical tradition is not just constructionist, it is also resolutely social and interactive. Individuals craft, memorize, and deliver speeches to audiences. These are speech acts in a pure form, aimed at persuading others. (To give structuralism its due, even these speech acts draw explicitly and thoroughly on the existing semiotic resonances of the words used.) Rhetorical theory is clear about the variations in orators, in audiences, and in arenas. Orators can be brilliant or mundane, present themselves as experts or as Everyman. As for audiences, there may be more than one: it is paramount to persuade the judge or jury, but orators also have an eye toward the public audience in a courtroom, upon whom their reputations depend. Arenas differ as well, especially in the goals and outcomes, but also in physical details such as size, availability of props, entrances and exits, seating, lighting, and so on.[28]

Most of all, rhetoric has a purpose. The orator hopes to acquit her client or inspire a vote for war. These are not stories and jokes told around a campfire or in a bar, intended only to amuse others—although amusement can be a powerful tool for orators. For this reason, rhetoric is especially useful in understanding meanings in political action, or more broadly strategic action, where people pursue their ends in conflict with others.

Another advantage of rhetoric is its explicit attention to emotions, so pivotal to human action and yet oddly absent from most analyses of cultural meanings. One of the purposes of rhetoric is to transform, guide, or liberate the feelings of the audience. These may be short-run emotions such as fear or anger; they may be medium-run moods such as excitement or optimism; and they may be long-run commitments such as love for one's nation or hatred of outsiders. Emotions invigorate rhetoric as well as narratives.[29]

One goal of orators is to shape the general moral orientations of their audiences by praising some people and actions and condemning others. Recognizing this, Aristotle described "epidictic" rhetoric, or the creation of general impressions about people, for example through funeral orations or hymns of praise (paeans). Epidictic differs from speeches aimed at decisions, either about future policy in the Assembly or about past actions in law courts. Its original meaning was to "show off," presumably because it lacks the immediate purpose of forensic or policy arguments. It reinforces moral values by praising those who uphold or embody them and condemning those who ignore or violate them. The greatest orators celebrated and shaped the city of Athens and its citizens, a tradition still followed by politicians today.[30] We will mostly use the terms "character rhetoric" or "character work" to refer to epidictic.

As Booth puts it, character rhetoric involves "attempts to reshape views of the present. An orator or a birthday-party friend can change the reality of how we value people and their creations. A hero can be revealed as a con artist, or a CEO turned from hero to villain."[31] Revelations and scandals do abrupt character work. Booth also notes that character rhetoric is undermined when it is too closely aimed at a decision, such as a vote—one reason that people tend to discount campaign advertisements, even though they may be affected by them without wanting to be. Claims to truth are undermined if they seem instrumentally self-interested. Here

Booth makes an additional point: rhetoric not only affects audiences' impressions of the characters directly portrayed, it also changes *the character and reputation of the orator.*

Booth emphasizes that we become better citizens through exercising our rhetorical skills, but we also affect our standing among others. Even the greatest orators have struggled with this: their main purpose is to burnish the character of their clients, but they also care about their own reputations. Cicero was constantly showing off in arguments, proving how clever he was, sometimes at his client's expense. It is difficult to fashion two characters at once with equal success.

Although Aristotle insisted that character rhetoric deals with general impressions, these are usually embodied in specific individuals and groups. Without concrete examples to point to, general moral claims end up sounding like dry principles, moral philosophy rather than moving rhetoric. Pericles spoke of Athenians' virtues, in his funeral oration for Athens' war dead that is often taken as the paradigm of epidictic. Although he mentions Athens' past valor and glory, he focuses on the permanent, ongoing character of Athenians, which includes a generous openness to outsiders and a meritocracy in which advancement in public life derives from capabilities rather than class background. He concludes with standard praise of heroism: "Judging happiness to be the fruit of freedom and freedom of valour, never decline the dangers of war . . . . To a man of spirit, the degradation of cowardice must be immeasurably more grievous than the unfelt death which strikes him in the midst of his strength and patriotism."[32]

Four hundred years later, Quintilian recommended encomia (praise) and invective as the first exercises to be assigned to an aspiring young rhetor. One of the benefits was to instill in the student good moral values, through the study of examples of good and evil. This was one of Quintilian's ways of dealing with the rhetorical anxiety, but it shows that we use rhetoric to persuade ourselves as well as others. Character rhetoric provides moral orientations for all of us, shaping how we think of ourselves. In the U.S. Congress even today, encomia make up a large proportion of members' one-minute speeches each morning.[33] How we allocate praise and blame is the core of our moral visions.

The Work of PR

Character rhetoric has never been so central to politics as it is today. Vast amounts of time and effort go into the character work known as public relations. Corporations advertise themselves as much as their products; politicians try to manage impressions. And yet, despite the ubiquity of corporate and political PR, the academic study of rhetoric has shrunk to a small specialty; the public-speaking courses once required of American college students have been universally replaced by "expository writing," purveying quite different skills.

Aristotle restricted epidictic to funeral orations and paeans, but today all the genres and the media contribute. The American president is a good example. His role has been inflated into that of a symbolic leader capable of nurturing the world's hopes, of betraying those same aspirations, of reassuring us during crises, or lecturing us about our own shortcomings. The media probe his every comment or past action for signs of character. Is he strong or weak? Good or bad? Is he doing too much or too little? All of this is character rhetoric.

The 2016 presidential race in the United States was full of epidictic. Donald Trump was the master, using the brevity of Twitter to sling wicked epithets at rivals, the media, and anyone who criticized him. Strength and activity swamped issues of morality among Trump's concerns—or rather, they *are* his definition of morality in a leader. In a throwback to traditional forms of masculinity, the important thing is not to be a loser; being a bully is fine. Early on, Trump ridiculed frontrunner Jeb Bush as weak, ineffective, phony, and pathetic. Journalist Katy Tur was incompetent and dishonest, George Will dopey, boring, and deadpan. Trump's favorite taunts seemed to target weakness and dishonesty—undermining the two main traits expected of heroes. As president, Trump has applied the same dismissive methods to world leaders, with one exception, Vladimir Putin, whose scary strength makes him the perfect hero in Trump's eyes. Trump's prolific tweets suggest that 140 characters are plenty to conjure up a villain or minion, but not enough to do much more. Heroes may take more extensive work. *Twitter is the perfect epidictic medium for invective.*

Rhetoric is crucial to a democratic polity because persuasion is expected to outweigh coercion and payment as strategic means for getting one's way.[34] As long as voters have choices, character rhetoric will be directed at them. Persuasion is as central to politics as payments are to markets or coercion is to war. But means and arenas are not perfectly correlated. In most arenas we find all three families of strategies. If politicians primarily deploy persuasion as a strategy, they also rely on money and even coercion at times. They can pay to promulgate their chosen image; they can use coercion to demonstrate their strength. Political players (and their opponents) combine the three in whatever ways seem likely to be effective. They all do character work.[35]

The very point of character rhetoric is to flatten characters, to portray them as having an unchanging, dependable character, whether good or bad. All members of a characterized group are alike, without subtle variations. They have no history, which would also acknowledge their ability to change. They are *incapable* of learning and reform, or they do not *need* to learn. Such distortions and selections of facts convey to the audience that we know in advance how a character will act: good people will do good, bad ones will do bad. Flat characters are easier to remember, more powerful as symbols, and arouse stronger, simpler emotions than round characters. They are easier to think with and easier to portray concisely in news stories.[36]

The field of rhetoric recommends that we keep clearly defined audiences constantly in mind: television viewers, legislators, judges and juries in courtrooms, the audience in a theater. Often the creator of messages is also one of the audiences, saying things for her own benefit, persuading herself at the same time that she persuades others. Blogs and social media provide a good example of this, as users respond to one another in a more equal conversation than traditional "broadcasting" allows.[37] We will look more closely at the many arenas of character work in chapter 4.

Performance

Just as the ancient Greeks elaborated the practice and theory of rhetoric, they invented theater as we know it. Players on a stage pretending to embody various characters can convey some messages that orators cannot, just as the latter have their own advantages. Mostly, the tricks and insights of the two traditions overlap. After all, it is the ability of orators to express ideas and feelings that they do not necessarily share—their capacity to be actors—that generates the rhetorical anxiety. Orators are nothing if not performers. In attacking rhetoric, theater, and images, detractors have expressed the same anxiety: that surfaces hide deeper, different truths, often by intention.[38]

But these anxieties prove the power of performances. Sociologist Jeffrey Alexander and his collaborators have used performance as a lens for understanding a range of political processes, including the creation of heroes. To the orator-speech-audience triad of classical rhetoric, Alexander adds social power and the mise-en-scène. By the latter he means the temporal pacing, the physical spacing, the gestures, and the other ways that the words are performed—a standard part of rhetorical theory. By social power he adduces the external factors that sociologists love and which shape a performance: who can rent an auditorium, who controls the media, who is allowed to be part of the audience and where they can sit (and what they can do), in other words, the theaters and arenas. In addition to these practical background factors, he usefully insists that cultural meanings (culture structures, he calls them) exist prior to performances and shape what is said and done and how it is understood.[39]

Alexander describes the performative approach as an example of "cultural pragmatics," which could also include rhetoric. Indeed, the term captures the strength of a rhetorical approach to culture. "The theory of cultural pragmatics," Alexander claims, "interweaves meaning and action in a nonreductive way, pointing toward culture structures while recognizing that only through the actions of concrete social actors is meaning's influence realized."[40] The French structuralists are right that there are meanings out there, like the words in a dictionary, but they do not do anything by themselves. Interaction and context must both be acknowledged.

Alexander has also, in writing about the civil sphere, described many of the traits implicitly associated with heroes and villains in modern society, or at least those who should be included and excluded from political participation. Although a residual functionalism leads him to see these traits as somehow demanded by the institutions of civil society, they are the traits associated with proper citizens and thus are subject to character work. Some have to do with strength: autonomous as opposed to dependent; rational not irrational; sane not mad. Others have more to do with moral evaluation: reasonable rather than hysterical, realistic not distorted, self-controlled not wild and passionate. Active versus passive is actually one of Alexander's binaries, and calm versus excitable is closely related to it. Although he sees cultural meanings as expressed in binary oppositions, he does not insist on the neurological underpinnings of the binaries that marred Claude Lévi-Strauss'use of them.

Alexander offers binary descriptions of civil relations that could easily be applied to public characters: heroes could be described as open, trusting, honorable, altruistic, truthful, straightforward, deliberative, and friendly, while villains are the opposite: secretive, suspicious, self-interested, greedy, deceitful, calculating, conspiratorial, and antagonistic. Citizens are not heroes in the traditional warrior sense, but they are indeed the heroes of contemporary democracy. They are weak as individuals but strong when they pool their powers.[41]

In other work, Alexander examines the construction of heroes in American politics when Barack Obama and John McCain battled for the presidency in 2008. "Heroes rise above ordinary political life," demonstrating their strength "by overcoming great odds and by resolving what seem to be overwhelming challenges." By looking only at heroes, Alexander misses an opportunity to apply his binary analysis by contrasting heroes with villains on the dimension of morality or with victims on that of strength. Instead, he subordinates character to plot: "In their earlier lives, heroes were tested and suffered, usually on behalf of something greater than themselves." The hero is created by a narrative: "The actions of a hero are caused by a meaning that becomes clear only after the heroic journey is complete. There is a purpose to the hero's life." When Alexander applies binary analysis, this is only to show that the two candidates endeavor to conform to common images of civil democracy.[42] But characters are not easily reduced to institutional rules any more than to a few simple plots.

Among other ways that performance plays to our expectations, it offers us familiar characters. Before Shakespeare, most dramatis personae depended on social stereotypes. Audiences expected different things from gods, nobles, and servants; from men and women; from young and old. Not everyone could be a hero. These stock characters have not entirely disappeared.

Stock Characters

Various literary traditions depend on stock characters: stereotyped portraits readily recognized by the audience. Aristotle's student Theophrastus famously defined thirty amusing character types, including the suspicious, the absent-minded, the shamelessly greedy, the stingy, the flatterer, the coward, the arrogant—and the lover of bad company. Stock characters are generally comical, meant to confirm the folly and weakness of humanity, not its nobility. In what is known as a charactonym, their name already suggests their character: GLOW's Liberty Belle versus Welfare Queen. But epithets play the same role in politics: Crooked Hillary.

The Theophrastean genre flourished in Rome and had an especially strong rebirth in seventeenth-century Europe. One of the most famous examples, out of hundreds, was Jean de la Bruyère's *Caractères*, explicitly indebted to Theophrastus. It is actually a long list of vices, of special interest to the French moralists of the time, and his characters were simply those who embodied them. Like Thomas Overbury's 1614 work, *His Wife*, this compendium was a warning not to be fooled. Flattery, cheapness, impudence, brutality, stupidity, and other traits can distort a person into someone to avoid. The social chaos of cities such as London or the deceits of courts like Versailles must have fed a desire to make sense of the sundry encounters of daily life through a search for stable character types beneath the ever-changing surface variety of other people.[43]

Shakespeare himself, great inventor of round characters, has dozens of flat characters, often borrowing from earlier stock traditions. His women are unpleasant shrews, cheating alewives, ambitious schemers pushing their husbands to evil deeds. Even the Bastard borrows elements of medieval stock types: the mischievous Vice, the social-climbing Gallant, and the more obscure Garcio, a rural, irreverent servant whose humorous commentary is lewd as well as subversive of the social hierarchy. The Bastard's initial impertinence turns into mockery of the disloyal barons and ultimately becomes a plea for national unity.[44]

Stock characters appear in most dramatic traditions, such as European medieval morality plays, Italian commedia dell'arte, and Japanese Noh and Kyogen. Thanks to its origins as street performance, commedia dell'arte's familiar characters all have clownish elements. We can work our way up the socioeconomic ladder, upon which every character has a clear rung. *Zanni* is a casual laborer or hobo, insatiably hungry but also lazy. Two Zanni are often paired, one strong but dumb and the other cunning (these two different sources of strength sometimes aid each other and sometimes cancel each other out). Zanni has several amusing, hyperactive styles of walking.

Next up the ladder, *Arlecchino* is a servant, physically active, often hopping like a bug. He can be quick-witted, even if incapable of long-term planning. Witty and cynical, *Brighella* is a jack-of-all-trades, often a shop- or innkeeper, who can get things done for other players—for a price. None of these characters rank high in morality: their cunning prevents that. They tend to be active (necessarily for slapstick comedy) and strong (especially by means of cleverness).

Pantalone is the rich old man, with long nose, bushy eyebrows, and a pointed beard, typically clutching at the same time his purse and his penis; he controls or at least employs the other characters. Physically weak but financially robust, he often falls flat on his back in the face of bad (usually financial) news and needs help to stand. He is the original Scrooge, who always tries, but fails, to buy love. Large and relatively immobile, *il Dottore* is the other old man: a quack, pedant, and know-it-all, nearly killing people with his "remedies" and sprinkling ornate Latinisms into his Italian. (All the characters speak with distinctive styles and regional accents.)

Young, handsome, well-spoken lovers also populate the commedia. The men—vain, impatient, and fickle—are also ineffectual and need the help of the servants and older men. They typically fall in love with Isabella, flirtatious daughter of Pantalone, intelligent (to deal with her lovers) but headstrong (to clash with her father). Her servant counterpart, and usually her personal maid, is *Colombina*: pretty, fleet of foot (always being chased), and patient, "the only lucid, rational person in *commedia dell'arte*. . . . Autonomous and self-sufficient, she has no negative attributes."[45]

There are also a number of more minor characters, including soldiers both fake (*il Capitano*) and real (*il Cavaliere*). Both fancy themselves ladies' men, and see themselves as strong, brave, and handsome. When threatened, however, il Capitano's deep bass turns into a squeaking soprano, likened to a castrato. Il Cavaliere is strong; il Capitano only pretends to be.

Japanese Kyogen is also comedy, often crude slapstick, frequently performed alongside Noh to contrast with the latter's solemnity. Dating from the same period as commedia dell'arte, Kyogen is also dominated by servants, often interacting with a master. In both forms, like most other premodern theater, servants are denied the morality or the strength to ever be heroes or serious villains. They are not moral enough to be victims. They are often feckless minions. But most of the time they are clowns, puncturing the moral pretensions of those around them and not aspiring to any morality themselves. Most Kyogen masks seem to be cross-eyed or otherwise unhinged.

In the loftier Noh tradition there are two hundred masks, some of them for specific roles. The main dimensions differentiating masks are age and gender. Those for younger women tend to express innocence, those of older women quiet dignity—but in both cases passivity and weakness. There are distinct masks for old men, mostly stately and elegant, and often representing gods or spirits who have taken human form. God-demon masks, in contrast, typically express wildness, a raw power; these characters are frequently the spirits of animals. A final set of masks represent vengeful spirits, whose disheveled hair contributes to their angry, demented, expressions. An interesting feature of the Noh characters is that the same masks are used by humans, gods, and spirits: there is no fixed, a priori distinction among these.

Strength in these Japanese traditions is best when tamed by age; otherwise it is wild and insane. This evokes Homer's version of Achilles, half man and half god, driven wild by his anger so that he was almost as dangerous to his fellow Greeks as to the Trojans. Strong characters, even when well intentioned, arouse ambivalence in those around them. In Noh and professional wrestling, power is expressed as a form of unstable insanity.

Wry commentaries on human foibles, comic traditions like commedia dell'arte and genre paintings tend to blur our character types in order to show that appearances can deceive. Characters who seem strong and brave on the outside are simpering cowards on the inside; the most moral individuals have dark secrets and ulterior motives; innocents are not nearly as innocuous as they seem. Even so, these subversive counter-traditions tell us a lot about the characters they mock. And for the most part, they are kept segregated from the noble, tragic, and serious traditions of characterization.

Humor reveals the world to be a complicated place, open to multiple interpretations, and this complexity undermines the exaggerations of our main characters. In particular, good people have to be simple to remain untarnished. Irony, skepticism, cleverness, and multiple layers seem to complicate and undermine their good intentions. This is true for both heroes and victims. Victims become less sympathetic if they are wiseacres, heroes less trustworthy. Villains and minions are more entertaining because they can have strata of complexity, even containing occasional nuggets of goodness. They can be funny as well, especially by mocking the pretensions and hypocrisies of good people. These complications work well in narratives meant to entertain, in the arts, but not so much in politics. (See the Appendix on the unsettling effects of humor on characters.)

Comedy is meant to entertain, but titanic battles between hero and villain are meant to defend a way of life, a moral vision, and to mobilize emotions for war and other sacrifices. Phil Smith speaks of "narrative inflation" when strong characters are involved. "Motivations become more ideal and abstract and less material and base." The main characters are stripped of ambiguity to become symbols of good and evil, with a great deal at stake. "The shades of gray that mark personalities in realist fiction, for example, are replaced by iconic, stylized character qualities that are emblematic of overarching moral positions." When it really matters, character displaces plot.[46]

Nor have the stock characters of old entirely disappeared. They may have simply occupied new genres. Molly Andrews finds "evidence to suggest that the morality play has re-emerged in the late twentieth and early twenty-first centuries, no longer in the theater (though productions of Everyman, for instance, are still performed) but rather in the realm of politics."[47] Andrews seems to be right, except that it is not obvious that the moral characterizations that motivated morality plays had ever really vanished.

In recent years narrative theorists have taken a cue from cognitive psychology to understand how humans actually read narratives. Monika Fludernik uses the unfortunate term "experientiality" to express how a reader understands what happens in a novel: people experience things. This brings her to the central importance of characters in how we read. "Readers' visualizations of experientiality are necessarily linked to the existence of a human subject, the experiencer."[48] Some of those human subjects are recognized characters.

Public characters embody what we fear and hate, admire and love, respect or pity. The lessons are explicit in religious traditions, but just as important in secular circles. Words are a key tool in character work, but hardly the only one. As performing arts, these dramatic traditions depend heavily on visual cues, especially masks and costumes but also an array of gestures, stances, and ways of walking. In some performances, pantomime replaces words altogether, consigning all the meaning to the visual. As we turn now to media that are more purely pictorial, we will see why visual images are the most powerful cues for character types. Because there is less scholarly theory about their impacts than there is about the impact of words, we will look at images directly more than at theories about them.

2 | Sights and Sounds of Characters

ISTORIAN JONATHAN ISRAEL CAPTURES THE essence of the propaganda war between the Spanish monarchy and the Dutch Protestants in the late sixteenth century, in the imagery of pamphlets that the Dutch printed and widely distributed: "the Dutch lion, the metal collar of subjugation, a deceitful king encased in armor, and a Pope presented as the real power behind the Spanish throne." The engravings, intended for popular audiences, in quick order present the hero, its potential reduction under the collar to victim, the boastful minion, and the real, more distant villain. A brilliant character summary.[1]

Most scholars work with words, so it is natural for them to understand narratives, rhetoric, and similar verbal efforts. Thanks to the influence of structural linguistics in French thought, and the more general acceptance of language as the model for how culture works, scholarly inattention to other carriers of meaning only worsened during the twentieth century. Even when we address those other carriers—images, music, performance—we tend to view them as vessels for verbal thoughts, as in the lyrics of a song.

When we don't ignore images, we view them with suspicion. Mistrust of images has deep historical roots in each of the great monotheistic religions, the Abrahamic religions of the book: Yahweh's prohibition on graven images, recurrent iconoclastic movements in Christianity, and Islam's diktat against the portrayal of living things (such inventions being in competition with God's acts).[2] The resulting acts of vandalism—especially against sculpture—are endless: King Hezekiah, the Protestant Beeldenstorm in the Netherlands, Paris in 1789, China during the Cultural Revolution, Eastern Europe in 1989, Bamiyan in 2001, Iraq in 2003. In 1529 the first bishop of Mexico, a Franciscan and supposed humanist, boasted to the king of Spain that he and his fellow priests were "very busy with our continuous and great work in the conversion of the infidels of

Public Characters. James M. Jasper, Michael P. Young, and Elke Zuern, Oxford University Press (2020) © Oxford University Press.
DOI: 10.1093/oso/9780190050047.001.0001

whom . . . over a million people have been baptized, five hundred temples of idols have been razed to the ground, and over twenty thousand images of devils that they adored have been broken to pieces and burned."[3] They were following in the footsteps of early Christians, who destroyed pagan statues whenever they had the chance.

Every revolution demolishes the images of the former regime. The core of iconoclasm is a suspicion that images operate directly on our emotions, short-circuiting our thought processes and leading to irrational beliefs and actions. Coming from vicious, destructive iconoclasts, it is an ironic charge.

And yet it persists. In a series of powerful histories, Stuart Ewen has castigated images for making us all into gluttonous consumers, undermining the rationality of politics, and protecting capitalism.[4] This supposed irrationality of images depends on a contrast with rational thought as uncorrupted, uninformed by the media, by framings, and by other packaging of meanings. It draws on a long tradition contrasting rational thoughts and murky emotions, the mind versus the body. As a Marxist, Ewen holds to this view even after most other social scientists have abandoned such a pure vision and hope.

Just as the rhetorical anxiety acknowledges the power of rhetoric and fears its misuse because of that power, and anti-theatrical prejudice sees the same dishonesty and power in performance, so iconoclasm abhors images because of their power to move us despite our will. In all these cases the perceived power is esthetic and not ethical: in fact it is contrary to ethics, for it is emotional rather than rational. For this reason Plato is the Western source for both iconophilia and iconoclasm, according to intellectual historian Alain Besançon, just as he was the main critic of both rhetoric and theater.[5] Besançon claims that the Talmudic and Koranic bans on images were efforts to discourage worship of competing gods, but the underlying assumption was still the irrational, seductive power of images.

Yet it turns out that the invention of the modern civil sphere in the Italian renaissance depended heavily on images. The sculptures of Florence are one of several examples we use in this chapter to show what public characters look and sound like.

Crafting Civil Society

The civic humanism of the Italian renaissance began as character work. In June 1402 Gian Galeazzo Visconti, Duke of Milan, after defeating the combined armies of Bologna, Florence, and their allies, occupied Bologna. He hoped to impose feudal rule on most of northern Italy, and Florence was to be his next conquest. Miraculously, the duke died six weeks later and the city was spared. It thereupon launched a civic campaign, primarily in sculpture but also in architecture and literature, to celebrate its status as a republic, in contrast to the Papal States to its south and the autocratic principalities to its north.

Taking republican Rome as its model, Florence enthusiastically re-made itself to flaunt the civic virtues that had disappeared for so many feudal centuries. Rhetoric, necessary for democratic debate, flourished, and public squares were opened where citizens could safely gather. Until 1537, when it finally ceased to be a republic, the city commissioned count-less statues for those squares that celebrated a distinctive form of heroic republican virtue. With the increasing dominance of the Medici family during this period, the effort became more of a publicity scheme than a re-flection of underlying political reality, but it was one of the great character-building projects of all time. And the loveliest.

In one exercise of civic pride, the church and guild center of Orsanmichele, completed in 1404, offered fourteen niches on its exterior walls to the guilds of Florence so that they could commission statues of their patron saints. Most were created by the three leading sculptors of the time, Donatello, Ghiberti, and Nanni di Banco. The saints are draped in ancient garb, a salute to the virtues of the Roman republic. Surprisingly for a Christian church, not one is portrayed as a martyr.

Instead, the iconography is mostly Roman and heroic. The figures look strong and dynamic, even though many carry books (The Book) rather than weapons. Most look slightly downward, as if to confront the Florentine crowds who would pass them as they walked between the religious center of the cathedral and the center of secular government, the Piazza della Signoria. (Orsanmichele itself fused religious and civic functions, serving as church, guild center, and granary.) Their realism makes the statues very human, but their elevation and larger-than-life size make them heroes.

One of the saints, George, had supposedly killed a dragon, making him a hero in the traditional martial mode. Around 1420 Florence's preeminent sculptor Donatello created St. George's statue for the Armorers' Guild, giving him a handsome shield (Figure 2.1). Beneath the butch figure of the saint is a panel depicting his famous deed, with a princess watching on the right, the writhing dragon on the left, and George on a rearing horse in the middle: the essential triad of victim, villain, and hero (Figure 2.2). There is also a striking contrast between the dragon's craggy rocks on the left and

FIGURE 2.1 George the warrior saint is allowed to hold a shield as he stares alertly into the distance.

the palace's arcade on the right, rough nature versus calmly balanced civilization. The panel, important in art history for its perspective and sensitive gradations, establishes characters through a single event without turning to a full narrative.

Despite the inevitable presence of saints, Florence's favorite hero was the Old Testament boy David, whose virtue helped him overcome the strength of the giant Goliath. Donatello created both a marble *David* and a (more famous) bronze version. The latter, from around 1440, is an epicene figure who has not reached puberty, his skin still smooth and soft. He looks down, modestly, more an object of desire than an active hero. He is

FIGURE 2.2 The panel shows the event for which St. George is famous, with well-proportioned culture on the right and rough nature on the left behind the victim and the villain.

innocent, not strong. He was also lucky, like Florence in 1402, overcoming steep odds in his battle with his villain. This was the first free-standing bronze male nude since ancient Rome. In the 1470s Verrocchio made a similarly boyish but cockier version, with the left elbow jutting out provocatively, perhaps reflecting the city's growing confidence.

Another Donatello sculpture portrays the beautiful Judith slaying the invading commander Holofernes, another case of a hero's virtue compensating for her physical weakness. Its inscription reads, "Kingdoms fall through luxury; towns rise from their virtue. See the neck of pride sliced by humility." A hopeful lesson for urban merchants asserting themselves against feudal kingdoms based on landowning. It continues more ominously, hinting that the republic was already bending to the will of its most powerful family: "Piero son of Cosimo de' Medici dedicated the statue of this woman to the liberty and courage lent to the Republic by the invincible, constant spirit of its citizens."[6]

By 1504, at the height of the renaissance, Michelangelo's *David*—by far the most famous—was no longer a soft boy but a powerful, brooding giant more than five meters tall, with massive hands and a snarling glare. The statue highlights his essential character—willful, alert, brave, defiant—at the expense of his action: there is no giant's head at his feet, indeed it is not obvious if he has launched his rock yet. This *David* is supremely confident, lacking the human vulnerability of Donatello's version. All hero, no victim. During the fifteenth century Florence had refigured itself, thanks to the Medici, into an economic and political Goliath, and its character work changed accordingly. Strength displaced virtue.

The renaissance turned to ancient Rome for its sculptural and architectural inspiration but also for its political lessons. The great orator (and character-worker) Cicero was the central influence on Plutarch, the primary inventor of the humanistic image of the modern individual. The democratic, or at least republican, political tendencies that this implied also had roots in republican Rome. Rhetoric and sculpture were an inevitable pair of tools in Florence's creation of its new heroic self-image.

Heroic Sculpture

Sculpture—expensive and durable—is especially suitable for the celebration of heroes, who deserve a place in history. Villains do not appear in bronze and marble, unless they are being crushed under the foot of a hero, like St. George's dragon. Minions are not worth the bother; neither are victims until they are transformed into martyrs or saints.

The audiences for speeches and for sculptures differ. Oratory is meant to persuade those who participate in governing in some way, who may be called upon to make decisions. Sculptures and buildings may also be aimed at them, but these large investments can also send something like the opposite message: this ruler is so powerful that any thought of protest or noncompliance is foolish. This message is aimed at subjects, not citizens, although using the same epidictic media. Dictators throughout history have made giant, fearsome images of themselves. Ramses II commissioned countless sculptures, in addition to carving his name on many others, with some of the largest ones, at Abu Simbel, twenty meters tall. The intended emotional impact was awe, intimidation, and worship. One Ramses was never enough: there are four colossi of the pharaoh at Abu Simbel. Saddam Hussein must have been envious.

This character work is a standard part of statecraft, as rulers attempt to persuade their subjects that their power is so great that they are divine and permanent. Not only statues, but memorials, gardens, and especially buildings are intended to reinforce this message. Sociologist Chandra Mukerji decodes the gardens of Versailles as a demonstration of France's engineering power to reshape and subordinate territory to the will and whim of Louis XIV.[7] Upon such artifacts the discipline of collective memory has been constructed.

Even without sculptures, architecture can be heroic, suggesting the glories of a ruler, a people, a political party, a city, or even the architect. Size, symmetry, long rows of columns standing like obedient soldiers, a uniformity of design and building materials all convey grandeur. Broad boulevards from which to view all this have the same effect. No wonder that in 1937 Mussolini, perhaps looking to impress Hitler on his first visit to Rome, cut the grand Via della Conciliazione through Rome to the Vatican, in celebration of the 1929 Lateran Treaty whereby the pope had recognized the fascist government. Such grand avenues are not themselves heroes, but they are the proper setting for heroes.

Subjects do not necessarily accept the messages that their rulers intend. They may fail to bow to the grandeur of imposing architecture and over-sized statues, reinterpret the intended meaning of heroes in devious ways, or most audaciously, simply ignore the objects in front of them, viewing them simply as a surface for pigeon shit. *In politics character work is inherently adversarial*, with one side's hero being the other side's villain. Common folk lack the resources to commission sculptures but they can always mock and deface their rulers' creations.

The statues in renaissance Florence were novel in not glorifying a despot, but in seeking to provide inspiration for normal citizens. Many were freestanding individuals, removed from architectural, especially religious, locations. Not everyone could hope to be a saint, but at least saints were real humans, not gods. David was neither saint nor god, just a shepherd. Instead of sending a message of impossible superiority, these epidictic statues were meant to inspire civic virtue in Florence's own citizens.

In the French revolution the people became the despot, but the character work looked similar. At the urging of the neoclassical painter Jacques-Louis David, the National Assembly adopted the image of Hercules, greatest of all heroes, who had once symbolized the monarchy, to demonstrate instead the triumph of the radical phase of the revolution in 1793: the National Assembly's victory over the decentralizing forces of federalism. Festivals now featured giant images of Hercules with his foot on the hydra, representing the many-headed counterrevolutionary federalists. Despite his tiny penis (a classical sign of virtue), his was a virile power, intended to displace the revolutionary figure of Marianne and—thereby—to discourage women's participation in the revolution. The men of the Assembly were beginning to fear the "hysterical"—and hence feminine—crowds of

Paris.[8] Heroism would later expand to encompass feminine virtues of endurance, but for now traditional macho heroes continued to dominate.

Caricatures

Later in the renaissance, Florence also seems to have invented a pictorial equivalent to stock dramatic characters, in what came to be known as *caricaturas*. At the end of the sixteenth century the brothers Agostino and Annibale Carracci, sophisticated artists, apparently amused themselves by drawing rough sketches of their friends that exaggerated their prominent features. They also seem to have invented the visual joke of transforming a human face into that of an animal or a tool—staples of caricature ever since. According to E. H. Gombrich, artists worked out the expression of emotions in the human face in this mocking realm, since serious art required too much decorum for such experiments: "the noble neither laugh nor cry."[9] The weak may laugh and especially cry; villains may laugh in an evil way; heroes do neither.

Even as Theophrastean character sketches faded in modern literature, they flourished in genre paintings, where familiar characters engaged in everyday activities, such as Nicolaes Maes' *The Idle Servant* or Gabriel Metsu's *The Poultry Seller*. These are really roles, fusing the person and the activity. Look at Frans Hals' famous work, *The Merry Drinker*, painted 1628–1630 (Figure 2.3). Although sometimes suspected of being a portrait of an innkeeper whom Hals knew rather than a true genre painting, its longstanding title recognizes the elements of a character sketch. This is not someone who happens to be drinking, but a man whose life is devoted to the task. (Almost all the subjects of Hals' portraits appear to be drunk, but only in genre paintings are they defined by this.)

Like sculpture, oil paintings are usually reserved for wealthy patrons and historical heroes. But not always. José De Ribera's painting of a beggar boy (Figure 2.4) expresses pity for this suffering victim, giving him the dignity usually reserved for full-length portraits of the wealthy. In a bit of romance of street life, intended to help rich patrons feel good about their own compassion and charity, the boy smiles charmingly and perhaps even wisely. He has a clubfoot but offers a note, in Latin, asking for help. He is well lit and not at all menacing. The Counter-Reformation forms the background emotions for the painting, suggesting that there is Christian insight in suffering, the basic human condition. There is sagacity among beggar philosophers. (And among Catholic leaders who

FIGURE 2.3 This man's character is devoted to drinking. He is not a hero, although he comes close in his single-minded devotion to his chosen role.

recognized the power of images to counter the austere iconoclasm of the Protestants.)[10]

Beggars were capable of dignity but not political participation. At the Spanish court only elites were portrayed as powerful. Philip IV may have been homely but he loomed large and strong in Velazquez's portraits. In the hierarchical Counter-Reformation, subjects were encouraged to be obedient not heroic. Florence's republican virtues went into eclipse until the American and French revolutions, when ancient Rome would again surpass Christianity as a source of moral heroes.

The neoclassical painter Sir Joshua Reynolds (1723–1792) had some simple suggestions for presenting heroic nobility in a painting. "To give a general air of grandeur at first view, all trifling or artful play of little lights, or an attention to a variety of tints, is to be avoided; a quietness and simplicity must reign over the whole work, to which a breadth of uniform and simple colour will very much contribute."[11] This simplicity of color, he goes on to say, can be achieved either with the heightened dark and

FIGURE 2.4 A smiling victim can cheer up potential patrons.

light of chiaroscuro or with distinct patches of the basic colors, blue, red, and yellow. He associates these bold colors with martial music, intended to arouse noble passions, as opposed to the subtle shadings that appeal to softer passions.

Bold, simple colors and lines are the means by which Masaccio and others developed an Italian renaissance style of painting out of the International Gothic style. The latter featured elaborate decoration and a delicacy of human expression that we might today code as feminine. This was not appropriate for an art that fashioned a heroic individual of considerable (male) strength. Heroes should look calm, quiet, and confident.[12]

Visual Propaganda

There are a number of hints that the presentation of characters changed in the art and literature of the late eighteenth century: high art's new preference for complex round characters and images; the emergence of "high art" itself, defined in opposition to more plebian forms; increased anxieties about the abnormal rather than about the malevolent; and a new Romantic emphasis on psychological depth. Changing tastes in characters (especially in novels) were related, in ways still debated, to the expansion of cities, flourishing of markets, increased influence of women as cultural consumers, and excitement around images of democracy.

In her discussion of this transformation, literary theorist Deidre Lynch argues, "Novel writing's claim to a singular distinction among the disciplines would be founded on the promise that it was this type of writing that rendered the deepest, truest knowledge of character." Criticizing structuralists for ignoring historical context, especially how readers and viewers were actually understanding the characters that they enjoyed, Lynch analyzes what middle-class British audiences *did* with characters (audiences in other countries would follow). "With the beginnings of the late eighteenth century's 'affective revolution' and the advent of new linkages between novel reading, moral training, and self-culture, character reading was reinvented as an occasion when readers found themselves and plumbed their own interior resources of sensibility by plumbing characters' hidden depths."[13] Traditional characters were too flat, too simplified, and often too distant from readers' own lives, to satisfy this need.

Because of these changes, traditional public character types migrated from serious art to political propaganda. It is worth looking at one example that spans the two, Delacroix's famous painting of 1830, *Liberty Leading the People*, in the Louvre (Figure 2.5). Liberty is powerful and armed, if a bit vulnerable with her bare breasts. This was a serious history painting, more than ten feet wide, and perhaps the last great allegorical painting in the European tradition; yet it suggests elements of a political poster (as it would repeatedly become in the decades to follow). Delacroix used allegory because his heroes, many of them already sacrificed in the foreground, were intended as political characters, part of a grand narrative of progress and revolution and all that.

When revolution settled down into politics, thanks partly to counterrevolution and partly to modern cynicism, traditional heroes declined: no one was all that good or all that strong. Characters would rarely again be absolutely, naively heroic. They would be more like the caricatures of Daumier or the American Thomas Nast. Nast, an immigrant from Germany, invented the image of the corrupt fat cat, in a fancy suit with a moneybag in place of his head: an image of the villain that would be used to portray both corrupt politicians and rich capitalists. In twenty-five years of work for *Harper's Weekly* he invented both villains, like Mr. Moneybags (Figure 2.6) or the

FIGURE 2.5 A heroine on the cusp between serious art and political propaganda.

Tammany Hall tiger, and heroes such as Columbia, the spirit of American liberty, who was virtuous but not physically strong (and later replaced by the stern but rarely muscular Uncle Sam).

Public characters continued to have their uses in politics, as "the masses" now expected to participate: to rally, to vote, to hold and express opinions. Character rhetoric would be revived to try to persuade them. The leaders whom they were asked to follow borrowed the conventional trappings of heroes; the villains against whom they fought were given the customary signs of evil beasts. Victims were constructed to arouse their sympathies and indignation.

Simple line drawings turn out to be one of the most powerful tools for character work, summing up someone's essence with just a few hints. An Egyptian historian comments, "the function of any cartoon is to influence the spectator for or against something, either by presenting it as a figure worthy of sympathy, or by distorting it into a figure of ridicule." Enemies can be ridiculed and made to seem less formidable, or inflated

FIGURE 2.6 A large figure with his motivation (and source of power) front and center.

into icons of true evil. As an ancestor to the cartoon, he finds a bas-relief from 2000 BCE mocking the keeper of the sacred baboons, tripped up by his charges.[14]

Beyond Graffiti

Every wall is an invitation to graffiti, an ancient form found on monuments thousands of years old. A wall, a billboard, the side of a bus all become media for political messages from all sides. Some are easy parodies of commercial products, often adaptations of advertisements. Some are works of art. In portraying a Guantanamo prisoner on a London wall, the artist Banksy makes him kneel, in a pained, manacled pose, so that passersby must look down at the image, to press home his victim status (Figure 2.7).

Most graffiti are not performing character work except on behalf of the artists themselves, who are placing their personal tags on as much territory as possible, in competition with other artists but also in combat with

FIGURE 2.7 Character work can appear anywhere, even if wall defacement rarely rises to the level of art, as it does in Banksy's *Guantanamo Prisoner*.

guards and police. They take risks as a way to demonstrate their courage (and in many cases masculinity), playing into tropes of strength and—in their own subculture—perhaps a morality of resistance. Not only the styles but the names themselves are often chosen to connote aggressive strength and control, such as Butch, Acrid, or Claw, and almost any nickname with a Z in it (these examples are from London and New York).[15] In their subcultures these artists are heroes, even if broader society views them as destructive minions.

Graffiti can consist of messages about the graffiti artist's position and values, but it also operates as a kind of jujitsu move in which the graffiti play off the original message. The featured politician receives vampire fangs or a Hitler moustache (Figure 2.8). A central word is covered to reverse the meaning, or a commentary is scrawled. A face is simply shredded.

Since the rise of modern printing technologies, walls have hosted a new form, the poster, that great medium by which average folk are exhorted to vote, buy products, and march off to war. The history of the political poster is the history of modern character work. The printing press allowed

FIGURE 2.8 In the French presidential race of 2012, Jean-Luc Mélenchon received the eyeless treatment as well as the Hitler treatment, with both moustache and bangs.

for the first posters, with an English example from as early as 1477. By the seventeenth century France already had regulations against the posting of printed bills without permission, an astute effort to control character struggles.

The form burgeoned with lithography, which by the revolutions of 1848 allowed ten thousand copies of a page to be printed in an hour. Political posters had appeared in large quantities during the French revolution, castigating the old regime but, even more, promoting the new. The personification of Liberté, strong and calm, became popular, along with liberty caps and the simple words of the revolution, Liberté, Egalité, Fraternité—and Unité. The people themselves became the hero.[16]

Ever since, political campaigns and military engagements have called forth posters and other advertisements designed to reinforce perceptions of moral and immoral characters. World War I vastly increased the production of such vehicles, divided into the mobilization of people and finances (war bonds) on the one hand and the condemnation of war atrocities—containing both victims and villains—on the other. Designers have learned to convey a message in a few lines and colors, in contrast to the impossibly busy scenes in eighteenth-century posters. Muscles make a hero, a squinty reptilian expression creates a villain. We'll look at the specifics in a moment.

New technologies continue to transform character work, from simple emoticons and emotisounds to elaborate visual editing. Just as Twitter encourages venomous character attacks like Trump's, all the more effective because they are as brief as a couple of lines in a caricature, so the ubiquity of cellphone videos has given the public a powerful tool for influencing the characters of public and semi-public figures. The most obvious genre consists of the thousands of videos taken of police actions, a number of which have damaged police credibility and reputations. These are ministories meant to establish public characters.

Out of a hundred or a thousand videos put online, perhaps one or two will resonate widely, partly because they seem to establish a person as a public character. Think of the UC Davis police commander in 2011, deliberately walking along a line of quiet protestors, already restrained behind a police tape, and dousing each one with pepper spray to the face. The chief's calm gives his action more depth, as a careful decision rather than a momentary accident, and so reflecting a demented character. The victims' calm also makes them seem more victimly, rather than the active players that protestors often appear to be. Like the Black students who sat at lunch counters in 1960, the UC students were simply sitting and waiting: and this is what they got for their efforts.

On Staten Island, Eric Garner's fatal arrest in the summer of 2014 was also caught on tape. He was an obese man, too large to run away, and apparently was simply standing there, while half a dozen cops wrestled him to the ground, partly by means of a chokehold around his neck. The hyperactivity of the police contrasts with his passivity. His only words are a repeated (eleven times), "I can't breathe." When a grand jury decided not to bring charges against Officer Pantaleone for the chokehold that helped kill Garner, it is not surprising that cities around the United States erupted in indignation, with people of all races attending large marches.

It is not easy to predict what combination of sounds and sights will "go viral" on the Internet, as these two cases did. The sheer amount of footage taken of protests and other interactions vastly increases the odds that one of them will take off. Villains and victims need to be presented in clear terms, and the general public who sees them does not have access to all the complexities that grand juries do (or to all the biases and rules that prosecutors introduce). Characters are produced in streamlined forms. (Heroes are also, although more rarely, created in these videos, as in the occasional video clip of a lifesaving deed.) Politicians are also filmed constantly, even in "private" settings. One slip can damage a reputation, as Mitt Romney learned in 2012 after disparaging the "47 percent" of the population who, he claimed, used social services but paid no income taxes.

Gender Advertisements

If Delacroix deployed character rhetoric to rally citizens for war, and if graffiti artists present themselves as heroes of resistance, corporations need to recruit people to be consumers. These are everyday characters, in which housewives are the heroes and grease and grime are the villains. But the same visual iconography is at work, whether it is Mr. Clean's bulging biceps or Aunt Jemima's warm glow.

Sociologist Erving Goffman, known for his brilliant analyses of interpersonal interactions, scrutinized advertisements from the 1960s in a book called *Gender Advertisements* that showed how ads reflect, exploit, and play with social expectations of how men and women behave.[17] First published in 1976, Goffman's close reading of advertising photos was part of a wave of research into the social construction of gender dichotomies that showed that these are not based in "nature" quite as much as they sometimes seem. The book is nothing short of a catalogue of visual signs of subordination, of strength and weakness.

Goffman reminds us of one meaning of the word "character," namely the essential nature of a person or object. Because we know that people can conceal their intentions, thoughts, and feelings, we look for signs that are difficult to fake, based on a lay psychology that he calls "the doctrine of natural expression." As a result of this "we routinely seek information about those of an object's [a person's] properties that are felt to be perduring, overall, and structurally basic, in short information about its character or 'essential nature'." And in fact he says, "there seems to be no incidental contingent expression that can't be taken as evidence of an essential attribute."[18] We unavoidably try to discern character beneath appearances, as we will discuss more in chapter 3.

And because we are *aware* that everyone constantly observes others for signs of their character, we normally learn a great deal about how to control our own expressions. Even expressions that feel to the actors and to observers to be "spontaneous and unselfconscious . . . uncalculated, unfaked, natural," are still learned, even though that learning can be hidden and unconscious. People "are learning," Goffman continues, "to be objects that have a character, that express this character, and for whom this characterological expressing is only natural. We are socialized to confirm our own hypotheses about our natures."[19] We believe in characters, and try to live up to those beliefs.

Goffman devotes so much attention to how we build facades of character that he has led many readers to doubt whether there is much behind those facades, any enduring moral person behind their many faces. Our approach is similar: we concentrate on how public characters are created and used, without asking whether the people portrayed really are villainous, heroic, and so on. But we do insist that these are useful, maybe necessary, tropes that help people to construct their moral visions, again without asking if they are accurate portraits.

Most of Goffman's observations are about the content of gender rather than characters more generally. Some reflect his interest in face-to-face interactions, especially how invested each person is in the interaction. Those who are not so invested cannot control the situation or initiate the next move. Goffman finds that the women shown in ads often adopt a puckish, childlike (or clownlike) expression, or wear clothes that suggest they are not taking their role seriously.[20] Distance from a particular setting can signal weakness or passivity, but in some forms it can also suggest the role of a powerful, distant protector, constantly watching over the others.

Many of these insights can be generalized from gender to character work more broadly. These are frequently matters of competence and control. Women in advertisements often caress an object—or themselves. "This ritualistic touching is to be distinguished from the utilitarian kind that grasps, manipulates, or holds." One is passive, the other active. Goffman observes that interactions among unequals often draw upon the model of a parent-child relationship, which runs as a theme throughout his analysis of gender. The subordinate person is often talked over or ignored, treated as not fully competent; she often solicits aid by acknowledging her helplessness or lack of competence and by expressing gratitude afterward, gaining some "mitigation of potential distance, coercion, and hostility." "Ritualistically speaking," says Goffman, "females are equivalent to subordinate males and both are equivalent to children."[21] Advertising photos have various ways to capture competence or subordination, as our Table 2.1 lists.

In the "bashful knee bend," someone stands off balance, with most of their weight on one leg and the other bent. The knee bend "can be read as a foregoing of full effort to be prepared and on the ready in the current

TABLE 2.1 Erving Goffman's Gendered Cues for Subordination*

CUTENESS:	LICENSED WITHDRAWAL OR FLOODING OUT:
Puckish, childlike expression, dress, or activity	Hands or fingers over mouth
Clowning posture	Playing with fingers
Smaller size, lower elevation	Averting one's gaze or head
Function ranked as less important (e.g., doctor and nurse together)	Faraway gaze, especially when touching an alert, powerful character
Light caress (as opposed to utilitarian grip)	Expressions of transported happiness
Bent knee, off-balance stance	Observing a situation from a slight distance or from behind a shield
Bent body or head	Turning toward or against another's body for protection or comfort
Expansive smiling	

* Erving Goffman, *Gender Advertisements* (Harvard University Press, 1979).

social situation, for the position adds a moment to any effort to fight or flee. Once again one finds a posture that seems to presuppose the goodwill of anyone in the surroundings who could offer harm." Often, the person with a bent leg leans on another for support. A bent body or head can send the same signal: "an acceptance of subordination, an expression of ingratiation, submissiveness, and appeasement."[22]

"Licensed withdrawal" from an interaction is another sign of weakness or incompetence as well as of subordination. For instance, "Women more than men, it seems, are pictured engaged in involvements which remove them psychologically from the social situation at large, leaving them unoriented in it and to it, and presumably, therefore, dependent on the protectiveness and goodwill of others who are (or might come to be) present." Goffman mentions "flooding out," when someone puts a finger or their hands over their mouth out of shock, remorse, fear, shyness, or laughter. Averting one's gaze or turning one's head has similar effects of withdrawal, which connotes a lack of power or control.[23]

Subordinates are potential victims. They express deference and weakness, of which stronger players may take advantage. One immoral act of victimization is all that separates victim from potential victim. Heroes cannot afford to withdraw, relax, or look away; they must remain vigilant and prepared to act.

Visual Signs

Cultural analysts in the social sciences concentrate on the words that humans use to convey meanings, slighting musical and especially visual vehicles. Even when we do pay attention to music or images, we tend to extract the verbal messages they contain without asking how they convey them. Music is reduced to its lyrics, easy to reproduce on a printed page, rather than the bodily sensations that we feel when producing and listening to it. Visual images are more easily reproduced in books and articles, but again, an idea is usually extracted and carried off.

This is an idealism that we need to move beyond. As sociologist Jonathan Turner remarks, "If humans thought only in words, they would seem very dim-witted, since language is an auditory mode of communication . . . sequential and very slow. Humans are a primate and, by virtue of this fact, they are visually dominant."[24] As much as one third of the human brain is devoted to processing visual information, such as color, light, motion, face and object recognition, and so forth.

This may be one reason that narrative theory, oriented toward words, has sometimes overlooked characters: in real life we assess characters more rapidly and regularly with visual means than with verbal ones. One could spin an evolutionary tale about why this is so: we need to evaluate threats before they are too close, and we need to do this as fast as possible, long before conscious calculations would be able to kick in. When humans were prey rather than predators, such assessments were essential to survival. Our ancestors did not have time to sit down and read a story. Visual information must be processed through rapid feeling-thinking processes, and more gradually through verbal means. In evolutionary terms, we needed to know if another creature had some reason to want to hurt us, was strong enough to do so, and was fast enough: morality, strength, and activity level.

In some settings, narratives are explicitly subordinate to images. Among magical items thought to contain special powers, Christian icons stand out because they sum up a saint's goodness as a way of directing the viewer's attention to God and her supplication to the saint for intervention. Stories about saints merely illustrate their inherent moral character. "A series of episodes that support narration," observes Cynthia Hahn, are "emblematic of various virtues or truths that are revealed as essential to the subject as a holy being. Together the episodes shape an aggregate picture, or icon, of the saint."[25]

Among the visual images deployed for purposes of characterization, those in the media are most readily available and most often studied. But political players themselves, whether in election campaigns or in protest movements, are the other main producers of visual images. In some cases, political players employ character workers directly. In others, it is artists and intellectuals only loosely associated with organized groups who produce the messages, including verbal means such as novels as well as visual ones like posters, theater, murals, films, and graffiti.[26] But artists and intellectuals are rarely dependable, often adopting complex or even ironic approaches to public characters. It's usually best to do one's own character work.

Dutch scholar Rens Vliegenthart shows why it is important to look at images themselves rather than trying to extract their ideas. Examining more than two hundred election posters for Dutch political parties, stretching from 1946 to 2006, he finds that over time they have placed less and less emphasis on ideology. Instead, they have increasingly highlighted visual information: party logos and individual party leaders.[27] Political consultants have realized that people think visually, even if scholars have not entirely caught on.

Much of the work of character assessment that our minds perform occurs outside conscious awareness. As we'll see in the next chapter, we decide to like or trust someone in a split second, without much time to calculate why. We scan their faces and body language for visual cues (Table 2.2).

Good intentions are signaled and interpreted visually above all else: a genuine smile, a friendly gesture, eye contact, physical proximity, and leaning toward the other person. Bad intentions also have their signs, in narrowed, "beady" eyes and shifty, sideways looks.

Visual cues also express power and competence: upright posture, expansive gestures, calmness, eye contact (again), thoughtful facial expressions, size and position. The strong are typically placed higher than others, and are sometimes at a slight distance, as though they cannot enter into the merriment while they are on guard. People appear grander when seen from below; they can be made to seem larger than the viewer.

TABLE 2.2 Visual Cues for Main Character Traits

BENEVOLENCE	Genuine smile, upward gaze, attractive face Brightly lit, glittering, shining Warm, reddish undertones Supportive posture and gestures
MALEVOLENCE	Shifty or beady eyes; false grin or smile Overly large or sharp teeth Twisted, ugly face, suggesting cruelty Grasping or clawed hands Shadowy; cold, bluish undertones Threatening posture and gestures Patently immoral acts or costumes Skulls and skeletons
STRENGTH	Large size, takes up a lot of space Symmetric or attractive face, body Higher than others Lit in chiaroscuro style Clenched fist, arms triumphantly in air Figure gestures or comes toward us Thick, well-defined muscles Holding up heavy weight, group totem, or children Thoughtful expression Moistened eye when sad Small group of massed individuals (five to ten)
WEAKNESS	Small size, underdeveloped physique Full crying when sad Ridiculous appearance, mocking Hands out in supplication Disabled or wounded Childlike appearance: large eyes in relation to face; large head in relation to body; small chin, round face Babyface Large crowd of individuals (more than ten)
ACTIVITY	In motion, curved lines Sharp, angular Thin bodies; upright posture Heat Alertness Clenched, angry fist; exaggerated gestures "Speed lines" in drawings Portrayed in action contexts
PASSIVITY	Horizontal posture Straight lines Dishevelled clothes Head shots only Cold Corpulent, rounded Leaning, lounging, or engaged in leisure activities Portrayed outside action contexts

TABLE 2.3 A Selective Bestiary of Visual Metaphors

BENEVOLENCE	Dog (loyalty) Horse (courage) Lion (brave, noble) Dove (pure)
MALEVOLENCE	Pig (selfish, dirty) Wolf (dangerous) Vulture (opportunistic) Monkeys (disruptive) Fox (sly)
STRENGTH	Elephant Ox Bear Owl (wisdom) Horse
WEAKNESS	Baby animals Small animals Rabbits
ACTIVITY	Monkeys Birds Bees, Ants Beavers Dolphin (playful)
PASSIVITY	Sloth Cows Sheep Plants

Nonhuman species are ready symbols of character traits (Table 2.3). Animal analogies for malevolence include both mischievous monkeys, up to no good, and more powerfully threatening figures such as bears. The baring of teeth is an aggressive threat, and is easily transformed into various other signs, such as rabid animals. Teeth can be shaped into fangs. In caricatures, large animals, especially those associated with work, connote power.[28]

So what do heroes look like? They are large, as well as strong and benevolent, calm but watchful. "We attribute virtue to healthy and beautiful bodies," observes William Miller, "and vice to ugly and sickly ones." This is why we speak of "standing tall, standing up, standing firm, of not taking it lying down."[29] Heroes are "larger than life," and we literally see them as bigger than they are. The legendary labor leader Big Bill Haywood was invariably described as "tall, tremendous, broad in chest and shoulders, erect and displaying physical powers that dwarfed [other men]," but when his jailers finally measured him he was a mere five feet eleven inches. Taller than average, but hardly the giant he appeared to those who knew his reputation.[30]

Heroes carry a quiet simplicity, Joshua Reynolds said. When *Time* magazine placed Hillary Clinton on its cover in January 2014, she did not necessarily look moral, but she looked strong and, most of all, just a giant pants-leg crushing tiny competitors. But Hillary is the gender exception. We do not have a well-developed iconography for women heroes, as we do for men. When women are portrayed as heroes they usually look masculine, except for long hair and a couple of awkward breasts stuck on a broad-shouldered, muscular male body (Figure 2.9).

Just as the best way to prove you have power is to use it, the best way to look powerful is to be seen actively exerting it. Heroes are not portrayed standing at attention like a line of toy soldiers who could easily be knocked over. They are coiled, like springs, ready for action, or in the middle of vanquishing a villain. Even statues of heroes are given a contrapposto pose, rather like an S, instead of being shown flat-footed and at attention. They may be calm, but alert. Or they may be gritting their teeth in determination. They may look alarmed. Proper heroes should look into the distance, or up in the air. When they look down, at those nearby, they can appear to be "looking down their nose" in a contemptuous manner.

Throughout history leaders have exploited the universal association of light with heroes, dark with stealthy, shadowy villains—none more successfully than the French kings beginning with Charles IX (a century before Louis XIV). "Heat and light represented the victory over error, hatred, evil, and death—the realm of cold and darkness. With countless variations, subtle twists, and little quirks, this solar imagery ultimately served as a continual reminder of the benevolence that the king showed (or should show) toward his kingdom. This benevolence was at times represented as a garden made fertile by the sun's rays or at other times as a ship guided by the light of the sun or other royal stars." Heroes emit a warm glow. Torches, beacons, candelabra, and pillars of fire were common symbols of the king.[31]

The weak are allowed to play, to look ridiculous, to distance themselves from their roles. They may adopt explicitly supplicant roles, with outstretched hands. They express emotions differently, especially allowing themselves to cry in uncontrolled ways. Seen from above, they appear smaller. Small animals, busy or not, intimate weakness.

FIGURE 2.9 Women have to become men to be heroes in traditional iconography.

There is also an iconography of weak innocence. In many modern cultures, indicators of childhood serve this purpose: great, glassy eyes, disproportionately large for the head; a head that is disproportionately big for the body. Such indicators of "cuteness" have been used to extend compassion to nonhuman species; animal rights ads inevitably show babies of a species. Activist Brian Davies describes his moral shock at seeing a seal killed: "He was a little ball of white fur with big dark eyes and a plaintive cry . . . he was only ten days old. He went to meet, in a curious, friendly and playful way, the first human he had ever seen and was . . . by that same human . . . clubbed on the head and butchered on the spot. He was skinned alive."[32] The story not only helps us visualize the innocence of a baby but also to appreciate its attitude toward the world around it. And there is a villain to the tale as well.

Visual cues for activity include a look of alertness, bodies in motion or tensed for sudden movement. Suggestions of active emotions, especially anger, include a clenched fist or heated facial expression. Passivity on the other hand is expressed through bodies that seem incapable of sudden exertion: lying down, lounging about, or engaged in distracting leisure activities. Hair and clothes may look disheveled, as though the subject were confused or inattentive. Slow-moving animals, especially those usually found in domesticated herds, suggest passivity.

Seated figures rarely look heroic. They are passive and smaller. A partial exception is the seated Lincoln in his memorial in Washington, D.C. His pose conveys both contemplation and weariness in the aftermath of the American Civil War. But his weak stance is countered by the enormous size of his marble statue, the grand temple in which it is housed, and the expansive grounds on which it is situated. These factors work together to dwarf those who come to visit a man who even in a weakened position is clearly presented as a hero. For the most part, standing figures look more active; figures on horseback look enormous as well as active, especially when one or two of the horse's feet are off the ground (frequently a sign that the rider died in battle, further accentuating their heroism). Ronald Reagan and Subcomandante Marcos liked to be photographed on a horse; Putin went further and rode shirtless.

We often read character back from the emotions that people express, especially reflex emotions that are easy to detect in the face. Anger, disgust, surprise, sudden joy or sadness, and fear all have characteristic effects on facial muscles that allow others to perceive what we are feeling. They can be faked, but not easily. Artists and actors learn how to capture such feelings, and audiences to read them. The latter have an easier time, since we see the same expressions in those around us every day.[33]

Different characters display different emotions. Fear and anxiety tend to suggest weakness; pride connotes power. Sadness, because it expresses loss, may also hint at weakness, while joy is linked to success and hence power. Sociologist Theodore Kemper explains why these emotions are related to underlying social positions, positing that power and status continually shape our expectations and behavior and hence our emotions.[34] His concept of power lines up well with our strength dimension, and his idea of status includes our moral dimension: heroes are proud, calm, trusting, and happy, victims are afraid and anxious, villains are hateful and contemptuous, and minions are envious and anxious. Not only do we have characteristic emotions about public characters, we expect them to display distinctive emotions themselves.

Much visual meaning depends on specific historical contexts. Individual politicians are familiar to audiences and carry their own load of meanings. But more general images can also be given specific content. A helmet on a soldier may suggest strength, but make it a German helmet of the Nazi era and it also connotes evil. For an audience that trusts its police, images of someone being arrested suggest that person's criminality, but if the same audience is opposed to their regime or sees it as repressive then the figure being arrested can become a hero or victim instead. Placing a figure on a donkey reminds Christians of Jesus, but for Muslims it is an insult.

Not all bodily cues are visual, of course. The human voice is a subtle instrument for conveying messages beyond words. In the early days of rhetoric, a loud voice, capable of reaching thousands, was crucial, but in today's world of mediated messages more refined cues are possible. For instance, Margaret Thatcher took lessons to lower her voice, to convey strength in a more manly way. Like Hillary Clinton, she had to conquer many gender expectations in order to appear heroic.

The Music of Character

Words and images are the basic tools of character work, but sound plays a role as well. Films, television, and video clips are ubiquitous means for character construction. A character's voice is central, but other sound effects can be added to suggest power or weakness. A squeak, rattle, or fart makes a character more ridiculous. A creaky breaking noise renders a vehicle or a robot inoperable—and harmless. The ominous, slow thuds of cowboy boots across a wood floor suggest a powerful threat. Deep, booming noises or the crack of Indiana Jones' whip suggest strength. Some of the best sounds are cheers and boos—an old trick of rhetoric which consists of telling the audience how to react by showing them another audience reacting.

But when it comes to character work, the most effective sounds come from music. The glue that binds collective action of all sorts, from marching to dancing to working together, music has long helped soldiers feel heroic solidarity with one another. As Emile Durkheim pointed out, groups acting in unison furnish each individual member a sense of being part of something larger, something sacred and grand. The proud beat and swelling chords that create heroes have their counterparts in the musical creation of villains and victims, even minions. Over the years composers have developed a precise musical vocabulary for performing character work, especially in movies.

A single character can be associated with a solo instrument, often with either a goofy or a powerful timbre. And since Wagner, characters have frequently had their own mini-melodies, leitmotivs that are associated with the subjective viewpoint of an actor, heard only when she is present (or about to appear) and possibly even mimicking the sound of her voice. Instead of a voice-over, this form of music expresses the character's emotions directly.[35]

Beethoven's great *Eroica* symphony is a study in the sounds of heroism. He uses broad, bold sounds, much like Reynolds' simple, noble colors, and the novel length of the work suggests a grand project. Heroes triumph in the end, and so music must shift from uncertain stress and struggle to a joyful outcome. Beethoven connotes uncertainty and confusion in the first movement, followed by grief, strife, even despair in the second by means of a funeral march, followed by a more joyful, triumphant scherzo and a playful but calming finale. It ends in reassuringly tonic E-flat major chords. Whatever the emotional ups and downs of the struggle, heroes leave us feeling safe, proud, and secure.

Heroes can also be constructed by showing what they confront, as with Ralph Vaughan Williams' haunting sounds of cracking ice and howling winds in the score for *Scott of the Antarctic* (1948). Chromaticism, says Alfred Brendel, "stands for suffering and insecurity."[36]

Films deploy every sort of music to support their character work, whether borrowing pre-existing pieces or composing new soundtracks. Clean tonalities and swelling orchestras alert us to heroes, especially if the music mimics or accompanies cheering crowds. William Walton composed a grand crescendo to accompany the French knights' charge at the beginning of the battle of Agincourt in *Henry V*, admiring their strength even though they were, strictly speaking, the enemy—and facing annihilation.

Music can also create threatening characters. Director David Lean described his character work in the scene in *Oliver Twist* when Oliver first joins Fagin's band of pickpockets. "Fagin as a character starts off in Oliver's eyes as an amusing old gentleman, and gradually this guise falls away and we see him in all his villainy." To demonstrate this, Lean interrupts a comic ballet in which the boys show off their talents, with a sudden, vicious kick from Fagin, aimed at two boys who had not performed well.[37] The story combines visual and aural character work.

Music has many straightforward emotional effects, and these emotions are in turn linked to public characters: the joy and triumph of a hero, the fear associated with villains, the pity evoked by victims. Minor tones make us sad, a feeling that accompanies our pity for victims, but they can also accompany the frightening music appropriate to a villain.[38]

An increasing tempo may signify the triumph of a hero or the approach of a threat. A slow tempo might accompany passivity: a victim, or a hero at rest. Leitmotivs for villains begin slowly but work their way to cacophonous crescendi. Think of the Wicked Witch of the West. The most recognizable villain motif of recent movies is not for a human at all, but for a great white shark, whose two-note theme assumes many variations as it slows and quickens to stimulate audience adrenaline.

Whether in music or voice, pitch also connotes character, especially strength or weakness. Minions speak in high tones, which we associate with small, ineffectual creatures. In the recent movies featuring them, they chatter and giggle nervously in their own amusing language. Childlike victims are also likely to speak in high tones. Deep tones come from large lungs, likely in strong animals and big men. Hence heroes tend to speak in handsome baritones and have deep themes, while villains also have gravely deep voices and leitmotivs. Volume has similar connotations of strength and activity (loud music) or weakness and passivity (soft volumes). The gender connections are unavoidable.

Different instruments suggest different feelings, as one composer suggests when he added "an Irish pennywhistle" to suggest "a certain purity and innocence."[39] Related to its color is an instrument's tonal range: "If you have a slow, four-part, quarter-note texture, it might seem most appropriate in mid-range strings. But if you condense the texture as closely as possible and put it up two octaves in a purely violin color, it suddenly goes from a pastoral feel to one of saintly ascension. Or if you take this same condensed version down three octaves in a low brass color, you have another totally different version that is dark with an ominous tone— very different emotions from the same music."[40] You have gone from the enlightened spirituality of a hero or possibly victim to the darkness of a villain.

Strong rhythms, especially those found in martial music intended to accompany or mimic marching, connote strength. Flowing rhythms suggest the power, grace, and accomplishment that we expect from calm heroes going about their heroic work. Uneven or broken rhythms, in contrast, connote excitement but also sometimes fear.

With a regular, flowing rhythm we easily perceive heroes marching off to war. But the same strength can take on an immoral feel, as composer Hanns Eisler long ago suggested in his analysis of *No Man's Land*, a pacifist film by Victor Trivas from 1931. At the beginning, individual men are reporting for duty in 1914. "The atmosphere is melancholy, the pace is limp, unrhythmic." But the gradual imposition of a stronger rhythm unites the men, indeed the entire community. "Music suggesting a military march is introduced quite softly. As it grows louder, the pace of the men becomes quicker, more rhythmic, more collectively unified. The women and children, too, assume a military bearing, and even the soldiers' mustaches begin to bristle. There follows a triumphant crescendo. Intoxicated by the music, the mobilized men, ready to kill and be killed, march into the barracks. Then, fade-out."[41]

This would seem to describe the creation of brave heroes ready to die for their community, but Eisler points out that the film is pacifist. What we see is the creation of a villain, "the transformation of seemingly harmless individuals into a horde of barbarians." He injects his own Brechtian desire for esthetic distance or alienation, fearing the emotional effects he describes. "The composition and performance of the music combined with the picture must demonstrate to the public the destructive and barbarizing influence of such musical effects. The music must not be continually heroic, else the naïve spectator would become intoxicated by it, like the men portrayed on the screen."[42] Eisler's anti-fascist concerns may lead him to dislike the impact of music that connotes militarized power, but its emotional impact is undeniable.

Would the musicality of heroism have been so clear if Beethoven's symphony had not been called *Eroica*? Music's strongest contributions to character occur *when it is joined to words and images*. Our immediate feelings upon hearing the music contribute to our abiding sense of a character that lodges in our brains. Those who compose soundtracks for movies have refined this musical vocabulary over the generations. Richard Wagner's operas were engagements among the protagonists on stage mirrored by musical interactions among their repeating leitmotivs. The film industry has refined the application of music to emotions over the past century, dropping the constraints of traditional forms so that it can concentrate on emotional impacts.

In songs, lyrics help create characters alongside the music that gives them passion. In fact, academic analysts of music's impact on politics have frequently concentrated on those lyrics while ignoring the music itself. A full analysis of characters must unite these different dimensions.

Traditional images of heroes may have migrated from marble sculpture to graphic novels and action-figure dolls, but elements of their portrayal persist in campaign photos, caricatures, films, and daily life. This is inevitable. Humans perceive and interpret visual cues about faces and bodies in an instant, drawing inferences about what kind of person would look like this. Music too tells us immediately how to feel about the images in front of us. Psychologists have examined many additional ways that we draw sweeping conclusions about people from tiny amounts of evidence. This kind of attribution has been central to social and cognitive psychology. If chapter 1 and chapter 2 have examined cultural products that convey character tropes, we now turn to the psychological mechanisms with which people interpret others as characters.

3 | The Psychology of Creating Persons

If you have brains and a heart, show only one or the other. You will not get credit for either should you show both at once.

—Friedrich Hölderlin

W E FIRST SEE JON SNOW as he tries to teach his ten-year-old half-brother to shoot an arrow. His good-natured smile tells us he is a decent guy, as does the color purity of his last name in a novel and television series—*Game of Thrones*—that relies heavily on color symbols. Other people refer to him in Shakespearean fashion as "the bastard," placing him outside the normal feudal hierarchy that governs most of the other characters and thus freeing him to earn his own place in society. To stress the point, we soon see his father Ned Stark, performing his duty as Lord of the North, behead a sympathetic guardsman for desertion. Stark explains, "The man who passes the sentence should swing the sword": a sense of social responsibility beyond normal good and evil. With more choice and agency available to him, Jon Snow can be morally superior to Ned Stark.

In the next scene Snow begs Stark to spare the lives of six orphaned dire-wolf puppies, one for each of Stark's children. They will grow into fierce protectors, even Snow's, the runt of the litter. In a similar kind spirit, Snow begins to bond with "the Imp," the scorned dwarf son of the kingdom's richest man. "All dwarfs are bastards in their fathers' eyes," the Imp wryly observes. Only in the distant future will the Imp's wit and intelligence prove to be useful sources of strength in this world of warriors, and his bond with Jon Snow will help unite several warring clans.

It takes longer for the series to reveal what a powerful warrior Jon Snow is, with strength to match his goodness. He also has supernatural

Public Characters. James M. Jasper, Michael P. Young, and Elke Zuern, Oxford University Press (2020) © Oxford University Press.
DOI: 10.1093/oso/9780190050047.001.0001

sympathies that permit him to be brought back from the dead, a neat trick that allows us to see this hero's willingness to sacrifice himself but also places him back in the next battle. One more thing: he is devilishly handsome.

This all appears significant only in retrospect, but it is planted in our view of Jon Snow the bastard. He seems a minor character at the start of the series, but he is destined for greatness. Like any sophisticated fictional product today, the series takes a long time—in this case seven seasons—to bring him to his full potential. By then viewers have learned that he is not a bastard at all, but the clandestine heir to the throne of the Eight Kingdoms. His own ignorance of his blood line helped Jon Snow to grow up to be stronger and more moral—and a better hero-king. Like Shakespeare's Faulconbridge, this son of a king was not raised with the pretensions of a prince. Good by choice or accident, strong through genetics and some supernatural aid, he is the perfect hero.

As good painters and storytellers know, humans fill in lots of missing pieces in the evidence they acquire about each other. If we know one small thing about a person or a group, our minds automatically furnish other information. A few dabs of red on a portrait, and we see drunkenness. From an adjective or two in a novel, we think we know a person's inner self. We begin to like Jon Snow from his handsome, diffident smile. Our nervous systems are so good at perceiving patterns that they may see patterns that are not actually there. Most famously, in the "halo effect," if we know that a person has one positive trait—often simply good looks—we think they have others. If we like them for one trait, we try hard to like them for others as well. As a result, what we learn first about a person often influences everything else.[1]

Attributing Personhood

One of the most enduring fields of psychology is the study of how people think and learn about each other. One of its practitioners, Daniel Gilbert, uses the term "ordinary personology" for "the ways in which ordinary people come to know about each other's temporary states (such as emotions, intentions, and desires) and enduring dispositions (such as beliefs, traits, and abilities)."[2] The packages of traits that we have been calling characters are one such tool that people use to summarize the enduring dispositions they perceive in others. We apply similar tools to public characters in the media and to people we meet at a party.

In the first half of the twentieth century psychologists assumed that we look at other people much as we would look at objects through a special lens: people display signals that we may or may not notice, may or may not interpret correctly. Judging other people was like judging the length of lines on cards, as in Solomon Asch's celebrated experiments on peer pressure.[3]

In another, equally famous experiment, Asch investigated how we form impressions of people, not black lines, by reading strings of adjectives aloud and then asking subjects about the person described. Different word orders change our impressions: earlier information shapes how we interpret later information. Asch, trained in Gestalt psychology, showed that our minds put together discrete pieces of information into a unified package that we recognize as a thing or a person. We make inferences about the whole from small parts of it: "the subject works to reach the core of the person through the trait or traits."[4]

According to another Gestalt psychologist, Fritz Heider (whose circle and triangles we encountered in chapter 1), we normally assume that people's behavior reflects underlying character traits, or "dispositional properties" that make the world a predictable place. Just as we accept that an object has not vanished simply because we have turned the corner and can no longer see it, we attribute to other people an inner stability that allows us "to integrate a bewildering mass of data in the most economical terms."[5] Our attribution of characterological properties is a learned but unconscious ability necessary for social interaction. We "know" what people are like, and we know what to expect from them. We cling to our expectations, all the more easily because they are rarely tested directly.

When we try to understand another person's action, according to Heider, we attribute it to the person's capacity and motivation. These are obviously close to our dimensions of strength and evaluation. Motivation, he elaborates, consists of both intention and level of exertion. Exertion, too, is not far from the third dimension of active versus passive that we will elaborate shortly. In Gestalt psychology, the overall configuration—our sense of a "person" in this case—shapes each piece of information we receive, at least as much as the information contributes to the configuration.

In 1967 Harold Kelley observed that people account for each other's behavior through the same logical processes that scientists use in explaining the world. People look for behaviors that persist over time ("this is not the first time I have seen him act like a jerk"), across different kinds of settings ("he acts like a jerk to me, but also to his wife"), and which distinguish that person as different from most others ("no one else treats me badly"). We look for patterns, just as scientists do. (Of course we use feeling as much as thinking to detect those patterns.)[6]

Since then, hundreds of cognitive psychologists have elaborated on how people make inferences about others. We tend to label actions in terms of the intentions of the actor (her beliefs, desires, and plans) and her basic personal traits (honesty, niceness). We then attribute the action either to the dispositions of the actor or to the situation in which we observe her. In the attribution effect, people tend to attribute actions to people's personalities and intentions rather than to the situations they are in. When a firefighter pulls a child from a burning building, news accounts extol his inherent bravery rather than describing the extensive training given to firefighters to elicit just that response, or the special equipment he used. We admire brave heroes more than disciplined professionals.[7] Characterization works because we expect character traits to influence how people act, in fact to have the most fundamental influence.[8]

A single word can affect the characters we construct, especially if it is the first piece of information we encounter, an effect called "priming." If we are briefly exposed to sentences that convey hostility, we will feel more negatively about someone we then encounter or see. Orators trying to construct villains and minions know this well. In contrast, the word "brave" can prime us to see people more positively, for instance seeing their actions as adventurous rather than reckless.[9] Small hints like this can color everything else we perceive and feel about a person.

Other people's faces are one of the most important tools we use to attribute character to them. We make judgments about faces in less than one tenth of a second—and when given more time we tend not to change our minds but simply to become more confident in our initial judgments.[10] We rely on and believe in visual facial cues.

What do we see in those faces? Two things, primarily. The main thing we decide about someone is how much we like them: how warm, approachable, attractive, and friendly we find them. Are we drawn toward them or repelled? We are immediately attracted to Jon Snow as appealing and good. The second thing we judge is how competent, dominant, or aggressive they are. Although different researchers label the two factors differently, they boil down to what we are calling morality and strength. Is someone good or bad, strong or weak?[11]

Psychologists have concluded that humans have an "implicit personality theory" that helps them impose coherence on scattered observations. As Gilbert puts it, "Observers do not think of actors as collections of unrelated dispositions; rather they use the dispositions they have inferred from behavioral evidence ('taciturn and scholarly') to construct unifying explanations ('brooding intellectual type') that allow them to infer new dispositions for which they have no evidence ('opera lover')." Gilbert notes, "Asch once suggested that the most important finding to emerge from his studies was that of his many subjects, not one was ever at a loss to explain how the most incongruous traits might cohere."[12] Public characters are a case of implicit personality theory.[13]

A business professor, Phil Rosenzweig, shows how these effects can be important in the real world. Books on successful or unsuccessful companies, he says, exaggerate the influence of CEOs on these outcomes, largely because of the halo effect: if a company succeeds, this must be the result of the leadership traits of the CEO, who is then described as decisive, flexible, or whatever current fad in management theory says a good CEO should be. We cannot believe that failed companies might be headed by good CEOs, or successful ones by bad CEOs. We underestimate the impact of luck and structural factors, such as industry decline or growth, and we make CEOs into heroes or villains.[14]

Fast Thinking

All this research into how we form impressions of other people suggests two conclusions: we form impressions of others in a fraction of a second merely on the basis of their faces and other surface signs; and the initial information we get about a person frames any later evidence we obtain. This is the reason that visual images are so important in politics, and why scholars often associate them with irrationality.

As we learn more about another person, we do correct our first impressions, but usually not entirely.[15] When we are particularly interested in the setting, we may assume that someone's behavior—looking nervous for instance—derives from the situation rather than her dispositions. We expect someone to be nervous before a debate, for example. But otherwise, we look to their character.

Psychologist Alexander Todorov and his colleagues have shown that our snap judgments of a politician's face give us an impression of her competence, which in turn affects how we vote. They asked their Princeton undergraduates to rate pairs of faces on a number of personality traits, not telling them that the photos were of actual candidates in U.S. Senate and House elections. They compared their students' judgments with who actually won the races, and found that the more competent-looking politician won in more than two thirds of the elections. Judgments of who was trustworthy and who was likeable had no effect.[16]

Like other researchers, they found that additional information about candidates dilutes the initial impressions, but does not erase them entirely. They sadly conclude, "Although research has shown that inferences from thin slices of nonverbal behaviors can be surprisingly accurate, there is no good evidence that trait inferences from facial appearance are accurate."[17] This conclusion does not fully avoid the bias against images that so many scholars harbor, but it confirms the deep impact of the visual. And we rarely form character judgments purely on the basis of a visual glimpse with no context or expectations. As we saw with music, sights, sounds, and words are usually packaged together.

The study of political life is a challenge for the great tradition of experimental psychology that we have been examining. A great deal of politics consists of slow thinking, not fast, as arguments are challenged, deliberations stretch out, and individuals are forced in some cases to justify their positions. In these messy processes, a number of factors intervene that cannot be reproduced in laboratory experiments: complicated affective attachments to groups and individuals, strong reflex emotions such as anger or fear that institutional review boards would never allow researchers to create, and sustained interactions that can lead in unexpected directions.

A lot of the cultural understandings that go into forming character judgments have not yet been replicated in experiments. Visual cues are crucial to our construction of impressions of others, and psychologists have studied what faces tell us. But what about a certain style of dress, a haircut, a way of talking that connotes class or party or religion? For example, Betsy Leondar-Wright has documented the gap between middle- and working-class styles of interacting in groups, from how they joke to how they feel about community leaders.[18] Experiments have not yet told us much about the many details that go into character readings.

For instance clothes suggest character. Cultural historians Stuart and Elizabeth Ewen discuss the messages of clothes in ways that resonate with character work, beginning with blue jeans. What had been work clothes in the nineteenth century became symbols of a simpler past in the twentieth. "In the movies, the range hands of the early cattle industry were reborn as icons of a noble, rural simplicity; rugged individualism; primal morality and law. Blue jeans were conspicuous within the moral landscape of media Americana. On the screen these pants taunted the imaginations of city folk as emblems of a simpler and uncorrupted life." Not only blue jeans but Indian beads and olive drab came to connote moral revolt in the 1960s. Advertising had already taught consumers the iconography of clothes. "Clothing of revolt became all the more possible among people schooled by a world in which meanings and images were infinitely manipulable. The consumer society, with its heavy implantation of imagery, had supplied its opposition with the visual terminology of revolt."[19] Visual signals are crucial, but character packages limit how we interpret them: they are not infinitely malleable.

Warmth and Competence

Because the principal traits that we attribute to leaders and other individuals are benevolence or malevolence and strength or weakness, cognitive psychologists have used these as schemas in research on how people think about and evaluate the social world, studying characterization without using that term. Psychologist Susan Fiske labels the dimensions warmth (similar to our morality dimension) and competence (one aspect of strength), tracing the processes by which we compare social-economic groups on the basis of these underlying components.

Fiske reports experimental research on the usual emotions felt toward different kinds of groups. We are *proud* of those we consider warm and competent (including, for Americans, housewives, Christians, and Americans themselves!). We feel *pity* for those who are warm but incompetent, like the "retarded," disabled, and elderly, and *disgust* for incompetents who we think lack warmth, such as the homeless. We *envy* those who are competent but cold, notably the rich. This is one way in which her social comparisons differ from our political characterizations: in politics we hate villains but do not usually envy them.[20]

Fiske's findings and our expectations about public characters are compatible in most ways. The rapid evaluations we make about another's warmth add up to a judgment of friend or foe, "which readies us to act: to give direct, active aid to friends (assisting, helping, protecting) or to do direct, active harm to foes (fighting, attacking, sabotaging)."[21] Interestingly, she finds that we are especially vigilant with those who are either trustworthy or untrustworthy, but not those who are neutral on this dimension: we want to know whom to approach or avoid. The moral dimension dominates.

Only after judging warmth, Fiske says, do we make judgments about the other's competence (although both judgments take place in a split second). "Because being competent to enact goals is a secondary judgment, we engage in passive but positive behavior with competent, high-status people, essentially going along to get along (cooperating with, uniting with, associating with). In contrast, scorned, low-status people merit passive harm (excluding, ignoring, neglecting)."[22] We cooperate with heroes, assist victims, fight villains, and avoid minions.

These judgments interact with a society's stereotypes about different genders, classes, sexual orientations, and racial-ethnic groups. In the United States, respondents typically rank men, white people, those with more education, and the famous as more competent. But lower-status groups are often viewed as warmer (more honest, nicer), and they especially view themselves this way.[23] There is some evidence that the "haves" of American society really are less nice.[24] Cultures have different expectations for different stereotyped groups, and these expectations determine how easy it is for members of those groups to be seen as one or another public character. Where women are thought to be weak, it is hard for them to be heroes—or villains. We'll return to group stereotypes in the next section, and to gender in chapter 9.

A student of Fiske's, Amy Cuddy, has applied this framework to workplace interactions and impressions. Judgments made about morality turn out to be more fragile than those about competence. When we find that someone we consider competent does not know how to ski, we dismiss this as an unlearned skill. We still think of them as generally competent. But one instance of bad behavior can devastate a person's moral reputation. We feel as though a curtain has been lifted and we are seeing the "real" person if we see her slap her child or find that she has lied. According to Cuddy, we *expect* people to hide their authentic intentions, so we look for deeper clues to their *real* moral fiber. (Signaling theory suggests that people "mimic" the behavior of good people, even if they are not so good.)

We see the same fragility of moral standing in organizational reputations: one lie can damage the credibility of an entire organization. In a study of the interactions between animal protectionists and their organizational targets, the largest blunder the latter could make was to be caught in a lie. Arrogance or nasty counter-tactics can also damage an organization's moral reputation; people often turn revolutionary when a dictator represses peaceful protests. Further, mistakes by a small part of the organization can taint the whole—although organizations try to isolate the damage by firing individuals and blaming "human error" (the treatment of whistleblowers is a familiar example). If an individual or organization is nasty or deceptive on one occasion, we assume that it will be on others too.[25]

These observations suggest that it is easier for a reputation to decline on the moral dimension than to rise. It is easier for a hero to be reconfigured into a villain than for a villain to be rehabilitated into a hero. Damaging revelations about victims turn them into minions more easily than sympathetic information about minions recasts them to appear more moral. Presumably, apologies can improve moral reputations, but the most effective rehabilitation probably comes when prior damaging information is proved to have been false.[26]

Cuddy confirms that people expect an inverse relationship between morality and power. "The more competent you are, the less nice you must be. And vice versa: Someone who comes across as *really* nice must not be too smart."[27] She and Fiske find the equivalent of our public characters in economic status hierarchies, but people react to them differently. In strategic settings, strong and malevolent players are feared and demonized; in social settings, they are often envied as well. Envy involves both admiration for their strength and resentment of their success. This is a common reaction not only to villains but also to heroes: we admire them and are grateful to them, but in many cases we do not really like them. We fear their power.

If a single bad action can ruin a reputation for goodness, it can establish one for badness. Few political players aim for reputations as villains, but among criminals this is a crucial job requirement. Sociologist Diego Gambetta has studied how criminals communicate with each other, starting from the observation that "the conditions that make having a good reputation worthwhile and effective—easy diffusion of reliable information, easy reidentification of previous partners, stability, and long-lived firms—are not common in the underworld." Conditions here do not support the normal logic of reputation. Except that one act of brutality establishes your willingness to engage in bad actions. Undercover cops don't commit murder; only true criminals do—proof of who they really are.[28]

Accepting that competence is often felt as threatening to others, Gambetta describes some ways that strategic players flaunt their *incompetence* in order to build the trust of their colleagues. If a player displays ineptitude at doing anything else but crime, he demonstrates that he has no alternatives and will remain loyal to his current job, organization, and boss. "If he were too clever," says Gambetta, "he would be a menace to the boss. In some respect, idiocy implies trustworthiness."[29] (He applies the same argument to the *baroni*, the powerful professors who control appointments in Italian universities, who, Gambetta says, are actually less competent and less mobile than the average Italian academic.)

Villains must be strong as well as malevolent, so criminals hide any weakness. As with professional wrestlers, it is more important for criminals to demonstrate physical strength, including a willingness to turn violent, than to demonstrate intelligence (a useful form of strength in most other arenas). In prison, Gambetta says, "fighting is crucial, for it generates credible information, which otherwise not only may be unavailable to display but may not even exist before the fight takes place."[30] One or two fights serve to establish a prisoner's strength, lessening the need for future fights. In prison systems that rotate inmates frequently, however, they must reestablish their reputations more often and do in fact fight more.

Psychologists Finke and Cuddy find widespread contempt for the weak, but this depends on judgments about their morality. For example the socioeconomic version of the category of the weak, namely the poor, arouses deep debate. What are their intentions? For conservatives, they are minions: ill intentioned, criminal, lazy, and deserving of their fate. For progressives they are victims: through no fault of their own they have ended up in economic deprivation. In this controversy, the activity dimension is also moralized: those who passively accept their situation are condemned; those who struggle against it by going to school or looking for work are admired—or pitied if they nonetheless fail despite their best efforts. The deserving and the undeserving poor: victims and minions.[31]

Social Groups

What is the relationship between stereotypes about social groups—based on race-ethnicity, caste, gender, sexual orientation, religion, social class, and more—and attributions of character? We have already seen, thanks to Fiske and others, that they are intimately related. We believe that two issues are often confounded. One is the definition of heroes, victims, and the other public characters; the other is the eligibility of members of social groups to play the part of these characters. We suspect that the availability of different groups to fit into the character slots varies more across time and place than the slots themselves do. Part of the reason is that the stereotypes used to denigrate oppressed groups vary quite a lot. Sexist stereotypes differ from racist ones for instance, and both differ from homophobic taunts.

Early in life, according to David Sears, people develop feelings toward images, words, and groups, which shape their reactions to political events ever after. These symbols, which can be abstract and remote from people's daily lives, arouse positive or negative feelings through rapid, automatic processes whenever people encounter political information. People think through their emotions. Some predispositions are stable over time, with considerable influence over related attitudes due to the elaborate cognitive work that people do to confirm and reinforce their predispositions.[32]

These affective commitments provide the raw materials for moral panics and other character work. In what Sears dubs "symbolic racism," people adopt stereotyped expectations of racial groups early in life and cling to them tenaciously.[33] In research with Jack Citrin, Sears used his theory to understand the surprising success of the movement to limit property taxes in California, culminating in "Prop 13" in 1978, which even today continues to constrain the state's budgets. Examples of "wasteful" government spending were those on behalf of poor people, which in turn was a racialized category, so that the campaign tapped into symbolic racism (although negative stereotypes about poor people are also powerful). As Sears and Citrin found, "The influence of symbolic racism on support for the tax rebellion among whites in California is still greater than that of either of the more usual partisan predispositions, party identification and liberal-conservative ideology."[34] Groups are frequent primary symbols, heavily stereotyped, with deep emotional resonances.

Although stereotypes can take many forms, strength and morality are usually part of the package. To deprecate a group as being "like animals" is to acknowledge a certain feral strength—enough to make them threatening—and at the same time to minimize their morality. As basketball-player Isiah Thomas controversially suggested in 1987, to call someone a "natural" athlete is to admire their beastlike power while denying their intelligence and hard work—highlighting one form of strength at the expense of others.

Many common stereotypes combine a threatening form of strength with a lack of morality. This makes a group into a villain, especially if individual members are threatening on their own, or at least into minions, if they are weak except when massed in large numbers. "Delinquents" are more threatening when they join together in packs of "wilding" youths. Many immigrant and ethnic groups around the world, including Jews, Armenians, Chinese, Arabs, and (in Europe) Americans, have been viewed as commercially savvy operators, a form of strength, and yet disliked as threatening for that reason. They are usually also characterized as immoral or at least disliked for their lack of appreciation of culture and the other good things in life.

Even those who wish to help a stereotyped group may end up portraying them as weak victims lacking the agency to help themselves. Middle-class commentators in the U.K., when they were not fearful of the working class in the early twentieth century, portrayed them as hapless victims. George Orwell and others "chose to represent the 'typical' unemployed man as apathetic, resigned, or impotently frustrated. These writers were unwilling to acknowledge that working-class people might have the capacity to be agents of social change without the leadership of a liberal middle class . . . . The only role offered them by either politicians or liberal social investigators was that of helpless victim."[35] They were not expected to mobilize themselves into a successful political party.

If they hope to reverse the stereotypes against them, stigmatized groups must try to portray themselves either—depending on the stereotypes to be debunked—as moral or as strong: Martin Luther King Jr. and the SCLC stressed the morality of Black Americans; the Black Panthers underscored their strength. This is a form of the naughty-or-nice dilemma: threatening others may get what you want, but at the cost of your reputation; more often, authorities intervene and suppress an aggressive group. Some groups win by having an assertive wing and a more moderate one, so that the former can be demonized and the latter accepted as good. The challenge is always to maintain distinct reputations for the two wings, a difficult feat.

Gender is probably the most studied set of group stereotypes. Most public characters are gendered. Men are supposed to be strong, women weak. Men are supposed to be active, women passive. So the stereotypes of most cultures expect women to be better victims, men to be better heroes—but also better villains. Only in fairy tales do female villains seem common: evil stepmothers, witches, and old crones stand in stark contrast to mothers, who are by definition good and virtuous. But here too heroes are overwhelmingly male: fathers arrive as rescuers and young men appear as charming princes.

Like race-ethnicity and other group stereotypes, gender is constructed on the building blocks of strength and activity. Thus when Sarah Palin, just before Russia invaded Ukraine in 2014, complained, "People are looking at Putin as one who wrestles bears and drills for oil," but "they look at our president as one who wears mom jeans and equivocates and bloviates," her main point in feminizing Obama was to accentuate his weakness.

Neither men nor women are necessarily portrayed as more moral, but their expected forms of morality differ. Through most of history men's morality was more prized (at least by men): the morality of protecting one's family and group through the glories of war, or the morality of embodying group aspirations as leaders, or that of articulating abstract principles through feats of intellect. Women's morality—nurturing others, showing sensitivity, and *not* impinging on others—came to the fore in nineteenth-century industrialization, as grubby capitalism made the public spheres of politics and commerce appear corrupt in comparison to the middle-class family home, that "haven in a heartless world."

Among psychologists from Freud to Kohlberg, women did not seem to possess the reasoning power required for them to be entirely moral, in the Kantian sense of calculating the correct action in the light of carefully justified principles. The pendulum swung back with Carol Gilligan, who saw women's ethic of care as morally justifiable to the same degree as men's morality of autonomous rights. Even today, to some extent, men's is the morality of strength and activity, women's of weakness and passivity. Women tend to be seen as good, weak, and especially passive, men as strong and active but not necessarily good. Women, we will see later, are frequently heroes of endurance.

Although some stereotypes portray women as more emotional than men, it is more accurate to say that men and women are expected to display different emotions. The active/passive dimension is especially gendered. Women are more likely to suffer from debilitating moods, such as depression, sadness, and grief, that discourage action, and to feel reflex emotions that also take them out of strategic games, such as shame and fear. Global rates of diagnosed depression (an extreme version of passivity) are twice as high for women as for men, a finding surprisingly consistent across countries.[36] As we saw, Erving Goffman catalogued many of the visual cues for this kind of flooding out of strategic engagements.

Men are expected to suppress fear and shame and other "passive" emotions, but they are encouraged to feel and display anger, *the* aggressive emotion. Anger often arises from a sense that one's rights or status have been violated, and men may well expect a broader range of entitlements than women usually do.[37] Anger is also generally seen as a sign of competence, or strength, and it indicates action rather than passivity. It is highly gendered.

Even if women and men do not differ so much in how many emotions they feel, they may differ in *how* they express them. Stephanie Shields contrasts "controlled expressivity," a manly emotion, with extravagant expressiveness. Controlled expression is a style that conveys an emotion in a subtle way, at the same time demonstrating control over that emotion. Shields' paradigm example is tearing up without actually crying, a display for which men get considerable credit (but women do not) as strong but also good. Extravagant emotional expression—such as loud crying and wailing—is considered appropriate to intimate relations, a sign of benevolence, but it undermines signals of power and control. Men may tear up but not weep (Figure 3.1).[38]

In research on the buildup to the 2003 invasion of Iraq, Wendy Christensen and Myra Marx Ferree found a sharp gender component in the character work undertaken by American media. It is a tradition straight out of the Western. "The cowboy," they say, "becomes an icon for a certain type of masculinity that presents physical strength, linguistic simplicity and autonomy as 'American' values, and arguments both for and against this masculinity place women, Europe, complexity, and consensus-seeking together in a category framed as the 'other'." Although they observe examples of this masculinity on both sides of the debate, it was George W. Bush's specialty: the dumb cowboy. His Texas twang hid his elite Yale background.[39]

Men who reject traditional cowboy masculinity—questioning its claims to morality—often have trouble combining strength and morality. At the extreme, Michael Messner and colleagues have studied male activists who have devoted their careers to fighting violence against women.[40] Those who are best at reaching audiences of frat boys and soldiers, in locker rooms and board rooms, can do so because they have many of the markers of traditional masculinity. They are big, strong,

FIGURE 3.1 The strong way to cry: expressing the emotion but at the same time tightly controlling it.

often former military or college athletes; they look like heroes. These same traits make the women activists they work with suspicious of their moral commitment to feminism. Relatively few in number, these men often grow more famous, and are in greater demand as speakers, than their female counterparts. The men's fame is a source of strength for the movement, but it raises controversies on the moral plane. This is a case of the powerful-allies dilemma that heroes always raise: the greater their strength, the more likely they are to use their allies for their own purposes rather than helping their allies win the allies' own goals. This is another reason it is hard to trust heroes entirely, in addition to the other dangers always inherent in strength.

Sexual orientation further reveals the gendered elements of public characters. Gay, bisexual, transgendered, transsexual, or cross-dressing men are rarely acknowledged as heroes, perhaps even less often than women are. For this reason gay athletes and actors who play leading-man roles have been slow to come out, and it is possible that it has been easier for women to come out than for men. Ellen DeGeneres came out two decades before Anderson Cooper. In this period a (female) comedian did not need to project strength and competence the way a (male) news anchor had to. But eligibility to be a hero is spreading.[41]

Basic Impressions

In the late 1950s social psychologists Charles Osgood, George Suci, and Percy Tannenbaum found that humans react to people and things in their environment by assigning them "affective meaning" along three main dimensions: evaluation (good or bad), potency (strong or weak), and activity (lively or sluggish), abbreviated as EPA space. In their surveys Osgood and his colleagues found the weights of these three factors to be remarkably consistent across a range of settings, with morality being most important: "evaluation accounts for approximately double the variance [in a word's affective meaning] due to either potency or activity, these two in turn being approximately double the weight of any subsequent factors."[42]

In what is now a charmingly dated example, from the three-way 1952 presidential race between Democrat Adlai Stevenson, moderate Republican Dwight Eisenhower, and conservative Robert Taft (in the race only until the Republican convention), Osgood and his collaborators asked 150 potential voters to rate a number of politicians and policies on the EPA dimensions. Unsurprisingly, subjects gave their own favored candidates high scores on all three dimensions: these were their political heroes, good, strong, and active.

Other results were more interesting. Even Republicans, while rating Franklin Roosevelt slightly negative on fairness (evaluation), rated him somewhat high on strength and very high on activity level. Supporters of each of the three candidates rated the new United Nations as fair and modestly active, but they differed on its strength: the conservatives saw it as weak, while the other two groups saw it as slightly on the strong side of the continuum. All three groups saw trade unions as strong and active, but both sets of Republicans saw them as malevolent while the Democrats saw them as good: one side's villain, the other's hero.[43]

In the 1970s sociologist David Heise and others adopted this EPA space to represent a kind of summary of what people think they know about an interaction. Drawing on what they understand from their culture, most people expect those with certain identities—defined by these three dimensions—to behave in predictable ways depending on the social definition of the setting. Fiske's warmth (and our morality) dimension lines up fairly well with Heise's evaluation dimension, and her competence (and our strength) dimension captures most of power and some of Heise's activity.[44] Given that sociologists have been criticized again and again for portraying humans as overly socialized, trapped in their roles, Heise was raising fundamental questions about the emotions that bolster social order. Our public characters are salient roles, or perhaps meta-roles, in this system.[45]

What came to be known as affect control theory (ACT) is a thoroughly cultural approach in that it portrays humans as walking around with stocks of identities that they use to understand and grapple with their everyday experiences. Through surveys, ACT researchers have established catalogues of the meanings that different cultures have for roles and actions. Our public characters—four out of the hundreds of identities studied— mostly have the semantic meanings we would expect. Heroes are good and strong; villains bad and strong; victims are weak (although not necessarily good).[46] But in addition to being distinct roles, we can also see our main characters as clusters of roles: anyone who is coded as good and strong is a kind of hero, and so on. A certain region of EPA space is heroic, another villainous; one region represents victims, another minions.

We not only have typical feelings toward each character, we also have regular expectations about how they will interact with one another. We expect heroes to protect victims, villains to attack everyone, and minions to make ineffectual threatening noises (although the word minion is not included in ACT catalogues of meanings). Because they follow our expectations, these classic interactions are satisfying to watch, especially when the ultimate gratification is delayed by suspenseful plot twists.

In many settings potency and evaluation are correlated. In some cases the relationship is positive, as we admire heroes for goodness and for strength. Osgood and his team found this in political judgments in the 1950s: "the group giving the lowest evaluation of a [political] concept attributes the least potency to it and vice versa."[47] People did not necessarily see the politicians they disliked as villains, but ridiculed them as weak. In other cases the correlation between morality and strength is negative: we fear strong players for what they can do to us. It is natural to fear malevolent villains, but we can also be anxious about heroes even as we admire and appreciate their deeds. Strength allows people to do bad things as well as good. We don't want to get in a hero's way.

According to Heise, humans are shocked when events do not match their expectations. Their negative emotions include surprise, anger, outrage, indignation, anxiety, even fear. The greater the gap between our expectations and what we see or learn (the "deflection," in ACT terms), the stronger the emotion. For instance we expect mothers to nurture their children; we have strong emotions when we instead see a mother starve or ignore her child. Normally we view mothers as very good, somewhat strong, and somewhat active, and we try to protect these basic cultural assumptions about mothers (we try to "control our affects").

The main way we control our affects after a shock is to change one of the elements in the subject-act-object triad: we may conclude that the mother herself has been weakened or made passive by starvation, even though she still has good intentions; instead of seeing her as a villain (a bad mother), we can see her as a victim (still a good mother, but weak and passive). Or perhaps we have misunderstood the action, mistaking illness for intentional starvation: the child is sick rather than starved. Finally, we may decide that the child is actually improving under her mother's nurturing care: the child is not her mother's victim; she is not suffering or deteriorating.

We do interpretive work like this not only in face-to-face encounters but also when we receive mediated news or propaganda, even from the other side of the globe. When we see reports of pedophile priests, brutal police, or unloving mothers, our expectations are dashed and we feel some form of shock or disappointment. (At least, those of us who expect priests to be gentle, police civilized, and mothers loving.) These emotions can be powerful, although continued exposure may eventually dull them through "compassion fatigue."[48]

If we cannot confirm our underlying sentiments by reinterpreting events around us, we sometimes take action to do so, for example by gathering more information or by intervening in some way. Just as we might remonstrate with the bad mom to act better, we might be primed for political action: if peaceful protestors are not supposed to suffer, and police are not supposed to act brutally, then we should intervene to help redress such wrongs. Or someone should intervene: the heroes.

Our expectations easily take on a moral tinge: many disruptions are not merely cognitively unexpected and emotionally engaging, but morally arousing. Many of our expectations are felt as moral imperatives. It is wrong to violate them. Presumably this is especially true for roles that are high or low on the evaluation scale. This is part of the emotional power of many characters, the reason that we call them public characters.

ACT theorists sometimes distinguish between characteristic and structural emotions. People experience characteristic emotions when they feel they are performing a role as it should be done. A hero's characteristic emotions would be to feel strong, kind, and vigilant (which define a hero on the EPA dimensions). These might merge into a feeling of pride. In interaction with others, structural emotions come out: in the case of the hero, she might feel generous or protective of those weaker than her. Structural emotions are derived from the EPA traits of both roles, which interact with each other. We feel characteristic emotions about ourselves, structural emotions about others.

ACT is not only about how we understand identities; it is a theory of action, of how we respond to what we experience. ACT suggests ways that emotions can contribute to political action, and its concept of "deflections" has parallels with the "anxieties" that have been shown to cause greater surveillance and information gathering among voters.[49] Often, we work to confirm existing cultural views and social structures. But the point of political propaganda can be, instead of to numb us, to shock our expectations in ways that cause us to act (or support government action) to change the world around us. Events trigger emotions depending on our background expectations. If we expect our government to be good, strong, and active, we are shocked when it fails to protect us (from hurricanes, for instance) or acts badly (killing its own citizens, for example). Unfortunately but realistically, not everyone expects her government to be good; cynics are hard to shock.

Lory Britt and David Heise have applied ACT to the well-known dynamics by which protest movements try to transform shame into pride, especially movements of those with stigmatized collective identities.[50] The key to mobilization, they observe, is to move people higher on the activity scale, in contrast to the shame that leaves people feeling vulnerable and deflated. But if recruits begin to see themselves as more active without also seeing themselves as more powerful and good, they will feel fear. Group members must instead feel anger, a dominant emotion. Activists stoke anger and indignation (morally tinged anger) by shifting the blame to external sources and by portraying those opponents as strong. In other words, by creating strong, evil, and active villains.[51]

Activity Level

Although the evaluative and potency dimensions define our main public characters, we can distinguish them further along the third dimension suggested by affect control theory: how active or passive they are (Table 3.1). This distinction helps us understand different kinds of public characters even better.

Among heroes, sleeping giants are roused to action in order to right a wrong, protect the weak or seek vengeance. Because of the widespread suspicion of those who initiate strategic engagements, heroes' initial passivity heightens their goodness, as they only fight when provoked. But fight they must, as heroes must accomplish great deeds. If they remain passive they are only potential heroes. It is the hero's transformation from passive to active that provides the emotional punch of many narratives.

In contrast, villains are rarely portrayed as passive: they are plotting even before they act. Rhetorically, there is no point in casting someone as a villain unless he is threatening, and he cannot be threatening unless he is at least scheming to do bad. In contrast to heroes, villains are always aggressing, always looking to start trouble. That's part of their evil. So activity level is linked to the evaluation dimension; initial passivity is generally good.

In the world of strategic engagements such as politics, the activity dimension is also correlated with strength. Weak players tend to avoid activity, since they lack the resources to compete effectively. Strong players initiate engagements, because they are confident (often overly so) in their ability to control events. But because the correlation between the two

TABLE 3.1 Characters by Power, Intent, and Activity Level

ACTIVE CHARACTERS		
	STRONG	WEAK
BENEVOLENT	Heroes Awakened Giants Judges, Donors Allies Converts (start in cell below)	Good Clowns Protestors Sidekicks
MALEVOLENT	Villains Outside Agitators Traitors (start in cell above)	Minions Bad Clowns Rioting Crowds

PASSIVE CHARACTERS		
	STRONG	WEAK
BENEVOLENT	Sleeping Giants Martyrs (start in cell above or across) Saints Survivors	Victims Good Clowns Passive supporters (can also be strong)
MALEVOLENT	Plotting Malcontents	Scoundrels Cowardly Bystanders Milling Crowds

dimensions is far from perfect, activity-passivity can reveal additional character dynamics.

Victims who manage to transform themselves into survivors through sheer endurance can be framed in two different ways. One is to portray them as gaining strength, a kind of toughness that allows them to exert some influence over their fate.[52] They may even be able to protect others, the key to being a hero. Alternatively, their activity levels can be highlighted, showing that through constant vigilance they can compensate for their weakness, for instance resisting through "weapons of the weak," for which they cannot be caught and punished. These may be anonymous, such as sabotage or poaching, or deniable, such as shoddy or slow work. Chapter 9 examines these heroes of endurance.

These nuances of low-activity characters help explain mixed attitudes toward victims. We tend to pity them, but that pity can shade into contempt to such an extent that the character tropes slide toward immorality. We are angry if we believe they could have done something to help themselves, as we saw with poor people. ACT research often discovers slight negative moral ratings of victims. If only they could become survivors, resisters, or heroes of endurance, we would instead admire them.

The figure of the overt protestor usually combines good, weak, and active elements. Activists are regularly depicted as well-intentioned but ineffectual, even while they are pictured as busy. The standard news image of protest displays a lot of people marching, chanting, shouting, holding up banners, and in general looking very busy. The very word "activist" suggests this. In ACT surveys, they are close to "boys": weak, active, and not especially good or bad.

On the other hand, in an interesting analysis of the Alcatraz occupation by American Indian militants from 1969 to 1971, Christopher Wetzel shows that news media typically portrayed these activists as lounging about, fishing, and waiting. Newspapers used head shots and other photos of activists outside any political context, rather than portraying them as speaking or making demands.[53] They appear neither active nor strong. This may have more to do with media stereotypes of American Indians than of activists, on the activity dimension. The media rarely portray protestors as heroes except in retrospect, after they have won. But within the activist group itself, members can see themselves as heroically strong, moral, and active.[54]

The activity dimension of ACT is meant to get at just that, how active a role is. But there are different ways to be active, and these can make a difference in politics. Table 3.2 distinguishes two components to activity level. One is between being the subject or the object of an action, the (active) initiator or the (passive) recipient. The other is the level of energy required. A hummingbird or a child can be active without affecting others, but an active pickpocket cannot. Minions are busy but incapable of initiating political projects; they are subjected to the villain's will.

TABLE 3.2 Two Components of Passive-Active Dimension

	SUBJECT	OBJECT
HIGH ENERGY	Protestors	Survivors
	Aroused Heroes	Minions
	Male	Female
LOW ENERGY	Normal or	Victims
	Disengaged Citizens	Attacked Heroes

Ineffectual activity does not threaten others, but action directed at someone else does. In strategic contexts, those who initiate engagements are not only taking risks themselves but also putting others at risk. We may admire them, if we are on their side and think they (we) will win, but we may also disapprove of them, if we feel we are taking too great a risk. When weak characters initiate action, they take enormous risks.

Action—and the distinction between those who are subjects and those who are objects—is more related to traditional gender distinctions than mere activity level by itself is. Women are expected to busy themselves with housework, caregiving, and other activities, but they are not expected to found businesses, attempt to seduce others, or initiate other actions. Traditionally, women could be high on the energy component, as long as they did not take the lead. When they did, they were usually coded as immoral, or in some cases desperate.

Activity level takes a back seat to power and morality because political characterization is about essentializing a player. A player is good or bad, weak or strong, no matter what they actually do. It is convenient if a villain acts badly, but his opponents try to demonize him whether he does or not. His actions merely give them ammunition for crafting their portrait. His high activity level merely makes a response more urgent; it does not change the underlying character construction.[55]

The purpose and the power of public characters come from their ability to point out "essential" traits of a group or individual, freezing them in a reassuring stability that will not change. "She is a hero" goes to the unchanging essence of a person, while "She is heroic" has a bit more distance from that core self, and "She did something heroic" almost seems accidental, as if next time she might not act heroically. Psychologists have studied the impact of nouns like hero in contrast to adjectives like heroic: the former are felt to be stronger and more stable. When applied to groups, noun forms facilitate stereotypes, suggest homogeneity of all the group's members, and encourage bias against "outsider" groups—basic elements of group characters.[56]

Erving Goffman famously drew attention to the ways in which we all try to manage the impressions others have of us, devoting his career to the many social settings in which we perform this work. We labor at these impressions, and in most cases those around us help us create and sustain the personae we want. What was missing from Goffman's descriptions are the cultural expectations we bring to our interactions—we do not start each one afresh. Social and cognitive psychology fills this gap, showing the influence of our pre-existing expectations. But how do our institutional environments affect these expectations?

In the first three chapters we have examined a number of cultural-psychological processes and physical embodiments of character, from the human voice to lithographs to novels. It is time to look at the public arenas in which character work takes place, ranging from the building of nations to electoral politics to the oratory of court cases. These arenas rely on images and words, and they show us what is at stake in character work.

4 | Arenas of Character Work

The moment we want to say *who* somebody is, our very vocabulary leads us astray into saying *what* he is; we get entangled in a description of qualities he necessarily shares with others like him; we begin to describe a type or a "character" in the old meaning of the word, with the result that his specific uniqueness escapes us.

—*Hannah Arendt, The Human Condition*

E XILED FOR HIS SMALL PART in the "Young Italy" uprising of 1834, Giuseppe Garibaldi spent the next dozen years in Latin America, where he developed a reputation as a pirate, bandit, and—not much of a stretch in those days—armed freedom fighter. After he formed the "Italian Legion of Montevideo" to help defend liberal Uruguay against authoritarian Buenos Aires, his successes and failures appeared regularly in European and American newspapers. He pointedly refused material rewards for his services. Giuseppe Mazzini, the leading figure of the Italian Risorgimento, used his journalistic contacts across Europe to model Garibaldi into a hero for the nation they both hoped to create.

Garibaldi played his part well, obtaining just enough military victories to feed his myth. He returned with 250 men to fight in the first Italian war of independence after the 1848 revolutions had disrupted Europe, winning several minor victories before the republicans' ultimate defeat. He was back in 1860, seizing Sicily and Naples from the Bourbons in highly celebrated victories. He was more interested in Italian unification than in republicanism and handed his gains over to the Piedmontese crown. He died in 1882 at the age of seventy-five, a hero of national liberation and unification.

Garibaldi's reputation benefited from media outlets that in the nineteenth century were bringing world news to Europe—and from later Italian

Public Characters. James M. Jasper, Michael P. Young, and Elke Zuern, Oxford University Press (2020) © Oxford University Press.
DOI: 10.1093/oso/9780190050047.001.0001

governments hoping to stoke nationalism through rituals, monuments, and heroes. As we'll see, all public arenas encourage some degree of character work as part of the strategic conflicts they allow. Who is strong or weak, who is creditable or blameworthy are important elements of war and politics, law and markets. This chapter draws on sociology and political science to suggest how different strategic arenas demand and shape character work.

Sources of Public Characters

In the 1970s there was a sociology of characters that linked them to the basic values of a society. Reflecting the structural-functionalism of the time, Orrin Klapp insisted that we use characters to position ourselves in relation to our society's norms and values. "Heroes, villains, and fools represent three directions of deviation: (1) better than, (2) dangerous to, and (3) falling short of, norms applied to group members or status occupants."[1] Klapp defined characters along one dimension, the moral: heroes embody the approved ethics, villains threaten them, and clowns mock them (intentionally or not). Another sociologist, William Goode, analyzed public honors as a means by which societies value certain activities and groups; the bestowal of prestige is a form of social control.[2] Characters offer moral lessons because of their relation to a group's fundamental moral values.

In the years since Klapp and Goode, social scientists have begun to look at societies differently: less as unified wholes, and more as sites of conflict and disagreement. Our views of cultural meanings have changed accordingly: instead of a unified system of symbols, we are more likely to see cultural meanings as a variety of symbols, images, and other meanings that can be combined in different ways according to the needs of individuals and groups. Jack Katz, for one, took a more interactive approach, examining the processes by which we impute character essences, linking them to deviance and charisma (inferior and superior capacities to respond in interaction) rather than to basic values. This allows us to view character work more strategically as a set of tools for demeaning or praising others.[3]

Our way of understanding how different kinds of character work can occur in the same society is to link that work to a variety of *strategic arenas*, which are institutional settings with their own players, rules and traditions, and something at stake. National elections, media production, markets, public opinion, wars, and diplomacy are all examples of public arenas. Family conflict, organizational operations, and academic department meetings are less-public arenas, but they feature many of the same strategic operations, including the construction of characters. Different kinds of rhetoric are effective in different settings, depending largely on who is to be persuaded: a spouse, a colleague, a stranger watching the news, a sworn enemy at war, a reader looking for entertainment in a novel. Every setting has its audiences for characters.[4]

Imagination and selection go into the creation of all public characters, but those of fiction are less constrained than those in strategic arenas where real people can act in ways that undermine their carefully constructed reputations. Artists can craft fictional characters to express just the right nuance of morality or strength, and they can also point to the processes behind those constructions. Humor in particular can both rely on public characters and cast doubt on them at the same time, a process we'll examine in the appendix. Art is real in different ways than the reputations of "real-life" groups and individuals are real. A novelist or actor can do interviews about her characters and roles, putting some distance between them in ways that a politician cannot usually use to distance herself from her own actions.

There is not as much difference between fiction and nonfiction characters as we would like to believe. Or as character workers would like us to believe. Good character work aims to convince us that the reputation of a politician or corporate manager is "true," a reflection of their deep character, their essence. But they use all the tricks of fiction in order to convince us, especially when they are doing character work on behalf of a collective character. A corporation or a nation is not "real" in the same way that Donald Trump or Brett Kavanaugh is real. Successful character work leads us to accept that a corporation has a personality and desires, makes choices, follows moral rules, and so on—just as an individual does. Effective character work invites us to imagine these entities as public characters.[5]

Throughout this book we turn to fictional characters to understand how public characters affect audiences, but most of our interest is in how the same characters are used in strategic settings. In the remainder of this chapter we try to understand some of those institutional settings.

National Characters

As a hero, Garibaldi the symbol was more influential than Garibaldi the military tactician, whose strength lay more in inspiring his followers than in making battlefield decisions. As a Romantic hero, his image was unparalleled. Foremost, in a period when lithographs began to appear in newspapers and magazines, was his appearance: "strong and physically imposing; he wears flamboyant clothes, and has abundant facial hair and flowing locks, piercing eyes (of indeterminate colour, perhaps light brown but often said to be blue), and a robust, athletic body." He was also graceful and serene, "with a kind and pleasant face." Historian Lucy Riall speculates, "it is perhaps this combination of strength and mildness, a combination so popular in the romantic literary hero, which best explains his immediate physical attraction." Plus he looked good on a horse (Figure 4.1). His Argentine opponents' efforts to demonize him as a dangerous corsair may actually have contributed to his aura, reinforcing his reputation for strength.[6]

As befits a hero of nation-building as opposed to a gunslinger, Garibaldi was an inspiring leader, not a lone hero. He arrived from Montevideo with his band of brothers, fellow Italians, and he recruited additional "Volunteers" wherever he went. He embodied *italianità*. He was both a rascally ladies' man—essentially abducting his first wife—and a saint living a simple life so that he could concentrate on the cause. The notion that one man could embody the will of a nation would reach its dangerous and absurd conclusion in fascism in the twentieth century, but in the early nineteenth, it inspired progressive change.

FIGURE 4.1 Daring and debonair, Garibaldi embodied the nation that Italians hoped to form.

Reputations are central to politics, shaping what players can and cannot do. Nelson Mandela's heroic aura—painstakingly crafted by the ANC—helped South Africa to retain its unity after apartheid, as well as to maintain high international prestige under Mandela's presidency. Hitler's reputation as the twentieth century's greatest villain has provided all sorts of rhetorical terms and analogies for those condemning others. Conversely, those who celebrate Hitler today have an easy way to demonstrate their disdain for society's norms. The deep victimhood of the Holocaust has driven and enabled Israel's policies, and the policies of other nations toward Israel, since its founding. Germans, as Günter Grass demonstrated, still find it difficult to criticize Israel.

Nations are built on the backs of individual heroes, constructed as founding fathers and (more rarely) mothers. Just as Pericles promoted a civic character for his fellow Athenians, so mythmakers of modern nations fabricate heroes who embody the essence of their people. Heroes do great deeds, and what greater accomplishment than founding a new nation and all its institutions, especially when that involves—it always does—struggle against perceived oppressors from the outside?[7]

Scholars of collective memory have catalogued the ways this fabrication is accomplished. There are physical objects and places: sculptures of heroes; buildings, roads, and airports named after them; walls designating martyrs; quotations chiseled into the marble walls of legislative chambers; museums and parks constructed where key events occurred. Curators learn how to package a nation's identity through both permanent and special exhibitions, often reflecting current preoccupations. A nation's heritage is sustained (and debated) through these sites and objects.[8]

Political parties and other organizations battle over just who will be honored, how, and when. The controversy over the Vietnam Veterans Memorial in Washington, D.C., pitted those who favored a traditional monument against those who preferred a monument for a "post-heroic era." Barry Schwartz describes the ideal type of the national monument, intended to celebrate founding heroes and their successors: "a statement engraved on the monument describing the cause for which it was built, idealistic human representation, larger-than-life physical dimensions, vertical preeminence, centrality and prominence of placement, lightness of color, grandness of size, prominence of national symbolism." He contrasts these with more recent monuments of the post-heroic era: absent or ambiguous statements about cause, abstractness of representation, horizontal lines (often walls hugging the ground or placed below ground), inconspicuous placement, darkness of color, smallness of size, want of national symbolism."[9] In the case of the Vietnam memorials, the post-heroic wall was built first, "nonpatriotic and nonheroic," whereas the more traditional statues were added in response to later complaints.[10]

Memorials often provide the backdrop for a second carrier of national identity, commemorations of founding events: parades, rallies, religious services, speeches, interments, concerts, and more. Memorial-site visits and commemorations allow political leaders to honor fallen heroes and to bask in the ideals of unity and strength that they represent. But as in all arenas, their selection of heroes and memorial sites and the interpretation of key historical moments also present opportunities for critics. Japanese politicians' visits to the Yasukuni Shrine consistently elicit protest, especially from neighboring states that bore the brunt of Japanese imperial conquest. The shrine honors two million people who died for the Empire of Japan, including civilians, priests, and soldiers, but also convicted war criminals. (Yasukuni also houses a museum that offers an unrepentant military history of the period 1868–1947.) Places shape these activities, but the activities also shape the meanings associated with the places (and sometimes the physical aspects too).

Conflicts play out over time. Heroic memorials built by one set of elites may not correspond to the values of a later generation, especially with the transition from a colonial to a post-colonial regime or from an authoritarian to a democratic one. Memorials built to honor colonial leaders like Britain's Cecil Rhodes in South Africa or Stalin in the former Soviet republics offended later generations. Citizens in these cases pulled down antiquated memorials in a bid to redefine the nation. These moments, and photographs of them, can be so powerful that some are staged, like the toppling of Saddam Hussein's likeness in Baghdad, in an attempt to bring about the change they seek to represent.

Different national heroes highlight different traits. In writing about Garibaldi, Lucy Riall traces his style of heroism to the French revolutionaries who, needing to craft new, non-aristocratic identities for their project, turned to ancient Greek stoicism with its "physical demeanor of dignity, reserve and authenticity" that became both an artistic and a political ideal. "The male hero—physically beautiful, morally virtuous, personally courageous and, until Napoleon, never living—came to be a powerful political symbol both for the revolution and for the heirs of the revolution." Throughout the nineteenth century, the rhetorical purpose of the hero was "to personify a political idea, to embody an elite or collective movement, and/or to sacralise a regime."[11]

Garibaldi was lucky; most heroes of nation-building must die in order to play the role of founding hero. The organizers of Ireland's Easter Rising in 1916 knew this well. They were quickly surrounded and cut off from one another in the Dublin buildings they had seized. The British occupying force no doubt felt generous in commuting seventy-five out of ninety death sentences, but the quick execution of the remaining fifteen produced national martyrs and rallied public opinion behind independence. Patrick Pearse, poet and ringleader, had predicted as much the year before, in a Periclean funeral oration that helped create the Republic: "Life springs from death; and from the graves of patriot men and women spring living nations . . . . The fools, the fools, the fools! They have left us our Fenian dead, and while Ireland holds these graves, Ireland unfree shall never be at peace!"[12] The Irish may admire martyrdom more than Italians, but they understand the emotional wellsprings of heroism.

Volumes have been written about nationalism, the affective allegiance needed to support nation building. But like research on other forms of collective identity—class consciousness, gender, race, and so on—nationalism is usually seen as a cognitive boundary drawn between "us" and "others." In some cases, scholars have acknowledged that these boundaries are not neutral analytic distinctions, but strongly felt emotional attachments. But scholars of identities or nationalism have not altogether recognized the central importance of individuals as carriers of those identities, of how heroes embody the ideals of the folk, and the struggle to establish the nation. Nation-building seems to require heroic founders for later generations to praise and celebrate.[13]

Heroes give focus to national narratives, symbolizing what the nation ought to be and so nudging it in that direction. In South Africa, Mandela embodied the ideal of national reconciliation necessary for a peaceful transition from apartheid. The party he represented, the ANC, worked hard to craft his worldwide image of strength in the face of his suffering during his long detention. Songs and t-shirts with the refrain "free Nelson Mandela" became part of popular culture. Upon his release from prison, formerly critical foreign powers also bolstered his moral image, obscuring his violent past and communist allies. Even as the decades have passed, the debate in South Africa today is not whether Mandela was a hero (he was) but who most effectively embodies his legacy. The ANC urges voters to continue to support the party of Mandela, while critics lambast it for not living up to the icon's promise. Heroes are useful to a wide range of actors.

Victims are a more problematic trope in nation-building, which ultimately requires public characters strong enough to carry institutions into the distant future. Victimhood can justify some redress and reparations, especially for special groups, but an entire nation cannot hope to survive if it portrays itself as weak. After a military defeat, like France's in 1871, the state may employ a shared sense of suffering to unite the nation. But even in such cases, the emphasis will usually shift from victimhood to survival, political rehabilitation, and revenge.[14]

Villains also play a modest role in most national-founding narratives. They should be foreigners who can be expelled, not a group who continues to be part of the new nation—a problem for whites in some African nations. But other than being defeated to clear the way for the nation, they serve little epidictic purpose, as nation-building unfolds mostly after they are gone. They may be useful as a contrast to define the virtues of the new people, especially if the former rulers persist as hostile neighbors. Most disappear or withdraw, leaving the field open for national character work. But villains, old or new, are revived and created when war threatens.

Going to War

Once they have nations, elites must still discipline, inspire, and mobilize the "masses" for a number of purposes, including voting, working in factories, and fighting in wars. In wartime negative character work is most salient, with opponents demonized as evil Huns, the Yellow Peril, or ruthless dictators with weapons of mass destruction. This propaganda—identifying an external villain but aimed at domestic audiences—notoriously quiets internal divisions, as "the nation" begins to dominate rhetoric both as character (victimized sleeping giant) and as player (patriotic war machine). Even in supposedly "peaceful" democracies, governments easily galvanize public opinion behind declarations of war, typically by promoting the idea that the nation has been provoked by some insult or assault. It is time for the victim to take revenge, to become the hero.

Players invent villains to gain sympathy for themselves, outrage at opponents, and a feeling of urgency. By demonizing Saddam Hussein, George W. Bush's administration overcame otherwise strong resistance to U.S. efforts to change foreign regimes. Surveys repeatedly demonstrated strong support for "removing Saddam Hussein from power."[15] But as "success" in rebuilding Iraq seemed less and less likely—threatening Americans' self-congratulatory images of their nation as omnipotent hero—support for the intervention fell dramatically. Americans support military force to respond to aggressive action against the United States, but not to alter the domestic politics of another country.

If opponents must be characterized as demonic, one's own side must be heroized (Figure 4.2). In war, heroism is especially gendered. According to Kristen Hoganson gender images were a kind of "mortar" that held together pieces of character rhetoric in the buildup to the Spanish-American war. The hawks insisted that the country needed to "fight for American manhood," as though its honor had been challenged. Manhood was the great symbol of strength, and men who opposed the war could be portrayed as wearing petticoats and being overly influenced by suffragists. They

FIGURE 4.2 Those who cannot become heroes by enlisting can at least support their government by lending it money at low interest rates.

were not "true men." Not only was war necessary to protect the nation, war would also improve the nation morally by forging "a new generation of manly, civic-minded veterans who would serve as the pillars of American democracy."[16] Their opponents responded by describing the hawks as brutish and uncivilized. Hoganson reports that one woman wrote to her senator characterizing war "as uncivilized as prizefights, and it degrades the world as prizefights do a community."[17]

As volunteer armies became the norm after the French Revolution, a new vocabulary and sensibility developed across Europe to make recruits feel like heroes. They were the sacred embodiment of the nation, literally wearing its symbols and shielding it from harm. They had to live outside the settled, domestic life that they were trying to protect, and many have been unable to return to that life. Until recently this ethic was restricted to men, "a moral posture exemplifying courage, strength, hardness, control over the passions, and the ability to protect the moral fabric of society by living a so-called manly life." These men were supposed to feel like heroes. "A desire for the extraordinary, for a sacred mission which might transcend the dreariness of daily life, will be found throughout the history of volunteers."[18] Many heroes of myth similarly set out in search of adventure.

Wars are the ultimate in drawing boundaries: literally, as frontiers turn into battlefronts. Cindy Kam and Donald Kinder discuss the role of ethnocentrism in the war on terrorism. Ethnocentrism, they argue "is a deep human habit, an altogether commonplace inclination to divide the world into ingroups and outgroups, the former characterized by virtuosity and talent, the latter by corruption and mediocrity."[19] They demonstrate the significance of general prejudice in support for the war on terror. "Americans who are predisposed to denigrate the character and capacity of *their fellow Americans*—white, Black, Hispanic, and Asian—are the ones most likely to lend their backing to the President and his policies."[20] Stark boundaries, it seems, make external wars easier, even when those boundaries are inside your own society. Morality is on one side, immorality on the other.

The powerful character tropes of war make it a tempting frame for understanding other kinds of events, and 9/11 fit neatly into this pattern. Americans expect their presidents, above all others, to do classic epidictic work "of providing existential guidance, addressing not only the symbolic matters surrounding collective identity—'who Americans are' as a people—but also even more fundamental human questions about the meaning of suffering, loss, and finitude."[21] Bush II was not especially skilled at this, and often appeared dumbfounded, but even he was able to take advantage of familiar ways of presenting villains, victims, and the sleeping giant that he was trying to awaken (even if only to go shopping).

The attacks of 9/11 were an extraordinary moment, which dramatically heightened Americans' perception of threat. But they were not unique. "Threat comes regularly in politics, and elites commonly rely on rhetorical weapons to pit 'us' against 'them'."[22] To portray insiders as good and outsiders as bad requires standard character work. Groups are easily personified, turned into characters every bit as vivid as the individuals who comprise them. Nations are the obvious example, but political parties, corporations, and protest movements can all be crafted into public characters.

Domestic Contention

Peaceful contention includes character work, as politicians vie in elections, lawyers present their clients in court, or protestors make demands on elected officials and other targets. All strategic and especially adversarial settings encourage character work. Our reputations matter across a range of public and private arenas.

Reputations have two different dimensions. One consists of its *content*: is someone seen as kindhearted, as goofy, as a prig; or in character terms, is someone good or bad, strong or weak, active or passive? The other dimension consists of *scope*: how many people are familiar with a person or group? We have reputations among our friends just as surely as President Putin has a reputation around the world. Having an extensive reputation means that a strategic player is a useful symbol for both supporters and opponents, available to be plugged into assorted arguments, exhortations, and condemnations. Various players find such people worthy of character investments, in ways that we are not. They are known public figures; we are unknown private persons—although reputational scope varies along a continuum. This book is about reputations of significant scope, but some of the same dynamics operate in the creation of local characters as well.

Our reputations among those we know personally matter as much as our reputations—if we have them—among a more anonymous general public. Our immediate audiences are central to any strategic action. As groups and individuals pursue their goals as players in a variety of arenas, they will have different reputations with different fellow players in those arenas. The arenas vary in scope. Some are face-to-face: conflict within a family, the dynamics of a classroom, or the debates of a legislature. Others are immense and mediated, like a national election or a multinational alliance or war. The way our spouse thinks about us has different sources than how Pakistani leaders think about the United States or about the American military.

Media vastly expand the scope of reputations. We may follow Juventus without ever going to a match and love its players without ever meeting one of them personally. In electoral politics, this is almost the case by definition: we have feelings about representatives we've no hope of ever meeting in person. And our opinions of foreign nations are often crafted in the absence of any first-hand experience with them (this gap is especially striking in the United States, most of whose citizens have never left the country). For individuals in the public eye, various kinds of dramatic encounters can be arranged that influence their reputations, ranging from safe, well-controlled ones (honorific ceremonies) to open-ended confrontations (debates, athletic matches).[23]

In *Difficult Reputations* Gary Alan Fine shows the work that reputational entrepreneurs do as gatekeepers of another's reputation.[24] Why would someone have an interest in someone else's character, even after they are dead? In some cases a person can be demonized as a scapegoat—especially when they are dead and unable to defend themselves.

Some people symbolize a political idea, group, or faction. "Why would one attack Martin Luther King today," Fine asks, "if one didn't intend to insult the African-American community?"[25] Some individuals represent an organization with ongoing reputational interests, such as a corporation, pitted against labor organizers and unionists or against government regulators who contest those reputations. Character work reflects underlying interests.

In addition to direct interests, reputations provide raw materials for collective memory construction. Those like Garibaldi with extensive reputations are ready-made symbols, like words in a language that others will recognize. Whatever they do or say will be noted and used in character construction. For Charles Horton Cooley, "the function of the great and famous man is to be a symbol, and the real question in other minds is not so much, What are you? as, What can I believe that you are? What can you help me to feel and be?"[26] Great names give us confidence and hope. (Names may also be charged with disgust, hate, outrage, and anxiety; the same name can arouse positive feelings in some, negative feelings in others.) Fine observes, "it is easier for reputational entrepreneurs to insert a public figure than to insert a nonfamous person into social discourse, and simultaneously harder to exclude him or her if such scrutiny is undesired."[27] We use the most convenient symbols as tools.

Our reputations directly affect our own individual well-being, through our self-esteem, but they also indirectly affect our ability to pursue practical goals and projects in the world around us. Sociologists have long put reputational accomplishments, such as status and prestige, at the top of their list of human goals, but—except for trust—they have paid less attention to their use as means. Our reputations affect how others treat us: with deference, contempt, or indifference, for instance. And how they treat our families, allies, and others identified with us. The impacts of reputation ripple outward across institutional arenas.

For political players, who must appeal to others for sympathy, contributions, votes, or alliances, reputation is possibly their most important capacity, affecting their ability not only to get things done but to obtain and remain in office. It is not just elected politicians who worry about their reputations; all those making claims on the public's attention try to present themselves in ways that will emotionally engage some portion of the public, whether through sympathy, admiration, or even fear. Protestors, for example, or other claims-makers in controversies over social problems, work hard on their public characters.

No player has full control over her reputation. Character work is itself an arena for conflict among multiple players. Strategic players try to shape others' reputations, for instance constructing "folk demons" to establish the severity of a social threat, using melodramatic characters to "declare war" on a new social problem.[28] Corporations try to tarnish the reputations of their critics as a way to blunt their criticism. When an employee blows the whistle on some illegal or unethical practice, her employers almost always go on the offensive: she is "disgruntled," unstable, a complainer, someone with a personal grudge. They cannot accept her own implied character claim to be an honest hero trying to right a wrong. Destroying her public character demolishes her argument.

It is not only corporations that protect their reputations in this way; governments zealously react to critics of their preferred characters. The U.S. government portrayed Edward Snowden as a traitor and even a Russian spy. Secretary of State John Kerry pronounced him both a "coward" and a "traitor," suggesting that he is simultaneously weak yet also threatening. House Intelligence Committee Chairman Mike Rogers argued that Snowden had likely received some "help" from the Russians, implying Snowden's inability to act on his own. The Voice of America dubbed Snowden a "High School Dropout," giving the impression of a dim-witted slacker. Snowden's supporters pushed back, most prominently with the release of *Snowden* and *Citizen Four*. Through an intimate extended interview format, the latter (documentary) film presents Snowden as an intelligent, thoughtful, and courageous individual who sacrificed his comfortable life for a larger cause. Both movies present him as a hero.

To complicate matters further, arenas overlap and interact. A politician pursues her goals by cultivating a certain reputation with the general public—usually for strength and probity—but also through personal interactions with rich donors, colleagues, or news gatekeepers. What transpires in one of these arenas can change reputations, resources, and possible moves in other arenas.

Marketing Characters

No one trusts merchants. Aristotle condemned them for engaging in the unnatural pursuit of money for its own sake. Others throughout history have perceived a propensity to cheat their customers. Few merchants have been strong enough to be feared as villains; even Shakespeare's merchant of Venice, demanding his awful pound of flesh, was casuistic and tricky in using the laws of contract rather than being powerful himself. (Anti-semitic stereotypes of the time prevented Shylock from being too strong.)

In the modern world merchants have performed systematic character work to make themselves appear good, even heroic, often in reaction to legislative threats to their property and flexibility. Some capitalists have been their own apologists, like Andrew Carnegie in *The Gospel of Wealth*, arguing that capitalists are heroes who save the poor by providing jobs and affluence for all and by philanthropically creating public goods in their later years.[29]

In the United States, the Supreme Court granted the corporation the legal status of a person in 1886, encouraging legislators and consumers to think of what kind of person each corporation would be. Giant corporations, something new, had the means to engage in extensive public relations as well as the incentive, namely anti-trust legislation that the Justice Department had enormous leeway in applying. The character contest was on for "the soul of the corporation," as Roland Marchand puts it.[30]

The size of the new corporations, especially monopolistic trusts, left little question of their power but considerable doubts about their morality. Some corporations responded by highlighting their origins in humble mom-and-pop shops, not only humanizing the corporations but suggesting that their growth was due to hard work and frugality rather than predatory acquisitions. Retaining a family name such as Ford helped this family-enterprise image. World's fairs, expositions, and parades allowed for personal interactions and even a glimpse into how factories worked. Corporations flipped their tentacle-like reach into every small town into an image of neighborly connection and support, especially "Ma" Bell's phone service. They promoted their stocks as a service to widows and orphans everywhere. Corporations operated heroically in "the spirit of service."

Public relations went further than rebuffing demonization, depicting the corporations' obvious power as sources of progress and wealth for everyone. Trucks, telephones, and electricity transformed the lives of farmers. The bigger the railroad, the more efficiently it could move goods. If "Ford" took the folksy naming route, International Harvester or International Business Machines adopted modern, scientific monikers. Companies built large, sleek skyscrapers for their headquarters. They aligned themselves with science when possible, for instance in Dupont's portrait of the lab technician as hero. The heroic image of the American corporation reached its zenith in World War II, as corporate America helped the Allies win through massive production of Jeeps, tanks, planes, and more—an astonishing triumph that immediately found its way into advertisements.

From the start, PR departments constructed the charismatic CEO as the embodiment of a corporation's character, including earnest statements from the great man in early advertisements. Henry Ford was frugal, straightforward, and hardworking, just like his Model T (although he was also anti-semitic and isolationist, showing the risks of embracing living characters as tropes).[31] Fifty years later, Lee Iacocca, son of Italian immigrants, abandoned Ford to take the helm at Chrysler, saving the latter by selling his bailout plans—and himself—to the U.S. Congress in 1979. His bestselling autobiography appeared in 1984, while he was still running the company. CEOs were again being cast as heroes.

According to Rakesh Khurana, the cult of the CEO-hero flourished in the 1980s, especially in the form of an outsider who could sweep in and save a failing company. These are celebrities who appear in advertisements, hire ghost writers to produce self-congratulatory autobiographies, and make their way onto magazine covers. Corporate boards and executives deploy character work to appeal to new audiences who influence stock prices, namely business media and stock analysts, instead of the corporations' own employees. CEOs pitch their companies to outsiders instead of actually running them. A CEO must be a "visionary, evangelist, role model, coach," says Khurana. "Becoming a CEO is now about communicating an

"Came Prometheus, the Fire-Bringer, he who snatched
from the sun's glowing chariot thrice-precious fire
and brought it, hidden in a fennel-stalk, to earth,
that men might live like gods in its pleasant warmth."
(Transl. Greek Myth)

THIS is today's Prometheus . . . . . Bringer
of comforts . . . . The Chemical Engineer!

One of civilization's pioneers, it is he who has
brought to mankind comforts and conveniences
that a century ago were only wishes.

It is he who, searching in the hidden depths of
Nature, has bared her secrets and laid at the feet
of the world's industries new substances, new uses
for them, new ways of using the present materials of commerce in the satisfying of man's wants.

It is he who, watching on the frontiers of science,
has seen in his test-tubes visions of industries yet
unborn that are to drive commerce to the far cor-
ners of the earth in the service of man's needs.

The world's debt to The Chemical Engineer is
one that can never be paid.

*This is one of a series of advertisements published
that the public may have a clearer understanding
of E. I. du Pont de Nemours & Co. and its products.*

FIGURE 4.3 Corporate scientists save the world, one test tube at a time.

essential optimism, confidence, and can-do attitude. In the process, indi-
viduality has become a desired attribute, not a liability."[32]

Corporate PR engages in epidictic contests with several audiences
in mind: consumers, shareholders, the general public, employees, and
legislators. Often, advertising was a direct response to threats in legislative
arenas, beginning with anti-trust battles. Even today, corporations often
respond to protest and pressure by increasing their own character work to
appear as heroically contributing to the public good.[33]

The Characters of Protest

At their heart, social movements try to persuade others, deploying the essential triad of villain-victim-hero to do so. Protestors pursue their projects

across many arenas, ranging from courts to elections to media coverage, addressing both internal audiences of their own members and external audiences of bystanders, opponents, and others. In some cases they hope to recruit bystanders to become participants, allies, or donors. Creating a victim is the first step to defining a social problem, a villain is a step to creating outrage around it, a hero a step toward demanding action.[34]

Victims are often the first character to be established, proof that an outrageous social problem exists. Most movements then aim to transform the victims into heroes, in famous cases such as the women's, labor, and civil rights movements. At the opposite extreme, such as movements to protect animals, children, or the environment, the victims cannot fight for themselves and need a heroic movement to help them. The pity we feel for victims—whether compassion for their suffering or a sense of unfair treatment—is central to the outrage and anger that animate protest.

Villains focus blame and indignation. Clifford Bob discusses the ubiquitous character work that advocacy movements conduct, especially demonizing opponents. "A network's promotion of its own goals is intertwined with struggle against its adversaries. To turn one's eyes from the clash is to miss decisive events. Of course at moments, rivals may engage in high-minded dialogue. More typically, advocates work to destroy their foes' reputations, ideas, and values."[35] The result is polarization, as "each side portrays itself as virtuous victim and its rival as pernicious perpetrator." Character work leads to "hyperbole and Manicheanism. We represent the public; they shill for the interests. We speak truth—to power; they lie—for power. We defend the good; they menace rights, lives—the very Earth itself. We are rational; they are deranged."[36] As befits victims versus villains, the contrast is primarily along the moral dimension, but it also portrays strength as immoral. In many rhetorical contests, the primary dualism features villains and victims.

For most protest movements, heroes are more complicated than victims or villains. In some cases experts carry the strength of scientific knowledge. In others virtuoso activists, like the Greenpeace volunteers who get in the way of whalers, risk their lives in classic, even macho, hero style. But most movements gain their strength from numbers, often demonstrated in rallies and marches. They lack other traditional signs of strength. But they are courageous, as well as certain that they will prevail in the end. Charles Tilly described their epidictic work as "WUNC displays": they assert their moral Worth, Unity, large Numbers, and Coherence as players. These imply strength (U, N, and C) as well as morality (W).[37]

In a dynamic we examine in chapter 9, many protestors must balance the characters of victim and hero. Nancy Whittier has studied the adult victims of child sexual abuse, finding that they sometimes relive their passive role as children and at other times reject that portrayal in favor of more heroic figures as survivors and protectors of others. Different epidictic settings encourage one or the other kind of character work: television shows often encourage regression to the weakness of childhood, while political arenas demand the strength of full citizens capable of making demands and pressuring other players.[38] More recently, staff in nonprofits have swung to the opposite horn of the hero-villain dilemma, discouraging their clients from telling victim stories, as these might re-traumatize them. Reflecting an ongoing rhetorical anxiety and denying the underlying dilemma, these professionals insist that more heroic narratives are both more ethical and more effective—even when their clients wish to tell their victim stories.[39]

Like other strategic players, protestors adapt their own public characters to the many arenas that they enter in their conflicts with others. Every one of those arenas includes character work, as players try to promulgate their own victim, villain, and hero tropes. This is the stuff of politics.

Voting for Characters

Character work is the essence of electoral campaigns, an arena even more directly adversarial than protest. Political strategist Paul Tully used to sum up the four rhetorical efforts made in a two-player conflict, using the case of an election race, through a four-cell "Tully box": What I say about my-self in the upper left, what my opponent says about me in the upper right, what my opponent says about herself in the lower left, and what I say about my opponent in the lower right. The four are equally influential, as are the characterizations that third parties make of the two competitors.

"American presidential elections are inherently personal contests," according to Martin Wattenberg.[40] Character traits such as integrity or trust-worthiness, presumed competence, and reliability have always played a role in voter assessments. Eisenhower stood out for his integrity, while Goldwater did for his presumed lack of competence or reliability. The Bush campaign's attacks on John Kerry, along with the Swiftboat Veterans for Truth advertisements, suggested Kerry's lack of reliability. But, as partisanship has increased, Wattenberg suggests that voters' evaluations of candidates' personal character have had less influence on their choices in presidential elections. But this is too simple, as there are many dimensions to character. Trump's character work clearly damaged his opponents, even if they also left many with a negative impression of Trump: villain to some, hero to others.

American parties still deploy characters to mobilize their own base and win over independents. "Democrats are most likely to identify Republican candidates as lacking in compassion, while Republicans will view Democratic candidates as weak leaders."[41] David Holian and Charles Prysby use polling data to demonstrate the importance of empathy for Democratic candidates, as Democratic voters are more likely to seek a leader concerned with economic inequality and sympathetic to the struggles that people like them face. For a party that focuses on social welfare through Social Security and Medicare and more recently the Affordable Care Act, empathy is a key moral trait. Republicans counter that Democrats' empathy is misplaced, ignoring the real working class in favor of undeserving minorities.[42]

For Republicans, national defense and traditional values lead to a focus on strong leadership. For the 2012 election, Holian and Prysby demonstrate Romney's poor standing on questions of empathy. More importantly for Romney's chances of electoral success, independents perceived Romney as roughly even with Obama on leadership, underlining Romney's weak showing in a key area of strength for most Republican candidates. In 2016 Trump projected strength to his voters, even at the expense of moral virtue. His speeches are riddled with comments on whether people and actions are strong or weak.

Character assassination was part of election campaigns long before Donald Trump. Jane Caputi collected political paraphernalia from some of the most vociferous attacks during the 2008 election campaign. Attacks against Hillary Clinton and Barack Obama commonly employed sexist and racist stereotypes. Clinton was frequently portrayed as a witch, reinforcing "the sexist canard . . . that whenever a woman works power, she works evil." One button portrayed her as the snake-haired monster Medusa; others used fangs and claws. Depictions of Obama employed racist images ranging from the jungle to the ghetto as well as attacks upon his masculinity. One button brought a number of these tropes together: "Hey, Obama! Can't You Control Yo' Mamma?" Such products are designed to attach negative emotions such as fear, discomfort, hate, and humiliation to public candidates. They reinforce negative perceptions of the "other" candidate among a committed base.[43]

Legal Characters

Legal trials were one of the primary settings for rhetoric in ancient Greece, as accusers and defenders had to create characters for themselves to persuade juries that consisted of hundreds of citizens at a time. Many lawsuits were transparent attempts to seize the defendants' property, just as 1500 years later Europe's elaborate heresy trials hid the fact that the properties of the condemned were frequently split between the accusers (often the Church) and the judges (often local notables). Outcomes frequently depended on the local reputations—the characters—of the alleged heretics.[44]

In courtrooms each side constructs its villains and victims, usually in opposition to each other. Psychologist Neal Feigenson found that juries for trials about accidents tend to construct melodramatic stories that focus on the victims, divide the parties into good guys and bad guys, and explain individuals' actions in terms of their character. Juries try to craft decisions that punish the villains and reward the victims.[45]

An arithmetic of blame suggests that the more damaged the victim, and the more moral she was before the crime, the worse the villain and his action. On the other hand, if the villain can establish himself as a good person, the blame is reduced: the act was uncharacteristic, not intended, not so bad, and so on. In most courtrooms, villains who act like villains (who do not show contrition, for instance) are blamed more, while victims who act like victims (showing sadness or depression) are thought to have suffered greater harm. People want harsher sentences when nasty villains harm sympathetic victims.

The opposite characterization is often useful in the case of victimless crimes such as drug infractions, where the accused harm themselves when they claim victim status; sentencing may be lighter when they take responsibility for their actions instead of claiming the passivity of the victim.[46] Accepting responsibility allows them to ask for forgiveness, itself a claim to good moral standing. Affect-control researchers have found that observers allocate blame and punishment based on their character judgments of villains and victims more than on their judgments of the actions alone.[47]

Legal procedures are often used to compensate acknowledged victims. The United Kingdom has a minister for policing, criminal justice and victims, while France appointed a minister for victims after the 2015 Paris attacks. The U.S. federal government created a Victim Compensation Fund for the survivors and families of those killed on 9/11. Following principles of tort law, the Fund offered different amounts of money for different kinds of victims, based on their age, number of dependents, and potential earning power. Life insurance and pension payments were deducted from the amount, but charitable contributions were not. Battles ensued between various groups who thought they—or their deceased—were being shortchanged. At a deeper level, those who accepted compensation from the Fund (averaging $1.6 million per deceased) had to agree not to sue the airlines. The legislation saved the airline industry from bankruptcy by excluding airlines from the category of villain: airplanes were only the vehicles used by the real villains, the hijackers.[48]

The well-documented trial of novelist Michael Peterson, convicted of murdering his wife Kathleen, suggests how hard it is for families and for juries to attribute awful suffering to "accidents." They seem to prefer to find a villain to match the victim. Gay porn and emails with a male hustler were allowed as evidence in this case, putatively to cast doubt on how happy the Petersons' marriage had been (all other evidence to the contrary), but in fact to make Peterson a bad person in jurors' eyes. "I don't know who that person is," complained Peterson, referring to the villain carefully elaborated by prosecutors.[49] This affluent writer was an easy target in North Carolina. The jurors seem to have dismissed the heavily accented testimony of a Chinese American, world-renowned forensic scientist Henry Lee, to the effect that the dramatic bloodstains could have been caused by Kathleen's coughing up blood after she had slipped on a staircase. Peterson was "other" enough to be transformed from grieving husband to premeditating murderer.

Although most trials are machines for designating villains and victims, political trials can also generate heroes. Protestors often see court trials as a way to promote their claims to broad audiences. Prosecutors almost by definition try to portray the violators—often those who have damaged property or trespassed, but sometimes even armed revolutionaries—as criminals: either misguided minions or threatening villains. But many activists see trials as opportunities to spread their heroic image, suffering prosecution for the greater good. Juries or judges must choose between the two characterizations.[50]

Media Frames

Fiction and nonfiction media both utilize epidictic rhetoric. The news media attract audiences by relying on fairly traditional public characters. Sociologist David Altheide shows how the media deploy images of fear and crisis. "The discourse of fear involves victims, indeed requires them." Audiences, he says, "expect victims to perform certain activities, speak a certain language, and, in general, follow a cultural script of dependence, lacking, and powerlessness, while relying on state-sponsored social institutions to save and support them." Officials are the usual heroes in media constructions. Victimhood is generated by "a cultural context that promotes fear as a common definition of the environment."[51] Different fears presumably generate different victims—and villains.

The media often transform victims into experts, who can talk about what it is like to experience crime whether or not they have the kinds of facts and percentages that could put the crimes into broader perspective. According to Barry Glassner, this is one of many tricks that the news media use to exaggerate crime and play on audience fears. Yet the media are torn between allowing victims (always "innocent victims") to own their own stories, a form of empowerment, and expecting them to act like victims: passive and pitiful. It is no accident, says Glassner, that the media pay more attention to victims who are women and white.[52]

Critics of the media naturally attribute most of the blame for misrepresenting crimes and victims to the media, not to politicians. Yet the literature on moral panics shows that politicians and others have just as much to gain from creating folk devils as the media do. No one has surpassed Stanley Cohen's definition of a moral panic: "A condition, episode, person or group of persons emerges to become defined as a threat to societal values and interests; its nature is presented in a stylized and stereotypical fashion by the mass media; the moral barricades are manned by editors, bishops, politicians and other right-thinking people; socially accredited experts pronounce their diagnoses and solutions; ways of coping are evolved or (more often) resorted to; the condition then disappears, submerges or deteriorates and becomes more visible." Working-class youth have especially "occupied a constant position as folk devils: visible reminders of what we should not be."[53] Cohen gave folk devils equal billing to panics, recognizing that the construction of a villain or minions is key to the whole panic.

Legal and media arenas interact in celebrated trials. Lawyers for high-profile clients—whether celebrities like O. J. Simpson or politically charged defendants like the teenagers convicted (falsely) of raping the Central Park jogger—use the media to shape public impressions, engaging in the kind of characterizations at the heart of traditional epidictic. Defendants symbolize protest movements, political issues, and forms of oppression that are controversial enough to raise doubts about whether they are villains, victims, or heroes. Press conferences, media leaks, and other PR are rhetorical venues that Aristotle could not have foreseen but would have understood.[54]

Some scholars believe that character work has increased in recent decades. Lynn Chancer points to a proliferation of media outlets and intensified competition among them.[55] Jeffrey Berry and Sarah Sobieraj see the emergence of an entire "outrage industry" in media such as radio, blogs, Twitter, and cable television. "Outrage discourse," they say, "involves efforts to provoke emotional responses (e.g. anger, fear, moral indignation) from the audience through the use of overgeneralizations, sensationalism, misleading or patently inaccurate information, ad hominem attacks, and belittling ridicule of opponents." In other words, the tools of creating villains. (Although similar rhetoric is used to claim victimhood for yourself and those like you.) They acknowledge the long history of character work, but they suggest that "Outrage today is found in a far greater number of venues, circulates quickly, has vast audiences, and often gathers momentum from the attention of conventional news organizations and the synergistic coordination between media organizations, pundits, bloggers, and politicos."[56] Old rhetorical tricks find new outlets.

In many cases the media are all too ready to rely on traditional flat characters, especially when they reflect unacknowledged group stereotypes. Mahmood Mamdani excoriates journalists for presenting "a simple moral world, where a group of perpetrators face a group of victims, but where neither history nor motivation is thinkable because both are outside history and context." They, or their readers, desire a simple moral story "that describes the victim as untainted and the perpetrator as simply evil." They are unable to understand situations where villains become victims and vice versa. They want "an African replay of the Holocaust," but this frame obscures the political roots of that continent's wars. In the case of Darfur, this character work allows, even demands, a hero: "It is a world where atrocities mount geometrically, the perpetrators so evil and the victims so helpless that the only possibility of relief is a rescue mission from the outside, preferably in the form of a military intervention."[57] The irresistible triad of villain-victim-hero.

Gossip, Rumors, Scandals

In all these arenas that we have examined, much character work occurs in sheltered forms such as gossip along networks of individuals. "Gossip was everywhere," says Joanne Freeman of the early American republic.

Then, as now, it was a normal part of politics. "Political gossip—discussion of revealing, immoral, or dangerous behavior learned and passed through unofficial channels"—allowed politicians to accomplish several normal tasks. "They formed alliances, developed political strategies, and agreed on common goals . . . . Their discussions were urgent and they disclosed hidden threats to the republic."[58] Gossip creates villains in a subtle way.

But like most character work, there was the opposed side: if discovered, gossip could be denounced as a villainous act, and the intended villain transformed into an innocent victim. The outcome of such contests—in arenas such as courts but also duels—depended less on the truth of the accusations than on the skills of the character workers. Freeman suggests that the fragility of the new state ("a government of character striving to become a government of rules") encouraged gossip as the only means to debate policies, through a version of metonymy by which policies and their proposers were conflated.[59] Even if gossip increases in unstable situations, it hardly disappears from normal politics. Individuals still symbolize policies.

Sometimes character work happens very rapidly, especially the construction of scary villains, and sometimes it spills across arenas. Scandals are more self-contained than moral panics, but they have similar dynamics. They tap into existing anxieties; the media use them to expand and titillate their audiences; moral entrepreneurs seize the chance to promote their own agendas. Some scandals provoke moral shocks that allow or force people to articulate their moral intuitions; others simply offer prurient details of celebrity lives. At their most political, scandals can focus public attention on the legitimacy of an organization or institution, as Watergate did.

Scandals are often strategic inventions, in the form of a denunciation or a smear campaign. According to Ari Adut, repetition and exaggeration can replace solid evidence, since people assume, "where there is smoke there is fire."[60] Within organizations that assume or try to impose a moral consensus, denunciations can take the form of "degradation ceremonies," as a victorious or simply more powerful faction attacks the strength and morality of another bloc, or of an individual representing it. Harold Garfinkel pointed out the essentializing and public nature of these character degradations, which claim that someone "is not as he appears but is otherwise and *in essence* of a lower species."[61] In medieval Europe accusations of heresy and witchcraft assumed, and helped define, this activity as public entertainment, often reflecting the dominance of one political faction over another.[62]

When one player in an arena has sufficient power, at least temporarily, it may impose a degradation ceremony on its opponents. In a case from the McCarthy era in U.S. politics, Gary Alan Fine singles out the nasty proceedings of the McCarran Committee, officially known as the Senate Internal Security Subcommittee, which was created by a bipartisan group of extremely conservative senators. They went after Owen Lattimore, a China specialist who both wrote books and served on diplomatic missions there. To them, and to their carefully selected witnesses, Lattimore represented a murky conspiracy in the State Department that had helped give China to the communists. As he complained, "Concerning my reputation and character, you have now for many months been publishing to the world an incredible mass of unsubstantiated accusations, allegations, and insinuations. For months a long line of witnesses has set me in the midst of a murky atmosphere of pretended plots and conspiracies so that it is now practically impossible for my fellow citizens to follow in detail the specific refutation of each lie and smear."[63] This committee was established to demonize him and others; he was hardly allowed to defend himself. Meeting during the Korean War, the primary goal of the committee's political theater was to malign and undermine Truman administration policies.

Controversies sometimes involve dueling scandals, or dueling accusations of scandal, like the usual spiral of mutual accusations between whistleblowers and their employers. Political parties are eager to exploit scandals across the aisle, as the reputation of a party is influenced by that of its individual members. Corruption scandals against members of Brazil's Workers' Party devastated the party under the leadership of Dilma Rousseff. They also provided fodder for opposition parties, popular protests, and eventually the triumph of neofascist Jair Bolsonaro.

But corruption allegations do not always harm a party or a politician, as supporters may view these allegations as mere political mud-slinging. Most effective is when the entire party has been tainted by some dubious arrangement or decision. After the end of apartheid in South Africa, the National Party, which had long campaigned on racial segregation and discrimination, faced a tough media battle. Its opponents barely had to remind voters of its role in the now thoroughly discredited system. As most of apartheid's former supporters now claimed they had never really liked the idea, the party that had established it disappeared with barely a whimper.

Rumors, along with the moral panics and scandals based on them, are efforts to make sense of events and situations, and they do this partly by drawing on reputations. They in turn reinforce or transform those reputations. In fact the logic of rumors often follows character expectations even to the extent of ignoring or distorting available information. Rumors tend to essentialize players by stripping that information to a bare minimum. One neighborhood hears that young men from another neighborhood are coming to rob and loot: the feeling of threat reduces the others to pure malevolence and exaggerates their strength. A message over a police radio condenses a complex situation into a perpetrator and victim. It does not help that the reduction follows stereotyped expectations about gender, race, and class.

Rumors can gain credibility when they have broad—even global—scope, since the "facts" that support them are entirely mediated. Gary Alan Fine and Bill Ellis examine the global networks for rumors that have emerged through increased migration, tourism, and trade. These can build on villainous reputations, suggesting for example that "evil outsiders deliberately conspire to import danger, sometimes with the connivance of our own fellow citizens." Sometimes it is only through rumors that full demonization can occur: "Rumor permits concealed sentiments to enter public debate, gaining an often sympathetic audience for assertions that might otherwise be deeply troubling."[64] Rumors and reputations have no special relationship to what we might call facts. They are powerful tools for character work.

Denunciations and rumors remind us that orators construct two public characters in their epidictic activity: their object of attention, but also themselves. A player's own actions help define its character, and these include its epidictic actions. When we ridicule or praise someone, those acts convey something about what kind of person *we* are as well as what kind *they* are.

What kind of person denounces another, creates scandals, spreads rumors? Heroes do not act like this. In one of the memorable moments of the 2016 presidential campaign in the U.S., Chris Christie savaged Marco Rubio for robotically repeating sound bites rather than listening and reacting to others in the debate. Rubio proved the point by repeating—word for word—what he had just said. It was a powerful hit, questioning Rubio's real intelligence: was he just another pretty face who could memorize good lines? A few days later he performed poorly in the New Hampshire primary, and his campaign never recovered. But Christie's own performance was even worse, and he immediately dropped out of the race. The exchange had crystalized Rubio's robotic image of slickness, but also Christie's image as smart but vicious.

———————

Part I has examined the sights, sounds, and words out of which we build characters, as well as the cognitive and emotional tricks with which we put the information together. We have also distinguished a number of strategic arenas where character tropes play salient roles. In Part II we turn to the specific public characters. Each has its "characteristic" words and images, with corresponding impacts on how players interact, and a variety of effects on our understanding of the world. We begin with the immoral characters, for without the threat they pose there would be little need for character work, or at least little struggle over it. Bad characters are usually more fun than good ones.

II | The Primary Characters

5 | We Fear Villains

The surest way to work up a crusade in favor of some good cause is to
promise people that they will have a chance of maltreating someone.
To be able to destroy with good consciences, to be able to behave badly
and call your bad behavior "righteous indignation"—this is the height of
psychological luxury, the most delicious of moral treats.

—*Aldous Huxley*

A S INVESTMENT COMPANIES, BANKS, AND personal fortunes
collapsed in late 2008, and as the global economy was heading
into the fastest downturn since the 1930s, anxiety, anger, and frustration encouraged the search for explanations and villains. Out of many
candidates, who made large profits by misleading their own clients, one
suddenly emerged in December as the greatest of all villains, Bernie
Madoff. Total strangers shouted abuse at him and his family on the streets.
 The image that seemed to crystalize his enormity was his return home
to house arrest, when he ran a gauntlet of photographers. He had a cap
down over his eyes and had what was quickly labeled a "smirk" on his
face. His mouth extended horizontally, his lips pressed together tightly in
a mysterious, sphinxlike half smile. Instead of being interpreted as a man
trying to contain pain through a polite smile, it was interpreted as a look of
disdain and triumph. There were actually many images, as his short walk
was captured on video. He was shouted at, jostled, and in one case shoved
rather hard by a photographer hoping for a better shot. An old man in pain
being harassed by paparazzi would not have fit the character work that
had immediately unfolded. No one would view him as a grandfather who,
missing his own ambitious targets, slid slowly into covering them up, always hoping that he would eventually make good on the losses.

Public Characters. James M. Jasper, Michael P. Young, and Elke Zuern, Oxford University
Press (2020) © Oxford University Press.
DOI: 10.1093/oso/9780190050047.001.0001

Madoff's villainy derived from the size of his Ponzi scheme, which mirrored the brilliance of his prior reputation as an investment wizard. Based on his supposed genius, he flipped from hero to villain with ease. Madoff's evil flourished to the extent that his many helpers were ignored or absolved, especially his wife and sons. His brother Peter's role as chief compliance officer was largely ignored in the media, even though he was sentenced to ten years in prison. No fewer than sixty-three character letters were sent in support of Peter before his sentencing; there were none for Bernie.

On paper there was 65 billion dollars in his clients' accounts, most of it put there by professional money managers on behalf of their own clients. Like the small fry, they wanted to believe in Madoff's wizardry, but unlike the little investors they should have known better, especially after an exposé appeared in *Barron's* in 2001. One, French aristocrat René-Thierry Magon de La Villehuchet, killed himself days after the scandal broke, having lost 1.4 billion dollars of his clients' money. His act suggested a dramatic contrast with Madoff, who now appeared more cowardly and self-serving, but it may also have deflected attention and blame from the rest of the professional minions.

Madoff's main minions were his assistant Frank DiPascali and his tiny staff on the secretive seventeenth floor of the building where the main offices were located. They were criminals but not villains, whereas the professional investors were large enough that they "knew or should have known" about Madoff's scheme, in the words of the suits against them trying to recover the victims' funds. Eventually an entire book was written about Madoff's relationship with J. P. Morgan Chase, which paid more than two billion dollars as a settlement. Even so, Madoff's evil seems to have prevented his case from becoming a broad critique of capitalism, even though plenty of money managers became just as rich by legally charging their clients 2 percent a year.

Bernie's evil depended on his eight thousand victims. Most of them had invested in funds and banks that in turn—through professionals—had passed their money on to him. There were also dozens of charities, again run by supposed professional financiers. The headline number of $65 billion reflects the Madoff team's fabrications over two decades; the original amount invested was $18 billion, 75 percent of which was recovered and repaid. ("An incredible recovery rate for a crime of this magnitude," but a story that, lacking the villain, did not make headlines.) Most of these clawback suits were against professional investors who earned money from referring clients to Madoff or who withdrew funds right before the collapse (the redemptions that brought down the Ponzi scheme). According to the lawsuits they "knew or should have known they were benefiting from fraudulent activity or, at a minimum, failed to exercise reasonable due diligence." In the shadow of Bernie Madoff, they never rose to the status of villains in the story.[1]

Madoff offered little defense, but privately he did what many con artists do: he belittled his victims. They were greedy, pleading with him to take their money even though—in a brilliant marketing strategy—he appeared to be reluctant to let them into his funds. He also castigated them for being willfully naïve (naïvety is a form of innocence, willful naïvety is not!). They should have known Bernie's returns were impossible, at least the professional money managers among them. In his view, they wished to shift the burden of worrying to him, the heroic wizard of Wall Street. He was responsible for the *best* returns as the hero, and the *biggest* fraud ever as the villain.

We see demonization in many arenas, but especially in politics. The federal government is evil, exclaimed Marco Rubio during the 2016 campaign. Planned Parenthood is a criminal enterprise, according to Ted Cruz. All professional politicians, in Donald Trump's eyes, are "highly incompetent people running our country into the ground." Europe is just as bad, said the Donald, run by nothing but "weak leaders." Hillary Clinton is a liar. We need not even repeat what the Republican candidates said about President Obama, or about opponents like Iran, ISIS, or North Korea. Whatever the politicians said publicly, ultra-conservative voters posted much worse—more racist and sexist—jokes and epithets on social media.

Fear and hatred of villains are among the most powerful emotions in any arena. Political leaders deploy anxieties and outrage to draw people out of their daily routines and prepare them for the sacrifices of public life and even war. Racist cartoons of Hirohito, Tojo, and Saddam Hussein helped prepare the American population for war; paranoid stereotypes of Quakers, Catholics, Mormons, communists, Jews, African Americans, and others have helped excuse horrendous repression throughout American history; American populists have featured corrupt bureaucrats and the idle rich as the embodiment of ill intention and action. To present villains as both powerful and secretive heightens our sense of urgency in stopping them, generates collective identities forged against the evil outsiders, and places god-fearing citizens in the role of protective heroes prepared for sacrifice.

Villains are bad and powerful, frequently more powerful than the heroes. Most of the time heroes need help against the villain, although sometimes their cleverness or sharp shooting can prevail against the strength of the villain. The more powerful the villain, the more we need a hero to stop him, the more the hero needs our help, and the more admiration we have for her. We feel relief when the hero arrives.

A villain's strengths come mostly from the same list as the hero's, transformed morally, as listed in Table 5.1. Intelligence in the hero becomes wily cunning in the villain; virility becomes disrespect for women, or worse. Wealth and nobility are corrupting, physical strength is now brutish. Bravery appears on the hero's list, but not the villain's, as it has an unavoidable moral admixture: villains are supposed to be selfish, not self-sacrificing. Recognition of an opponent's valor would transform him from villain into hero, at least in part.

On the (im)moral dimension, villains can be cruel, arrogant, greedy, hypocritical, sacrilegious. Just as heroes can be superhuman, with godlike qualities, so villains can appear inhumanly strong. Evil sorcerers traditionally had magical powers.

Just as people can become heroes through one brave, generous act, so villains can be constructed on the basis of a momentary choice or

TABLE 5.1 Sources of Strength and Examples

	HEROIC VERSIONS	VILLAINOUS VERSIONS
PHYSICAL POWER, PERSONAL OR MILITARY	Hercules, Achilles, champions of lone combat	Invading armies, ogres, monsters, dragons
TECHNOLOGICAL POWER	Gunslingers, U.S. military	U.S.S.R. in Cold War
INTELLIGENCE	Scientists advancing progress	Scientists out of control
NUMBERS	Protest movements	Mobs
BRAVERY: WILLINGNESS TO SACRIFICE ONESELF	Medal of Honor winners	Foe's bravery (rarely acknowledged, or criticized as disregard for life)
WEALTH	Philanthropists	Conspiratorial elites
TRUST, MORAL CHARM	Charismatic leaders	Demagogues
OFFICIAL POSITION	Commanders, presidents	Dictators
ENDURANCE, SURVIVAL	Abuse survivors	Unrepentant convicts
ENERGY, ENTHUSIASM, CONFIDENCE	Leaders	Fascists, invaders
SUCCESS	Wealthy entrepreneurs	Colonial occupiers

action. One lie, one betrayal, can ruin a player's moral reputation forever. Observers are not content to judge only the action, but attribute abiding traits to the person behind it. We create characters from actions. And when one act stands out in a person's life, maybe only his death, it is easy to shed complexities and create pure characters. We are not satisfied with "circumstantial villains."

We construct villains for the powerful emotions they inspire in audiences who fear and hate them. They focus blame, transforming anxiety and frustration into indignation and purpose. Villains are usually "others," outside our moral community, even if they are suspected of having infiltrated us. If nothing else, we expel them from our circle of moral concern when we condemn them.

It is less clear how many players actually see themselves as villains, or what they feel if they do identify themselves that way. If they break the "rules of fair play" it is usually because they do not see them as fair at all, but as imposed dishonorably by their opponents. Even the most callous villains frequently portray themselves as victims. Yet there *are* people who welcome bad reputations, we'll see later.

Passive villains are rare. The character work of creating villains is usually done by others, especially opponents, who typically want the villains to appear as threatening as possible. Being active is more threatening than passivity. *A passive villain is usually a defeated villain.* If initiating strategic action is ordinarily bad, then villains must be seen as doing just that. And they must bring energy and enthusiasm to their evil. Activity can sometimes compensate for relative weakness, as with Shakespeare's Iago, whose assiduous innuendoes set in motion all the action in *Othello*.

Villains are thought to be secretive, heightening our sense that we cannot trust them. Their dishonesty is one source of power that heroes lack. We are anxious that they will catch us off guard, surprising us when it is too late to resist. Secrecy is not passive, but an active effort to keep something from others. We cannot admire their duplicitous ways. Attacking Obama in late 2015, Donald Trump mysteriously said, "There is something going on with him that we don't know about." A villain brought down the Greeks' greatest hero, Hercules, but in a delayed, devious way that depended upon his wife's jealousy (the centaur Nessus gave her a shirt that he promised would make Hercules faithful to her but in fact poisoned him). To poison someone is not a hero's vengeance, but a villain's.

Conspiracy theories seem to have existed in all times and places, based on belief in villains so evil that they can hide their work from normal people. The lack of credible evidence merely proves the villains' power to those who believe. Every time a public figure dies suddenly, a nation loses a war, an airplane disappears, or a favored team loses a match, conspiracy theorists crank out their analyses. Adapting conspiracy talk to a new arena, Justice Brett Kavanaugh attributed his confirmation problems in 2018 to "a calculated and orchestrated political hit" by unnamed people seeking "revenge on behalf of the Clintons," while his supporter Senator John Cornyn decried "the screams of paid protestors." (Paid by George Soros, no doubt.) Many conspiracies are readily named—Jews, Opus Dei, the deep state, the Koch brothers—but in some cases the conspirators are so deft that they cannot be identified. Or they are too frightening and omniscient for us to speak their names aloud, like Harry Potter's nemesis, "he who shall not be named." New technologies, medicines, and far-flung bureaucracies seem to provoke these anxieties.

According to sociologist Orrin Klapp, there are villains who *threaten* the social order, usually criminals of some type; villains who improperly *usurp* or *abuse* their place in the social order, such as dictators; and those who *have no place* in the social order, outsiders, strangers, deviants, or other pariahs. In our view this third category become villains proper only when they are developed into folk demons. (Klapp also mentions traitors, sneaks, parasites, and others too weak to get what they want openly: public characters that we would call minions.)[2]

Villains are central to political theory. Since the Greeks, much theorizing has focused on the distinction between heroes and villains in the special form of just and unjust rulers. Given that monarchs and other potentates are almost always strong, how can we judge whether they are also good or bad? And who is to make that judgment? Questions of democracy lurked just beneath the surface of these theories, sometimes rising to the top as explicit models.

The Germanic tribes who brought down Rome believed that warriors had to consent to follow a king, through processes of acclamation and homage. Augustine and a thousand years of Christian theorists argued that humans are so depraved that almost any authority is better than allowing people to choose their own rulers, but even these thinkers recognized that certain rulers are evil. Their transgression typically consists in placing their own personal wealth and desires above the good of the community, acting against the law and against God. Aquinas' famous distinction between usurpers who had seized power unlawfully and tyrants who pursued their own goals condemned unjust rulers on the one hand for being too powerful, and on the other for being malevolent.

Even if a ruler could be characterized as a villain, there was still the question of who had the right or obligation to overthrow him. John of Salisbury offered a unique solution in the twelfth century. A tyrant's political subjects had no right to overthrow him, since he was not breaking any political agreements that he had made with them. He was doing something worse, violating the laws of God. So the rebel had to be someone acting as God's agent, a charismatic figure from outside the system. In other words, it required a special kind of hero to overthrow a sovereign villain.[3]

Demonization

Demonizing your opponents is one of the oldest political strategies and still plays a role in politics today. You exaggerate their strength, their malevolence, and their activity levels. They may be either superhuman or subhuman, but urgent action is required to thwart them. They are always busy, looking for your weaknesses.

In political arenas there are many advantages to extremism in character work, crafting your opponents into the most evil villains (and you and your allies into the most good and powerful heroes). Painting policy advocates with whom you disagree as "too extreme" or "radical" is common enough, a way to attack people rather than engage their demands. This has been the fate of many protest movements. Journalists often take their ideas, but not them, seriously. "The extremism tactic," note several psychologists, "builds on the public's presumption that even admirable values such as gender equality or environmental protection can be taken to unreasonable lengths."[4] A political player who needs to attack a popular position that is based on widely held values can indirectly go after the character of its proponents. The extremism taint is compatible with ill-intentioned villains, but also with misguided minions.

Villains provide a rough-and-ready explanation of adverse events. The initial reaction to an attack is almost always to select and demonize a supposed perpetrator, with "terrorists" serving as the great villain of the twenty-first century. After two bombs exploded in the Moscow subway system in March 2010, Russian President Dmitri Medvedev called the terrorists "beasts, simply." Prime Minister Vladimir Putin called on the police to "drag them out of the bottom of the sewer and into the light of God." Such malevolence could not be human. The following day, in contrast, Medvedev discussed the poverty and unemployment found in the North Caucasus, re-humanizing the terrorists: "People want a normal and decent life, no matter where they live." He admitted his government's responsibility for helping them achieve such a life, implicitly assuming a portion of the blame for the terror.[5] We don't know why the rhetoric suddenly changed, but the retreat from the initial, gut-level villainization was striking.

Some forms of demonization represent ongoing character work against real or imagined opponents. Rival political parties maintain a constant barrage of innuendoes and accusations against each other, which they put aside only if they find themselves in a coalition government together. And sometimes not even then. If things go bad it is better to be the junior minion than the senior villain.

Although demonizing opponents is usually a sound political strategy, it can backfire if other players see these assaults themselves as immoral—as we saw with scandal accusations. A truly good player does not try to smear others. For this reason heroes try not to sully themselves with such attacks; their followers or third parties often do it instead. It's easy to see why. In March 2004, the governing Spanish Popular Party thought it had found a winning reelection strategy in blaming the Madrid bombings (three days before the general election) on its traditional demon, the Basque separatist group ETA. The interior minister's statement that "The government has no doubt ETA is responsible," quickly unraveled in the face of contrary evidence, and inspired indignant protests against the attempted manipulation. "My horror at the massacre doesn't impede my ability to recognize the leeches that try to gain something from it," wrote one person on a listserv. "The same rage turns into disgust at the spectacle of how they try to benefit from tragedy."[6] Sympathy for the victims could actually be used in this case to resist too quick a demonization of the wrong villains. The demonizers were demonized instead. The Popular Party lost the election.

Efforts at villainization often throw all sorts of accusations into the hopper together. The history of homophobia provides a tediously long list of indictments meant to conflate all condemned practices into one. To take just one example, Supreme Court justice Antonin Scalia, in his unhinged dissent to the *Lawrence* ruling that nullified U.S. sodomy laws, complained that it would now be impossible to uphold "state laws against bigamy, same-sex marriage, adult incest, prostitution, masturbation, adultery, fornication, bestiality, and obscenity." The equation of gay sex and bestiality, in an effort to maximize disgust, is a favorite trope of homophobic tirades, leading one columnist to mock the "man-dog marriage panic" over "petaphilia."[7]

Historian John Dower catalogues the rhetorical figures that Americans deployed to demonize the Japanese after Pearl Harbor. No distinctions were made among Japanese, who were often referred to collectively as "the Jap." They were subhuman or nonhuman: "animals, reptiles, or insects (monkeys, baboons, gorillas, dogs, mice and rats, vipers and rattlesnakes, cockroaches, vermin—or, less directly, 'the Japanese herd' and the like)." They were a swarm, a beehive, or an octopus with its tentacles strangling Asia. A float in a 1942 New York parade showed, according to one journalist, "a big American eagle leading a flight of bombers down on a herd of yellow rats which were trying to escape in all directions." The small size of rats suggests minions, but they were threatening enough when homogenized together into a large swarm or herd.

This war required an epidictic transformation of the Japanese from minion to villain, Dower suggests. At first "most Westerners found it difficult to take the Japanese really seriously . . . . then, shocked and stunned by the military successes of the Japanese in the months that followed the outbreak of war, they erred in the opposite direction by exaggerating the enemy's material and psychological strength." They went from subhuman to superhuman, minions to villains, from cockroaches to King Kong (Figure 5.1).[8]

It is easiest to demonize another group when you believe in literal demons, based on one cosmology or another. This is the specialty of dualistic religions that posit a great clash between the forces of good and evil, which raise to eternity the stakes of this struggle. Christianity has developed an apocalyptic vision of one final battle, the staging of which requires accurate identification of the "anti-Christ." The list of candidates for this role is long: American Indians, the Church of England, Jews and Catholics, communists of course, but also feminists, the U.N., and King Juan Carlos of Spain. These villains are wily, using zip codes and supermarket bar codes to keep track of us all. The conspirators are cunning in hiding their tracks. Interestingly, one strand of this thinking grants humans considerable agency to fight the forces of evil, while another grants all power to God. We do not have to be the heroes, only loyal followers, when we have Him on our side.[9]

Not All Bad

There are some advantages to being acknowledged as a villain. When strength is the most advantageous asset in an arena, people may cultivate villainy to boost their reputation for power. There are benefits to being feared by others, who as a result will think twice about attacking you.

How Tough Are the Japanese?

They are not tougher than other soldiers, says a veteran
observer, but brutality is part of their fighting equipment.

FIGURE 5.1 When the Japanese proved their military strength, King Kong became a better trope than rodents and insects.

Where you fall on the moral spectrum matters less in these settings, where it is always better to be a feared villain than a contemptible minion.

Like many stigmas, demonization can bond those on the wrong side of the moral boundary. In his study of the underworld, Diego Gambetta posits, "Groups whose members have transgressions to hide from public view and whose members share knowledge of these transgressions with each other will enjoy a comparative advantage in their ability to support their internal cohesion."[10] Although Gambetta is thinking about crimes that could be prosecuted, other villains may come to revel in a bad reputation, using it to get their way by intimidating others. Alexander the Great was a villain to those he conquered, but his fearsome reputation led many a walled town to open their gates to him rather than risk destruction.

Bad characters face choices, and sometimes dilemmas, over their most advantageous characterization. When facing charges in court, it is preferable to play the minion, shifting blame for a crime onto those who are more powerful. But when your audience is your fellow criminals rather than a skeptical judge or jury, it can be useful to play up your misdeeds to establish your strength.

There are other settings in which people accept a villainous reputation because strength is the dimension that matters most. Paul Watson, captain of the *Sea Shepherd*, purchased for him by Friends of Animals, has said in interviews that he wants Japanese whalers to think that he will do anything, perhaps even sink their ships. He left Greenpeace over their commitment to nonviolence. To some extent this character work is simply about strategy: keeping them guessing, and a little afraid. But Watson's reputation as being a bit crazy helps him pursue this strategy convincingly. (And he did ram one whaling ship in 1979, a semi-legal whaler that was damaged and then retired from service.)

Because his approach relies on physical interference, coercion, rather than communication and persuasion, Watson must emphasize his strength more than his intentions. He wants the whalers to think of him as a villain, a reputation that grants him strength. They would think of him negatively along the moral dimension at any rate, but he would rather be seen as a villain than a minion. Even here, when coercion is central, the players are still trying to persuade one another of their characters. The same is true in war. There is no such thing as pure coercion; there is always some persuasion as well, some character work.

Like Alexander the Great, the Watson example reminds us again that one side's hero is the other's villain, a battle made easier because both characters are high on the strength dimension, and usually on activity as well. Contrasting moral assessments are the core of politics. Watson's real dilemma is his reputation with his financial backers, who may stop seeing him as a hero if they disapprove of his tactics. Alexander did not have to answer to a board of directors.

It is easier to agree about a public character's strength than her morality. Their strength is proven by their impressive deeds, the kind that enter historical chronicles, the kind that people talk about: what used to be known as *glory*. But glory involves destruction. His fellow Macedonians celebrated Alexander's conquests; the conquered were presumably less pleased. Later writers could hardly deny his accomplishments, whatever they thought of them morally. Among Romans, Seneca declared him "a robber and plunderer of nations"; to Lucan he was "a pestilence to the earth, a thunderbolt that struck all people alike, a comet of disaster to mankind."[11] But his strength was undeniable: it is what made him great to the Macedonians and a pestilence to others.

There is another kind of villain, with the potential to be converted into a hero when we come to admire them for their strength. Marlies Danziger finds these "heroic villains" in the tradition of the sublime in the eighteenth and nineteenth centuries. In most literature, the sublime has nothing to do with morality, only with power, pushing the hero and villain together. "A highly gifted villain may change and eventually perform deeds of extraordinary virtue, whereas the ordinary man, without the strength of mind and sensibility of such a villain, is likely to remain a moral nonentity."[12] As long as they are art and not reality, depictions of horror and sorrow delight us and feed our souls. This line of esthetic theory eventuated in Nietzsche's superman "beyond good and evil." Again, the elimination of the moral dimension collapses heroes and villains, a useful move in literature but not in politics.

The proximity of villains to heroes on strength sets up an important type of plot: conversions. A villain becomes an instant hero when he sees the light, and he brings his welcome strength with him. The conversion of minions is celebrated, but it can never matter as much.

Enemies

The categories of villains and of enemies overlap, even though they are not quite the same. In some cases demonization may occur before we enter a conflict against opponents, but more often demonization is part of that conflict. We try to portray our enemies as vicious and threatening in order to motivate and justify action against them, action that goes beyond normal competition in peacetime arenas. Enemies are inherently evil, not simply opposed to us.[13] As conscript armies replaced professional mercenaries, the mobilization of antipathy became a vital ingredient of war. Epidictic flourished as emotions replaced money as the prime motivator for soldiers.

The essential triad of villain-victim-hero is important in most politics, but crucial for going to war. The order is decisive: a nasty action that has caused suffering, the allocation of blame to evildoers, and the arousal of a sleeping giant to action. Heroic protectors repulse evil aggressors. Professional armies can be commanded into limited incursions, but large, sustained wars require a level of support from the public that can only come about through their feelings about basic public characters. Bush II pushed the United States and several other countries into a deranged invasion of Iraq through a super-simplified character triad—although the shock of 9/11 almost required some such character work.[14]

Wars demand some demonization of opponents, but the definition of who is foreign and opposed is flexible and contested. The obvious case consists of citizens and immigrants of foreign descent. The United States' participation in "modern" wars, that is to say the "world" wars, brought intensive character work to bear against those associated symbolically with the nation's enemies. At the outbreak of World War I, roughly 10 percent of Americans were of German ancestry: eight million people. There were lively German-language newspapers, schools, churches, and associations. Most German Americans argued for neutrality until 1917, but immediately changed their stance after Germany sank several U.S. vessels and Woodrow Wilson declared war.

This support did not prevent a vicious demonization of all things German American. German-speaking immigrants were required to register, and were banned from living near arms factories. A series of laws targeted "enemy aliens," and the German press was shut down or boycotted by distributors. Immigrants Americanized their names and stopped speaking German to each other in the streets. Crowds attacked German businesses and homes, and lynched at least one person. Grassroots sentiment and official state action encouraged each other. It did not help that German spies actually did blow up a number of sites.[15]

Even more notorious was the incarceration of 120,000 Japanese Americans during World War II, based on character work that homogenized everyone of Japanese descent. The "Japanese race is an enemy race . . . the racial strains are undiluted."[16] In the concise characterization of General John DeWitt, "A Jap's a Jap." In a typical form of self-reinforcing boundary work, more than five thousand internees were willing to return to Japan as the only way to get out of the prison camps. In surveys, three quarters of Americans said they would not hire those of Japanese ancestry, and two thirds felt that all of them should be sent to Japan.[17] Although there were some German spies and saboteurs at work during World War I, virtually all German and Japanese Americans were patriots in both wars and no threat at all. But they were easy targets, swept up in wartime demonization of America's enemies. Decades later, the interned Japanese were refigured into victims—and heroes, as 23,000 of them served in the U.S. military.

The German assaults on American ships in 1917 and the Japanese attack on Pearl Harbor are only two occasions when American politicians and opinion makers called on their sleeping giant of a nation to rouse itself and take revenge. The attacks of 9/11 were another, although it took more cultural work to identify the villains, thanks to George Bush's obsession with Saddam Hussein. Other provocations had to be entirely manufactured to justify action against predefined villains. "Remember the *Maine*"? Remember the Gulf of Tonkin "incident"? Both were flimsy excuses for the sleeping giant to lash out. Enemies must be framed as villains for popular consumption. (As often happens, the press, especially Joseph Pulitzer and William Randolph Hearst, took the rhetorical lead in the character war against the perfidious Spanish in 1898, pressing a reluctant McKinley into a real war—as a Civil War veteran, McKinley knew the awful difference.)

Dangerous Locations

The modern world has created its own categories of villains and minions who are not necessarily grounded in dualistic theologies or the exigencies of war. In *The Art of Moral Protest* Jasper suggests certain types of people who have been singled out again and again as villains or minions: foreigners, or those defined as foreign (wartime antagonists are obviously the ultimate example); young people, who have not (yet) been socialized into the norms that their elders hold; those at the cutting edge of economic and technological transformations; those at the bottom of the economic ladder, who are dangerous because they naturally resent being there; but also those at the top of the ladder who are resented for their power.[18]

Cities, which many cultures contrast with the supposed simplicity and harmony of the countryside, are the places where all these villains and minions congregate. They are dangerous, "polluted" places, full of impurities. The rich and poor are thrown together. Foreigners appear, and representatives of foreign powers. New techniques, such as large factories, are tried out, often by employing newcomers without other options because they have no place in existing social structures. New subcultures emerge based on shared interests in music, drugs, sexual orientation, and other activities that can be framed as "sins."[19] Villains, minions, and potential victims abound.

In addition to our emotions about place, villains can be manufactured out of a sense of time. Feelings for past, present, and future—and how they are connected—are central to all cultures. In many cases, nostalgia is constructed around the idea that life is not as good as it used to be, and some group is found to blame for the decline. Newcomers are predictable heavies in nostalgic narratives.

Foreigners and immigrants are easy to fear (as villains) or to mock (as minions). They often speak a different language, so that it may be hard to communicate with them. They may look, dress, and act differently. They eat different foods. Sights, smells, and bodily differences can be woven into a sense of disgust against these groups. For all these reasons they may keep to themselves, even when they are not forcibly segregated. They may not have the social connections, material resources, or cultural knowledge to defend themselves in character battles. To make matters worse, "worthy immigrants" may succeed by presenting themselves—or being portrayed by others—as the opposite of "unworthy immigrants."[20]

Jasper discusses a number of examples of demonized groups. In early modern Europe accusations of witchcraft, for which a hundred thousand people were put to death, tended to fall on poor and elderly women who had no morally recognized place in the emerging markets and nation-states, and whose families avoided their traditional obligations to them. The Khmer Rouge brutally emptied Cambodia's cities, especially Phnom Penh, seen as the hotbed for foreign influence and corrupt puppet regimes. They wished to create a "new socialist man" by returning to the glories of the Angkor period a thousand years earlier. To do this they had to purge their society of the "microbes" who had infected it: "invisible, pervasive, and deeply rooted."[21]

The creation of villains relies, like other character work, on what Jasper dubs "the violence of abstractions": the use of rigid binary contrasts, deduction from abstract principles, and political programs to remake the world according to these blueprints. Such visions tend to see societies as totalities, with interlocking parts, so that a problem in one part threatens to pollute the rest. Villains are at work everywhere in this paranoid hallucination. Abstracted worldviews "hold out the hope of purity, an escape from ambiguity, compromise, and pollution."[22] Villains cannot be reformed; they must be eradicated. Individuals are reduced to their functional roles in the system, and if they perform dysfunctions they can and must be eliminated. By this logic the Red Brigades felt free to kill bankers and public officials, and the Khmer Rouge felt obliged to destroy numerous class enemies.

This reductionist thinking homogenizes groups: every member of the group has the same character, shares the same goals, and acts in predictable ways. As a result the group appears more unified than it is, and thus potentially more dangerous. Unaware of differences within the group, opponents lose the strategic capacity to pit different factions against one another. Endless wars and suffering have resulted from this reductionist character work, as one side fears a united opponent. American colonists treated all Indians alike, mostly as Satanic villains, with the self-fulfilling result that eventually more and more tribes became enemies. Lord Kitchener later set the Middle East on a tragic path through simple-minded assumptions about Muslims, notably that they were united by their religion, behind the caliph, whom the British therefore had to control.[23]

The Decline of Evil

Social scientists do not believe in evil. As a result they have had a hard time explaining what most people consider evil: a deliberate, incorrigible malevolence that is almost beyond our ability to understand. But character workers know how to deploy images of evil, and do so with abandon. Evil transcends human logic. Just as the greatest heroes partake of the divine, the greatest villains are driven by a force that is not part of normal human motivation. Mythic villains were often equal to the heroes: their fallen, rejected brothers, for example. In the end, Professor Moriarty kills Sherlock Holmes, not the other way around. In dualistic religions villains are gods every bit as strong as the benevolent deities. And villains are usually more interesting: delicious Iago, compared to dull Othello.

Part of evil is to seem capricious or incomprehensible. To understand a villain's reasons would be a step toward empathy. But some of the awe and fear we feel for prodigious villains is that we simply cannot comprehend them (Figure 5.2). Shakespeare's two greatest villains, Iago and Aaron the Moor (in *Titus Andronicus*), have no obvious reasons for doing the immense harm they carry out with such energy and assiduity. Iago claims to be jealous of Othello, but even this motive is a bit circular: only a mean person would be this insanely jealous of another's happiness. We spot evil at the point where the human imagination fails.

Mysterious evil is not the only source of villainy. Strength, we have seen, inevitably threatens others and as a result it can be morally suspect. In American iconography, but with roots in Faust legends, intellectuals often appear as being so concerned with scientific facts that they have lost touch with their mortal (and moral) souls, and also with "common" people. This condemnation is often reinforced by a claim that they are outsiders as well. "No specialists from the outside," said William Jennings

FIGURE 5.2 In Francisco de Goya's etchings depicting Napoleon's occupation of Spain, the perpetrators are almost faceless, going about their destructions for reasons that elude the viewer.

Bryan in the notorious Scopes monkey trial that crystallized images of the godless expert, "are required to inform the parents of Tennessee as to what is harmful." Villains are often portrayed as too smart for their own goodness.

Not all villains are smart. Some are viewed as forces of nature, beastlike predators who are powerful and threatening but incapable of reasoning. Many of the folk devils of moral panics are characterized this way, like the young African Americans accused of "wilding" and related delinquency in recent decades. Evil is sometimes associated with beasts, with other species that have not attained our moral discernment. If some villains are superhuman, others are subhuman. Just as brute strength and intelligence are contrasting sources of power for heroes, so they are for villains.

African American men have been subject to centuries of simian slurs, from gangs of silly monkeys to big, scary gorillas. One result is that many audiences see Black men as larger and more dangerous, a misperception that can have deadly consequences when it is held by armed officers of the law. Media accounts often include apelike descriptions even today, and the result of such associations is frequently harsher sentences.[24]

Bestiality takes many forms. Legal scholar Patricia Williams describes American racism as the portrayal of Blacks as entirely devoid of will, or having "anti-will" as she dubs it. "We live in a society where the closest equivalent of nobility is the display of unremittingly controlled willfulness. To be perceived as unremittingly without will is to be imbued with an almost lethal trait."[25] The lack of will that has been attributed to Blacks is connected to a perceived subhuman lack of self-control. This lack of will usually marks someone as a minion not a villain, dangerous only when massed in large numbers (in gangs, riots, swarms, wildings, and other behaviors coded as almost instinctive rather than conscious).

Often, when we portray opponents as forces of nature with whom reasoning does not work, physical coercion seems the only way to stop them. The strategy of "containment," used by American leaders against communists during the Cold War, was based on a physical image like a dike or a levee. You don't bargain with a flood, you block it. Islamic martyrs and fanatics, willing to die for their cause, are often portrayed as beyond reason, again in an effort to justify force against them rather than negotiation with them. Their opponents—and politicians trying to frighten voters—inevitably portray them as dangerous nuts.

If a lack of intelligence can be bestial, ineptitude can at least save someone from imputations of malevolence: U.S. President Warren Harding was seen as inept, not evil. Deflecting moral blame from him (he was simply a poor judge of character, too loyal to his friends) meant placing it on corrupt cabinet members, whom he could not control. He had to be seen as weak, a minion not a villain. But after Harding died, those "friends" pushed back, blaming him in order to avoid their own prosecution.[26] The arithmetic of blame demands a perpetrator. Here is a broader dynamic of alliances, known to social-movement scholars as the radical-flank effect: one faction or leader is constructed as reasonable—someone to bargain with—while others are portrayed as out of control, as radical, dangerous, or evil. The symbolic leader's reputation is saved by condemning an underling or ally as the threatening villain. The alliance itself may sometimes benefit from presenting itself as split in this way.

Fewer and fewer people in the modern world find evil plausible as an explanation, and villains have been correspondingly reduced on both the strength and the morality dimensions. Now, they are more likely to be all too human, minions rather than true villains. Gone is the divine mystery that made them so powerful and so evil. Villains are not what they used to be.

Diminished Villains

As Lionel Tiger put it, "Once upon a time, evil was personified. Evil was Mephistopheles or the Devil. Colorfully costumed. Almost flavorful, altogether identifiable, a clarified being from another world." In other words, a public character. In the industrial world, Tiger says, the production of symbols has been as technologized as that of consumer goods. "Malefactors are harder to spot. They no longer boast horns and wear suits with tails, but rather three-piece suits and sometimes turtleneck sweaters of cashmere wool or magenta blouses of tailored silk."[27] Mass-produced villains are shallow compared to Mephistopheles.

In the psychologized modern world, personality disorders often play the role once allotted to evil. Anti-social personality disorder, for instance, entails lack of empathy for others, allowing immense cruelty. Narcissistic personalities also lack empathy, while paranoids actively expect harm from others. Thomas Szasz famously saw diagnoses of mental illness as serving the same function—making us feel good by castigating others as bad—once fulfilled by accusations of witchcraft and other forms of demonization.[28] The diagnosis of mental illness more generally is often a form of character work, in which episodes tend to be construed as signs of abiding personalities, hints at a deeper character.

Even when problematic people and their actions are "medicalized" so that they seem to be suffering from an illness instead of bad intentions, moral judgment often remains. There used to be some moral taint to cancer, as Susan Sontag pointed out, and today addiction is the best example of moralized illness. We often admit the overwhelming force of addiction but nonetheless blame addicts for having allowed themselves to start down the wrong path. The very word addict is a character claim fully defining them as a person.

However we explain them, crazy people are alarming, whether they are villains or minions. In one of the most famous political ads of all times, Lyndon Johnson's 1964 campaign ran a commercial known as Daisy Girl. A cute blonde three-year-old—all innocence and vulnerability—is plucking petals from a dandelion and counting from one to nine. She suddenly looks up, and an image of an exploding nuclear bomb fills the screen. We hear Lyndon Johnson's voice: "We must either love each other or we must die. These are the stakes, to make a world in which all of God's children can live, or to go into the dark." The spot begins with the perfect victim, adds the ultimate danger, without even naming the villain crazy enough to push the button, and then turns to the hero who can protect us from Barry Goldwater's aggressive insanity (although without showing Johnson, so that his image would not be directly associated with the bomb).

Cleverly, the Johnson campaign was prepared for indignation over such a strong commercial, and not just from the Goldwater camp. So they were ready to pull the ad as a generous concession. If they seemed too nasty in airing the commercial, they could make a conciliatory gesture by stopping. In fact, the ad ran only once, during NBC's "Monday Night at the Movies" on September 7th. But the message was clear. As Goldwater himself later expressed it: "Barry Goldwater would blow up the world if he became President of the United States."[29] Stanley Kubrick's film *Dr. Strangelove* had appeared earlier that year, inventing a pro-bomb villain with whom Goldwater was instantly associated.

Here was a villain who was clearly dangerous. His malevolence was not intentional; it was crazy and reckless. But the threat was the same. Goldwater's inconsistency on a number of issues was also exploited as evidence of his instability. In a speech three days after Daisy Girl aired, Johnson warned of "reckless factions, contemptuous toward the will of majorities; callous toward the plight of minorities; arrogant toward allies; belligerent toward adversaries; careless toward peace."[30] Nuclear weaponry was so dangerous that its user need not be evil in order to be immensely threatening. In a way, the Goldwater character concocted by Johnson's team suffered from weakness as much as from malevolence. Senator Hubert Humphrey warned that Americans did not want a "twitchy, nervous, emotional hand on the atomic bomb. I want to be sure that whoever is President of the United States is calm and strong and resolute, and does not think with his blood."[31] Goldwater was part scary villain and part unstable minion.

Selfishness is a modest, modern form of malevolence, seen less as a distinct personality than as a grubby universal motive. In December 2004, Augusto Pinochet was at long last indicted in Chile for human rights violations under his regime. Part of the reason was a shift in popular characterizations of the former dictator. As the *Economist* magazine put it, "Support for General Pinochet was undermined earlier this year by the discovery that, contrary to his supporters' belief that he did not profit from power, he held several secret bank accounts in the United States."[32] His moral standing—already highly contested—was further tarnished by the perception that he was acting out of self-interest rather than some collective or ideal interest. Even though the revelations were irrelevant to the human rights charges, they were an important strand in the struggles to characterize Pinochet as a villain. He no longer stood for arguable principles but for petty greed.

A similar damaging claim is that a person's proposal or position is "politically motivated," which ironically implies that they are after personal gains rather than the public benefit that they pretend. An example came to light in 2005, when the *New York Times* quoted emails from an advisor to Governor George Pataki to the New York State Thruway Authority, advising them to reply to the State Comptroller by calling his damning report on the Metropolitan Transportation Authority "politically motivated" (doing his job as comptroller, he had accused the authority of keeping two sets of books, itself a self-serving breach of public trust).[33] This kind of attack works best in a culture like that of the United States, where many people already see politics as thoroughly corrupt. A "political" act is debased. But Pataki's intervention appeared just as petty and political when it was "revealed."

Cases like these can be interpreted in two ways: the revelations show that the politicians are more malevolent than realized or that they are more petty. In one case heroes become villains. In the other, if they are motivated by tiny interests rather than powerful ideologies, they take a step toward being minions.

Corporations attack whistleblowers in much the same way, deflecting blame for corporate malfeasance onto personal pathologies. The case of Jeffrey Sterling, convicted of giving information about the CIA to the *New York Times*, continues the pattern. The prosecution "painted Sterling as a disgruntled employee who leaked the information because of unrelated grievances stemming from a racial discrimination complaint filed by Sterling, who is African American, against the CIA."

"He felt he'd been mistreated," prosecutor Eric Olshan said. "He was angry. He was bitter. He was done keeping the CIA's secrets.""The defendant put his own selfishness and his own vindictiveness ahead of the American people," Olshan claimed during closing arguments. "For what? He hated the CIA and he wanted to settle the score."[34]

Americans may have clung to traditional images of heroes and villains more than Europeans have. Perhaps this is because they are more religious than Europeans, with one third of Americans believing the Bible is the unerring word of God. Dualistic religions view the world as a continual struggle between evil and good, or villains and heroes. This is a perfectly logical theodicy, or account of suffering, as long as evil and good are relatively balanced, but Christianity began to have logical difficulties when it combined dualism with its view of God as omnipotent. In a world of innocent victims who suffer terribly, God cannot be both completely good and completely powerful. Perhaps this logical gap explains Christianity's long obsession with identifying great evildoers who can almost rival God. In European politics, many hero and villain tropes have a more mocking, ironic tone.

Blame Balancing

The basic public characters revolve around an arithmetic of moral blame. Villains and victims are positively correlated: the greater the victimhood, the greater the villainy. If the victims prove to be less innocent, or less harmed, then the villains appear to be less bad. As diagonal opposites in our tables, villains and victims must be paired in order to heighten the impact of character rhetoric on both. Villains and heroes are also correlated: the more powerful the villain, the greater the hero who vanquishes him. In contrast there is a zero-sum relationship between villains and minions, or between various villains: the more one is blamed, the less the others are.

The reconstruction of Rwanda after its notorious civil war revolved around a clear villain-victim pairing typical of war reportage: the Hutus were the villains, the Tutsis the victims. As Cyanne Loyle and Christian Davenport observe, this character work requires almost exclusive attention to the genocide, not to the civil war, reprisal killings, or the post-genocide government's repressive activities. These more complicated stories— starting the blame narrative slightly before or after the genocide—would make the villains less villainous, and sometimes transform them into victims, and would make the victims into occasional perpetrators of violence.[35]

Children make the purest victims, implying nastier villains who harm them. Mark Jordan analyzes the rhetoric that Anita Bryant deployed to create a homosexual threat when she put aside singing and selling Coca-Cola and orange juice to battle Dade County's new gay rights ordinance in 1977. It was vital to have victims, so she named her campaign "Save Our Children," whom she insisted were being infected and recruited by gay people. Never mind that the root metaphors of infection and of re-cruitment are so different: they both convey a threat. Gays had organized themselves, she said, into a militant, secret, but well-financed organization to advance their "agenda." But their evil overflowed any specific goals, as Jerry Falwell told a Bryant rally: "We are dealing with a vile and vicious and a vulgar gang. They'd kill you as quick as look at you. If you don't think that, you don't know the enemy."[36] Gay people are not usually stereotyped as powerful, much less as brutal and ruthless—except when they band together in shadowy, miniony conspiracies.

Bryant's character work ironically accepted the emerging essentialism of the medical community—and of much of the gay community. Instead of speaking of particular acts, "she assimilates the acts to the identity, she thinks of the acts only in terms of the identity. Indeed, when she wants to talk about these sexual acts, she uses the odd locution 'the act of homosexuality'."[37] Gays are so powerful that their only worthy adversary is God himself, and Bryant turned one county's human rights ordinance into an epic battle between good and evil.

To do this she had to do some fancy epidictic footwork. Teenagers became innocent children: perfect, vulnerable victims without any will of their own. Gay adults were all-powerful, in contrast, with silver tongues ready to recruit young people. "Anita prefers not to talk about troubling adolescents," Jordan comments. "She wants either innocent children or sinful adults, but not changeling adolescents, half victims, half predatory."[38] Like villains and heroes, villains and victims make a powerful contrast, stoking the heat of moral indignation.

In another example of how villain and victim characters are entwined, a team of psychologists examined the speeches given by Australian Prime Minister John Howard in the six years following the 9/11 attacks. The first theme they looked for were statements about the villains as evil and threatening: "This is no isolated act of terrorism: this is the product of years of careful planning, it is the product of evil minds." A serious program of action, years devoted to the task, and careful planning all suggest the power of the villain.

The psychologists also found themes about the dangers facing Australians: "How the situation specifically affected the listener, was bad for them, or placed them in danger. It included the use of inclusive words like 'us' and 'we'." They were potential victims themselves, unless their government responded firmly.

Third was moral outrage over the actions, including remorse, hatred, and disgust. Here it is difficult to separate characterizations of the villains from outrage over their actions, and the thrust is still villainization. "It is an act of terror. It is an act which is repugnant to all things that we as a society believe in." The indignation arises from the contrast between an evil them and a respectable us.

Finally, there were uncertainties about how to cope with the threats from terrorism. The last theme appeared more strongly when Howard tried to galvanize support for his policies, for instance in the run-up to the 2003 invasion of Iraq: his "statements suggested to listeners that they were in danger, at risk of terrorist attack, and unable to ensure their protection against such risks."[39] Part of the plea for support, for action, was that Australia had to become heroic, not only to avenge past victims but to prevent Australians from becoming future victims.

Villains' blame is calculated according to the victims they abuse, the heroes they battle, and sometimes their fellow wrongdoers. Gary Alan Fine gives an example in his discussion of Benedict Arnold, one of the great villains of American history. To make Arnold into an arch-traitor, historians have largely refused to place any blame on John André, the British officer with whom Arnold was conspiring. Although André, captured by American soldiers right after meeting with Arnold, was hanged as a spy, his moral reputation revived as Arnold's fell. He came to be seen as a soldier following orders, a minion at worst.

The other contrast is with George Washington, Arnold's patron and commander, who often made excuses for Arnold's failings. Fine points out that Washington could easily have shared some blame for the Arnold episode. "Instead, Washington is uniformly believed to have been betrayed by the deceitful Arnold, and his *betrayal*, rather than his naïve complicity in Arnold's schemes, enhances his reputation as a moral hero." As commander-in-chief, Washington could not be framed as a victim, too weak and passive a character. Washington was everything good, Arnold everything bad. Strong villains demand strong heroes, and vice versa.[40]

As we've seen, one side demonizes whom the other side deifies. No one illustrates this better than John Brown, whose reputation since his Harper's Ferry raid in 1859 has been a constant battleground between Transcendentalists, Black Americans, and labor radicals on one side versus Confederates and their later apologists on the other. Abolitionists naturally embraced him, but conservative efforts to reincorporate the Old South from the 1880s to the 1950s had to demonize him. Robert Penn Warren wrote a 1929 biography of Brown that at least acknowledged his bravery but otherwise demonized him as a lawless nut. For African Americans Brown remained a hero, so that W. E. B. Du Bois could proclaim, "John Brown was right." Recently a more balanced view has emerged, recognizing that his cause was just even if his means were dubious, and allowing historian

David Reynolds to label him "a deeply religious, flawed, yet ultimately noble reformer."[41]

Villains are handy symbols of immorality, every bit as essential to moral orientations as symbols of good—heroes and victims—are. They hold special risks for modern societies, which have been known to strenuously prosecute and exterminate those labeled as villains: not only opponents in wars but internal groups such as heretics and minorities. Constructions of villainy tend to erase any possible doubts about the use of extreme measures.

Villains are also defined by how they differ from the character with whom they are morally associated, minions, as blame is apportioned among the wicked. Villains' only defense, in many subsequent arenas, is to claim minionhood. But minions are crucial to most villains' plans. Satan took almost half of God's angels with him to create Hell. The evil Queen of Narnia relied on an extensive network of spies. And Simon Legree needed Sambo and Quimbo to torture his other slaves. In literary and political examples, minions are often the most entertaining of the characters, subject to amusing ridicule.

6 | Ridicule and Contempt for Minions

Wrongs are often forgiven, but contempt never is. Our pride remembers it forever.

—*Lord Chesterfield*

THE ANIMATED FILM *DESPICABLE ME* introduced viewers to a band of diminutive yellow minions given to high-pitched chatter and giggles, indeed a range of excited little sounds. They steal the show from Gru, the accented villain, and within a few years they ended up with their own movies. Hoping to "serve the most despicable master they could find," they hop like insects and look like a cross between Cheetos and fire hydrants. Easily distracted and more easily entertained, they are accident-prone and inadvertently destructive, doing more to help opponents than to aid the villain they serve.

The recent movies get it right: minions are those manic little helpers who show up in cartoons making a lot of noise. According to the Oxford English Dictionary, the origins of the word are unknown, but it can be found at the beginning of the sixteenth century as meaning a darling, a beloved object, and especially a lover or "lady-lover." But it immediately seems to have taken on the disapproving connotation of the favorite of an arbitrary ruler or boss, to whose indulgence the minion owes everything. In the words of the OED, the minion "is ready to purchase its continuance by base compliances," and there is a hint of scandal and corruption (Figure 6.1). The minion is something like a pet, a creature kept for the amusement of the powerful (who, by keeping minions, lose moral credit and slide toward villainy).

Inept characters cannot be too threatening and thus need not be punished or repressed too thoroughly. They will go away, self-destruct, or see the

Public Characters. James M. Jasper, Michael P. Young, and Elke Zuern, Oxford University Press (2020) © Oxford University Press.
DOI: 10.1093/oso/9780190050047.001.0001

FIGURE 6.1 Size alone usually differentiates minions from the villains they serve.

error of their ways with little outside intervention. It is hard to blame them. Villains are the real threat. Portraying your opponents as ineffectual is a way to discourage their potential backers and to undermine their own confidence, but it also may relax and demobilize your own team. There is little need to rally against minions, despite the crucial role they sometimes play in carrying out villains' intentions. Their dastardly cowardice is more disgusting than frightening.

Character work tends to portray the weakness of victims—paradigmatically women and children—as the lack of physical power, whereas the weakness of minions lies more in their ineptitude, and in an overexcitability that undermines effective action. Groups can be demeaned as immature, gullible, and childlike, or as bestial, smelly, and dangerous. Minionizing stereotypes bounce back and forth between children and animals as root metaphors, sometimes assigning one to women and the other to men. At the height of American racism, movies like *Birth of a Nation* portrayed Blacks as both silly and threatening at the same time: the demeaning minstrel show on the one hand and hysterical lynchings over fabricated accusations on the other. The British looked at the Irish in the nineteenth century much as white Americans looked at Blacks in the twentieth: too much sex and intoxication, not enough work and intellect. They are amusing—until they band together in mobs.[1]

Contempt is something we frequently feel toward those who are inherently weak, passive, and bad. They have not just made mistakes, but are contemptible, unworthy of respect. They are something less than human. In individualistic cultures like the U.S., they blend into the crowd rather than attaining moral autonomy. In cultures more oriented toward groups, like Japan, minions are more likely to be those without a clear place in any group. In hierarchical cultures like India, minions are those at the bottom, a source of amusement for their superiors. Many dramatic traditions cast servants in this role.

One common element in the construction of minions is to portray them as childlike. Just as John Dower describes the demonization of the Japanese after Pearl Harbor, he also lists the ways in which they had previously been ridiculed as minions. They were believed to be inferior pilots, due to poor eyesight and inner ear problems apparently thought to inflict the entire nation. They were said to be ill equipped, weak in morale, and afraid of the jungle. They were depicted as pre-rational and pre-scientific (stereotypes often applied to women in those days). They were stigmatized as skilled at flower arranging and haiku, not war. Pearl Harbor was thus quite a surprise, but even then "most Westerners regarded Japan's initiation of war as high folly, an incredible miscalculation of America's pride, its wrath, and its bountiful resources."[2] The conversion of Japan's minions into villains after 1941 would take time.

As their military prowess became clear, these "children" became "savages." The British and Americans only grudgingly granted them villain status: "Special powers assigned to avowedly lesser men and women take many forms, including physical prowess, sexual appetite, intuitive genius or 'occult' skills, fanaticism, a special capacity for violence, monopolization of certain forms of knowledge or control, even an alleged capacity for 'evil'. Such uncomfortable evocations of the superhuman also may rest on sheer numbers: an impression of the enemy as Other as being quantitatively huge, and consequently a serious and even unfair threat as a collectivity."[3] Minions become villains only when massed together into a single unified player.

Ridicule is a frequent response to minions, and it can be devastating. Ronald Reagan ravaged Jimmy Carter in their 1980 debate with an apparently friendly but actually condescending, "There you go again." The implication: Carter was too intellectual, too wrapped up in his own arguments, to be a strong and effective leader. It diminished Carter, who already faced the challenge of being short by presidential standards (5 feet 9 inches) instead of looking tall and presidential (although Carter looked taller than he was partly because he stooped a little, which is what a tall person does to talk to shorter people).

A minion, put in a position of authority, can do foolish, desperate things. To return to the 1964 presidential campaign, we can see the Johnson White House's efforts to make Goldwater appear ridiculous, like Humphrey's effort to portray him as emotional and nervous. Jack Valenti, then a special advisor to LBJ and later president of the Motion Picture Association of America, advised, "We ought to treat Goldwater not as an equal, who has credentials to be President, but as a radical, a preposterous candidate who would ruin this country and our future." The method of attack should be "Humor, barbs, jokes, ridicule . . . . We must make him ridiculous and a little scary." (Note: only a *little* scary.) Vice Presidential candidate William Miller should be depicted "as some April Fool's gag." In contrast, Valenti argued, the "President stays above the battle. He is the President and acts like one."[4] He won by a landslide.

The long war in Syria against Bashar Assad used ridicule as well as artillery. A series of puppet shows posted on You Tube was called "Top Goon: Diaries of a Little Dictator," using size to diminish his stature. One episode was called "Who wants to kill a million?" When a leaked email from his wife revealed her "pet" name for him, graffiti immediately began referring to him as a duck, a small and not especially threatening animal. Visually, this was a gift to cartoonists that connected to his large upper lip. Sadly, ridicule was insufficient to drive him from power; Assad proved more villain than minion (Figure 6.2).

Ridicule hints at the characterological proximity of minions to clowns, who are usually weak and not necessarily good. We laugh at clowns (although many clowns laugh at us at the same time). By saying that minions and clowns are "beneath contempt," we imply that they are not full strategic players in our engagements. They are usually subordinate to others. They lack that element of divine power that we still associate symbolically with heroes and villains.

The Feckless Mob

Minions tend to be cowardly, and it is popular to portray them as the members of a "mob."[5] Familiar from a long line of pseudo-scientific critiques of crowds and mass society, mobs combine demagogues, powerful and malevolent villains, with weaker individuals who may or may not be ill intentioned but who are "suggestible." Such images ironically justify fuller repression on the grounds that such people are not themselves

FIGURE 6.2 Bashar Assad as Donald Duck. What is sillier than a trouserless cartoon character? In the end ridicule was not enough.

ready for democracy. Jeffrey Alexander lists some of the terms used to describe these characters: passive, dependent, irrational, hysterical, excitable, passionate, unrealistic, and mad.[6] Their social relationships, he continues, are characterized as secret, suspicious, deferential, self-interested, greedy, deceitful, calculating, and conspiratorial. They are "enemies" of the democratic order, and everything that heroes are not. They are bad, weak, and mostly passive—until "stirred up."

Fears of the mob date back to ancient Athens. Poor decisions in the Peloponnesian War and the condemnation of Socrates in one of the first recorded moral panics persuaded Plato and other elites that skilled orators could flatter the assembled citizens into voting for unwise policies. In contrast, speakers who told the Assembly hard truths took risks in doing so (or so they flattered themselves into feeling like misunderstood heroes). Crowds came to be seen as ignorant, selfish, and fickle—easily swayed by the passions of the moment. They are the perfect image of the minion: weak and easily influenced, venal rather than self-sacrificing, and prone to easy choices and actions.[7]

Crowds are also coded as feminine, a further way that sexist traditions have demeaned them as weak, passive, and fickle. Euripides helped define the mob with his depiction of the Bacchae, women followers of Dionysus who, intoxicated, were capable of great joy and wild violence. Gustav Le Bon, the great crowd theorist of the late nineteenth century, also described mobs as feminine in their suggestibility (although also in their occasional willingness to make sacrifices).

Mobs are typically passive, watching and listening to others. But the threat of action is always there. They do not initiate action, but they can become busy, in the manner of insects and rodents. The very term "mob" suggests that the action is likely to be bad. If we substitute "public," the possibility for arousal is still there without the pejorative implications. Publics can do good or bad when roused from their passivity. But in most bad versions it takes a demagogue to rouse them; he (almost always he) is the active villain.

The 1950s saw an American moral panic over crowds, as intellectuals tried to both understand fascism and express their distaste for communism. Concerns over the other-directed personality, the organization man, the authoritarian personality, mass society, and others, all shared Plato's anxiety that people, brought together in crowds, do things that otherwise would horrify them. What's worse, they are willing to do such things outside immediate crowd settings, since entire societies are now supposedly "massed," creating blindly obedient people who cannot or will not think for themselves. Individuals administer electric shocks to strangers when men in white coats tell them to; families watch television rather than reading newspapers; workers go out on wildcat strikes rather than accepting the contracts their union leaders have negotiated.[8]

Postwar anxieties even left their trace on that traditional font of simple characters, the Western. Will Wright perceives a shift around 1950. Before then, the lone hero is eventually reconciled with society, often by the woman he loves, and the two settle down in the town he has rescued. After 1950, Wright says, she tends to join him in leaving the town to start their own little community on a ranch elsewhere. "While the hero is still 'good', the conceptual weight of 'bad' is now carried by the townspeople, or society, rather than by the villains." Villains still have their minion helpers, but average citizens have also become minions, willing to tolerate evil out of their own weakness.[9]

Minions demonstrate one of the forms of being active; indeed they are hyperactive. But they are ineffectual. They lack the other aspect of activity, namely initiating action. This is due partly to their subordinate status to a villain, and partly to their ridiculous hyperactivity.

Since minions face ridicule, the proper rhetorical medium is often comedy. Thus *Saturday Night Live* skewered the large field of Republican presidential candidates in the fall of 2011. In portraying one of the many Republican debates, the comedians placed the candidates in locations that reflected their centrality to the race: only two were at the podium, another was in a chair in the corner facing the wall, two were down the hall in a locked janitor's closet, one was outside in the parking garage, and homophobic Rick Santorum was in a crowded gay bar in San Francisco. The skit was funny because it played on the audience's sense that all the candidates were weak and inept but also vaguely malevolent.

In a nastier historical example from 1856, South Carolina Congressman Preston Brooks, after nearly killing abolitionist Senator Charles Sumner, bragged about his accomplishment. "The fragments of the cane are begged for as sacred relics. Every Southern man is delighted and the abolitionists are like a hive of disturbed bees. They are making all sorts of threats. It would not take much to have the throats of every Abolitionist cut."[10] A hive of bees: weak, and dangerous only when disturbed and banded together in large numbers. They are spineless, invertebrates, insects. Their threats are hollow. For his manly action, Brooks became a hero to the South, a villain to the North.

The Brooks episode suggests the kind of political interests behind much character work, especially contempt. One of the founders of subaltern theory, Gyanendra Pandey, has shown how important it was for the British to construct a history of India as a primordial, incessant conflict between Hindu and Muslim communities. The colonial rulers compiled lists of communal riots going back hundreds of years, grounded on a form of crowd theory in which primal religious affiliation plays the role of other crowd emotions in driving normal people to do awful things. The epidictic message was clear: this vast but childlike nation would fall apart without a strong, paternalistic British presence.

An 1809 disturbance in the holy Hindu city of Benares (Varanasi) becomes an emblem of colonial historiography for Pandey, who traces the successive reports that culminated in this 1907 summary of the event: "The city experienced one of those convulsions which had so frequently occurred in the past owing to the religious antagonism of the Hindu and Musalman sections of the population."[11] Every problem is attributed to primeval and irrational affiliations that were partly held in check once the British brought "civilization" to the subcontinent. The British were rational, with their sense of fair play, while the Indians were childlike and emotional in their primitive faiths and their ability to lapse into lethal mobs.

Pandey documents one hundred years of distortions that led to the 1907 report, almost an exact contemporary of Durkheim's formulation of the collective effervescence of crowds. Even the number of dead rose from twenty in an early account to "hundreds" by 1907 (the exact numbers hardly mattered; minions are faceless and uncounted). Some groups are stereotyped as strong, such as "fighting castes" like Rajputs or Muslims. The mobs are manipulated by local elites. The origin of every street fight is assumed to lie in religion, even though there is no evidence for that in the Benares case. In a primitive religious ritual, the excitement is seen as naturally, inevitably, leading to rioting, criminality, and "a helpless, instinctive violence" between groups who have always and will always detest each other.[12] No other explanations are needed, or looked for. This is the way India has always been, and will always be.

Pandey leaves out one thing: since 1947, indigenous groups have stepped into the story-telling role, with a similar interest in the construction of India as convulsed by religious conflict.[13] Hindu and Muslim leaders mobilize their followers by portraying Indian history as a long battle between primordial forces, although they tend to represent the other side as formidable villains not laughable minions. In almost any political arena—electoral or colonial—a player can gain rhetorical advantage by depicting others as an emotional mob.

If the mob is feckless, how does it ever become a threat? One strong hero should be able to scare them off, and in fact Western literature is full of such stories. Huckleberry Finn encounters the formidable Colonel Sherburn, part hero and part villain. The colonel calmly shoots and kills harmless Old Boggs, "in town for his monthly drunk," who has taken to insulting Sherburn. When a mob goes to the colonel's house to lynch him, he stands on the roof of his porch and frightens them off, contemptuously observing that none had "grit enuf" to kill a real man. Sherburn describes the villain-minion dynamic that gets justice done: "A MAN goes in the night, with a hundred masked cowards at his back and lynches the rascal. Your mistake is, that you didn't bring a man with you; that's one mistake, and the other is that you didn't come in the dark and fetch your masks."

Twain's earlier description of the men who would soon become a mob is priceless: "There was empty drygoods boxes under the awnings, and loafers roosting on them all day long, whittling them with their Barlow knives; and chawing tobacco, and gaping and yawning and stretching—a mighty ornery lot. They generly had on yellow straw hats most as wide as an umbrella, but didn't wear no coats nor waistcoats, they called one another Bill, and Buck, and Hank, and Joe, and Andy, and talked lazy and drawly, and used considerable many cuss words. There was as many as one loafer leaning up against every awning-post, and he most always had his hands in his britches-pockets, except when he fetched them out to lend a chaw of tobacco or scratch." Talkers, not doers.[14]

Villains are not so easily scared; like heroes their courage can be one source of their strength. So the mob needs a villain to lead them. Later on, in the arithmetic of blame, having a villain permits minions to seem less guilty. Hitler's enormity allowed compliant German citizens to avoid much of the blame. It is often convenient to place all the blame on a group's leaders rather than on the group itself. In a study of ethnic mobilization in Romania and Slovakia, political scientist Sherill Stroschein found that groups tend to blame the mobilization of their opponents on the other group's elites. (They do not attribute their own mobilization to elite manipulation, of course.) She sees this attribution as a way for people to keep interacting with normal members of the other groups in daily life, as neighbors, shop clerks, and friends. They are not to blame. They are minions, not villains. The cost is that they are not fully autonomous human beings, either.[15]

Reducing Villains to Minions

Cicero was a master of epidictic, epitomizing villains with particular zeal. His most famous work of demonization was his rendering of Catiline, whose conspiracy we know about primarily from Cicero's speeches. "Can any man be a friend of someone who has murdered so many victims? He has fouled himself in all manner of vice and crime. He is soaked in the blood of those he has impiously slaughtered. He has robbed the provincials. He has violated the laws and the courts." Cicero conjures threats by talking about secret (but luxurious!) meetings, vague conspiracies. He may have even been the source of the rumor that the conspirators sacrificed a young boy to swear an oath on his entrails (eating them afterward). In this case he probably inflated a minor minion into a treacherous villain. Thanks to Cicero the term Catilinarian has come down to us as a synonym for a heinous conspiracy.

In the slanderous world of Roman rhetoric, Cicero's ribald wit could also reduce villains to clowns: still nasty, but ineffectual. In the case that made Cicero famous in 80 BCE, he attacked a freedman, Chrysogonus, for his luxurious lifestyle. "Look at the man himself, jury members. You see how, with his elegantly styled hair and reeking with perfume, he floats around the Forum, an ex-slave waited upon by a crowd of citizens of Rome, you see how superior he feels himself to be to everyone else, that he alone is wealthy and powerful." Effeminacy was a frequent means of ridicule in Rome. It was all right to be a top, but not a bottom.[16]

In a modern version of minionization, Peter Maas describes an Iraqi television show called "Terrorism in the Grip of Justice," in which detainees confess to a variety of crimes. It debuted in January 2005, right before that nation's parliamentary elections. He makes an interesting comment that goes to the heart of character work: "Those being interrogated on the program do not look fearsome; these are not the faces to be found in the propaganda videos that turn up on Web sites or on Al Jazeera." In other words, these people are not being demonized. Instead, they "come off as cowardly lowlifes who kill for money rather than patriotism or Allah." God and country connote power in ways that monetary transactions do not. "They tremble on camera, stumble over their words and look at the ground as they confess to everything from contract murders to sodomy." They are being shamed, a way of stripping them of agency and power. Then we find out why. "The program's clear message is that there is now a force more powerful than the insurgency: the Iraqi government, and in particular the commandos" who have captured these petty criminals. The detainees are bad, but not powerful: minions, not villains. Because of their weakness they are not appealing role models for Iraqi youth.[17]

If you wish to stoke fears and mobilize supporters, it is best to demonize your opponents, but if you wish to lend confidence to your supporters it may instead be better to dismiss your opponents as silly and weak. In other words, reduce them to minions. This is a central strategic dilemma of character work: *the villain-minion dilemma.* Do you play up the power of your opponents or play it down? We can make them seem more threatening or less, villains or minions. In the latter case, it is often desirable to portray the minions as clowns, more ridiculous than dangerous.

Our choice has a rhetorical impact on our own team: do we mobilize them through anger and a sense of threat from villains, or give them confidence by reassuring them that they will defeat their miniony opponents? The impact on our opponents' team is simply reversed: they may not like being characterized as villains, but this at least gives them a sense of power, which claims of minionhood in contrast deflate. Outside this seesaw of morale, there may be no dilemma when you appeal to certain audiences: in front of judges, for example, you want to hammer your opponents with the full moral condemnation that villains deserve, with no mitigating excuses.

European and American rhetoric about Islamic terrorists reflects this dilemma. For years, Muslim extremists had been portrayed as inept, but after 9/11 U.S. politicians had to adjust this judgment to justify war and the expansion of surveillance, much as an earlier generation had done with the Japanese following Pearl Harbor. It was morally ineffective to admit that the bin Laden gang had simply been lucky, finding a way to turn jet planes into bombs—and that with slightly better airport security and stronger cockpit doors their feat was unlikely to be repeated. Instead, U.S. politicians now portrayed them as an extremely effective, secretive, highly organized network in order to justify the massive spending used to fight them. The media ran footage of secret training camps, with men in sleek black uniforms going through their drills. This approach persists despite a long line of bumbling shoe bombers, underwear bombers, and would-be jihadists who managed to blow up only themselves.[18] Terrorists had to be pumped up into out-and-out villains. (Saddam Hussein had to be reworked in the same way to justify invading Iraq.)

It is especially humiliating to be defeated by those whom you have dismissed as minions, as in both Pearl Harbor and 9/11. The same thing had happened a hundred years ago in Palestine, where Arabs held a "traditional view of Jews as inconsequential weaklings." When, time after time, they were defeated and humbled by Jewish settlers, this was especially galling. "Such slights the Muslim world found difficult to countenance; such a situation could not be allowed to endure."[19] In the late 1940s the Arabs learned too late how mistaken their characterizations had been.

Iris Murdoch captured the ambivalence of the media—or perhaps their confusion in the face of the villain-minion dilemma—in her novel *Under the Net*. The narrator is reading the newspaper after a day of street battles between labor activists and the police. Referring to a prominent activist whom he knows, he reports, "Lefty's name occurred quite often; and once a whole editorial was devoted to him, couched in terms designed to suggest simultaneously that he was a serious public menace and that he was a petty street-corner agitator who was beneath contempt."[20] Logically, the media can't have it both ways, but character work is based on emotions not strict logic. The line between villain and minion is fuzzy because the dimension of strength is a complicated continuum; the moral boundary between good and bad is usually firmer.

The Minion Defense

Those portrayed as villains may themselves adopt a "minion defense" to deflect blame, especially in court proceedings. You did not have the strength, competence, or authority to perform an evil action, or you were ordered to do it by someone with greater authority (the real villain). Sometimes you need only present yourself as weak, frail, and alone. As one journalist commented on the trial of Serbian strongman Slobodan Milosevic, he "sits by himself at the defendant's table, and it is likely he is purposefully trying to convey the impression that he is acting entirely on his own, overmatched by the overwhelming resources of what he calls 'the Other Side'." This actually goes beyond minionhood, and the journalist comments that Milosevic was trying to be a hero: "This tactic plays very nicely into the Serb myth of the hero—stubborn, indomitable, and courageous, particularly when faced with certain doom."[21] Milosevic could not hope to make the leap from bad to good in the eyes of the judges, but he certainly could in public opinion back home.

Those who were not heads of state during war crimes can take a more pure minion defense when formally indicted, insisting that they were simply carrying out the orders of their superiors. This is known as the Nuremberg Defense, after the Nazis who adopted it in 1945 and 1946. Already inflated into the great villains of the century, they could hardly hope to shift the moral boundary in their favor, so they went after the strength component of character. They were simply following orders and lacked the strength to say no to superiors. Adolph Eichmann, captured fifteen years later and brought to Israel for trial, articulated the minion defense. "I never did anything, great or small," he claimed in his final statement, "without obtaining in advance express instructions from Adolf Hitler or any of my superiors."[22] The minion defense sometimes succeeds, especially in trials by the accused's own side in or after a war—suggesting that moral sympathy remains a factor. But the minion defense did not work for Eichmann.[23]

In a recent book Bettina Stangneth devastates Eichmann's minion claims, showing how self-consciously ideological and unrepentant he remained. So he was malevolent. He had also been powerful, with considerable discretion and responsibility for the fate of Jewish prisoners—he even bragged about his creativity and leadership from 1945 until his abduction to Israel in 1960.[24]

Hannah Arendt famously analyzed the Eichmann trial, and almost as famously became "American Jewish Public Enemy Number One" for portraying him as a minion rather than a villain.[25] But Arendt was interrogating the nature of modern villains, not excluding Eichmann from that category. The banality of evil, for her, was "the phenomenon of evil deeds, committed on a gigantic scale, which could not be traced to any particularity of wickedness, pathology, or ideological conviction in the doer."[26] She despised the anti-intellectual, petty-bourgeois Eichmann, so susceptible to unthinking clichés and banalities. He was "neither monstrous nor demonic," in her view, but an ambitious bureaucrat eager to please his superiors. This banality was actually *more* frightening to her than traditional evil villains. Eichmann felt his way through the world according to what would help him to advance personally. He lacked the awesome power or evil vision to be a classic villain. He was a thoroughly modern, careerist bureaucrat of a villain, lacking the imagination of his leader Adolf Hitler.

Historian Christopher Browning offers a similar case from World War II. A German military unit of 500 men was given orders to massacre the 1,700 women, children, and elderly of a Jewish village in Poland. Such events had not yet become commonplace, and the commander offered his troops (composed of police, not Nazi ideologues) the chance to refuse this horrendous duty. Only a handful did at first, joined by some others during the long day of killing, even though almost all later claimed to have been shocked and disgusted by the orders. After the war, there was an investigation and a small number of trials, during which the participants explained their decisions.

According to Browning, the reason that most went along was group conformity. "To break ranks and step out, to adopt overtly nonconformist behavior, was simply beyond most of them . . . . Why? First of all, by breaking ranks, nonshooters were leaving the 'dirty work' to their comrades." Their refusal could have been seen as a moral reproach of their comrades. "Most, though not all, nonshooters intuitively tried to diffuse the criticism of their comrades that was inherent in their actions. They pleaded not that they were 'too good' but rather than they were 'too weak' to kill."[27] They claimed to be sick or to have nerves that prevented them from firing accurately. They did not wish to be villains, enthusiastic killers of babies, but they did not want to be moral heroes. They modulated the strength dimension and became minions.

The men who initially refused, and the many more who abandoned their duties during the course of the day, ran the risk of being labeled cowards (a characterization that would have prevented their future advancement in the police ranks). Their choice to be weak minions did not challenge the moral system of the Nazi regime, either in its violence or in its macho values. In postwar judicial inquiries, a high moral road was closed to them, and so they insisted that they had been minions following orders. But that also seems to have been the story they had told themselves and their officers at the time of the massacre.

In other situations, the minion option disappears. As it apparently did for most of the men in Browning's example: the policemen who needed to prove their strength, to themselves or others, could only be full villains, prepared to rip into innocent victims. Arne Johan Vetlesen finds that, in settings where normal moral options are stripped away, people perceive the world along one dimension only, that of strong or weak. Those who see the world as a war of all against all, such as those imprisoned in concentration camps, do not believe in innocence (a moral judgment). Being a victim "is tantamount to utter powerlessness—and this is a destiny too terrible to contemplate in a world where power is the only currency. . . . To be in the role of the victim is considered as tantamount to being nobody."[28] No one seeks pity in those situations. As we suggested in our discussion of villains, it is better in immoral settings to be a strong villain than a weak minion or victim. Only later, in saner arenas, does the minion defense become attractive.

In some settings morality simply collapses, making it impossible to allocate blame clearly and precluding normal character work. We saw in the last chapter that a reputation as a villain can be advantageous in prisons, based on strength without reference to morality. Auschwitz survivor Primo Levi describes the Sonderkommandos, special squads of prisoners who carried out the worst tasks in exchange for a few extra weeks of life: he calls these squads the Nazis' most demonic crime. "No one," he insists, "is authorized to judge them, not those who lived through the experience of the Lager and even less those who did not." In this moral grey zone, where survival was the only possible goal, "This institution represented an attempt to shift onto others—specifically, the victims—the burden of guilt, so that they were deprived of even the solace of innocence." Forcing Jews to kill each other was the ultimate humiliation. Morality was impossible; only strength was left. The victims were degraded, not sanctified. Such a setting confounds our need to judge, says Levi, who killed himself in 1987 after finishing his book on the subject.[29]

Public authorities grapple with the villain-minion dilemma in courtrooms as well as in media arenas, and especially when the two overlap. In some cases officials may wish to inflate minions into threatening villains—for instance if they are seeking resources for their crusade against them—but sometimes officials prefer to reassure the public by highlighting the state's strength and the opponents' ineptitude. It is better to be dealing with stigmatized minor criminals than a political challenger who wishes to take over the state.

Truth commissions, which offer freedom in return for a full account of offenses and orders given and received, offer villains the chance to portray themselves as minions. They also provide societies scarred by violence an opportunity for reform. One prolonged attempt at a minion defense was made by the man the South African press dubbed "prime evil." Eugene de Kock, an apartheid-era police colonel who ran the infamous Vlakplaas death squad, was a master of kidnapping, torture, murder, and disposal of remains. He was initially sentenced to 212 years for crimes against humanity but as a result of his revelations and his assistance in finding the remains of murdered activists, he was released in 2015. While the state acknowledged his minion status and argued that his release was in the "interests of nation-building and reconciliation," the general public was less fully convinced and his release date and location remained secret.[30]

Pumla Gobodo-Madikizela, a clinical psychologist focusing on trauma and forgiveness, interviewed de Kock in prison and published the gripping book (later a play): *A Human Being Died that Night*. She details her struggle to engage with him and eventually to forgive him, and argues against retributive justice. She contends that we need to consider the broader political and social forces that allow such crimes to occur. Unlike Eichmann, de Kock shows remorse, and unlike Arendt, Gobodo-Madikizela argues for reconciliation.[31] Part of this process is to transform de Kock from master villain (prime evil) to minion. He certainly stood out for his horrific actions, but he completed these actions in a system that employed him and praised him for his seemingly inhuman brutality. Understanding him as a minion provides an opportunity, not yet realized, to change the broader context nationally and internationally that allows such racism and brutality to persist. Villains provide scapegoats and thereby let the rest of society off the hook more easily. Minions dilute, but at the same time spread, culpability.

————

Minions can be made to appear so ridiculous that they are not a threat, and even more, that they are not morally responsible characters. Willingly or not, they are under a villain's hypnotic spell. They become clowns that no one takes seriously: fools, in medieval parlance, suffering from a madness that relieves them of moral responsibility for their actions and words. Fools are only one form of clown, but clowns of all types shadow the system of public characters, mocking it, ridiculing it, and undermining its pervasive morality. We'll return to clowns in the appendix.

Minions provide comic relief in fiction, but in politics they serve two main functions. When character workers paint opponents as minions it is to undermine their strength, credibility, and confidence. When players present themselves as minions, it is usually to escape blame, especially in later arenas when circumstances have changed. We turn next to the good characters of political dramas, the heroes and then the victims. Villains and minions only make sense when they are contrasted with characters on the other side of the morality boundary.

7 | We Admire Heroes

Whenever the Government appears in arms, it ought to appear like a
Hercules, and inspire respect by the display of strength.

—*Alexander Hamilton*

Show me a hero and I will write you a tragedy.

—*F. Scott Fitzgerald*

JOHN MCCAIN WAS A TRUE American hero. All the obituaries said so
after he died in 2018. Commentators across the political spectrum
declared their admiration for his honor, candor, integrity, courage,
optimism, dignity, and selfless service to his country. Endless photos
of McCain with Ted Kennedy—who died of the same kind of cancer
nine years to the day before McCain—suggested his ability to work with
Democrats on occasion, in line with his "maverick" reputation. On several
issues—campaign finance, immigrants' path to citizenship, torture—he
had proven himself independent of Republican ideology.

Like most heroes, McCain had been born to greatness, the son and
grandson of famous admirals. But he rebelled against these expectations,
graduating from the Naval Academy near the bottom of his class, 894 out
of 898. If anything, that rebellion made him more likeable, more human,
and he demonstrated an ability to excite and command others. He proved
his toughness during five years of torture at the Hanoi Hilton, suffering
painfully for his country and comrades.

Whatever the raw materials they had to start with, character workers
had another reason to lionize McCain after his death. In many ways he was
an anti-Trump, a conservative Republican who was honest and dignified.
Only Trump, reducing heroism to success, quibbled with the label of hero

Public Characters. James M. Jasper, Michael P. Young, and Elke Zuern, Oxford University
Press (2020) © Oxford University Press.
DOI: 10.1093/oso/9780190050047.001.0001

for McCain: "I like people who weren't captured." But for most audiences, sacrifice and suffering are a frequent ingredient of heroism.

In contrast, in one of the memorable moments of the U.S. presidential primaries in 2004, fringe conservative Ann Coulter called Senator John Edwards "a little faggot," alluding partly to his super-expensive haircuts. He worked too hard at those boyish good looks, something that a confident hero would not do. Coulter was not seriously questioning Edwards' sexual orientation, but pointing to his lack of manly strength. He was too young, too cute, too small to be an electoral hero. And with that epithet, summing up many voters' already-existing reservations about Edwards, Coulter helped to end his candidacy. He was no hero.

Strong, good, and active, heroes are the players who must set things right and protect others. A protest- or interest-group presents itself as heroic in its fundraising letters: it can and must prevail against evil. An American presidential candidate offers to save the nation from moral malaise or from radical Islamic terrorists. Heroes must struggle, which is why they are admirable—and also why they need our cooperation, votes, or financial support. American politicians describe the United States itself as a hero in the world, intervening on behalf of less fortunate nations threatened by villains, whenever they need domestic support for major wars.[1]

The combination of good and strong leads to bravery, actions that run the risk or reality of self-sacrifice. Hero portraits can remind us of the hero's past victories, but also of the powerful forces arrayed against her. Strong enough to protect herself, the hero's goodness requires that she act on behalf of others as well. This is the difference between heroism and success: an individual's accomplishments, such as earning a fortune, may not help anyone else (although apologists for the rich usually insist that they do help others, making capitalists into heroes). Because strong figures can be threatening, character work on a hero highlights her goodness by this focus on her brave willingness to sacrifice herself for others.

Admiration is what we are supposed to feel toward heroes. We revel in their glory. We appreciate what we could not have done ourselves, due to cowardice or weakness or simply a lack of skills or confidence. Our esteem may be mixed with gratitude, if we directly benefited from what the hero has accomplished. We may not like the hero, but we certainly want to be on her side, and to have her on ours. Heroes deserve praise.

Heroes cannot be altogether passive; they must act if they are going to protect someone. But in the passive category we have "sleeping giants" who must be awakened to do their duty, moving into the active category.

The sleeping giant can be portrayed as unfairly attacked so as to justify its action ("you picked on the wrong guy"). This has been a favorite symbol of American politicians trying to goad their country into war. We'll see later the importance of "who started it."

Vladímir Propp's donor trope may be a near-hero of this kind: clearly powerful and good, but active only in supporting the main hero, not in fighting the battle. Less active than sidekicks, donors and advisors are often older and wiser, former heroes: Obi-Wan Kenobi to Luke Skywalker, George Soros to the civic organizations he has funded. Chewbacca is a sidekick, Yoda a sage advisor.

Throughout much of human history, kings, warriors, and athletes have sought glory. This has almost always been a man's game, involving competition and triumph over others, deeds of such an impact that people talk about them long after the hero's demise. (In the modern world, artistic accomplishments can establish fame for their creator, but we rarely speak of artistic glory since artists are not triumphing over anyone else.)

The most glorious heroes are usually dead, in part because they have made the ultimate sacrifice of martyrdom for others. They have become pure symbols, gaining a kind of second life this way. If admiration is the key feeling we have for heroes, their death can only deepen it. Great warriors, and all those throughout history who have sought glory, have recognized this. Even in the United States, hardly a culture prone to glorify self-sacrifice, most Congressional Medals of Honor are awarded posthumously.

In contrast, living heroes can always do something that disappoints their team or other audiences, such as defecting to the other side. The longer ago the hero lived, the less likely someone can dig up discrediting dirt on her. Heroes become moral examples by transcending their times, and their goodness and power can both be exaggerated in the mists of memory. The dilemma for living heroes is that, if they seem too superior to normal folk, no one can hope to join their cause, no one can be worthy or strong enough. Long-dead heroes have an advantage here: they are no longer trying to recruit allies and so they avoid many of these pragmatic dilemmas.

Traditional heroes partake of the sacred. They may be avatars (earthly embodiments of gods), as in the great Indian epics, or they may be the product of mortal-immortal couplings, as in ancient Greek myths like that of Hercules. They transcend humanity. In many cultures the awe-inspiring strength of heroes (and villains) could only have divine origins. Joseph Campbell summarizes the myth associated with this type of hero, who "ventures forth from the world of the common day into a region of su-pernatural wonder: fabulous forces are there encountered and a decisive victory is won: the hero comes back from this mysterious adventure with the power to bestow boons on his fellow man."

Campbell traces an historical shift from myths about gods as the pri-mary causal forces in the universe to legends in which heroes play that role, down to the beginnings of history when "the heroes become less and less fabulous." By modern times their divine aura has diminished, part of the disenchantment of the world wrought by the great monotheisms. It persists as charisma, often but not necessarily seen as a divine gift.[2]

The purest heroes survive today in comic books. As fantasy, they re-flect the supernatural lineage of older heroes. One of them, Blade, is the offspring of a human and a vampire. They fly, they save victims, they en-dure unspeakable torments from their villains. Clark Kent, Bruce Banner, and most others keep their secret hidden behind a second persona, as they know that normal folks are uncomfortable with their dangerous strength. Today there are more female superheroes than there were a generation ago, and their powers are often a bit different: Jean Grey can read minds; Kitty Pryde can loosen her own molecules enough for her to pass through solid objects. A male superhero would simply blow them up.

Many superheroes began as villains before converting to good, and some are portrayed as hovering on the boundary between good and bad, such as the darker versions of Batman. Others began as bullied weaklings before discovering their superpowers. They also have a variety of attitudes toward their gifts. Batman went to great lengths, converting his industrial resources into technological powers for himself. Spiderman was not happy when he learned of his special talent. But most, like the heroes of ancient myth, are fatalistic about their responsibilities. Yet comic-book heroes can be complexly human, especially in the Marvel universe, and they often struggle with their own weaknesses and moral uncertainties as well as with the villain.

Campbell also notes the essentializing nature of character work. "The makers of legend have seldom rested content to regard the world's great heroes as mere human beings who broke past the horizons that limited their fellows and returned with such boons as any man with equal faith and courage might have found. On the contrary, the tendency has always been to endow the hero with extraordinary powers from the moment of birth, or even the moment of conception." If someone is predestined to be a hero, he says, this is a matter of inherent character rather than of biography.[3]

Inherently great characters are hard for normal folk to emulate, unless they also happen to be spawned from a god. Campbell mentions Jesus Christ, whose followers can imitate him if he is seen as a man. But if they see him as a god who took on human form, then "the hero is rather a symbol to be contemplated than an example to be literally followed."[4] This challenge remains even for today's shrunken heroes: if they are too strong, they do not need allies to join them; if too weak, they cannot protect their followers. By being equally divine and human, Christ inspired one of the most successful religious movements ever.

Heroes are more popular when they suffer than when they are distant, Olympian figures to whom everything comes easily. We can turn to the playwright Bertolt Brecht to see the poignancy of the long decline of heroes that Campbell mentions. A communist who did not believe in heroes, only in social classes grouped together, Brecht put this bit of dialogue in *Galileo*: "Unhappy is the land that breeds not heroes." The reply: "No, unhappy is the land that needs a hero." We miss the strength of traditional heroes, but we only need them when we are facing a severe challenge. Brecht points to the democratic heroism of us all, working together for that bright future that Marxism promised its followers.

Heroes and villains may not be divine any more, but they tend to be involved in important actions and situations, not trivial, everyday ones. We don't see heroes squeezing melons at the market, as we might see victims and minions doing. Clowns are the masters of everyday life, with its challenges and foibles and reminders of human frailty, a sure source of humor because less is at stake. Titanic clashes between good and evil are less amusing.

When heroes wear uniforms, as firefighters or soldiers, they gain a sacred aura by representing their nation or city, embodying civic values. In New York after 9/11, those who had died in uniform received more attention, respect—and charitable donations—than the dead civilians. The firefighters were heroes, the stockbrokers and secretaries were victims.[5]

Orrin Klapp sees three common modes of being a modern hero: helping others, winning some kind of test, and being martyred for a cause. The most perfect heroes combine all three. "The safest confrontation for a hero is with a needy party, to whom he generously makes a gift and who is in an inferior position and is showing gratitude." One risk "is that the needy party will not show appropriate gratitude and thus make it hard for the benefactor to play his role without incurring suspicion that there is something wrong with him rather than with the recipient." Klapp mentions U.S. foreign aid as an example, but U.S. military interventions are an even better case. The ingratitude of Iraqis and Afghanis cast doubt on the heroism of the U.S. military forces that occupied their countries for years. In the case of heroic tests, the best type is against a villain, since "any good effort against a villain receives some credit," because "the badness and strength of the villain make the hero look all the better."[6] Heroes and villains go together. (We'll examine Klapp's third type, martyrs, in chapter 9.)

Klapp also lists various ways that a public figure can orchestrate her own heroic reputation. Being colorful—dressing or acting oddly—can attract media attention, but not necessarily of a positive kind. It's better to act "in such a way as to deliver the greatest possible thrill to an audience. A colorful actor seeks high action, plunges, challenges others (in his own game, of course), solves crises, and performs feats." Such performers make their feats appear harder than they are, often through carefully prepared stunts.[7] Audiences usually dismiss heroes who too obviously are trying to do their own character work.

Types of Heroes

There are different types of heroes, based on different sources of strength (recall Table 5.1). They are not all compatible in the social imagination. Personal physical strength (Hercules), intelligence (Barack Obama), various technical skills such as firing a gun (the Lone Ranger), virility (Ibn Saud), creativity (Beethoven), bravery (firefighters or soldiers), aristocratic birth (Robin Hood), supernatural favor or lineage (Achilles), wealth (Donald Trump), even moral purity (Martin Luther King Jr.) are capabilities that allow a hero to get things done. When we move beyond the individual, strength can also come from large numbers or from the social connections necessary to mobilize others. Except for the inspirational power of moral purity, these are also the capabilities that make villains strong.

Heroes' sources of goodness also differ enormously: innocence, protecting others, conformity to valued norms, a willingness to sacrifice oneself for others, generosity, or merely being helpful. Most forms of goodness are associated with weakness more than with strength. You can still try to protect or help others without being powerful, although power helps you succeed. Because generosity is in proportion to one's capacities, the weak (or the poor) can be as generous as the strong. Conformity to norms does not necessarily require strength either. Innocence is usually associated with weakness, although strong figures can afford to be naïve, and are coded as morally superior as a result.

Jane Tompkins comments on the ideal of strength in Western films and novels. Its components "are qualities required to complete an excruciatingly difficult task: self-discipline; unswerving purpose; the exercise of knowledge, skill, ingenuity, and excellent judgment; and a capacity to continue in the face of total exhaustion and overwhelming odds."[8] (This is only the strength dimension; villains might be described in similar terms of cunning, obsession, and persistence.)

Not all these strengths are used directly in running a nation or saving a victim, but they all augment a player's reputation: John Kerry's macho windsurfing, Mao swimming in the Yangtze, Reagan on his ranch, riding horses and cutting brush. These all enhance a traditional heroic image, of an especially masculine kind. Even if these skills do not help a political leader do his job, they symbolize health or virility, powers that are assumed to be generalizable, thanks to traditional macho stereotypes. For some, the ability to father children (boys, at least) is linked to the ability to govern a nation—a kinky twist on Robert Filmer's seventeenth-century argument in *Patriarcha* that the king was the father of his country.[9]

The Godfather Don Corleone and President Donald J. Trump are a form of hero for whom strength outweighs morality, in what we can recognize as "amoral familism."[10] The only morality that counts is protection of one's own close network, if we can charitably call this morality. The ancient Greeks would have approved. "Strong" is Trump's favored term of praise, as in "President Putin was extremely strong and powerful in his denial today," when Trump once again asked him about Russian meddling in U.S. elections. Not persuasive, eloquent, or compelling, terms that might be used to judge a rhetorical claim. Through a kind of metonymy, Putin is strong, so his assurances are too.

In today's Russia Vladimir Putin has orchestrated a symphony of traditional motifs of masculine power in a kind of amoral nationalism. Many focus on athletic prowess: the judo black belt, shooting a Siberian tiger, photo ops with athletes during the Olympics, horseback riding—notoriously shirtless (Figure 7.1). A few stunts linked him to other macho figures such as a motorcycle gang or firefighters. In most Western nations these images would appeal to male voters, much like Trump's core supporters. But Putin has additional rhetorical appeals to women. Far from a reckless adventurer, he comes across as a force for stability. Women find him "reliable, responsible, sober (literally), and strong."[11] His much-vaunted sobriety puts him at odds with macho heroes celebrated for their

FIGURE 7.1 Vladimir Putin has mastered the signs of traditional heroic strength, impressing not only Russian voters but President Donald Trump.

drinking capacities, showing how different character traits can be packaged for the needs of different audiences. His vicious homophobia has apparently played to both men and women, and those who ridicule him often play the same tune, suggesting that he is gay—the ultimate denigration of a macho hero's strength.

Some heroes are born, others are made: categorical heroes and circumstantial heroes. The formers' innate, ascribed traits make them heroes, or at least raise expectations of great deeds. Those who are divine or of noble birth are positioned for greatness, like Superman. Circumstantial heroes unexpectedly achieve things despite their lack of known or pre-existing capacities; they have greatness thrust upon them, like the reluctant Spiderman or George Washington. Over time, character work tends to make circumstantial heroes into categorical characters by finding early hints of greatness, signs of divine favor, and so on. Even circumstantial heroes need the right attitudes, especially confidence and determination. But they need not have independent sources of strength, beyond their ability to do this one thing: to pull someone from a burning car or guide an army to military triumph. (Robert E. Lee is usually treated as a categorical hero, despite being a traitor to his country, whereas Ulysses S. Grant is viewed as a circumstantial hero who failed at everything except war; part of the reason is their personal appearance—and a concerted effort by Southern apologists.)[12]

Nothing proves manly heroism like war, and nothing proves a war to be moral better than circumstantial victimhood. Pearl Harbor justified the greatest military mobilization in history. Even dumb wars must be justified as heroic. The disastrous invasion of Iraq in 2003, which might have killed as many as a million Iraqis, had to be reinterpreted so that the U.S. forces and their handful of allies appeared as heroic. One trick, after the invasion, was to claim that the carnage would become even greater if the invaders withdrew. "Just how many Iraqis would die if the United States withdrew is anyone's guess," opined *Time* magazine, "but almost everyone who has studied it believes the current rate of more than a thousand a month would spike dramatically."[13] Because of their strength heroes are destructive, there is collateral damage. But things would be worse without them.

Sports competition is like warfare but within stricter bounds, and so it is tempting to see strong athletes as heroes. To the extent that they play team sports or represent their nations in the Olympics and other international venues, symbolizing some sacrifice for a greater group, they can be assimilated to heroes. To the extent they make money for themselves, this is more difficult; they are like singers or models, people who have one singular physical talent and make a career from it. Most athletes are celebrities, not heroes.

Some heroes' power comes from their intense concentration on their moral cause. They are portrayed as living simple, saintly lives, which implies that they do not personally gain from their activities. Dr. Jack Kevorkian, whose passion was an individual's right to physician-assisted suicide, presented himself in his trials as valorous and virtuous. "He pursued a simple lifestyle, buying his clothes from the Salvation Army. The jury was told about his integrity (he called the police after every assisted suicide because that was the law, and he refused to take a fee for his work); his compassion (his intent was to relieve suffering and to help all suffering people, and he sometimes cried when they died); and his courage (he stood up to the bullying local prosecutor to promote needed changes in medicine and law)."[14] Integrity, compassion, and courage are all moral virtues that burnish a hero's reputation. Americans especially tend to value sincerity above intelligence in their leaders.

While some heroes have a moral focus, others can concentrate intently on their technical task, such as shooting a gun or piloting an airplane. Unflappable control, even under pressure, can be part of their strength, even if it has little to do with morality.

There is often a contrast between a hero's power and a hero's bravery. The more powerful she is, the less brave she needs to be in order to face dangers. She is almost sure to prevail. But some heroes triumph despite their lack of pre-existing capabilities, through cleverness, confidence, or luck. David defeated Goliath by recognizing what no one else did: a small rock could be turned into a deadly weapon. David became a symbol for the ages, especially for towns like Florence that want to portray themselves as the righteous underdog. In some cultures, moral virtue wins the favor of the gods (or of God).

When heroes succeed without effort, this is a token of their power: "don't let them see you sweat." Alexander the Great famously slept late on the morning of his great battle of Gaugamela against Darius III, and his attendants had a hard time waking him—so confident was he despite the formidable odds against him (one suspects a carefully planned performance). Part of Barack Obama's appeal is that he is unflappable, apparently capable of dealing with anything ("no-shock Barack," "no-drama Obama"). The hero's confidence suggests an inevitability to her victory; if she can convey this to both followers (who need to be energized) and opponents (who need to be deflated), the expectations become self-fulfilling. (This worked better for Alexander than for Obama.)

And yet Obama was often *criticized* for his lack of ardor and indignation in the face of wrongs that needed to be fixed. Confidence can be read as moral coolness, so that the strength dimension undermines the moral. Heroes need to be exercised about the villains they face, before they calmly go about dispatching them. They need to participate in the character work of denouncing villains (but doing it fairly) and sympathizing with victims. They need to display righteous indignation.

Smart Heroes

Machiavelli famously asked if it was better for a leader to be feared or to be loved. Ideally a leader would be both feared and loved, he said, but that is a hard combination to pull off. Love is too fickle. For the most part, the Prince should be feared because that will keep him alive longer. But Machiavelli qualified even that advice: the fear must not develop into hatred of the ruler, which makes life dangerous again. The heroic leader can be loved as a symbol but feared as a decisionmaker. Here again we see a fundamental difference between living and dead heroes, the latter being incapable of predation. We no longer need to fear them.

Because people fear the power of heroes, they try to entice them to be good as well. Brute strength and acute intelligence are both capabilities that can arouse anxieties in others, since they do not have moral qualities built into them (recall the rhetorical anxiety discussed in chapter 1). It is perhaps no accident that the Hindu god Shiva creates and protects—but also destroys.

Intelligence especially tends to undermine impressions of goodness. Many cultures contain themes of suspicion concerning smart people, who are too clever and may threaten others; the sly fox, the clever monkey of fables. They are more likely to begin engagements, to initiate strategic interactions, with all the risks that involves. "Cunning suggests *clever*, not *wise*," remarks Don Herzog. "Cunning brings to mind crooked, shifty, slippery, elusive, and evasive." The suspicion would seem to lie in the fact that we imagine intelligence to generate ends as well as to be a means of attaining them. Smart people are ambitious: they will be thinking up their own projects rather than helping us fulfill ours, and they will often not reveal their own goals.[15] Dumb heroes who rely on physical strength may be less dangerous to their teammates, or at least more morally reliable. Odysseus, the smart hero, was not popular among his fellow Greeks. Like Cassius, he had that "lean and hungry look."

In today's world experts, who create and testify on the basis of the power of scientific knowledge, are heroes of intelligence. The products of Hollywood trace the rise of the expert. A few decades ago, films about World War II celebrated the grit demonstrated by normal men suddenly plucked from their daily lives who, with no special expertise or special weapons, managed to cohere as a band of brothers to defeat fascist evil. Think of *Midway* or *The Longest Day*, or the more recent *Saving Private Ryan*, about a platoon led by an English teacher. Most war movies today are different. In some, such as those about Vietnam, war is simply Hell. But when movies take a heroic turn, they emphasize elite commandoes (*American Sniper*), the CIA operatives who manage them (Tom Clancy's Jack Ryan), or both (*Zero Dark Thirty*). They are cool professionals with expensive weaponry.

To the (limited) extent that science has replaced religion as the source of truth, experts have great power in the public sphere, consulted like the ancient oracles. Their credibility is an extension, often unwarranted, of their ability to invent new technologies, discover new peptides, cure diseases, and simply to do their work as scientists. They promise magical control over the world. The transferred credibility is especially dubious when social scientists, who have contributed fewer practical benefits to humanity than natural scientists, borrow some of the charismatic aura of the latter. Cleverness and knowledge are not wisdom.[16]

Notoriously, experts disagree with each other. And when they do, the debate typically shifts from the power dimension—the strength of their knowledge—to the moral dimension. We rely on experts because we trust them, not only to be right but also to be well intentioned. But when each side has its own experts, we realize that they are partisan and cannot be so easily trusted. Disagreements among experts undermine their credibility; we no longer presume them to be disinterested. Policy debates then become character contests, says Gary Alan Fine. "Judging a person is more efficient than evaluating specialized knowledge."[17] In fact, we turn to experts because we *cannot* evaluate their specialized knowledge ourselves. But we think we can evaluate their character.

Fine points out that contemporary governments frequently justify their policies on the basis of expert knowledge, and they search for scapegoats when things go wrong. "In the case of dramatic failures, it is often insufficient to assert that experts provided mistaken judgments, but their advice is transformed into moral discourse, the basis for attacks on the character and motivation of the expert and on those who relied on her."[18] Even when things do not go wrong, experts rely on character work to bolster their credibility.

For experts to be taken seriously in public life, they must embody the main traits of heroes. "For an expert's reputation to be preserved," according to Fine, "the expert must be defined as competent (having an appropriate background), innocent (taking a neutral stance), and influential (providing relevant information)."[19] Competence is a form of strength, innocence a form of goodness, and influence perhaps a form of activity. Controversies often arise over experts, as political players try to demonize or heroize them. (Or sometimes they are described as the minion dupes of evildoers, such as corporate shills.)

One way to make smart heroes morally acceptable is to focus on their contributions to peace and prosperity. In the mode of Prometheus, knowledge and creativity can combine with the moral contribution of practical benefits for humans, converting inventors into heroes. Commercial societies are especially likely to prize inventions that can be used to make and market products. After 1815, for instance, as the United States settled down from a period first of revolution and then the odd little war of 1812, its idolization of the average man combined with a furious pursuit of commerce, leading many observers to find Republican heroes among those who "invent useful arts, or discover important truths which may promote the comfort and happiness of unborn generations in distant parts of the world."[20] The cult of the inventor-hero would only grow, culminating in Thomas Edison but continuing in corporate PR of the twentieth century. What makes them heroic rather than simply clever are their contributions to humanity but also their need to surmount obstacles, whether ignorance, mockery, disbelief, or humble origins.

Military Power

Of all the sources of strength heroes can have at their disposal, military power is the most frightful because war always brings devastation. "Acriter et Fideliter," the motto of the Vatican's Swiss Guards, means courage and loyalty. The courage connotes strength, while loyalty assures goodness. Military combat, along with some team sports, combines individual prowess with obedience and sacrifice for the team: strength and morality are fused. This is the reason that combat has provided such perfect examples of traditional heroes.

It's a sad fact of human history that nation-building has usually required armed struggle. As we saw in chapter 4, the founding heroes are often combatants, and their monuments frequently put them on horseback or in uniform. Because nation-states developed as war machines, and their survival continues to depend on military capacities, their leaders encourage admiration for the nation's military heroes. National heroes are rarely treated with irony; conveniently dead, they are fairly pure heroes in the traditional mold. And as symbols of the nation, an insult to their character is an insult to the nation. Those who ridicule or deflate them often do so *in order* to criticize the nation as a whole.

In Jean-Marie Apostolides' reading of Western history, heroes are necessarily violent because of their strength. Adopting Freud's postulation of an aggression drive, Apostolides argues that during wars heroes are praised for their courage, sacrifice, and glory, but in times of peace they are feared for their brutality, violence, pride, even criminality. Warriors without a war do not fit into normal social life. Privateers working for the crown when a nation is at war become pirates disrupting the state during times of peace. A person becomes a hero, Apostolides says, through a dramatic act, a rupture with stable social life: an extraordinary, exemplary action that changes history. It is often a founding gesture, creating a new political or social order—and at the same time destroying the old one. Nations are created through such acts, violent acts, and so nations always have their heroes.[21]

The hero's embodiment of the nation reached its apotheosis, like many elements of nationalism, with the fascists. "By the late 1800s the connection between hero and fatherland or nation was close to perfect, at least in Germany," recounts philosopher Josef Früchtl. "Whereas at the beginning of the [nineteenth] century, influenced by romanticism and culminating in Wagner, the artist was the chosen figuration of the hero, by the end of the century it was the warrior." The man of violence replaced the artist as the great enemy of bourgeois mediocrity and complacency. "At the end of this process are the totalitarian forms of state and society. They carry to extremes a development that could ironically be termed the 'democratization' of heroism." With obligatory military service, all men were heroic, not only famous commanders, and monuments began to list all the fallen. But Hitler and Mussolini embodied the nation more than others did.[22]

There was once a time when heroes could be seen to combine many of the sources of power. Or at least their image makers tried to combine them all. Listen to Robert Hughes' description of the wonderful statue of Marcus Aurelius that once stood (a replica still does) on Rome's Capitoline Hill: "It is by far the greatest and, indeed, the only surviving example of a type of sculpture which was widely known and made in the ancient pagan world: the hero, the authority figure, the demigod on horseback; human intelligence and power controlling the animal kingdom, striding victoriously forward."[23] This is the only one to survive because Christian iconoclasts—concerned with the power of images—melted all the others down, sparing this one in the mistaken belief that it was the Christian emperor Constantine.

It is still possible today to combine sources of strength. Look at this photograph of Subcommandante Marcos (Figure 7.2). He decided to arrive at La Realidad on horseback, a traditional pose for warrior heroes. The rifle peeking over his shoulder, reminiscent of Pancho Villa, sends further, perhaps threatening, signals of coercive strength. And yet the pipe connotes an intellectual, the writer and thinker, roles that Marcos also played. Intelligence and military valor do not always go together, but this very contemporary hero pulls it off, even with his shirt on.

FIGURE 7.2 Marcos the pipe-smoking warrior rides down from the hills.

Smart versus Strong Heroes

Even for Vladímir Propp, heroes use either force or cleverness in seizing the object of their quest, suggesting two basic types of action but also—if he had cared about characters—two types of hero based on either physical strength or intelligence. He also recognizes that the hero and the villain are similar in strength, as "heroes sometimes employ the same means adopted by villains for the initial seizure."[24] On the strength dimension, many heroes are too much like villains for us to be entirely comfortable with them.

The 2008 presidential election in the United States involved the two distinct kinds of heroes, one based on wartime bravery and valor, the other on analytic intelligence, a classic contrast between types of heroes (think of Achilles and Odysseus). John McCain had been a fighter pilot, already a heroic activity, and had endured five years in a prison camp as he refused to allow himself to be released without his men, a self-sacrificing, protective gesture. As Jeffrey Alexander observes, he was given a hero's welcome: "Though he still hobbled on crutches, McCain returned home, resplendent in a gleaming white naval uniform. He was greeted by triumphant headlines, a weary but grateful nation, and a celebration at the White House."[25] His damaged body was a constant symbol of his military heroism, which he parlayed into political office. Like many warrior heroes, Alexander observes, McCain's autobiography, *Faith of My Fathers*, suggests that he had been destined for great things from birth, given his naval patrimony. Nobility will out.

Barack Obama's claim to heroic power was based on an entirely different—almost contradictory—strength: his intelligence. He was articulate, intellectual, a professor of constitutional law. This kind of candidate rarely wins national office in the United States, where a large swathe of the population has a populist or fundamentalist mistrust of eggheads, but the global financial crisis of 2008 seemed to demand careful analysis. Obama's confidence in the face of this crisis contrasted with McCain's confusion.[26] (Otherwise, the Obama campaign downplayed his formidable intellect, and played up his triumph over obstacles such as racism.) Intellectual candidates may fare better in France, where intelligence is more valued in leaders, but even there traditional military heroes like de Gaulle or swaggering paratroopers like Jean-Marie Le Pen have followings. In the United States, parts of the electorate (on the right) are wary of the strength of intelligence and expertise, while other parts (on the left) fear more the strength of military force.

There are several related dilemmas here. Orrin Klapp mentions how heroes can establish their reputations. They should appear to act alone. They need to seek confrontations, especially with stronger opponents. Both stratagems presumably enhance their reputation for strength. But Klapp recognizes the engagement dilemma: "The one who starts things off runs the risk of being unpopular or a troublemaker or some other kind of villain, but, unless he takes this risk, he may never find himself winning the grand prize." People love a winner, Klapp implies, and success can crowd out other moral judgments. But he also says that a hero takes risks to protect his followers. He uses his might on others' behalf, thereby reducing their anxiety about his strength.

The hero can also demonstrate moral goodness in her style of action. Klapp suggests that the hero has more straightforward forms of aggression than the villain. Whereas the villain exhibits "sneakiness, backbiting, innuendo, mudslinging, bullying, domineering, quarrel-picking, and cruelty," the hero relies on "pluck, cockiness in an underdog, audacity, humor, satire, honest man-to-man slugging, and non-violent pressure."[27] Satire is not obviously more straightforward than bullying, but it gets a crowd on one's side.

Among forms of action, a hero can even show her emotions in a strong way, in contrast to our usual expectations of emotional performances that they reveal weakness, vulnerability, and passivity. We normally expect people to display emotions *instead of* action. But heroes—male and female—can display "manly emotions" by simultaneously demonstrating control over the emotions: instead of crying loudly and wailing, one tears up, bites one's lower lip, and gives a look of determination to get through it all.[28] Hillary Clinton is every bit as skilled in this as Barack Obama (although he gets more credit for it: people like sensitive men more than tough women). Anger, especially of a righteous, indignant sort, is also an emotion that heroes can display without undermining their strength. Heroes can suffer emotions to establish their goodness, but they cannot show them too much.

General George Custer is an all-American specimen of the contrast between physical bravery and intelligence. That he had graduated last in his class at West Point only highlighted the foolhardy bravery for which he became known during the Civil War (unlike McCain's poor scholarly performance, which was coded as rebelliousness). Apparently too dumb to fear anything, his death in "Custer's last stand," when he led two hundred soldiers against several thousand Lakota and Cheyenne fighters, epitomized his life. Some heroized him for his "sense of duty, love of country, courage, and self-sacrificing heroism" while others dismissed him as egotistical, "foolhardy, unprincipled, and vain," either a villain or a ridiculous minion.[29]

Prophets

In discussing charisma, Max Weber observes that prophets perform miracles: a pure form of strength, summoning supernatural powers to do things that humans cannot, to break even the laws of nature.[30] In some cases the prophets are also associated with more human forms of strength—virility, physical stamina, bodily strength—but often they are an alternative kind of hero, weak in most of these other ways but strong in just one, their connection to divinity.

Miracles are not the prophets' main medium, words are. In prophets, we see a sacred dimension of heroism different from the hero's traditional divine parentage. Prophets are communicative media. "God is raging in the prophet's words," said Rabbi Herschel. "God has thrust a burden upon his soul, and he is bowed and stunned at man's fierce greed." He describes prophecy as a crossing point of God and humankind, the traditional position of heroes.[31]

Michel Foucault too observes that the prophet "does not speak in his own name. He speaks for another voice; his mouth serves as intermediary for a voice that speaks from elsewhere."[32] The prophet's authority comes from the supernatural, always a convincing source of credibility. Foucault contrasts the prophet with other characters from ancient Greece: the sage, who expresses his own accumulated wisdom, the teacher, who offers technical skills, and the "parrhesiast" who tells unpleasant truths to the powerful. The sage and the teacher tend to appear in political narratives in the guise of Propp's donors, offering something useful to the main protagonists. The prophet and the parrhesiast are more powerful, sometimes heroic characters, especially the parrhesiast, who takes considerable personal risk in speaking truth to power, with the intention of helping the collective. In the final years of his life, Foucault developed the parrhesiast into a kind of philosopher's hero.[33]

Verbal attack is, in some ways, a form of strength, but it can feel more ineffectual than strong. Are fiery prophets heroic figures, or objects of ridicule? Their benevolence threatens to shade into self-righteousness, their strength into a loud squeak. The power of persuasion can be enormous, but it can also be an alternative to other sources of strength, such as armed force—John Brown being a notable exception who combined the two (Figure 7.3). In modern societies the figure of the protestor has filled these shoes: moral and active but ineffectual, annoying, and sometimes a bit comical ("that dreary tribe of high-minded women and sandal-wearers and bearded fruit-juice drinkers," complained Orwell about middle-class socialists).[34]

Prophets define themselves by their verbal attacks on villains and minions, not by their protection of innocents. For many prophets, like those of the Old Testament, there are no innocents to protect, so that

FIGURE 7.3 With both guns and books, John Brown was a warrior and a prophet, a rare combination.

their jeremiads are gloomy predictions of punishment—although usually accompanied by blueprints for salvation. Their audiences must save themselves. They cannot turn to the ranting prophet for protection, only instruction, so the prophet can only be a partial hero.

Prophets have no roots in present engagements, appearing suddenly outside the main drama. In this way prophets might be clown figures, commenting on the action rather than fully participating in it. But in contrast to clowns, whose ridicule undermines the importance of the action, dour prophets promote its vital urgency.

The Confidence of Gods

When heroes are so strong that they do not have to suffer in doing good, they transcend the category. They become gods. Gods do not die, and they are not subject to the same suffering as humans (Jesus is the obvious exception, being fully divine *and* fully human).

Most gods are very strong and very good, although there is a potential contradiction between these two attributes, a version of the challenge we have already examined: how can strong players not feel threatening to others, even their allies? In what Leibniz called the problem of theodicy, how can an all-powerful god allow horrible things to happen to his own creation, humans? He can be totally just or totally powerful, but not both at the same time. Of the many efforts to solve this challenge, according to

Weber, the Hindu concept of karma is the most consistent, seeing human suffering as punishment for transgressions in a previous life. Dualistic solutions make God a little less potent, adding an equally mighty evil force to their vision. Other answers turn to the passive-active dimension, making god an impassive or distant being who does not intervene in human affairs, due to his concern for free will or for other reasons.

To bring the tension back down to earth, powerful leaders suffer the same inability to appear both strong and good when bad things happen. Several scandals rocked the Mitterand administration, and Monsieur le Président pleaded ignorance. The problem was obvious: "If the President did not know about it, he was a weak president."[35] The minion defense only works for underlings.

Humans with god-like strength are normally the stuff of comic books and myths. But military forces frequently engage in similar character work. If you are about to go into battle, it is reassuring to believe that your commander is invincible, even part-god. That kind of confidence can allay the normal fears of battle that may otherwise be paralyzing. All heroes inspire courage in their followers, but superheroes have magical powers alongside the mundane forms of managing fears in battle, such as "boasting, faking, exhortation, rum rations, giving or taking orders, small-group cohesion, various self-deceptions regarding confidence, cultivating rashness and seeking thrills."[36] In the heat of battle soldiers want to believe in their commanders' superpowers: "The men turn to their officers for protection as though [they were] their saviours endowed with power from above."[37] The supernatural power of magic persists in the modern world.

Weapons can take on magical powers, in what Thomas de Zengotita calls the *glamor of gear*: our (male) fascination with the gloves, the robots, the ammo clips, the gleaming guns, skies full of fighter jets, fleets covering the sea as far as the eye can see.[38] The strongest heroes bring overwhelming force to their tasks. The equipment helps transform the passive giant into the active hero, and it can fuse the virtues of experts and warriors. Iron Man and Batman are strong only because of their accouterments. But this massive firepower can tip over on the moral scale, into large, dark bureaucracies, who are tamed by morally plucky heroes, underdogs who bring down the vast militaries: Luke Skywalker versus the Death Star.

Heroes reassure followers through their own confidence, a useful resource in all strategic action. Calmness, combined with strength, is reassuring to audiences. During the 1964 presidential campaign in the United States, an assistant wrote a memo to Bill Moyers concerning how to characterize President Johnson at the Democratic National Convention. "To the extent possible, his appearance should convey qualities of courage, political bravery, candor, as well as *convincing* compassion. Among other things, this means the President saying—for deliberate effect of courage, independence, and freshness—some things public and press would not expect him to say before his own Party." In addition, the president should "convey strongly the image of experience, safety, stability" even while offering voters the sense of something new;[39] new but strong.

Another Johnson aide emphasized the active dimension of heroes: "the inevitable flood of speeches [should] be intermingled with action or doing situations. That should also help reinforce the emphasis on his ongoing President role rather than candidate position." The activity dimension should be combined with the strength of the office. "While the President has to get around the country and show vigor and closeness to the people, he should also get back to the White House frequently and have showcase opportunities arranged there. In brief, he needs to be President as much as possible."[40] What better stage set for highlighting a heroic character than the White House, with associations of victorious wars, worldwide power, and all the good intentions of democracy?

Cognitive psychologist Daniel Kahneman describes a cluster of mental processes that generate over-optimism, into which heroes probably tap—for both themselves and their followers. "In terms of its consequences for decisions," observes the great expert on cognitive biases, "the optimistic bias may well be the most significant." Yet some people are more optimistic than others, and "[o]ptimistic individuals play a disproportionate role in shaping our lives. Their decisions make a difference; they are the inventors, the entrepreneurs, the political and military leaders—not average people. . . . Their self-confidence is reinforced by the admiration of others. This reasoning leads to a hypothesis: the people who have the greatest influence on the lives of others are likely to be optimistic and overconfident, and to take more risks than they realize." These people are heroes.[41]

Part of our confidence develops because we do not take full account of the many mistakes and bad luck that can occur. Kahneman calls this the planning fallacy: it is easy to think of the things we need to do to succeed, partly because they are under our control; it is harder to think of the many things that might interfere with our plans. Those interferences might include conscious efforts by our opponents to block us. We know our own skills, plans, and resources better than we know theirs, and so weigh our own capacities more heavily. We understand our hero's powers more than we grasp our opponent's (although for purposes of mobilizing followers as opposed to planning, it is frequently useful to exaggerate our opponents' power: Bush II exaggerated Hussein's power at the same time that Pentagon planning called for too few troops).

Kahneman understands that in some settings action is crucial, including most political and strategic engagements, and "When action is needed, optimism, even of the mildly delusional variety, may be a good thing." It offers "resilience in the face of setbacks": people keep at it.[42] And because we attribute almost-magical causal powers to individuals, we follow heroes who seem confident.

As we saw, confidence can go too far, like all character work. Ironically, the stronger the heroes, the more prone to tragic overconfidence they may be. Jasper describes the Titan's Hubris as just this kind of risk: if you believe in your own strength too greatly, you are more likely to underestimate your opponents and leave yourself vulnerable to unpleasant surprises.[43]

Heroic Suffering

Most heroes suffer deeply, even short of death. This makes them more admirable. For one thing, heroes are frequently isolated from ordinary society due to their dangerous power. The Western gunslinger rides off to another adventure: the same restless energy that makes him alert and powerful frequently prevents him from settling down to raise a family or run for a seat on the town council. He must endure loneliness.

When heroes do not realize what risks they are taking, this means that they are heroic mostly in other people's later constructions. The firefighters who went up the stairs of the twin towers on 9/11 did not know the towers were about to collapse, although they knew very well that fighting fires is risky. Whistleblowers know even less about what is in store for them when they go public with their organization's transgressions. "It will cost you your career and your house and probably drive you into bankruptcy," says Fred Alford. "It is not a comforting story or an inspiring one. 'Federal employees should not have to be martyrs', is how one psychologist who specializes in working with whistleblowers puts it. By the time they get to him most already are."[44] They do not start off as heroes, much less martyrs. Circumstances—the hostile reactions of those they criticize—turn them into martyrs.

Worse, the character work that others do on behalf of the whistleblower is often of no comfort, serving primarily the political ends of the character worker. " 'The little man who stood up against the big corporation and won' is a type of folk hero. But that is just the problem. He is a type of folk hero, that is, a stereotype. Everyone wants to hear about the stereotype, but no one wants to know how vulnerable we are to power and how much it can take from us, including the meaning of our lives. It is this the whistleblower has to teach, but no one wants to learn."[45] Alford mentions one whistleblower who feels he is part hero, part victim, and part co-conspirator. The organizational backlash against whistleblowers is so vicious that the heroes are reduced to victims—or villains.

By attacking powerful organizations, whistleblowers ignite a vicious character war, with their own reputations at stake alongside that of their employers—and a seesaw battle between them. Is the organization the villain, or is the whistleblower? Whether or not whistleblowers are lucky enough to have good-government or social-movement organizations on their side, portraying them as heroes or victims, they certainly have opponents painting them as villains or ridiculous minions.

Self-sacrifice is especially admired in Japan, according to Ivan Morris. In *The Nobility of Failure* he traces 1600 years of warriors who accepted defeat and death in order to maintain the purity of their spirit. They see "the inherent value of the sincere, self-sacrificial act, a value which is entirely irrelevant to its practical effectiveness and which may, on the contrary, be given additional validity by failure."[46] Here, the hero's strength and bravery lie in his refusal to submit to petty rules, social conventions, or political intrigue.

Morris describes the kamikaze pilots as this kind of hero. They represent an effort by Japan's military leaders to find an alternative source of strength in the face of overwhelming American superiority in ships and planes. A suicide plane, with a ton of explosives in its nose, was "a method that allowed pilots with minimal experience, flying almost any kind of craft, to damage, perhaps even sink, the seemingly impregnable [aircraft] carriers, the core of the American threat." These volunteers lacked the technical expertise and experience that normally give fighter pilots their heroic capacity. Instead, they believed that "their ultimate strength lay in moral superiority,"[47] a skyful of young Davids aiming at Goliath.

Farther along this Romantic path we find heroes who are anti-heroes, rejecting the very system used to judge heroism and accomplishment. They eschew normal standards of strength in order to listen to their own, internal alternatives. The Romantic hero suffers both for rejecting the mores of her society and simply because she is so sensitive to the world's woes. Most cherished are those who die young, full of inner promise rather than accomplishments (which can always disappoint). One of the most famous was Thomas Chatterton, a poet of medievalist works who killed himself in 1770 at the age of seventeen, immortalized by painters of the mid-nineteenth century. In this tradition, it is more difficult, and requires more spiritual strength, to be a nonconformist. But by the normal social standards of the majority, anti-heroes are not especially good, just weird. They often become heroes only to later generations.

Michel Foucault describes the puzzling rise of the Romantic artist as a kind of hero, speaking of "the moment when the stories of heroes gave way to an author's biography."[48] Traditional heroes have not disappeared; they have been joined in Romantic imagery by the artist as a hero of creativity and sensibility, a brave genius who towers over and leads the rest of us in the esthetic and emotional realm, and who suffers for it.

Most heroes suffer, and their travail becomes a symbol of their character: they are brave, self-sacrificing, stoic. "Taking pain is an action, not passive suffering," observes David Morris, "and the ability to absorb punishment becomes a semiheroic sign of courage and endurance. Taking pain means refusing to surrender."[49] The endurance of pain establishes the hero's strength. As sociologist Tyson Smith says of professional wrestlers, "pain can be flaunted, but it must not be construed as a sign of weakness or vulnerability."[50] Heroes are heroes because they do battle with villains strong enough to hurt them. We will revisit these martyr-heroes in chapter 9, since they trouble the boundaries between heroism and victimhood.

As part of their suffering, many heroes die for their community or cause, and their dying words are given special significance. This is a perfect rhetorical moment, as audiences are primed to expect a pithy message for which the hero will be remembered. "The final histrionic flourish," remarks one historian of the theater, "affirms the performer's chosen essence for the last time, and settles his claim to be what he has represented himself as."[51] He becomes his character.

A hero's final contribution to her community is often some kind of encouragement and blessing in the form of final words about the importance of sacrifice, moral lessons, not dying in vain, grace under fire, and so on. Yosef Trumpeldor's famous words, "It is good to die for our country," became part of the founding lore for Israel, the country he helped to create. But the statement is almost too heroically good to be true, and skeptics have debunked it, observing that Trumpeldor's Hebrew was too poor for him to formulate it in this elegant manner. Critics even claimed that his real last words, when he realized he was about to die, were a Russian curse that roughly means, "Fuck your mother." In the hands of ironists, "the revised text transforms Trumpeldor from the prototype of the New Hebrew man into a Russian immigrant, from a prominent Zionist figure who provided the nation with a sacred slogan into a soldier who broke into profanities, and from a self-sacrificing hero into a reluctant victim."[52] Profane fears of death can bring a hero down to earth.

Admiration and Antipathy

Heroes may be morally good on one dimension—their willingness to protect us—but not on others. This complicates our emotional reactions. Admiration, based on a sense of relief from the fears of threat, remains the core response. But what other emotions do we feel for heroes?

Heroes are valued but not necessarily liked. Their power can make them dangerous, for it can be used toward new ends. In a distant parallel, combat soldiers often dislike the snipers in their units, whose deadly accuracy accounts for a disproportionate number of casualties inflicted on enemies, but whose cool manner and efficiency undermine their goodness.[53]

Many heroes are stronger than they are good, and this can generate tragedy. In the ancient Greek notion of hubris, their very strength could lead them to overdo it. Their vengeful rage could lead them to humiliate their opponents or to break the rules of combat. Today we are more likely to use the word to describe those who lack humility, a fault that comes easily to those who are powerful. Their overconfidence can lead to their downfall.

Some heroes have disreputable friends, whose knowledge of criminal networks may ultimately aid the hero. The hero, who is supposed to be good, is polluted here by the dirty-hands dilemma: certain goals are only available through unethical means—but they may be necessary anyway. A hero may have to consort with unsavory characters, deceive others, and find ways to raise money. In many settings violence itself is unsavory, for instance with suicide martyrs.[54] The hero may risk her reputation as good in order to preserve her strength, or risk her strength in order to preserve her moral aura.

Other polluted heroes have done something in their past that can never be forgiven, or only partly forgiven. Hard-boiled detectives such as Sam Spade once did something that forced them off the police force, but their transgressions usually turn out—after much suspense—to have been a moral stand against a corrupt system or hierarchy. The cloud over their moral goodness is lifted, at least for the viewer.

At the other extreme, heroes can be *too good* to be liked. Heroes can be just as confident in their morality as in their strength, but this form of confidence can make them stubborn, self-righteous, arrogant—and unpopular. An interesting literature on those who took great risks to rescue Jews from the Nazis suggests that one of their central traits was unquestioning belief in their own moral compasses. This was sometimes attached to religious faith, but not always. It allowed the rescuers to achieve great heroic deeds in the face of enormous risks.[55]

Popular images of many protestors suggest that they are abnormal in their ideas and sympathies: bleeding hearts whose self-righteousness is annoying. The modern character type of the "protestor" is, sometimes in stereotype and sometimes in reality, unpleasant, so confident of having the Truth that popularity does not matter. As the original, Martin Luther, said, "Peace if possible. Truth at all costs." Truth is more important than peace, at least when god is on your side. (Protestors tend to see themselves as vaguely heroic, while their opponents disagree with their morality and the media tend to doubt their strength.)[56]

Psychologists Craig Parks and Asako Stone, much to their surprise, uncovered a similar antipathy to generous players in their research on behavioral fairness.[57] Undergraduate subjects were set at computers to play a money game with four other players (actually the computer). In each round, each player was given ten points, which the player could allocate to her own account or to a common account. Points placed in the kitty would be doubled. Each player could also withdraw from the kitty up to one quarter of what the other players had added, in other words dividing it up. However, after the last round (the subjects did not know when it would be), they would receive a bonus if the kitty exceeded a certain amount (also unspecified).

Parks and Stone were interested in how students would react to a rogue "player" who took more than her share. As a control, they programmed the rogue to sometimes be unusually generous instead. After the game, students reported that they would not like to play with selfish players again. But they also did not want to play with the overly generous players, either. The selfless players made them feel ungenerous: "He makes us all look bad." Protestors and heroes make the rest of us feel guilty—*especially* when we agree with their goals. Heroes may also not leave much for the rest of us to do. When Barry Diller gives 130 million dollars to New York's High Line Park, he is a hero, but the rest of us feel less need to contribute.

A hero's strength gives her autonomy, which in turn detaches her from social life. Will Wright sees the Western hero's strength as his ability to live alone and to take care of himself. He is one with the wilderness: he is seen alone, hunts his own food, has been a trapper, and is associated with caricatured American Indians. He has none of the effete culture of the East, which "is always associated with weakness, cowardice, selfishness, or arrogance." Wright also detects the market ideal of an individual entrepreneur: "The hero is free from dependence on the will of others, and he is essentially the proprietor of his own person and capacities, for which he owes nothing to society."[58] Not all heroes are so detached from their social surroundings, but the extreme individualism that emerged in nineteenth-century capitalism still influences character work in politics today. Autonomy is strength.

Because groups within societies disagree on moral values, the same person can be a villain to some and a hero to others, as with most protestors and politicians. Electoral campaigns are structured so that each party demonizes the heroes of the other parties. Bandits throughout history have sometimes been idolized by the masses and denounced by the authorities and wealthy from whom they steal. Koose Muniswamy Veerappan is a recent example, carrying out a variety of crimes including kidnapping and murder in the forested hills between the Indian states of Karnataka and Tamil Nadu. He was famous enough to be known by only one name, Veerappan, and at one time his merry band of thugs numbered more than one hundred. His reputation for strength came from his passion for killing elephants, beginning at age fourteen. The rather clownish and corrupt police who tried to catch him—a special task force numbering more than 750—contributed to his aura of strength, attributing their own inability to catch him to his near-supernatural powers. Veerappan boasted of bribing police and politicians, a claim that many Indians found all too plausible. His strength was never doubted, even as his goodness was contested. When the police finally killed him in 2004, twenty thousand attended his funeral.

Sleeping Giants

Given widespread suspicions about first movers, heroes are repeatedly portrayed as being forced into action by the villains. The passive/active dimension commonly has a moral tinge: heroes should be vigilant but not aggressive. The hero gains moral credit by being, at first, reticent to engage the villains. She holds back until she has been pushed too far. At that point, "retaliatory violence becomes not simply justifiable but imperative." Discussing Western heroes, Jane Tompkins says, "What justifies his violence is that he is in the right, which is to say that he has been unduly victimized and can now be permitted to do things which a short while ago only the villains did." This feeling of supreme righteousness, she says, is "delicious."[59]

American politicians inevitably justify their foreign adventures by portraying their country as a sleeping giant, minding its own business until forced to act. Longstanding myths about American moral purity, which precludes complex diplomatic engagements, force American leaders to insist that they are only acting to punish great evildoers. World War II remains the paradigm, alluded to in almost all war rhetoric since then.

George W. Bush, a president especially driven by platitudes, announced the switch from passive to active only a week after 9/11: "This country will define our times, not be defined by them." He consoled a grieving nation, but hinted at a firm resolve to get revenge. In November, he placed his country squarely in the hero mode: "It is also a reminder of the great purpose of our great land, and that is to rid this world of evil and terror. The evil ones have roused a mighty nation, a mighty land. And for however long it takes, I am determined that we will prevail." Once roused, the giant does not sleep until evil is vanquished.

Several months later, in his 2002 State of the Union Address, Bush insisted that "History has called America and our allies to action, and it is both our responsibility and our privilege to fight freedom's fight." Heroes can be reluctant, but what makes them heroic is that they live up to their responsibilities. When the decisive moment in the great battle arrives, the hero is ready. "In a single instant," Bush went on, "we realized that this will be a decisive decade in the history of liberty, that we've been called to a unique role in human events. Rarely has the world faced a choice more clear or consequential."[60] His speeches were liberally peppered with references to Pearl Harbor.

The original attack on Pearl Harbor allowed FDR to bring the United States officially into World War II (and conspiracy theorists believe he allowed it to happen for just this purpose). It became the great exemplar of the sleeping giant forced to act. Political leaders have tried to exploit or manufacture similar events, as Bush did or as Johnson did with the Gulf of Tonkin incident in 1964. But when these crises come to be seen as staged or exaggerated, public opinion easily reverses the roles of villain and victim. Controversies unfold over just this type of characterization: when a scandal is discovered to have been staged it becomes an affair instead, with the kind of dueling accusations we saw in chapter 4.[61]

We admire heroes less if they seem calculating, if they pause for a moment to assess the risks they are taking. We want them to act recklessly on gut instinct, revealing their essential nature. Everyday heroes, for instance, who save the lives of others by jumping into icy ponds or charging into burning buildings, never report any hesitation, any momentary thought of self-preservation. This might be because those people who hesitate are not recognized as heroes; or it might be that a moment's reflection reduces the impulse to save others and produces bystanders instead of heroes. Either way, calculation undermines our images of both morality and strength.

The Zionists who helped to develop Israel's national ideology made a great deal of the difference between passive and active heroes. Many Jews suffered during their long exile from their homeland, at the extreme undergoing *Kiddush ha-Shem*, or death for the glorification of God. But the New Hebrew Man of Israel often rejected this entire period of Exile as a shameful pollution. The Jews who had suffered and even those who were martyred in Exile could not be full heroes, a title that young settlers hoped to reserve for those who died for the cause in Israel, because only they could be fully active and strong. To this day these are the traits that Jewish Israelis have claimed in their character work. They commemorate the Holocaust on the anniversary of the heroic Warsaw ghetto uprising and not—like American Jews—on that of Kristallnacht, an event of victimhood.[62]

Supporting Heroes

Many heroes are surrounded by helpers: sidekicks who accompany them, donors who provide necessary resources, judges who can reward them, sages who counsel them, even bystanders who may cheer them on. Most are involved indirectly or sporadically. The *donor*, one of Propp's characters, helps the hero at some point without otherwise getting entangled (though perhaps watching from a distance). Those who send money to Greenpeace without themselves confronting whaling ships are a good modern example, descended from Merlin and other magicians who gave magic potions to fairytale heroes. The power of the donor is the power of the resources she provides. She is more powerful than active.

Another remote character is the lofty individual who appears at the end of a narrative to set things right or to comment on the action. This is often a *judge* figure who represents an unquestioned morality or power. King Richard arrives just in time to save Robin Hood; in other dramas, it is frequently a noble who fixes things but also summarizes the moral at the end, much as gods descended in their machines in Greek drama. Today any third party may play this role by offering moral verdicts about the conflict. Judges have the power that comes from holding a position in some arena.

It is reassuring to find an apparently neutral party who believes justice is on your side, whether it is a judge figure who can decide in your favor or merely observers who offer comments. If the judge decides against you, however, you try to refigure her as an "outside agitator," an inappropriately activist judge who misunderstands the situation or has a personal interest in the outcome. In other words, she is no longer an impartial judge but a partisan player.

Donors and judges do not depend on popularity for their power, and so they devote less effort to character rhetoric. Bill Gates has just as much money to support the heroic efforts of public health officials whether we like him or not. Yet the media write about these indirect players, sometimes in positive and sometimes in negative ways. This can matter, especially for those in institutional positions.

In traditional stories, the young (virile) hero is often guided by an older, wiser man. Today, these could be experts with specialized knowledge or an elder statesman endorsing a politician. The hero has to seek out these guides for advice, already demonstrating some dependence on others or at least some recognition that he is not strong enough to accomplish his chosen feat on his own. It takes Luke Skywalker a long time to find Yoda and almost as long to recognize Yoda's powers. Donors are more like judges, remote figures of unquestioned power.

Benefactors have various powers and assets, from magical potions to special knowledge to financial resources, but they do not put themselves at risk the way the hero does. Just as the Greek gods let humans fight their battles for them, so today's benefactors still have an Olympian position above the fray. In particular they do not risk their reputations in the dirty-hands dilemma.

In addition to those who support the hero while remaining above the fray, the hero has followers who help to the extent they can, or at least cheer her on. Just as the villain has his malevolent followers, minions, so a hero has well-intentioned supporters. As weak and good, they belong in the same table cell as victims, but by being on the hero's team they can share or at least feel some of her strength. They can be either active sidekicks or passive bystanders, aiding the hero on the one hand or simply cheering from the sidelines on the other. But as we saw, they risk looking like minions if they refuse to take action when the hero asks.

Proper heroes generously acknowledge and reward their helpers. Otherwise, the hero could not represent a group or a shared vision. Even the heroes who are loners must be fighting for someone and something, otherwise there is no audience to praise them and craft their heroic reputation. "Mandela's first speech after his release," observes Thomas Olesen, "was almost entirely devoted to crediting his freedom to others and to paying homage to those who had lost their lives in the struggle." He was free, Mandela explained, because of the sacrifices of so many others. A hero must share a moral vision with others.[63]

We have devoted considerable attention to heroes because so much of the action centers on them: they fix things, they found institutions, they pull groups together, they enter strategic arenas. They offer pride and exhilaration, the promise and joy of victory—some of the sweetest feelings in human life. In the next chapter we remain on the good side of the moral frontier, but we turn to the weaker counterparts of the heroes. Without victims or potential victims, there would be neither heroes nor villains. The victims' suffering defines the villainy. And yet we also see that, even in a modern world skeptical of the power of villains and heroes, there can still be victims. In the risk society they can be victims of human technological systems (godlike in their scope and power) rather than of villains.

8 | We Pity Victims

You can't be suspicious of a tree, or accuse a bird or a squirrel of subversion, or challenge the ideology of a violet.

—*Hal Borland*

The victims' innocence is a necessary precondition for terror.

—*Michael Gross*

THE LOVELY PÈRE LACHAISE CEMETERY in Paris is a tangle of tiny lanes full of famous figures, mostly heroes of culture and politics. In a distant back corner it also offers a history of victim celebrations. Near the wall against which the final holdouts of the Paris Commune were massacred in May 1871, a broad path is lined with monuments to those killed by others. Most were victims of the Nazis, with memorials to those exterminated in each of the main camps (Figures 8.1 and 8.2). Others evoke those killed fighting the fascists in the Spanish civil war or communists slain in police raids. (Other communists are buried here too, as if their beliefs were sufficient to grant them victimhood.) The most recent are monuments to those killed when airplanes went down—mainly due to bombs but also to technical failures. Villains slaughtered most of the victims remembered in this corner of Père Lachaise, although in modern societies there are also victims of technology.

If character work can establish that there is a victim, then there must be a wrong to be righted. Moral indignation requires victims, even when we have to use our imagination to come up with them.[1] In politics, the establishment of a victim usually precedes mobilization for redress via the search for a villain and a hero. The most sympathetic victims are weak, passive, and morally worthy. We pity them and want to help them. It is hard to watch them suffer.

Public Characters. James M. Jasper, Michael P. Young, and Elke Zuern, Oxford University Press (2020) © Oxford University Press.
DOI: 10.1093/oso/9780190050047.001.0001

FIGURES 8.1 AND 8.2 What better images of victims than those systematically starved and incinerated in concentration camps by the twentieth century's ultimate villains?

Victims can arouse pity, horror, and indignation in audiences. But those very emotions can make the victim seem something less than human; these are the same emotions we feel in watching animals suffer. We can empathize with their pain, but we cannot appreciate their subjective point of view. Victimhood creates a gap between viewer and viewed, objectifying the victim and freezing her outside the possibility of will or reasoned action.[2] Victims lack agency. They speak only to narrate their victimhood. They are objects, not subjects. Victimhood is thus a risky self-presentation, as with victims of rape or abuse who are sometimes criticized for not having done enough to save themselves. Children and animals, never in full control of their destinies, seem doomed to remain in the victim table cell, like the damsels in distress from an era when women were expected to be like children.

In presenting yourself as a victim in need of saving, you deny your own capacities for successful action: in exchange for aid, you give up some recognition as a full player, maybe even as a full human being. The women's movement had to fight hard to move women from the victim to the hero cell, capable of fighting their own battles, a process that we'll examine in chapter 9. Pacifists confront a similar fate and have worked to round their flat image by characterizing themselves as "peaceful warriors," calling for peace armies, and teaching that non-violence in the face of hate requires great courage and strength.

Victimhood is the lack of the many "capabilities" which, according to Martha Nussbaum and others, make for a full human life. These include health and control over one's body, the ability to exercise one's imagination, to interact with other species, to feel a range of emotions, to control one's material and political environment, and more.[3] Not all the capabilities are quite the same as strengths, but they allow for a normal, even rich, human life. Without them, you depend at least partly on others, and your actions are limited.

The most promising victims are small and quiet; the starving children in televised humanitarian pleas stare without crying. To return to the psychology we examined in chapter 3, people also attribute a number of victim traits to those who have round, wide-eyed "babyfaces." They are seen as weak, submissive, naïve—in a word, childlike. But they are also seen as honest and warm.[4]

Crying is the action that most represents victimhood. It is a plea for pity and help, a flooding out of the situation so that one abdicates adult responsibilities, a display of internal suffering that demands attention, a mode of corporeal communication that does not require words. (There are tears of joy as well, which suggest triumph not victimhood.) Full, open crying—wailing—especially suggests weakness, passivity, and often shame, unlike the "manly" crying we saw earlier. Many cultures associate crying with children, women, and other weak persons.[5] One of the traits often attributed to victims is emotionality, as we'll see later, on the assumption that emotional expression is an alternative to "real" action.

Other than the ability to communicate need, victims tend to cut themselves off from social life, often exhibiting a shame that leads to withdrawal. If evil consists of making others suffer, Emmanuel Levinas describes this suffering as the experience of "extreme passivity, impotence, abandonment and solitude."[6] Victims are not only weak and passive, but existentially alone, without the solace of full human connection. And yet they can cry out to attract attention and sympathy.[7]

If we think of our two forms of passivity—a lack of activity on the one hand or being the object of someone else's action on the other—victims are especially associated with the latter form. Being an object or means for someone else impedes a full, capable humanity. Even the *victim* of a shameful act—those who have been in concentration camps, those who have been raped—can feel shame. "The shame of passivity, the passivity of shame, is intolerable," remarks Arne Johan Vetlesen. "It is felt as incompatible with dignity, with self-respect." There is shame in not being able to prevent something terrible from happening, either to oneself or to others. An Auschwitz survivor compares his torture to rape. "Logically, it is the rapist who ought to feel shame, but in reality it is the victim who does, for she cannot forget that she was reduced to powerlessness, to a total dissociation from her will."[8] The strength and activity dimensions overpower the moral dimension of the action.

Vetlesen describes the bodily component to this shame. "No longer a natural and trustworthy source of pride, of self-esteem and self-identity, the body is all of a sudden turned into the opposite: a thing-like 'object' that one drags around, reminding oneself only of the body's fall from grace; a transition, that is, from a subject of willed action in the world whose every move exhibits her sovereignty, to an object of abuse at the hands of an alien will." The forms of shame reinforce each other.[9] Our many bodily limits and failures can become sources of moral shame, whether or not they begin as physical humiliation.

As we saw in chapter 6, victims shade into minions when morality—the boundary usually distinguishing them—dissolves. In nightmarish settings like Auschwitz but also less extreme prisons, survival crowds out morality. "To be in the role of victim is considered as tantamount to being nobody, to being devoid of agency, indeed of anything that would induce respect from others."[10] The boundary is all the more porous in that, as we saw, minions have little volition of their own.

The Pain of Others

Victims suffer, and our ability to construct them as victims depends on our reactions to the pain of others. We must feel compassion for them, as fellow humans, mammals, or simply creatures that can suffer: frontiers of sympathy that vary considerably across different times and places. Pain and humiliation can reduce someone's humanity to a bundle of nerve endings and traumatic neuroses.

Does violence—mental as well as physical—necessarily turn those subjected to it into a thing? Susan Sontag asks this, in a book about representations of suffering. "No, retort those who in a given situation see no alternative to armed struggle, violence can exalt someone subjected to it into a martyr or hero."[11] This exaltation depends on the character work of others, who find meaning in the victims' suffering, transforming them into saints or martyrs by placing them in a moral metanarrative. In a long revolutionary tradition Frantz Fanon saw colonial subjugation as a violent act that justified violent resistance as the only way to end it. Because "it rids the colonized of their inferiority complex, of their passive and despairing attitude," violence can be a "cleansing force" for victims.[12]

Art regularly offers characters for contemplation, as we saw in chapter 2. Greek and Hindu traditions favor heroes, Christian traditions martyrs. Sontag comments, "The sufferings most often deemed worthy of representation are those understood to be the product of wrath, divine or human. (Suffering from natural causes, such as illness or childbirth, is scantily represented in the history of art; that caused by accident, virtually not at all—as if there were no such thing as suffering by inadvertence or misadventure.)"[13] Sontag is not quite right: Breughel painted Icarus' accidental fall, but giving it the moral twist Sontag finds elsewhere. His father Daedalus had crafted wings to allow humans to soar too high, a lofty form of hubris that had to be punished. But it was a heroic form of suffering. (Many heroes bring pain to their families, in all sorts of ways.)

"The practice of representing atrocious suffering as something to be deplored, and, if possible, stopped, enters the history of images," according to Sontag, with the religious wars that devastated Europe in the seventeenth century.[14] Artists began to depict the horrors inflicted on civilians by rampaging armies. The apotheosis of this genre was Goya's etchings, *Los*

Desastres de la Guerra, made between 1810 and 1820 but not published until 1863, decades after his death (Figure 8.3). Goya had been shocked by the brutality of Napoleon's troops when they invaded Spain to quash the rebellion against French rule.

Goya provided condensed horror. "All the trappings of the spectacular," Sontag observes, "have been eliminated: the landscape is an atmosphere, a darkness, barely sketched in. War is not a spectacle." And the essence of victimhood is removed from any narrative that might pretty it up, or make it meaningful. "Goya's print series is not a narrative: each image, captioned with a brief phrase lamenting the wickedness of the invaders and the monstrousness of the suffering they inflicted, stands independently of the others. The cumulative effect is devastating." Romanticism gave us a greater appreciation for the suffering, feeling individual. "With Goya, a new standard for responsiveness enters art."[15]

Sontag also provides a capsule history of war photography, with its carefully crafted interplay of war casualties and patriotic successes. Only with the war between the United States and Vietnam did the practice of staging war photographs lose favor. One reason, she speculates, may be that "in Vietnam television became the defining medium for showing images of

FIGURE 8.3 At extremes victims are dead; here they are faceless, limp, unable to move or act any more; the ultimate in passivity.

war, and the intrepid lone photographer with Leica or Nikon in hand, operating out of sight much of the time, now had to compete with and endure the proximity of TV crews."[16] As that war became less and less popular, the journalist became more of a hero than the soldier, standing up to the government as a critic rather than following immoral orders.

"Images have been reproached for being a way of watching suffering at a distance, as if there were some other way of watching. But watching up close—without the mediation of an image—is still just watching." Such reproaches, she says, are often due to a frustration felt at not being able to do anything to relieve the suffering portrayed. But to look is to stand back and think, and as she says, "There's nothing wrong with standing back and thinking. To paraphrase several sages: 'Nobody can think and hit someone at the same time'."[17] (She was writing around the time that Bush II decided with little apparent thought to invade both Afghanistan and Iraq.)

A generation earlier, in *On Photography*, Sontag had famously argued that news events become more "real" when captured in photographs and film images, but that repeated contact in turn makes them less real.[18] We are exposed to such a barrage of images that we cannot concentrate on any of them. They create sympathy for distant others, then erode it. This is an old complaint about the overwhelming chaos of modern life and the surfeit of communication it brings. Our compassion is piqued only momentarily.

Sontag later worried that she was being associated with cynical postmodernists like Guy Debord and Jean Baudrillard who provocatively claimed that reality had become merely a spectacle. We can acknowledge, even analyze, the political and professional intentions of those who produce the images without falling into this "breathtaking provincialism" of wealthy Westerners far from the very real violence being framed and interpreted. "Some people will do anything to keep themselves from being moved," Sontag says, having spent many months in Sarajevo while it was under siege and apparently changing her mind somewhat about the clout of images.[19] Some images are so potent that they always retain their ability to move us—even though that power depends on formal properties reflecting the craft of the photographer as well as on what is portrayed. Suffering exists independently of images, but victims must be constructed to arouse pity and indignation in audiences.

Our compassion for suffering others is notoriously limited by national and racial-ethnic boundaries. We identify with our own group, however we define it, and can feel more easily the experience of those who are "like us." But our sympathies for distant others have increased enormously in recent centuries, for a variety of reasons that include global trade networks, better understanding of mammal biology, and media that can bring us the details of other peoples' lives with gripping immediacy. Many of us feel compassion for members of other species, which our ancestors could never have granted the status of victims.

Weak and Innocent

The same attributes that make heroes appear strong also make victims—who lack them—appear weak: a soft or feeble physique, small size; a lack of experience, intelligence, wisdom, wealth, offices, or special skills. Victims cannot protect themselves or maneuver in the political realm or other strategic arenas. Victims must also be good, summed up in the word "innocent" that is inevitably paired with "victim." One thing this means is that they were "minding their own business": they did not start the engagement. They are passive recipients of action, objects rather than subjects.

Small children fit the bill perfectly. They are the most sympathetic, pure victims, untrained in worldly ways that might protect or at least inure them to attack. The great historian of childhood, Philippe Ariès, sees the first stirrings of our modern image of children in the sixteenth and seventeenth centuries, when European children began to wear distinctive clothes. "A new concept of childhood had appeared, in which the child, on account of his sweetness, simplicity and drollery, became a source of amusement and relaxation for the adult." This indulgent "coddling," embraced especially by affluent mothers, would be joined and partly displaced by a sterner concern for children's moral discipline and development, especially on the part of clerics and moralists. But both visions would transmute the perceptions of sweet simplicity into a certainty about children's innocence, making them into perfect potential victims.[20]

American culture may be especially prone to sentimentality about the innocence of children, given Americans' extreme religiosity, especially the Christian dualism in which the world is starkly divided into villains versus heroes and victims. American Protestantism has also contributed to a prudishness about sexual matters, and an emphasis on so-called family values, as well as a popular culture full of simplistic moral visions designed for children. (Think of Disney.)

Victims need not have rational capacities, but this aspect is rarely emphasized one way or the other (although opponents of animal protection sometimes assert—mistakenly—that animals, because they are incapable of understanding what rights are, cannot be granted any). Victims' innocence is sometimes constructed on a lack of intelligence. The very smart cannot be trusted; the very clever are not usually innocent. As a result the media are often sympathetic toward people who have mental disabilities, such as those with Down Syndrome, who seem especially well-intentioned and incapable of guile.

On the other hand, many market-oriented cultures find ways to blame a person for not acquiring the experience or skills necessary for life in a competitive environment. Sympathy for weak, benevolent characters can easily slide into contempt, as observers want the person to stand up for herself. Even weak characters can at least be active rather than passive, audiences believe. The Yiddish word "nebbish" captures some of the frequent contempt we feel for ineffectual people, especially ineffectual men. They are pitiful, not pitied. The difference is often this: *could* the victim have developed the skills had she desired to, or were there constraints that blocked her despite her best efforts?[21]

Shakespeare was, among other things, an epidictic apologist for the Tudor regime. His character work was often brilliant poetry, but it was still character work. Those who had opposed the Tudor lineage or who might undermine its legitimacy became delicious villains in his hands, most notably Richard III (the sitting king that Henry Tudor slayed to seize the crown). In the play devoted to Richard, we see how important a pure victim is in the construction of a pure villain. Let's face it: if you find that your victims have been dubbed "the little princes," you have lost the character war.

Just as humans can be described in terms usually reserved for non-human species, animals can be anthropomorphized. What is more innocent than a kitten or a puppy? Animal protectionists discovered long ago the power of baby images. The Fund for Animals ran a typical advertisement. At the top, the irresistible face of a wild kitten stares at the reader. "She needs her fur more than you do," the headline blares, relying on widespread tendencies to see babies as innocent and females as better victims. "In the wild, animals suffer for hours or days in steel-jawed leg-hold traps, chewing through their own limbs trying to escape. And in fur factories, animals live their entire lives in tiny cages, their misery ending only when they are gassed, anally or genitally electrocuted, or have their necks broken. With the many warm and elegant alternatives, fur is unnecessary animal cruelty. Choose not to wear fur or fur trim. In the 21st century, compassion is the new fashion." The vulnerability of the tiny creature is harshly juxtaposed to the tortures that await her.

Admission of any slight guilt can ruin a victim's blamelessness. Women who fight back after years of abuse lose some of their victim status in courts. Oppressed groups must learn to express their anger, but this can tarnish their reputation for innocence. An abused domestic worker, telling her story to claim victimhood, must downplay her own agency; she neglects to mention that she ever fought back against her employer. Although this omission makes her more sympathetic, "we have less of a sense of her as a real person, with her frustrations, anger, and pain."[22] She is less human but a better victim. Character work is caricature and simplification; it is not accurate biography.

Defense attorneys in rape cases continue to question the innocence of victims, pointing to provocative dress, flirtatious emails, or promiscuous pasts. Any evidence that a woman actively pursues or controls her sex life deflates the passivity associated with innocent victims. The only way to make the accused less of a villain is to make the accuser less of a victim.[23]

Not all who suffer are sympathetic, especially those who "externalize" their hurt through verbal or physical aggression. They are neither weak, good, nor passive—unlikely prospects for recognition as victims. Therapeutically inclined social scientist Paul Hoggett remarks, "Sometimes the subjects of social suffering ['victims' of inequality and prejudice] are not those who easily elicit our compassion, since they do not comport themselves as innocent victims, but as aggressive, resentful, or suspicious beings whose hurt is directed at others."[24] We also fail to grant victimhood in these cases of structural suffering because it is difficult to find villains to blame.

In a study of political assassination, Ron Eyerman offers the interesting suggestion that there can be "evil victims" such as the Black Panthers gunned down by the police a generation ago.[25] He seems to be defining victim in terms of the simple action of being killed, not as character rhetoric to be contested. Downed Panthers were victims or martyrs to their supporters, but to the forces of order they were not victims at all but rather criminals who got what they deserved. (They were either villains or minions, depending on how threatening they seemed.) Eyerman is interested in cultural traumas that result from high-profile assassinations. In our view, this kind of moral shock is possible only when good people are killed, not when bad ones are. The shock arises when heroes are killed, or when large numbers of victims are. Evil victims are either not evil, or not victims.

Blame and Indignation

Victims have long been a staple of research into protest rhetoric and the construction of social problems. Indignation over injustice is the core motivation behind protest, and it follows that there must be someone who has been treated unjustly. Victims testify, their stories are elaborated in detail, photos of their wounds are published, all in an effort to arouse moral anger. "Without victims there would be no social movement dramas."[26]

Bad things happen to many people who suffer as a result. Some of these—floods, forest fires—come from nature or are "acts of god." We pity these victims and wish to help them. Other bad things come from human action: fraud, war, oppression, crime. In this case we not only pity the victims, we also are outraged at the perpetrators. One family of victimhood demands villains and political action, the other does not. Villain-victim-hero is the essential triad of most protest movements. (The boundary between human blame and natural disaster shifts according to political and cultural framings, especially as government has taken over responsibility for more and more areas of life, such as preventing floods and forest fires.)

Controversial wars generate debates over victims, following in Goya's footsteps. After the U.S. invasion of Iraq, iraqbodycount.org estimated deaths far surpassing the figures given by the U.S. government in order to demonize the latter. Debates over drone warfare have also focused on civilian deaths, with critics' estimates twice as high as those given by the Obama administration for example.[27] Victimhood drives arguments over the justice of every modern war. Do we view wars as a calculated plan, or as more like a natural disaster with inevitable collateral damage?

Battles over blame are so important to politics that even villains try to claim victimhood, along with the resulting indignation. The Nazis insisted that Germans were the victims of Jewish malice and the Treaty of Versailles, a vengeful punishment that ruined their economy in the interwar years. According to an expert on psychopaths, "In an ironic twist, psychopaths frequently see *themselves* as the real victims." John Wayne Gacy, who buried thirty-three boys and young men in his cellar, blamed his own childhood. "I was made an asshole and a scapegoat . . . when I look back I see myself more as a victim than a perpetrator."[28] It is difficult to ask for sympathy or to mobilize supporters without some sense of past victimhood or the prospect of imminent victimhood.[29] Gacy and the Nazis operated on different scales, but their character pleas were similar.

Alexander and Marguerite Mitscherlich, in *The Inability to Mourn*, claim that Germans after World War II did considerable character work in private to justify their country's and their own actions, "secretly blaming others for their own humiliation, for their various defeats, for things having gone so badly with them, and, consequently, for their being so misunderstood." Who wants to admit to being a villain? In this case, where victims were (almost) impossible to deny, a villain had to be found: Hitler and the Nazi leadership, who forced normal Germans to go along. Germans were unable to mourn, according to the Mitscherlichs, because they could not accept any guilt, and hence they repressed their memories of the fascist period. The best way to deny guilt is to claim victimhood, becoming good, weak, and passive at the same time.[30]

Choices about character roles are at the forefront of trials and reparations that follow horrors like the Holocaust and apartheid. We already looked at the minion defense, but victims also face strategic decisions. Do you have trials to punish the villains, or do you try to honor and compensate the victims?[31] Victims themselves must decide the extent to which they will replay their victim roles in court and other proceedings, thereby remaining stuck in the past to a certain extent, or instead throw off that role and look to future action. A permanent victim identity can be crippling. Collectivities that wish to be political players cannot at the same time present themselves too extensively as weak, passive victims. It is hard to be a victim and a player.

A Holocaust frame highlights victims; a Nazi frame focuses on villains; a D-Day frame centers around heroes. Various contemporary players have reasons to focus on one or another way to remember the 1930s and '40s in Europe.

Governments are not above constructing victimhood in order to pursue reparations. Victims arouse guilt not only in former perpetrators but in those who could have helped but did not. The narrative promoted by the Kagame government in Rwanda suggests that Western governments abandoned the country when it needed them, thus discouraging any criticism of his current policies. These include the not-so-subtle promotion of the idea that Hutus were the villains, Tutsis the victims (now survivors), maintaining a moral hierarchy even though ethnic labels have been outlawed. Philip Gourevitch, author of the popular account, *We Wish To Inform You that Tomorrow We Will Be Killed with Our Families*, captures the suffering of victims turned survivors during the genocide.[32] But in the process of highlighting the plight of victims and the heroism of Kagame's forces in ending the genocide, he accepts Kagame's reconstruction of the truth, ignoring war crimes and post-war violations of human rights by Kagame's forces. It is difficult to blame both the perpetrators of genocide and those who fought to end it. Rwandans and experts on Rwanda who sought to correct Gourevitch's account failed to draw the same attention that his clear narrative of nasty villains and innocent survivors received.[33]

After the genocide, Kagame expertly used the guilt felt by many outsiders to garner support and resources for rebuilding. Only after two decades of mounting human rights violations, including the assassination of Rwandan dissidents at home and abroad and the funding of rebel groups in neighboring states, did major donors such as the United States, European Union, and the United Kingdom publicly criticize Kagame's government and withhold funding. Victimhood that plays on the guilt of others can be powerful. Israel's national mythology involves a similar drama, in which former victims became tough survivors but remain above criticism in honor of their past suffering.

We negotiate everyday life, and not just politics, by attributing blame, drawing on our cultural "knowledge." Jack Katz has analyzed the indignation felt by automobile drivers, for example.[34] When we are cut off in traffic, we not only demonize the other person, but—since we don't know much about them—expatiate about them as a "type": BMW owners are . . . ; women drivers are . . . ; and so on (we draw on culturally plentiful stereotypes). We find ways to portray ourselves as victims who must get revenge, thus restoring our own sense of agency as we transform ourselves into avenging heroes. Our opponent is either a villain or an inept clown. We invoke a broader moral community to condemn those who have offended us and to assert our superiority over them—even if we must wait for the dinner table to do so in recounting our story. Reflex emotions of the moment, especially anger, are remade into moral emotions of indignation and contempt. These are rhetorical strategies found in a wide range of settings, even in the absence of anger. Again, villains and victims are tightly, inevitably paired.

Indignation is an energizing emotion, pushing one from passivity into action, possibly even strength. It offers an escape from victimhood.

Victim Arithmetic

If victims can become heroes along one boundary, a process we'll examine in the next chapter, they are still defined mainly through their contrast with villains and minions. We discussed the nearly mathematical processes in the allocation of blame in chapter 5, in which greater goodness in one character demands more badness from others. This is especially true of villains and victims, who compete to shift the blame back and forth by attributing the initial causal action to the other; the starting point of the narrative determines who is cast as villains, who as victims.[35] Victims are more pure if they did not know the villains who attack them, as social relationships introduce shades of complexity to the moral claims. And the nastier the villain, the more sympathetic the victim. Many or most character conflicts are over who is the victim, who is the villain, or what political scientists have called "competitive victimhood," with Hutus and Tutsis a paradigmatic case.[36]

A victim who is not well intentioned may be no victim at all, but a minion. This is the essence of blaming the victim, tarnishing her moral repute. For example con artists often appeal to their victim's greed. In addition to a dependable human motivation, this allows the criminals to blemish their own view of their "marks." Erving Goffman observes, "the con man protects himself from remorseful images of bankrupt marks by arguing that the mark is a fool and not a full-fledged person, possessing an inclination towards illegal gain but not the decency to admit it or the capacity to succeed at it." The weakness dimension remains intact, but a shift in the mark's moral standing pushes her from victim to minion. The victim's "beefs and complaints are a sign of bile, not a sign of injury."[37]

As in the case of villains, one's political position suggests who is an eligible victim, and villain-victim debates unfold around many oppressed groups. Women and racial-ethnic minorities are not worthy victims in the eyes of American conservatives who have mobilized to push back against the political gains these groups have made. Instead, they see themselves as the victims: "those individuals who have been ostracized, censored, and punished in other ways by political correctness, affirmative action, hate speech codes, and similar manifestations of injurious victim politics."[38] The sinister forces of liberalism are blamed for "playing the victim," when they are not really victims. The conservatives agree that women are weak, but they are not so moral or passive. As feminists, they are minions undermining American values of self-reliance. Trump's election in 2016 shows how widespread this backlash is in the U.S.

In the politics of blame, there is a crucial difference between characters who seem permanently relegated to victim status and those who find themselves victimized: categorical versus circumstantial victims. The latter are in a victim situation, but they can mobilize resources and act, becoming perhaps awakened giants. We have different reactions to permanent victims and situational ones. We may pity permanent victims, but we do not expect them to suddenly become heroes. We do not embrace them as allies, since they have no strength to offer. But we trot them out as symbols of evil in order to blame our chosen villains.

Children will, with luck, develop into autonomous and possibly strong adult humans one day. Animals will not. Even when we humans sympathize with other species we rarely view them as beings capable of controlling their lives—at least when they are domesticated and under human control. Activists have promoted the idea of animal rights in recent years, but with little impact. It is easier to want to "save the animals" than to "free the animals," the former indicating a passive creature while freedom connotes a strong and active one.

Candace Clark, a sociologist who has written about how and when we sympathize with others, notes that we feel compassion for "victims of illness, natural disasters, and abuse, as well as errant souls who repent and people in extenuating circumstances." On the other hand, "a person who claims sympathy directly may appear self-pitying or weak," or strategic, and therefore not truly passive. To complicate matters, we often admire victims who are strategic in fighting their villains more than those who appeal directly for our sympathy. It is more effective to have others seek sympathy on your behalf than to demand it for yourself.

Although Clark mostly examines sympathy in personal life, she also notes the arithmetic of sympathy in the notorious Clarence Thomas hearings in 1991. "To have sympathy for Hill's distress meant having little or none for Thomas. Having sympathy for Thomas's crisis meant blaming Hill for causing it. The more sympathy one side could win, the more the other lost." Thomas won the victim battle by displaying more pain and emotion (to the point of controlled tears), supported by former secretaries, coworkers, and family members who expressed indignation. Hill, whose suffering was long over, appeared sincere but not emotional, sending out "nonverbal cues of embarrassment and distress but not of humiliation or devastation." Thomas displayed victimhood; Hill mostly described it.[39]

The dilemma of the victim trope is this: is it better for a group or individual to be pitied, with the attention and aid this may bring, or is it better to mobilize capacities to fight back? Morally good players who find themselves at the receiving end of blameworthy treatment are victims, but they need not stay that way. They may turn out to be less weak than they are reputed to be, finding bursts of strength capable of transforming them into heroes. They may even be sleeping giants, passive only until they are provoked but then seeking moral vengeance. Their transformation lies at the heart of revolutions, social movements, and many other political struggles.

In Part Three we complicate our story of public characters. To remain political players in today's world, victims must become heroes. Chapter 9 shows various ways that they do this, by looking at heroes who differ sharply from traditional warrior demi-gods. Chapter 10 then examines modern twists on public characters, especially the erosion of heroes and villains from demi-gods into mere mortals.

III | Variations and Transformations

9 | From Victims to Heroes

I'm calling for steadfastness. The important thing is to hold on. Holding on
is a victory in itself.

—*Mahmud Darwish*

I am not suffering. I'm struggling.

—*Alzheimer's patient in Still Alice*

N BOTH THE OCCUPIED TERRITORIES and the refugee camps in Lebanon,
Palestinians undertake extensive character work. Schools, hospitals,
and streets carry the names of those killed fighting for Palestinian justice and independence. Every home has at least one martyr poster on its
walls, and public walls are often plastered with these tiny memorials. The
placards represent "both the person who was killed and the martyr that
person has become": their deaths, whether intentional martyrdom or not,
open the way to considerable character work around them, efforts they can
no longer resist or undermine.[1]

Some of the dead fit a traditional heroic mode, as part of armed resistance, especially those killed during the years of PLO dominance and the
Lebanese civil war and more weakly during the intifadas. In recent years
more Palestinians have accepted the tragedy and humiliation of victim
roles, pleading for international sympathy, aid, and recognition—yielding
the hero role to outsiders. "We know we are Palestinians because we suffer
so much," said one young woman interviewed in 2002.[2] If traditional
heroes were most often men, it is Palestinian women who are more likely
to acknowledge their weakness as victims.

The Palestinians have also elaborated a third configuration of character
and story, summed up in the concept of *sumud*, or steadfastness in the
face of adversity. Steadfast heroes, who came to the fore in 1982 after

Public Characters. James M. Jasper, Michael P. Young, and Elke Zuern, Oxford University
Press (2020) © Oxford University Press.
DOI: 10.1093/oso/9780190050047.001.0001

the vicious massacres by Phalangist militias and the Israeli forces who supported them, helped their friends and neighbors by finding enough to eat, by educating their children, by rebuilding homes that had been torn down. These were not traditional heroes who sallied forth into glorious military battles. But they had hope for the future, refusing the desperation and resignation that would have been so easy to feel.

These *heroes of endurance*, we will call them, were mostly women relying on the routines of their daily lives. Throughout human history, women have kept future generations alive, struggling to feed and protect the family, while men went off to seek the glories of war. Only in the modern world, as gender hierarchies have been challenged, have we come to recognize these survivors as a kind of hero rather than as victims to be pitied.

Oppressed groups must figure out how to jump the boundary from victim to hero, and we will look at several ways they do this. The first method is martyrdom, in which weak characters manage to pull together enough strength for one final heroic action, making a sudden leap from victim or potential victim to sacrificing hero. Heroes of endurance instead find strength through a form of passivity that eschews active aggression, making a less dramatic transition to survivor and then to hero. We admire them for their ability to survive rather than to dominate others. A third—very modern—possibility is to gain strength through numbers, either resisting through weapons of the weak or taking advantage of democratic arenas in which ordinary people can influence the world. These heroes are not individuals but groups, sometimes anonymous groups.

In the West, the construction of hero and victim tropes usually features individuals, who are made more human through personal stories and faces. Across the moral boundary, villains and especially minions are frequently faceless masses, not quite human as a result. In many other regions of the world, morality consists more in being a dependable part of the group, not standing out in contrast to it. For that reason traditional heroes may be especially salient in more individualist countries, which use personal autonomy as a positive moral indicator. In less individualistic countries, heroes of endurance—who can remain faceless and collective—have been familiar for a longer time.

Heroes of Example

Martyrs are heroes made from victims: they suffer because they are part of some political effort that is presented as heroic. They are resonant characters who arouse both the sympathy of victims and the admiration of heroes. Their intentional sacrifice differs enormously from the unwanted suffering of victims. They establish their morality by their urgent refusal to "take it anymore," having been pushed beyond the limits of what humans may endure. Only death can restore their dignity.

Not all victims become martyrs, and they lose some of their innocence when they do. To become martyrs, victims must be refigured as strong rather than weak. They must be seen as having intentionally sacrificed themselves for the cause, so that their action can be seen as an act of strength, for the movement at least but also usually for the individual. The child killed by an inebriated driver may inspire her parents to join or found a protest group, but she remains an innocent victim not a martyr. Mohamed Bouazizi, who by setting himself on fire helped to spark the Arab uprisings of 2011, could be recast as a martyr, even if his personal motives differed somewhat from those of the movement he inspired. But that movement benefited from portraying him as an intentional martyr and from redescribing his motives to match their own.

The death of victims is often dismissed as pointless, unlike the pointed sacrifice of martyrs. Palestinian poet Mahmoud Darwish discusses the massacre of the village of Kufr Qasem in 1956 at the start of the Sinai war. "The inhabitants of this downtrodden and neglected village did not engage in anything that should rouse anyone's anger. . . . They fought only against harsh nature and black despair. Why then did they die? They did not die for our sake at all. They were victims, not martyrs." He goes on, "We could say that they died so that our hatred of oppression and usurpation would grow deeper and our worship of the land would grow deeper. We do not need such savage facts. We are perfectly capable of developing our sense of love or hatred without this death for nothing." His answer is also couched in public characters: they died "Not for our sake but for that of the killers, so that Zionists may feel they are capable of playing a role in history other than that of victim. Killing tastes delicious when it is done for such an aim. 'Either be the killer, or be the one killed'—this is the narrow choice they have set before themselves."[3] The Israelis cared less whether they were heroes or villains, as long as they demonstrated strength.

Indian specialist Paul Brass also distinguishes martyrs from victims, and connects them to heroes. "Most often, the hero is perceived as acting against great odds regardless of the prospects of success, while the martyred resister acts with the certainty of defeat and death." Martyrs are just further along the continuum of the risky odds that heroes face. He confirms that the difference between victims and martyrs lies in the latter's association with a political cause. "They were not chosen or selected," Brass says of one case, "because of their race, creed or ethnicity; they were targeted because they acted, and their actions were greeted by undue force."[4] Among the Sikhs he studied, a claim of victimhood for their community feels degrading to the men, who pride themselves on their warrior ferocity. They can accept the label of martyrs, but not victims.

Some victims are hard to reconfigure into martyrs. A person who predeceased the political mobilization cannot be seen as a martyr in the full sense of knowing what she suffered or died for, unless she is portrayed as a pioneer in the sensibility on which the mobilization is based. Normally, a predecessor is painted as a victim. The same goes for people who suffered as children, before they were capable of the power necessary for heroes, or even the level of power that is normal for adults.

True martyrs know what they are doing. They are heroes in a conflict so important that they are willing to sacrifice themselves to promote victory. They are often religious believers who see in violence "an almost cosmological reenactment of the primacy of order over chaos."[5] Suicide bombers are weak players only in relation to some organized military force. Instead of direct military confrontation, they find arenas where they are less disadvantaged. They are traditional military heroes, except they are not operating in military arenas. But they are thinking and acting strategically.

Saints are a Christian twist on the martyr, in which Christ-like suffering itself has transcendent value. The early saints almost all suffered death for their faith. More generally, saints may accomplish important things, often (like Mother Theresa) helping victims, but they live in such a way that a saint's greatest accomplishment is her life itself. She influences others through example rather than forcing changes through strategic action. Saints are *heroes of example*, parallel to heroes of endurance in that they find non-traditional sources of strength, indeed turning some of their weaknesses into strengths, *moral* strengths.

In part this is a change in ideals brought about by Christianity. The ancient Greeks admired the carousing and anger of their heroes, who were defined by their power rather than their kindness. Charity and humility came to the fore with Christianity, so that the power of the ancient hero would thereafter be tainted by arrogance. Turning the other cheek is victimhood as spiritual heroism. Although Nietzsche held this slave morality in contempt, it is today acknowledged as a form of strength.

In the same Roman imperial culture that nurtured Christianity, a pagan equivalent emerged, especially as recounted by Livy (59 BCE–17 CE), a historian engaged in character work on behalf of the emperor Augustus.

Among the great heroes of Roman legend, as Livy catalogued them, Lucretia emerged as one of the most popular. A virtuous married woman, she was raped by Sextus Tarquinius, son and heir to the last tyrant at the end of the sixth century BCE. After extracting a promise of revenge from her father (a prominent magistrate) and others, she killed herself in front of them. In Livy's telling, the event was a kind of moral shock to the Romans, who rose up against the king and installed the Republic. One weak person managed to have enormous influence through her self-destruction, which transformed her from passive to active. Her death made her into a shining symbol of virtuous resistance to tyranny, able to inspire others. Among later republicans in Florence and Holland, such as Botticelli and Rembrandt, she would prove a favorite subject for paintings—but not for sculptures, reserved for more traditional heroes (Figure 9.1).

Jean-Marie Apostolides, who emphasizes uncontrolled violence as the defining trait of the hero, contrasts saints and heroes. "If the hero tends to fuse with a warlike collective, the saint is distanced from his

FIGURE 9.1 Are they real? Painters used to create heroes out of women by plopping breasts awkwardly on a masculine body, misconstruing their sources of strength.

community. . . . The hero relies on will, determination, and brutality, the saint on renunciation, interiority, and innocence. They push toward two extremes, one toward absolute incarnation and the other toward disembodiment."[6] In Christianity, goodness requires a complete renunciation of every kind of power—except for that of moral example. And even that must not be allowed to grow into pride. Humility is everything.

Yet Apostolides shows how the Catholic church created a category of "heroic virtue" for those saints who were virtuosi of religious devotion. It first used the phrase in the canonization of Saint Teresa of Avila, founder of the Carmelite order, in 1602. Instead of one's own glory, these new heroes worked for God's glory. It was a heroism open to women, and especially suited for peacetime. Apostolides also mentions an especially feminine form of heroic nationalism, a passive heroism, "characterized by endurance and the acceptance of the inevitable—like the death of a loved one—and unconditional love for those willing to die for their country."[7] We can put a more positive spin on this, seeing these women—like their Palestinian counterparts—as keeping the home front intact in the absence of their warrior menfolk.

Suicides like Lucretia's are a common form of self-sacrifice, especially outside Christendom, offering control over one's body and destiny. From Lucretia to the self-immolation of Vietnamese monks, from the IRA's hunger strikes to Mohamed Bouazizi, suicide requires great courage. It is a striking form of power, for those who have no other—provided the proper character work is accomplished, either before (Lucretia) or afterward (Bouazizi). Killing oneself in the act of killing opponents, like suicide bombers or the 9/11 hijackers, is a more traditional form of heroic self-sacrifice.

Heroes of Endurance

Suffering by itself keeps someone a victim, even if it is accepted voluntarily but especially if it is endured passively. But that suffering can be resisted, at least in mental attitude. Even heroes must frequently suffer, as that boosts our admiration for them. Victims can transcend their characterization through a spirited defense. Endurance is more active than survival is (Anishinaabe scholar Gerald Vizenor suggests the term "survivance.")[8]

William Miller contrasts the strengths of offense and of defense. One is "ineffably martial, confrontational." In contrast, "Defense's courage is different. It expands readily beyond its narrow martial confines to find ways to exercise itself usefully in wider settings in which it merges with virtues like perseverance, patience, forbearance, and constancy." Although he cites Socrates and Seneca, the early Christians were the true devotees of endurance, including large numbers of women, to whom the courage of the battlefield was prohibited. "The warrior is displaced by the martyr as the purest exemplar of courage, a courage that now means suffering with acceptance."[9]

A scholar of literature, Mary Beth Rose, also contrasts this heroics of endurance with the earlier heroics of action, pointing to the gender differences between them. They represent the choice between killing and dying, which plots onto power, morality, and activity dimensions. In the modern world, there are increasing doubts about the morality of reckless violence, and hence of warrior heroes. In early modern English literature Rose finds a valorization of everyday life that allows for heroes of endurance. These are not always women, but even the male heroes of endurance often disguise themselves as women. "The terms which constitute the heroics of endurance are precisely those terms used to construct the early modern idealization of women: patient suffering, mildness, humility, chastity, loyalty, and obedience."[10] (But not exclusively modern: Penelope fits the bill, waiting ten years for Odysseus and putting off her suitors by secretly unraveling her day's weaving each night.) Passive and weak, yet morally tough.

Endurance is a trait found even in some traditional heroes. Joseph Campbell identifies a "deluge hero" who does not go out looking for adventure and confrontation but has them forced upon him. "The deluge hero is a symbol of the germinal vitality of man surviving even the worst tides of catastrophe and sin."[11] Even standard heroes of myth often endure a long period, such as a childhood in the wilderness, in which survival against the odds is their only feat. The modern equivalent is the hero who overcomes humble beginnings to achieve greatness.

Heroes of example and heroes of endurance solve one of the challenges to heroism that we have pointed out several times: suspicions about the strong. They persuade us rather than coercing us. Heroes of example and endurance are strong, but not in ways that threaten physical harm to anyone else—although exemplary heroes such as saints can be annoyingly self-righteous. The types of strength that yield glory, whether physical might, military arms, money, or even intelligence, are all more frightening than the capacity to survive, endure, and inspire.

In some cases heroes of endurance become traditional heroes by seizing power. The most thrilling example is possibly Nelson Mandela, whose quarter-century in prison had prevented him from communicating with a broader public. On the outside his myth grew under the careful guidance of his ANC colleagues and international journalists. On the inside, he not only endured prison but grew into a better leader, capable of mediating conflicts among fellow prisoners, inspiring a loyal network, and developing a deeper wisdom and openness. As he withstood Robben Island, heroic character work on his behalf prepared him to lead a new South Africa.

Heroes of Resistance

Heroes of endurance can still fight wars, blurring the line between them and traditional military heroes. Modern wars of national liberation—"colonial wars" to the other side—took a bite out of traditional military glory. Guerilla freedom fighters can lose every battle (itself an outmoded concept) and yet win the war simply through their endurance: by being an elusive target, able to blend into the countryside because of support from local populations. These heroes of endurance can afford to lose far more men and women—and they inevitably do—because they typically have large populations from which to replace them.

George Washington's eight-year war against the British, the first great modern war of liberation, shows that heroes of endurance can be celebrated as traditional military victors. Washington lost six of the nine battles in which he commanded, nine itself being a surprisingly low number which shows that Washington's main strategy was simply to elude the British in order to keep his ragtag army together. In the last major campaign of the revolution, Nathanael Greene's strategy was to elude, divide, and exhaust the pursuing British under Cornwallis. Greene lost every pitched battle he fought but imposed heavy costs on the British each time, until Cornwallis' tired army portentously arrived at Yorktown.

The heroics of guerilla warfare have contributed to the decline of traditional heroes like Achilles. Peasants and farmers, poorly equipped although often intelligently led, are hardly the divine champions of epics. They are victorious precisely because they are ordinary folks, able to blend into the population when necessary. They are not born and bred as warriors, but turn to war out of necessity. Afterward, most become normal citizens again.

We quickly see the character work, the mythmaking, behind many of these farmer-guerilla narratives. Many, perhaps most, received more material support from allies, typically enemies of the colonial power. George Washington would not have won without the French; the North Vietnamese Army (NVA) supplied and fought alongside the Viet Cong. The Soviet

AK-47s proved more reliable than the new M16s that U.S. forces carried. Morale is not everything, except in character wars.

Heroes of endurance shade subtly into heroes of *resistance*, and so they fit well with contemporary images of power. Michel Foucault taught us that power extends into every interaction, into very local institutional settings such as families, schools, and hospitals, operating in subtle ways through how we feel and what we know, in addition to more traditional and obvious mechanisms such as a centralized sovereign barking orders. Power operates by commanding us, not only by forbidding: by constructing our worlds and our selves at the deepest possible levels. Revolutionaries who battled the State had a way of becoming the next Leviathan, and so political resistance has to take more subtle forms if it is to avoid that fate. In other words, heroes' traditional strength, especially in military forms, is today seen as a trap.[12]

Endurance and martyrdom are contrasting reactions to oppression; one is resistance by living, the other by dying. In one case you are available to take care of others, in the other you hope to live on as a symbol. Or to find glory in the afterlife: martyrdom makes more sense to those who believe they will be rewarded for their actions later. The gender differences are obvious but striking, with men often more interested in their own honor than in their survivors' welfare. There are other cultural differences. "It is easier for the West to tell stories of triumph than of death," writes one feminist. Speaking of the young Pakistani viciously left for dead by the Taliban, she says, "Malala survives and fits our idea of a hero. We are not used to heroes who die. . . . It makes us uncomfortable."[13]

Types of heroism can be combined. Mahatma Gandhi lived an exemplary anti-colonial life, invented paths of nonviolent resistance, which included the suffering of endurance, and in the end was martyred—although ironically in a different battle of religious conflict rather than colonialism. His tiny size made him more heroic, not less. With hunger strikes and other tactics of nonviolence he transformed passivity into activity. Characters whose apparent frailness is deceptive are perfect as heroes of endurance. In many ways Gandhi was unique; in other ways his form of heroism was simply puzzling to those accustomed to Western images of strength.

Everyday Heroes

If strength is easily seen as menacingly immoral, "little guys" are often portrayed as virtuous. A lack of innate strength does not prevent people from becoming heroes by relying on bravery and virtue—or "pluck"—rather than muscle power. We saw the example of Florence after the republic was saved in 1402. Social movements often adopt the same kind of character. Says Rob Benford about a civil disobedience training session in the 1980s, "tales about the effectiveness of nonviolent direct action . . . typically took the form of Goliath and David tales, recounting how 'ordinary people' such as Rosa Parks overcame insurmountable odds for the cause of peace and justice." She was portrayed as an ordinary person who was simply fed up with the injustices of Jim Crow, rather than the dedicated civil rights activist she in fact was. Her very normalcy suggested "an eventual victory of the forces of good against evil."[14]

Sociologist Randall Collins advocates a theory of emotional energy that suggests why people might follow weak heroes. Emotional energy—we might call it enthusiasm or excitement—comes from enjoyable, face-to-face interactions that leave people feeling good for hours, days, or months. Certain individuals, "energy stars," have high levels of emotional energy, awaken that energy in others, and are the center of attention in the interactions. Not surprisingly, they also tend to work at organizing future interactions. Because emotional energy makes us feel good, Collins believes it motivates a great deal of human action.

Heroes have high emotional energy: they are positive symbols, and people want to be near them to feel some of that emotional energy [EE], or charisma. "Dominant persons are not intrinsically heroes," Collins observes, "but . . . they often appear that way. Persons with lower amounts of EE are impressed by those who have accumulated a lot of it; such people have an EE-halo that makes them easy to admire. They are persons who get things done; they have an aura of success around them." People join their entourage, take orders from them, or simply admire them from afar.[15] Every social circle has its energy stars; they need not have the traditional trappings of heroes.

Our friends and coworkers can have some of those trappings. If the most admired heroes are dead, one reason is that the strongest, most traditional heroes are difficult to live with. It is easy for ordinary people to see the heroes' flaws, suffer from their pursuit of glory, and be harmed by their self-destructive quests. It is easier to portray them as heroes after they have left us. In today's world, everyday heroes are admired for their modesty, when they downplay their feats, refuse to take credit, and avoid bragging about what they have done. In a book about the heroic deeds of a mountain search-and-rescue team in Colorado, Jennifer Lois actually says that rescuers must be humble in order to be considered heroes: "they cannot self-identify as heroes; the title must be granted by others."[16] This partly reflects a contemporary American (and gendered) definition of niceness and gentleness as components of moral goodness. It also shows once again that it is more effective to let others do your character work for you.

These rescue heroes are created in a different rhetorical context than political characters: their fellow rescuers create and sustain their characters, aided by grateful victims and the occasional local news report. This more personal setting means that heroes must be pleasant to live and work with, and not "larger than life." In these cases there is no political machinery with an interest in exaggerating a hero's virtues and strengths. Even here, though, the raw materials of character work are familiar: in addition to the ability to change history (saving a life), Lois finds "three aspects of rescuers' heroism: their willingness to intervene in urgent situations; the acts they performed during the missions; and their exceptional individual characters."[17] They are brave, they are strong enough to pull off miracles, and they are inherently good people.

Traditional heroes fought valiant battles, defensive or aggressive, but helping others in more personal ways is another source of heroism, related to endurance. We ourselves bear sufferings and assaults, but we also help those around us endure them. A World War I memoir describes "a wisp of a man with a permanently troublesome knee," quite unpromising as a war hero. He has survived some of the worst fighting, yet "under the foulest conditions, his spirits have never flagged." Morale is an element of heroic confidence. Even more, "when, by all the laws of nature he ought to have dropped half-dead, he has appointed himself to the role of Florence Nightingale, and has not even left himself room to lie down. I cannot sleep for thinking of him."[18] Florence Nightingale (never just Nightingale) is the pure feminine type of a hero of endurance, showing bravery under battle not in order to inflict harm but to help those already harmed.

Participants in most social movements deploy a similar image of heroism as a series of small, everyday actions that help others. In the modern world movement organizers have become serious players in political arenas, not because they arrive at the gates on white horses but because they persuade others, pressure their legislators, promote new ways of seeing the world. As individuals, protestors are weak, but joined together in campaigns and rallies they attain considerable strength and attention. (Much as minions, on the other side of the moral boundary, become strong only when massed together.) As individuals they are supporters to heroes; massed together they *are* the hero.

Dilemmas of Victimhood

We can reformulate martyrdom, endurance, resistance, and everyday heroisms as a cluster of strategic dilemmas for those who need the sympathy victimhood brings but also need strength to carry on a battle. Nancy Whittier unravels these dilemmas for the survivors of child sexual abuse. At one extreme they can be portrayed as the victims they were as children, the preferred framing of many television talk shows: "The fortyish woman on television tells a horrific story. Her speech is halting and her vocabulary childlike as she recounts her experience of physical and sexual abuse, and she periodically cries. She is accompanied by her male therapist, who pats her arm comfortingly and explains the nature of her symptoms and the prevalence of child sexual abuse to the audience."[19] Television producers often give teddy bears to guests to encourage and signal this kind of regression to pure victim status, inviting therapists to interpret their experiences for them as the heroic experts.

But these are not children; they are adults, engaged in a movement to stop the kind of abuse that they once endured. They rally, march, and shout, wearing buttons that say "Proud Survivor" and conveying other images of strength. To do this they must be heroes, not victims. They must be "ex-victims." Whittier lists the emotional displays appropriate to each role: "the emotions of trauma which include grief, fear, shame, and helpless anger, and the emotions of resistance which include pride, happiness, love, safety or confidence, and righteous anger (that is, anger not associated with shame)."[20] Victims and heroes operate in different emotional tonalities. Victims are not simply more emotional than heroes, they have *different* emotions.

Activists "believe that the display of feelings of strength, pride, or anger is strategically stronger than the display of grief, pain, or fear. The emotions of trauma, they argue, suggest that people are permanently damaged by child sexual abuse and, ironically, ultimately contribute to perceptions of survivors as unreliable witnesses who are incapable of shaping policy on the issue. In contrast, they see the emotions of resistance as suggesting that people can recover from child sexual abuse and as encouraging survivors to mobilize in order to prevent others from being abused."[21] The victims transform themselves into heroes of endurance by surviving, and then into more traditional heroes by saving others.

Both victims and heroes wish to mobilize others, but in this case the victim mode is an effort to draw in professional experts—in the legal system, psychiatry, the media, foundations, and interest groups—who will then "own" the problem of child sexual abuse. The hero mode is a self-help approach to mobilize survivors themselves. Both are standard strategies for social movements, and this movement too tries to balance the two: "I think what we've kind of aimed for," says one activist, "is a bit of a balance between, like, 'We were totally victimized, and now we're almighty and powerful.' . . . A little bit of balance between what's really vulnerable in our movement and what's really strong about us."[22] Such character tradeoffs are not easy to negotiate.

Whittier gets at the limits of victim characters as players in politics. "Displays of pain evoke feelings of pity and horror in observers, which in turn reify the boundaries between people who have been sexually abused and others by suggesting that the pain and experience of child sexual abuse is so severe as to be incomparable to any other experience. By rendering child sexual abuse so horrific as to be outside everyday experience, displays of hurt make it easier to see abuse as a rare aberration rather than a widespread social problem." As a result, "feelings of pity and horror are not particularly conducive to mobilization."[23] To the extent that members of the movement adopt the victim role, they hand control over to psychologists, the hero-experts who are masters of an unemotional discourse supposedly based on scientific fact.

Victims then become *patients*. If attributions of blame settle on biology rather than social causes, if afflictions are seen as diseases rather than as offenses, character work is "medicalized." Doctors or other professionals become the keepers of the victims, the healers. The border between the political and the biological is no longer as obvious as it once seemed, thanks to a generation of social constructionists, but the apparent certainty of biology continues to have rhetorical appeal.

Mental illness is a good example. The National Alliance on Mental Illness insists: "Mental illnesses are medical conditions that disrupt a person's thinking, feeling, mood, ability to relate to others and daily functioning. Just as diabetes is a disorder of the pancreas, mental illnesses are medical conditions that often result in a diminished capacity for coping with the ordinary demands of life . . . . Mental illnesses can affect persons of any age, race, religion, or income. Mental illnesses are not the result of personal weakness, lack of character or poor upbringing. Mental illnesses are treatable." There is no one to blame for mental illness (NAMI was started by families of the mentally ill, who were especially eager to criticize models that blamed family dynamics). Patients are pure victims on the strength and activity dimensions (they are weak and passive), but the point of medicalization is to remove them from the moral dimension altogether. They are patients, not victims. There is no one to blame, because there is no moral offense. (Chapter 10 revisits this contemporary reworking of victims.)

Underdogs

One solution to the tension between heroism and victimhood has proven popular. Politicians, protest movements, and even nations frequently present themselves as underdogs in contentious contests in order to garner sympathy. If there are underdogs there must be an overdog: a powerful, frightening bully of a villain. Underdogs are good and weak, like victims, but they avoid becoming victims by being "scrappy." They win despite the odds. To a large extent, their success rests on their being extremely active instead of on being strong.

John Mearsheimer and Stephen Walt, in questioning the United States' unrelenting support for Israel, examine how Israeli apologists have built a moral case through decades of character work. Israel is democratic, surrounded by authoritarian regimes; it has held itself to high standards in war and diplomacy. Further, the story goes, the Jewish people have been victims in the past and so deserve considerable sympathy and aid.

Part of the case is also that Israel is small and weak compared to the Arab nations that surround and menace it. "Israel is often portrayed as weak and besieged, a Jewish David surrounded by a hostile Arab Goliath. This image has been carefully nurtured by Israeli leaders and sympathetic writers, but the opposite is closer to the truth." Even in the 1947–49 war, Mearsheimer and Walt argue, the Jewish forces outnumbered and vastly outgunned both the Palestinians and the armies of the five Arab states that invaded. Today, they say, "Israel is the strongest military power in the Middle East. Its conventional forces are far superior to its neighbors and it is the only state in the region with nuclear weapons." Yet the underdog character work continues, although with decreasing plausibility.[24]

This is not the full story, for a great deal of recent character work has been devoted to showing Israel as strong, even impregnable. In the world of spies, Mossad is often portrayed as the baddest of the bad, the most competent and secret of any nation's intelligence services. Israel's military victories have likewise burnished a legend of invincibility and power. Some underdogs are tough, not weaklings. Even more, Israel may be mutating from an underdog to a hero, with all the moral risks that involves.

As Machiavelli suggested, it is better to be strong than moral, it is better to be feared than loved.

Gendered Victims

The passivity and weakness of victims is easily tied to traditional expectations of women in most cultures. Jocelyn Hollander has shown how Americans attribute weakness and passivity to women, even in the face of contrary evidence. Women are seen as potential victims of men's violence, just as men are portrayed as potentially violent. "In everyday life, it is often impossible to tell from the outside appearances whether an unknown (or even a known) man may be aggressive. What is important to others around him—for example the woman walking past him on the street—is the cultural equation of masculinity with dangerousness."[25] Vulnerability—weakness and passivity—make one a potential victim. In their attributions, people tend to downplay women's active resistance in favor of our characterological stereotypes.

The traditional strengths of heroes and villains are extremely masculine; only the modern strength of endurance can easily accommodate women. Brute strength and martial success are thought to correlate with virility and penis size. This last trait would seem to have disappeared from the modern repertory of strengths, except for the 2016 U.S. presidential election, which saw Marco Rubio pointing to Donald Trump's small hands, while Trump bragged about his endowment and disparaged "little Rubio." Women can take on the moral trappings of heroes without such virility—perhaps more easily in the era of MeToo.

According to Jocelyn Viterna, the FMLN guerrillas in El Salvador were able to present themselves in a more moral light because they had women in their ranks (approximately one third of the guerrillas). Because men tend to be seen as violent by nature, an all-male force could have been dismissed as just a bunch of armed thugs. The cultural expectation that women are peaceful and passive meant that the women fighters were assumed to be driven by strong moral imperatives such as the protection of their children, their own honor, or sheer survival. Women's unaccustomed strength must be tempered (or explained) by high levels of morality. In the face of military assaults, heroes of endurance had to arm themselves.[26]

The FMLN also recruited women by suggesting that they would become victims—in particular of rape—if captured by the government's troops, a claim with some truth behind it. The FMLN would instead arm women so that they could gain strength, changing from victims to military heroes. After the civil war, Viterna says, these same women—now cast as strong heroes—had difficulty returning to gender-stereotyped civilian roles, due to an electoral majority who were eager to embrace traditional life after the trauma of war. Those who have assumed strong and active roles, even once, may have trouble claiming later that they are inherently weak and passive. Had they remained only heroes of endurance they would not have had this challenge.

The Mothers of the Plaza de Mayo in Argentina faced a similar dilemma. They were the perfect image of motherhood: previously apolitical, wearing headscarves, driven to action by their desperation over losing their children without even knowing what had happened to them. But by showing up weekly in the center of Buenos Aires they traded their passivity for activity. They retained some air of weakness, or else the regime would have felt its manhood threatened and retaliated more completely. But for some Argentines, passivity is an essential part of femininity, putting the Mothers' moral standing at risk. Observes Marguerite Guzman Bouvard, "Because the Mothers defy not only the Argentine political culture but also a society that still upholds the image of woman as homebound and submissive, disapproval is not unusual."[27]

The Mothers and the Junta engaged in two characterization battles: who were the Mothers, but also who were their children? To their mothers, the disappeared children were innocent victims of the regime, while the regime painted them as criminal and subversive villains. In one narrative the regime acted first, and arbitrarily; in the second the state was simply responding to aggression. In describing the systematic brutality of the state, the Mothers made the regime into the initial actor as well as an immoral one. The characterization of their children determined that of their mothers: if the disappeared children were innocent victims then their mothers were avenging heroes; if the children were criminals then their mothers were misguided minions.

Through their own actions—and their outrage—the Mothers came to feel their own strength, although this was often hard to admit because it rested on their being mothers (the source of their goodness). They also asserted their own human dignity, itself a source of strength. The regime tried hard to portray them as clownish minions. "As a tactic to isolate and weaken them the government deliberately ridiculed the women as an example to any group who might wish to oppose the regime. The carefully designed campaign labeled the Mothers as *las locas* (crazy women), effectively discouraging people from associating with them."[28]

Not only were they isolated, but the Mothers themselves were affected by such images, torn as they were between activism and motherhood (they were still responsible for husbands and other children). Many lived two lives: strong and active in one and weak and passive in the other. They carried some of the heroics of endurance with them: they could no longer save their children's lives, but they could still protect their children's reputations.

Women who move from victim to hero images remind us that virtue can—rhetorically—overcome weakness, especially in older character traditions that saw divine grace as a hero's source of strength. The child David could bring down the giant Goliath because God smiled on David's innocence (and on the chosen people he represented). Who is stronger than God? (Of course, this reward of strength for virtue may operate only in monotheistic traditions where God is both just and omnipotent.)

Delicacy—inevitably applied to women—can retard the transformation of a victim into a hero on both the strength and the moral dimensions. Under decades of military rule in Burma, Aung San Suu Kyi had little trouble winning the character struggle among most audiences, especially those in other countries. Journalists inevitably described her as delicate, a lady, "radiant as a lily," or a "Burmese Audrey Hepburn." In contrast, the generals were stupid, mediocre, crude, even "blubbery lipped."[29]

When Aung San Suu Kyi became leader of the opposition, a merely mortal politician, her reputation was a bit tarnished, as she could no longer appear to be so weak and delicate. Later, as "State Counselor," she proved tough indeed, and less and less moral as ethnic minorities were slaughtered on her watch. "We created a saint and the saint has become a politician," noted Kofi Annan, "and we don't like that."[30] We especially dislike it when politicians tolerate genocide.

The challenge for many women has been—and still is—to break out of the private sphere in order to play a role in the public. This is partly a move from passive to active, and partly from weak to strong. Women have had to learn to express their anger, an emotion associated with action and assertion. Their role as mothers often allows them to adopt the more heroic stance of protecting those who are even more vulnerable, whether they are fighting abortion or environmental hazards. In addition, "bound up in the strategic use of motherhood as a basis for activism is an ongoing concern with the reproductive consequences of toxic exposure."[31] In order to nurture children one must first create them. Because they are traditionally expected to be passive, women can put their apparent passivity to good use. They can make it a sign of moral goodness, following tradition. But they can also derive the confidence and stubbornness that give them the strength to endure.

A final example. Ileana Rodriguez claims that in Central America only men have the machismo to be heroes for a revolutionary movement, although strong women can be adopted as heroes by movements dominated by women, such as feminism.[32] Nonetheless, "The Uprising," a mural by Diego Rivera, features a heroic woman, solid and muscular, protecting a worker as well as a baby (Figure 9.2). This is not women's work, nor a movement primarily for and by women. This is active, not passive resistance, but it is protection rather than aggression. She is reacting to aggression, not starting it. At least one artist thought that women were appropriate heroes, although we cannot judge the mural's epidictic success.

As we saw in chapter 3, an oppressed social group usually tries to recast itself to be more heroic as part of its project of political assertion, but it may instead try to revise the definitions of what political heroes are like. While the broad women's movement has tried to reshape images of women to be less passive and weak, a subset of feminists—mostly intellectuals— have challenged what heroism is. They hope to extend the category in

FIGURE 9.2 Once again a woman is made strong by inhabiting a man's body, hiding her sexuality but allowing her to protect others.

ways that include heroes of endurance; in fact feminists were crucial in the rethinking of victims into survivors that we saw in chapter 8. In chapter 10 we will see that they helped to shift how we explain misfortune, moving toward trauma and away from traditional characters.

Victims who have been oppressed and injured can demand compassion merely as sentient beings deserving basic rights, but to be acknowledged as political subjects they need the strength to speak out, to be heard and seen and respected, to *matter* in strategic arenas. Victims must figure out how to retain sympathy while also crafting images of strength. We have looked at women's efforts to do this, but many other groups have faced the same challenge. Several new kinds of heroism have become available to them in the modern era.

Our basic public characters remain alive and well in today's world, and they appear regularly in the cultural work that goes on in strategic arenas everywhere, even with new media. But they have also changed. We see heroes of endurance, who would never have been admired in most warrior societies in history, just one way that women's challenges to traditional gender expectations have transformed all the main public characters. Heroes and villains have fewer supernatural powers than they used to. Victims have also changed, gaining their character from technological and other social problems unimagined or unacknowledged in the past. We turn, in the last chapter, to a number of other ways that the essentialism of character work is challenged, through various attitudes that range from medicalization and skepticism through cynicism and irony.

10 | Beyond Characters?

WHEN THE SENIOR AUTHOR OF this book was in kindergarten in the naïve world of 1962, the boys' favorite game was cowboys and Indians. The action was rigidly stereotyped. The boys would round up some compliant girls to play the settlers. Then a group of boys would come whooping in to torment them, in the role of nasty Indians. When all seemed lost, a larger group of boys would rush out of the capacious coat closet—the cavalry—and quickly subdue the Indians. The essential triad of villain, victim, and hero was played without irony or any sense of racism. No boys were willing to play the role of passive victim, leaving the wagon train in the girls' hands. But boys were often happy to play the villain, as making girls shriek was always a favorite pastime. But without a doubt, being the invincible cavalry was best.

This sensibility was about to change, fortunately. Through heroic acts of self-assertion, the American Indian Movement rejected villainous stereotypes and recaptured some of the Indians' warrior past, as one of many movements demanding rights and dignity. Some of those girls be-came feminists unwilling to put up with passive roles like that of victims, waiting to be saved by men on horseback. And more generally, many Americans and Europeans came to ridicule the flat characters of traditional stories, even in Westerns.

In movies the essential triad was already dissolving. In many films of the 1950s townsfolk had changed their moral valence from slightly good (victims) to slightly bad (minions), even while remaining weak. In the late 1960s heroes would lose their goodness even while remaining strong. In films like *Butch Cassidy and the Sundance Kid*, *True Grit*, or *Rio Bravo*, the gunslingers became professionals, hired to do a job at which they are very good. They are experts, often arriving as a group, and they are paid. The heroes and villains often merged, and audiences rooted for train

Public Characters. James M. Jasper, Michael P. Young, and Elke Zuern, Oxford University Press (2020) © Oxford University Press.
DOI: 10.1093/oso/9780190050047.001.0001

robbers Butch and Sundance, not the lawmen chasing them. (Butch and Sundance had a classic division of labor, with one having brains and the other deadly aim.)

For many filmgoers the turning point was 1966, when the Good, the Bad, and the Ugly competed to find $200,000 in buried Confederate gold. With their squinty eyes all three looked like villains, but even within that rubric they fractally echoed a hero (bounty hunter Blondie, played by Clint Eastwood), villain (ruthless Angel Eyes, Lee Van Cleef), and minion (comical, fast-talking Tuco, Eli Wallach). Since the money belonged to a government, and an evil one at that, there is no central victim, appropriate for the film's cynicism. But there are no real heroes either, and Blondie actually kills more people than Angel Eyes.

Cultural sensitivity and irony undermined faith in the supernatural powers once required of villains and heroes, trust in the earnest innocence of damsels in distress, even the plausibility of unfathomable evil. Strength and morality both grew more complicated. And yet we still have long-suffering heroes like Nelson Mandela and more hastily fabricated heroes like Viktor Orbán and Donald Trump, whose neo-nationalism remains grounded in the essential character triad. The world today is torn between those who mock the traditional characters and those who cling to them nostalgically. Both rely on classic public characters.

A Post-Heroic Era?

The decline of heroes began long before the 1960s, even if it took a great leap forward with that era's irreverence for authority. In Europe the driving force was the decline of traditional Christian faith in world history as a grand battle between good and evil. No characters had the strength of God or of Satan on their side; people were mere mortals going about their business in a mundane way. Liberal Christianity was about community and service, not about the Apocalypse. (Apocalyptic thinking went underground, but it did not disappear.)

Conservative thinker Robert Nisbet attributes the decline of heroes to new secular images of humanity in the nineteenth century, especially those proposed by Darwin, Marx, and later Freud. How could any character have a divine aura after these thinkers? And yet, Nisbet points out, the thinkers themselves self-consciously crafted several heroic attributes for themselves: unshakeable belief in their own superiority, denial of their predecessors except as prophets of their arrival, great books capable of functioning as sacred texts, exile or ostracism as they suffered for their originality, and finally, treacherous enemies and heretics. Their isolation from all but a small circle of true believers became a sign of their greatness, which could not derive from mere popularity (much as they craved this) but from some other world. With these modern intellectual heroes, it is the world of truth and no longer that of God that guarantees their superior status.[1]

In a study of the 1992 Rodney King riots, sociologist Ronald Jacobs shows that news media can erase the responsibility of characters through "tragic narratives." Journalists typically look for heroes: either the politicians who make decisions, direct resources, and fix problems, or sometimes the journalists themselves as heroes fighting for truth and justice. (The 2015 film *The Spotlight* and *The Post* from 2017 are examples.) When the jury found the police officers not guilty in the King beating, making obvious the wretched state of race relations in the United States, it was hard to find heroes since there were no accomplishments to boast of. "In a tragic narrative," says Jacobs, "the protagonist or hero ultimately fails in his or her mission, either because of the inevitability of fate or the violation of a moral law." Politicians lose their legitimacy. Jacobs intuits the two dimensions of heroes: in the case of failure, "either they are ineffective, or they are immoral." Narratives of tragic failure "encourage the audience to adopt a mood of resignation and somber isolation, an attitude which acts as a conservative brake against the potentially progressive belief that civic engagement and participation are worthwhile things."[2] Tragedy leaves victims but no heroes.

The nation-state partly replaced religion in the nineteenth century as the great creator of moral meaning. In periods of war, leaders have summoned collective identities using the most traditional tropes of heroes facing villains, as we saw in chapter 4. With World War I, the national heroes became the masses of men who died in the trenches, worshipped at new Tombs of the Unknown Soldier, first invented in France and Britain. Although all military cemeteries became places of pilgrimage after the war, the return and interment of unidentified remains became a supercharged ritual of national heroism. The whole nation had suffered—and for some countries triumphed—together, but these soldiers had done more than most. Pericles would have been proud of the epidictic oratory.[3]

For most audiences fascism discredited traditional hero tropes even while it gave the world powerful new images of villains and victims. To the nationalist idea of the nation itself as a hero (and sometimes as victim of treachery), fascists added a defense of dictatorship in the claim that one person could embody the entire nation, or at least the "true" nation. Their hero worship of il Duce and der Führer justified any and all actions by political parties that turned into massive criminal operations. Such is the power of character tropes. In reaction, European character work would tilt from heroes to victims in decades to come. In the charred moral landscapes of Europe after fascism, heroes could only be mocked (Figure 10.1).

Many national leaders, and the institutions they directed, lost considerable authority in the late twentieth century, as the postwar pact between capital and labor unraveled in the late '60s and '70s. For Americans, World War II was the last unambiguous war between evil and good; wars since then have been more controversial—and remained so even after their completion. The messianic, triumphalist vision of the American mission shrank to a minority of the public, even if one large enough to elect Trump. It has been joined by a tragic sensibility suited "for grappling with moral ambiguity and for engaging in reflective self-examination, even self-criticism."[4] Americans grapple with the ambiguities of Hiroshima and Nagasaki, not

FIGURE 10.1 East German Georg Baselitz (born 1938) painted this in 1966 as part of his series of ragged, bleeding, insecure "heroes" often set against a desolate landscape.

just the moral certainties of Pearl Harbor. Heroes are sometimes tarnished; villains not so completely evil; and victims not as innocent as they seem. Morality becomes complicated, full of dilemmas and tradeoffs.

We no longer believe in "great men," says Barry Schwartz, who cites a number of other institutional trends in the twentieth century that have been used to explain the decline of heroes: "the rise of analytic psychology, investigative journalism, deconstructive television and film, a new history emphasizing the achievements of ordinary people and the shortcomings of traditional heroes, fading nationalism, waning belief in the sacred, weakened tradition and authority, erosion of moral values, spreading of doubt, egoism, and cynicism, self-realization replacing commitment to the social good, and lack of critical challenges, including threats to the nation's existence."[5] Some of these proffered factors are more plausible than others, but they add up to a diminished respect for national leaders. War memorials replace commanders on horseback with long lists of those killed (Figure 10.2).

We occasionally invent new types of heroes, applying the epithet to "inventors, athletes, actors, politicians, and scientists." These are fine role

FIGURE 10.2 With the decline of narratives of national greatness, combat becomes a trauma; the dead are named but not glorified. These Romanians died fighting Nicolae Ceaușescu.

models, according to Philip Zimbardo and Zeno Franco, "but they do not demonstrate . . . bravery, fortitude, gallantry, and valor," the character traits that stirred past generations. We have moved away from admiration for warriors, but also for self-sacrifice.[6] Bush II mobilized America for his wars on the promise that no sacrifices would be needed.

Schwartz adds his own hypothesis, that increased democracy, tolerance, and respect for minority groups in the late twentieth century undermined the traditional myths of American history. "Nationalism, racism, and belief in the importance of great men are all rooted in the same social condition: a clearly bounded world in which the lines dividing nations, racial, class, and religious communities within nations, and individuals within communities, are clear and invidious."[7] A hierarchic order places great men at the top doing heroic deeds to which the rest of us must accommodate. They found nations, vanquish villains, and save victims. Since World War II, these narratives have become less plausible. Schwartz also points to an increased sympathy for victims in the new sensibility, displacing admiration for heroes.

The democratization of heroes has another side: skepticism about political leaders that comes from cynicism about government on the right and about political parties on the left. The great revolutions, led by Lenin, Mao, Che, and others, did not turn out as well as many had hoped. Even the progressive movements of the 1960s soured when their leaders turned into celebrities. Since the 1970s, protest movements of the left have self-consciously tried to avoid creating those prominent leaders. Building political parties can retard change, so resistance must be decentralized.

Schwartz was writing before Donald J. Trump revived nationalism, racism, and belief in great men, or at least emboldened those Americans who had never stopped thinking this way, the 26 percent of eligible voters who put him in office. Strong heroes remain plausible to many. It is hard to predict the direction of history.

The Risk Society

According to Akiko Hashimoto, Japanese collective memories of World War II grew less contentious in the 1970s. "Even if they disagreed on whom to designate as heroes, victims, and perpetrators, or how to remember Asian suffering inflicted by Japan during the war, they shared a memory of their own losses and could not deny the visible hardship that was around them."[8] Cultural trauma was shared by veterans and civilians, pacifists and militarists, left and right. A new form of suffering victimhood no longer required villains to blame or heroes to beseech. All were victims.

As audiences have grown aware of the complexities of modern life, it has become harder for them to direct blame for social problems at concrete characters. As Ulrich Beck, Anthony Giddens, and others have discussed, we tend today to attribute misfortunes to impersonal forces, especially large environmental and technological systems with complex risks that are difficult to understand. Although of human origin, these systems are more like impersonal forces of nature, which discourage the clear identification of victims or villains. The medicalization of villains and victims into patients is part of the same trend.

Blame has become diffused because we are more aware of the fragility of social action: those who initiate a course of action rarely see it turn out as they had hoped, and much of our action follows bureaucratic and technological routines rather than individuals' intentions. In discussing the kinds of stories that we tell about politics and policies, Deborah Stone distinguishes stories with intended or unintended consequences, and with actions that are either purposeful or unguided.[9] Only the purposeful actions that attain the intended outcomes are fully blameworthy or praiseworthy (assaults, oppression, conspiracies, but also policy programs that succeed, she reminds us), while at the opposite extreme the unguided actions with unintended outcomes are blameless acts of god or nature (earthquakes, storms, and—at least in modern societies—complex technological systems).

Stone's two mixed categories have correspondingly mixed forms of blame. Courts can pin down some responsibility for unintended outcomes through the category of negligence, and we more generally assign some blame for carelessness or omission. Unguided actions with intended consequences, such as machines doing their job or people who have been brainwashed to act like machines, allow some indirect blame of those who designed or trained them to start with. In such cases, few outcomes can be attributed directly to heroes or villains. Agency is diffused.

In *The Empire of Trauma* Didier Fassin and Richard Rechtman extend this idea of dispersed blame.[10] Looking at conditions such as posttraumatic stress disorder, responses to 9/11, and humanitarian psychiatry in war zones and occupied places like the West Bank, they see trauma as a new kind of character work that bears witness to a shared humanity. Thus U.S. veterans who did horrible things in Vietnam are suffering, just as their Vietnamese victims suffered. It need not be the same kind of pain. Not only survivors and their families, but everyone who watches a disaster on television, shares some of the collective trauma and deserves sympathy. No longer does a society deny soldiers' "shell shock" in order to preserve their military heroism. The idea of pre-existing character traits dissolves: anyone who experiences or even sees the same horrors will suffer. We are all circumstantial victims.

Jeff Alexander links cultural trauma to the basic construction of collective identities and moral visions. "However tortuous the trauma process, it allows collectivities to define new forms of moral responsibility and to redirect the course of political action." They do this in "a sociological process that defines a painful injury to the collectivity, establishes victims, attributes responsibility, and distributes the ideal and material consequences." Because responsibility can be defined as having *caused* the trauma or as the job of *fixing* it, the trauma process identifies the triad of villain-victim-hero.[11]

French sociologist Ewa Bogalska-Martin describes diverse types of victims in the public imagination, all of them enduring some kind of trauma: "those struck by violence, those subjected to prejudice, especially illegal prejudice, those suffering an injustice and, because of that, in pain."[12] We can imagine murky perpetrators behind this suffering, but the focus is on the psychic and physical pain that results, dogging victims forever.

We have seen that the passivity and weakness of victims makes it easier to place women in that role than men, and this continues with trauma victims. Even when claims of victimhood are the only language available for asserting a group's moral rectitude, men often resist the label, as we saw in the case of the Sikhs. When repressive regimes kill political activists, they create martyrs, not victims.

But the *families* of those killed can be portrayed as victims. In Northern Ireland, where more than three thousand people were killed in sectarian strife, a team of psychologists found widespread perceptions that everyone in the community was a victim, but also that the families of both the killed and the killers were victims. Individuals were reluctant to call *themselves* victims, however, despite some recognition that there might be legal and political benefits to doing so. "Group victimhood can be a powerful label, and it can bring support from powerful others and highlight the plight of the situation faced by the group, but for the individual the label victim is negative as it threatens their agency and masculinity." Once again, character work is better done by (or on behalf of) others.[13]

Families of deceased victims, themselves secondary victims of trauma, often "own" the rhetorical power of victimhood. They can pull off the trick of combining compassion for victims with the assertive agency of heroes, in that they are speaking *on behalf of* others. The judge in the murder trial of Michael Peterson felt constrained by the vociferous sisters of Peterson's alleged victim, who blocked any plea agreement for years, even after an investigator was shown to have fabricated evidence in the case. The widows and other family members of those killed in the World Trade Center had enormous influence over the memorials built there. Since at least Pericles, speaking for the dead offers enormous power.

There is a direct historical link between the tropes of trauma and the gendered heroics of endurance, because it was an alliance of feminists and psychologists, constructing domestic violence as a social problem, who developed much of the discourse of trauma. Those treating patients for child sexual abuse, especially using recovered memories, and those treating Vietnam veterans had common cause to promote diagnoses of post-traumatic stress disorder, or PTSD, which first appeared in the DSM-III in 1980. Perpetrators and victims (and audiences) suffered due to their shared humanity.[14]

Because modern victims often have legal paths of redress, there are elaborate, well-financed procedures for creating social categories of victims. Sociologist Stéphane Latté studied the creation of victims in the aftermath of the explosion of a chemical factory in Toulouse on September 21, 2001. There were 29 deaths and 2,500 serious injuries, and two thirds of the windows in the large city were destroyed. Insurance companies paid out two billion euros, providing big stakes to the legal definition of victims. Latté places this event in the broader emergence of a category of victim that combines victims of crime, of the Algerian War, and of environmental catastrophes—and which in 2004 led to the creation of the French Secretariat for the Rights of Victims.[15]

Latté makes a number of observations about the infrastructure of character definition. For one, the state—this being France—played an active role in financing certain types of associations of victims while marginalizing others. Organizations looking for reparations, and thus keeping victims in that sympathetic, passive role, were favored, while those more critical of capitalism, or which tried to transform victims into heroes, were undermined. The new ministry for victims' rights had its own agenda, to create a broad category of victim that authorized a variety of public interventions. Yet it lasted less than a year, a casualty of its own success at legitimating the category of victim: many other ministries adopted the same rationale for intervention, making the special ministry unnecessary. Victims became *clients* in several agencies.

Another major player, the medical and especially the psychiatric establishment, also saw an opportunity for expansion in the new categories of victims. By positing a distinct and shared state of trauma for victims of diverse events, and by gathering epidemiological evidence for it, biomedical specialists found yet another case for the "medicalization" of a number of social problems, and the transformation of victims into patients.

The construction of victims, according to Latté, also served the interests of protest groups and trade unions, which were able to mobilize a number of demonstrations, especially several silent, grieving marches. He implicitly relies on the rhetorical approach we utilize, arguing that, rather than the emotions of shock and grief leading directly to action, activist organizations were able to deploy grief as part of their activities. The emotions associated with victimhood, while strong, often lead to passivity rather than to action. It takes considerable organizing effort, often by established groups such as unions, to bring people into the streets. The rhetoric of victimhood demands certain kinds of actions—marching to commemorate the dead, giving witness of events, seeking legal compensation—rather than others. In many cases one group marches heroically on behalf of others, the passive (often deceased) victims.

Daniel Cefaï draws similar lessons from the vast research on disasters. Despite large differences in the pre-existing networks and organizations and in the official responses to catastrophes, "in the short run a suffering community emerges, with its own schemas for interacting, with a strong solidarity based on their shared experience and not on official statuses." They invent their own forms of self-help. Their solidarity, which tends to submerge previous cleavages, often persists through commemorations and organizations formed to press for aid. When official "humanitarian aid" eventually begins to flow from government and other organizations, Cefaï suggests, the displaced survivors are transformed from heroes in charge of their own fates into official victims.[16]

The same social and technological transformations that make us all victims may also be eroding the character of the villain. In an analysis of blame in the U.S. legal system, Nan Goodman finds a loss of any sense of individual human agency in cases involving product liability or toxic substances. In the late nineteenth century, agency was thought to reside in individuals who could be blamed for negligence. By the late twentieth century "the assumption is that agency is very often collectivized" because of the complexity of nuclear electric production or the creation and disposal of hazardous wastes, the effects of which may not be apparent for generations, long after the companies that produced them have disappeared. These may be tragic outcomes, but they are difficult to connect to individual characters who could be held responsible.[17]

Like Ronald Jacobs, sociologist Christina Simko notes an alternative to character-based moral plots, in the form of tragedy more appropriate to the danger society. Commemorations of 9/11 in Shanksville and at the Pentagon, she observes, follow the familiar script based on traditional characters: the crash sites have become battlefields where heroic first defenders sacrificed their lives for the cause of freedom, so that others might live. Since not all those killed made conscious decisions to sacrifice themselves, this discourse can also portray them as innocent victims, but they "did not die in vain." According to George W. Bush, their loss "moved a nation to action in a cause to defend innocent lives around the world."[18] Obama, Biden, and other political leaders did similar character work.

That is not the only possible 9/11 story. Commemorations at the World Trade Center largely avoid the villain-victim-hero triad by offering a tragic plot instead of a Manichean one. If Shanksville is referred to as a battlefield, the Trade Center is described as a burial ground, and participants tend to evoke grief and loss through literary references rather than heroism and sacrifice through political plots. "The tragic mode exhibits a subtle temporal structure," says Simko. One reviewer described the 9/11 Memorial Museum as "grief on a loop," with videos replaying the towers being struck, burning, and collapsing.[19] "In the early years, speakers focused on giving voice to suffering without attributing meaning to loss. Over time, the commemorations more frequently incorporated texts positing that suffering has meaning and encouraging hope or healing."[20] Even so, these speakers and texts rarely seek that meaning in world conflict; death and suffering are existential conditions, not calls to arms. Character work becomes unnecessary.

There are limits to the idea of a danger society. Even though we increasingly believe that there are hazards in all aspects of a modern life, this does not always return us to the fatalism of, say, a peasant or a fishing community. They accept acts of God and of nature as inevitable, but we continue to find players to blame. With our government acting as the responsible party of last resort, we have not entirely given up on victims or villains in our moral and legal dramas.

Normal and Abnormal

The concept of trauma reflects a modern rethinking of human subjects. We are today acutely aware of the processes by which people are characterized as "normal" or "abnormal," a twist on the moral dimension in the construction of characters. In the same process of psychologizing that assaulted flat characters in favor of round characters with deep inner lives, psychiatry, criminology, and other disciplines have created an aura of individual subjects who can be cajoled, shamed, and coerced into a variety of activities. Social control has been medicalized, as "diagnosis provides a cultural expression of what a given society is prepared to accept as normal and what it feels should be treated."[21]

Abnormality is an accomplishment of character work. Michel Foucault showed how judgments of character in the modern world have migrated inward away from actions and toward propensities, always the essence of character. Speaking of the character of the delinquent that emerged in the nineteenth century, Foucault says that expert psychiatric opinion aimed "to show how the individual already resembles his crime before he has committed it," through a series of acts that are not quite illegal. The series is not an illness, but rather a moral fault: "this series is proof of a form of conduct, a character, and an attitude that are moral effects while being neither, pathologically, illnesses nor, legally, offenses." Characters have become more important, not less, in his view, even if they are not quite the traditional public characters we have traced. The miscreant's desires, and not simply his actions, are bad, and he is punished for both. "Magistrates and jurors no longer face a legal subject, but an object: the object of a technology and knowledge of rectification, readaptation, reinsertion, and correction."[22]

With this concept of normal and abnormal, the moral dimension of character crowds out the others. Delinquents, masturbators, sexual deviants, and other monsters are dangerous because they pollute others, not because they are powerful. They are categorized as contagiously ill, not as villains. But they are not simple objects of scientific knowledge, as the emerging professions pretended; they are also public characters, perhaps a new twist on minions. The emergent professions were moral projects as much as intellectual or scientific ones.

Criminal law has long grappled with the line between making an action punishable and criminalizing a person's character. Racial-ethnic groups are stereotyped and treated differently; immigrants are distinguished by inherent traits (hardworking versus lazy and criminal). The U.S. Supreme

Court decided in *Robinson v. California* (1962) that Lawrence Robinson could not be jailed simply because he had track marks on his arms and admitted (possibly) to being an addict. In 1968, on the other hand, it ruled that public drunkenness was a behavior that could be punished. Public opinion no doubt sides with California, condemning addicts for their urges and not only for their actions. When addicts and others are recognized as having an illness, they no longer have agency and choice in the matter: they either step out of the character chart altogether, or they move from active to passive cells.

Foucault is clear about how abnormality replaced evil in the modern world. He interprets texts and institutions to show that, where Europeans had once acknowledged an existential battle between good and evil, around the renaissance they reduced this great conflict to a matter of the intentions of individuals. "The arena where the sacred and the profane had done battle vanished, and was replaced by a world where previously powerful symbols were reduced to the status of tell-tale signs betraying evil intent . . . . The day would come when the sole import of profanation and its tragic gestures was to serve as an indication of a pathological obsession."[23] Villains were replaced by people who suffered from mental illness, inflicted by error and confusion: impertinent, malevolent, perhaps even worthy of the term evil, but hardly the grand terrorists of religious myth.

Folk devils, we saw, are similar to the mob in being dangerous despite (or perhaps because of) their lack of intentionality. They are constructed as abnormal out of a society's fears and anxieties without usually being political players themselves. They are symbols, not creators, of society's melodramas. Says Stanley Cohen, "In the gallery of types that society erects to show its members which roles should be avoided and which should be emulated, these groups [mostly working class youth] have occupied a constant position as folk devils: visible reminders of what we should not be." Such delinquents can be hostile or menacing without quite rising (in the public's view) to the status of full human actors. Cohen emphasizes the character work behind folk devils: "Groups such as the Teddy Boys and the Mods and Rockers have been distinctive in being identified not just in terms of particular events (such as demonstrations) or particular disapproved forms of behavior (such as drug-taking or violence) but as distinguishable social types."[24] In other words by their characters, not their actions.

In moral panics a number of players see opportunities to advance their interests and ideals by exaggerating some threat. Police departments can increase their budgets; news media can increase sales; politicians can raise funds and secure votes; religious leaders can fill pews and feel self-righteous. These parties appeal to different but overlapping audiences, but in each case they construct minions who—in sufficient numbers—are threatening enough to add up to a collective villain.

Abnormal groups are threatening, if only to our complacent norms. Foucault discusses psychiatry's representation of madness in the nineteenth century as both an illness and a danger. This emerging profession "made the knowledge, prevention, and possible cure of mental illness function as an absolutely necessary form of social precaution against a number of fundamental dangers." Toward this end, he says, "the notion of degeneration provides a way of isolating, covering, and cutting out a zone of social danger while simultaneously giving it a pathological status as illness." The dimension of good and bad intentions disappears with the rise of "the normal," but the danger persists.[25] Villains have been humanized through modern medicalization, tamed into being mere minions, but without an evil agent behind them.

Foucault also suggests a close connection between minions and victims in the construction of the abnormal. The medical and the judicial discourses are joined, he says, by means of "the reactivation of what I would call elementary categories of morality that are attached to the notion of perversity; those, for example, of 'pride,' 'stubbornness,' nastiness,' and so on." Character work is unavoidable, especially if judicial judgments are required. This discourse can only be derisory, according to Foucault. At its kindest, it is "the discourse of parent to child, of the child's moralization." As in so many moral panics, children are both victims and potential perpetrators, depending on whether or not their socialization succeeds. A ten-year-old victim becomes a fifteen-year-old minion.[26]

Sinners are a Christian character related to the minion. They do wrong more out of weakness than malevolence, often tempted by true villains (the liquor interests, foreign purveyors of drugs or pornography, Satan himself).[27] They are capable of redemption, as their true inner selves are basically good, as long as they are not led astray. Addictions and other temptations have stripped them of their will. This was the early abolitionist view of most slaveholders: they were redeemable sinners whom the abolitionist might hope to convert.[28]

Emotionality

Morality, strength, activity, and normalcy are hardly the only tools that political players and the media use to create public character tropes. One of these other elements is the level of emotionality a person displays. Emotionality is a trait attributed to the weak, not the strong, to the passive not the active. Except for anger, emotionality is usually understood to undermine activity levels, in that the expression of emotion is often seen as an alternative to action. Emotions are a "safety valve" for energy that would otherwise have to find other outlets. They are thought to be "expressive" rather than instrumental, turned inward toward the self rather than outward toward other strategic players.

The supposed contrast between feeling and doing is thoroughly gendered, as the active-passive contrast is so strongly assigned to males and females. In social movements dominated by women, protestors are frequently dismissed as "bleeding hearts"; they in turn claim to be scientific and rational.

Julian Groves has described efforts by the animal rights movement to control this aspect of characterization. "Emotions don't win arguments," said one of his interviewees. Another contrasts activists with scientists, who "come across as the pinnacles of respectability, educated and rational people who are respected by society." Animal protectionists must mimic scientists' emotionless display. "We need to project a professional, well-educated, rational, non-emotional image in order to get our point across." Anger and outrage are necessary, but they must be linked to an intellectual justification. Thus philosophers were the "high priests" of the movement. Frequently, Groves found, protest groups selected men to be their spokespersons, hoping that they would come across as sober, strong, and unemotional.[29]

In affect-control terms, to be "emotional" typically undermines one's reputation for power: strength is associated with suppressing emotions, not expressing them. This is a highly gendered tradition as well. The exception is various kinds of anger, which are active, even aggressive, and so do not undermine power. Politicians are encouraged to express some emotions, such as indignation, but not others, such as sadness or depression. Men are allowed or encouraged to display anger more than women are.

Emotionality itself seems neutral on the evaluation dimension. Some emotions are good, and others possibly bad. But this depends on their display in appropriate or inappropriate settings. Hurt, frustration, and bitterness may be acceptable in family and romantic interactions, not in politics—but again, the reason they are inappropriate in politics is that they suggest weakness and passivity in a player.

Ironic Characters

When George W. Bush visited the Queen of England in 2003, several activists created the Clandestine Insurgent Rebel Clown Army to meet him (Figure 10.3). Armed with water pistols and feather dusters, dressed in camouflage and traditional clown costumes, with made-up faces, the clowns came to meet the president they considered the greatest fool of all, who had made up a fantasy story of weapons of mass destruction to justify the invasion of Iraq. Clown armies quickly sprouted throughout Europe, devoted to mocking heroes, villains, even victims, to undermining earnest practices of protest, to making police officers laugh while blocking and arresting them. And after arrest, the clowns produced so many odd objects from their deep pockets so as, once again, to undermine the entire proceeding. Authority dissipated. Ridicule ruled.[30]

In a cynical age, it is difficult to believe in the power or morality of heroes and easy to mock them into clown status. In nations with robust news media, it is precisely this muckraking role that makes them robust. Parodies, political cartoons, and caricatures are designed to help citizens challenge and question their leaders. They are a form of free speech especially crafted to amuse their audiences and annoy their targets. We are not supposed to bow reverently before authorities.

Disbelief in heroes presumably reaches its extreme in repressive nations where it is difficult to mock one's leaders in public. Political scientist Lisa

FIGURE 10.3 Satirists like the Clown Army can erode any claims to strength or morality.

Wedeen describes the cult of Syrian president Hafez al-Assad (1930–2000), not only the "father" and "first teacher" of his nation but also the "premier pharmacist" who "knows all things about all issues." Such exaggerations necessarily produce private irreverence, and yet the regime spent vast sums on this apparently empty character work. "Although people may not uniformly believe the cult's claims," she says, "they structure the images and vocabulary both for complying with the regime and for contesting it as well. Asad's cult, even when it is not believed, is thus a powerful, albeit ambiguous, mechanism of social control."[31] Character work mobilizes large numbers of people to be present for hero worship even when they are not worshipful—although there is always some risk that their real feelings may come out, as Romania's dictator Nicolae Ceauşescu discovered too late in 1989.

We have seen a number of trends that suggest the decline of public characters in political rhetoric. Heroes and villains have lost some of their religious aura. Individual warriors have given way to mass armies, although these often still represent the sacred nation. All of us are victims now, through a variety of traumas that afflict observers as well as direct players. Many modern governments display regret over past actions, rather than exclusively celebrating triumphs. Normalization and medicalization are less directly moral than villains and heroes are. The rediscovery of emotions in social science and popular writing, and their revaluation, suggest that we all have a variety of emotions. Fear is not confined to victims, confidence to heroes. And people, especially women, are no longer excluded from public life because they have emotions. Most of this adds up to a reassuring vision of progress, and it is no wonder that academics have embraced most of these developments. Which is why they were poorly prepared for their reversal in recent years.

The New Nationalism

Certain kinds of traditional characters may be out of fashion in parts of Europe, thanks to the Clown Armies and others. But in the world's two most powerful nations, the United States and China, heroes are thriving. In the Chinese media, we hear this character work on behalf of the president, in a widely circulated music video: "If you marry someone, marry someone like Uncle Xi; Swift and decisive, conscientious in everything he does."[32] Xi's heroic character prepared the way for his elevation to permanent president in 2018. Putin, Erdogan, and Orban have similar PR programs, pitting their heroism against a familiar litany of internal and external villains.

Heroic charisma persists, perhaps especially among those who retain some religious faith. Arlie Hochschild describes a Trump supporter in Louisiana, waiting for his hero to descend from his airplane in 2016. "To be *in the presence* of such a man!" She senses awe, reverence, even ecstasy. The fan expects great things from his hero, if not healing powers then the power to transform America, to make it great again.[33]

Drawing on the trauma literature, we saw, Christina Simko perceives a complex tragic sensibility that has emerged in American political culture alongside older good-evil narratives: Obama versus Bush II. Writing during the Obama presidency, she naturally thought this politics of regret was the future, despite the "enduring power of the anger, defiance, and desire for revenge that Bush's earliest speeches sought to evoke."[34] In fact, what we saw in 2016 was a repudiation by many voters of complexity, tragic dilemmas, and any acknowledgement of American guilt in world affairs. In Trump's neo-nationalism, he is the hero, and other world leaders are losers. The United States itself is heroic in some of his formulations, a vague entity that he can manipulate according to what he admires at the moment. Like classic fascist leaders, he *is* the nation, and his interests are our interests.

Trump's election was no accident. Around the world nationalism is reviving. With the generation of World War II almost entirely gone, politicians can revive some fascist tropes without disturbing their followers. Orban, Putin, and Trump are strong saviors of the nation, battling imagined villains such as immigrants, EU technocrats, liberal media, or the conspiracy of scientists promoting fluoridation and fears of global warming. Populist themes blame bankers, politicians, and of course minorities such as Jews and Muslims. We are far from a world free from the essentialist spins of character tropes. Because characters have a powerful effect.

The resurgent nationalism is in some ways a war over compassion. What do we owe to foreigners? Why should we care about the poor and other losers? The nationalists do not even feel they owe allegiance to proper legal procedures, or any respect and rights to their opponents, who are evil and deserve no mercy. Apocalyptic religious language lends the battle a sense of do-or-die urgency. Boys are mostly trained to lack sympathy for others, as a sign of weakness, and the new nationalism has a macho toughness that rejects compassion. Heroes and villains may be transformed into winners and losers, but the forces of hate continue to take them both seriously.

The historical perspective that has taken hold in the last two hundred years—the idea that people are different in successive periods—encourages skepticism about public characters and other efforts to ground politics in timeless morality. We have seen many other trends undermining traditional certainties about the powers of heroes and villains. Public characters have indeed been transformed, especially with the rise of heroes of endurance, but our awareness of that transformation need not lead to a rejection and cynicism toward any character work. Ignoring characters leaves secular folks at the mercy of religious and nationalist leaders who still unabashedly use the apocalyptic argot of moral struggles between heroes and villains. Leftists and secular humanists will be more successful politically if they name their own villains—and Donald Trump has proven a useful one for them.

Modern feelings about characters reflect our attitudes toward politics. Most citizens shirk their duties, avoid talking about politics, and view politicians with the utmost cynicism. Anti-political parties and movements, from Italy's Five Star to Spain's Podemos, from Zuccotti Park to Rio de Janeiro, reject the entire political system as deeply corrupted. They hope for an escape, in some cases into the arms of a would-be hero, in other cases into resignation. In many cases they have lost or rejected the language of heroes, villains, and victims, and to lose public characters is to lose the morality of politics. We can invent new words, but it will be difficult to develop a politics entirely free of public characters. Cynicism and irony are no basis for mobilization. Indignation, fear, and hatred of villains are powerful, perhaps unavoidable, tools for mobilizing people—for good as well as bad purposes. The decent, compassionate liberal-left has forgotten this to its detriment.

We will place irony in a longer tradition of humor in the appendix. Comedy is often used to disrupt the most potent character work and even the entire schemes of character, and it has been a core tool of orators throughout the history of rhetoric and images. We have seen it at work in a number of places, but because of its disruptive force we will segregate our main discussion of humor outside our main text. In the meantime, we conclude with the usual reflections on our book's implications, but also a brief dialogue with a scholar of narrative, sociologist Robert Zussman.

Conclusion

THE POLITICS OF BLAME

OST POLITICAL PLAYERS ARE AWARE of the fictional qualities of public characters even while they use them anyway to shape their audiences' common-sense understandings. In the United States, for instance, ACT UP joked about its own character work, beginning one 1991 meeting by announcing, "No hissing, except for the usual villains, who are not in the room at this time."[1] It was all right to have villains, so much so that it became a ritual. But they had to be elsewhere, distant targets whose feelings would not be hurt. Here, in ACT UP meetings, everyone is united despite numerous disagreements. ACT UP was always witty and playful. Not all character work is so lighthearted or capable of self-mockery. Some players believe wholeheartedly in the characters they create.

Our discussion of public characters offers lessons for how to understand culture more generally, especially in strategic settings. Cultural meaning is built out of tiny bits of information, out of sights and sounds and words that our minds put together into meaningful packages. We have emotions about these bundles. Public characters are a familiar example of such packages, but there are many others, from group identities to organizational plans to institutions such as marriage. Every instance combines familiar and novel bits to form unique examples of victims, say, or of marriages. Characters offer helpful examples of how these myriad combinations recur, in different contexts, sometimes fresh and startling and sometimes stale and forgettable.

Cultural sociologists and others have struggled with how to understand resonance: why some symbols and meanings grab us and others leave us cold. Part of their failure is due to their reliance on formal carriers—narratives, frames, and the like—rather than emotions in their explanations.

Public Characters. James M. Jasper, Michael P. Young, and Elke Zuern, Oxford University Press (2020) © Oxford University Press.
DOI: 10.1093/oso/9780190050047.001.0001

Part is due to the generality of their terms and their apparent reluctance to get into the minutiae of cultural meanings, especially visual meanings. Public characters help fill both gaps. They can be described in great detail, as can the emotions they arouse in audiences.

In coming to appreciate how people think, social scientists have concluded that, for most people, concrete cases and examples are more memorable and compelling than abstract statistics. A good story is better than a graph, an individual more gripping than a survey average. If you want people to donate to your charity, give them Malala, not facts and figures about women's status in various countries. Nothing encapsulates information better than simple characters, or makes it as gripping.

Another lesson for those who study culture is how public characters travel across different venues, appealing to different audiences. Our characters originated historically in fictional works—although fictional is not quite the word for epics and myths that purported to explain the origins of the universe, of royal lineages, of tribes and peoples. (And they appear to us to have arisen in these works only because these are the artifacts that have come down to us; the works themselves were no doubt part of broader epidictic projects: the *Aeneid* alongside ten thousand busts of Augustus mass produced and distributed across the Roman empire.)

Bits of the same characters appear in a number of strategic settings in which players and audiences try to take action, and the characters are adapted to each of those audiences. Cultural meanings such as characters are ammunition and opportunities to influence the world. They are complicated enough that some facets can remain familiar while others are novel. The sometimes-stunning creativity of new character tropes lies partly in their authors' attunement to new circumstances and surroundings.

This book has political implications, not simply intellectual or analytic implications. Public characters are an unavoidable part of morality and politics, helping us all work out our sense of right and wrong, admirable or shameful, serious and ridiculous. They are extremely useful forms of culture, handy for many tasks. But they are also frequently deceptive and dangerous. (What is handy for the deceiver is dangerous for the deceived.) Hatred and mistrust of icons and rhetoric are just as old as the products they attack, with good reason.

Exemplary characters can be a *part* of rich public debates—personifying facts and trends, reinforcing and transforming widespread feelings and intuitions, representing groups—or they can *substitute* for all that. This is the rhetorical anxiety in a nutshell. According to Kathleen Hall Jamieson and others, political oratory and public relations have been dumbed down to hot buttons that discourage analysis and solid evidence, a trend that reached its apogee with Donald J. Trump. By signaling (and simplifying) complicated arguments, characters and other tropes may discourage conversation and testing of those arguments, instead appealing directly to audiences' emotions.[2]

Robert Zussman, who reviewed this book for Oxford University Press, offered his own version of this critique, which we include here:

———

I love Public Characters. *Not least I love it because it's fun to read, something I would say about precious few other works of sociology, let alone sociology that is so relentlessly analytic. I love it for the range of examples, from Ancient Greece to Renaissance Italy to the comic books I grew up on to the Space Opera movies whose release I still eagerly await. Most importantly, I love it because it gives me a new set of tools for thinking about social life—about what happens when friends gossip and colleagues clash as well as about social movements, emotions, and cultural life more generally.*

I also disagree strongly with what I take to be a major premise of the book. I am altogether convinced that character construction is a major part of social and political life, that character construction is one of the ways we articulate and communicate fundamental values, that character construction evokes powerful emotions. I am not convinced, however, that any of this is inevitable and I am even less convinced that any of this is a good thing.

To be sure, the authors do acknowledge that character construction, in the words just above, is "frequently dangerous and deceptive." To be sure, there are occasional snipes at Presidents Bush (especially the younger) and Trump, against racists, anti-Semites, and charismatic leaders of what used to be called "totalitarian" states more generally. Fair enough. But very little of that tone persists in discussions of characters and movements the authors feel more sympathetic to or in the dominant tone of their book.

That dominant tone is much more positive. The authors of Public Characters *write, also just above, that characters can be "extremely useful forms of culture, handy for many tasks," that "exemplary characters can be a part of rich public debates—personifying facts and trends, reinforcing and transforming widespread feelings and intuitions, representing groups." Much of this makes good sense. Character construction can help mobilize supporters. It can help identify like-minded people. It can evoke emotions. But I am much less sure that it can contribute much to "rich public debates." I will own up that I sometimes feel tears welling up when I listen to Martin Luther King's "I Have a Dream" speech or Bob Dylan's rasping version of "Blowing in the Wind." I still cheer for Spiderman and Luke Skywalker. But this is not public debate and even comic books and Star Wars allow more nuance than we find in much political character construction. Spiderman and Luke Skywalker both have flaws, recurrent crises of confidence, moments of disbelief, temptations of self-interest. Similarly, villains are not pure evil, in the essentialist sense, but motivated characters, driven to villainy by lost love and failed ambitions, as shown in the endless origin stories of comic books, significant enough to justify the dreadful prequel of Star Wars, Parts I through III. In contrast, the pure hero and the pure villain actually preclude debate. If Mao or even Pol Pot is simply a villain, how can we appreciate that the disasters of the Great Leap Forward and the Khmer Rouge were driven by deeply egalitarian impulses? If the American Soldier is simply a hero, how can we make sense of My Lai or Abu Ghraib? Real debate requires complexity, tensions, and ambiguity. Real debate requires a lack of moral certainty. The construction of heroes and villains undermines all of that.*

The authors of Public Characters *wrote most of their manuscript before Trump's election and did most of their revisions in the first year of his presidency. I am writing one month into his third year, a day after his declaration of a "national emergency" on the border with Mexico. I have lived through more than two years of Trump's villainization of individuals (lyin' Hillary, crazy Bernie, "Pocahontas," and a long list of critics who are simply "disgraceful") as well as of whole categories of people (Mexican rapists, "shithole nations"). Trump has used virtually every technique of character construction outlined in* Public Characters *and done so more frequently and more intensely than any political figure in my memory. Has he been successful in evoking emotions from his supporters? Apparently so. Has he contributed to "rich public debate?" That seems much less likely. I do not count screaming matches on CNN or Fox News as "rich public debate." It is much more like professional wrestling (one of Trump's influences), with scripted heroes and villains playing out simple morality plays meant to reinforce the very biases its audience came to express.*

Efforts to find reason in political and social life have a long history— stretching from Plato through Hobbes to most economic thought and its extensions in contemporary rational choice "theory." As empirical descriptions, these efforts fall short and, in many cases, it is not clear that they were even meant descriptively. So too, many screeds

against "irrationality" in politics now sound badly dated, thinly dis-
guised objections to democratic movements and social change. Yet nei-
ther of these observations should discourage us from acknowledging the
dangers of emotions or the possibilities of reason, as an ideal if not a re-
ality. European fascism, far more than European liberalism, was based in
emotional appeals and simplifications, on the construction of heroes and
villains, built out of and intensifying racism and nationalism. So, too, con-
temporary rightwing populism, in Hungary, Turkey, Brazil, and the United
Kingdom as well as the United States and elsewhere, seems to depend
on the construction of a racial and national other as a villain. I may be
wrong but I would like to think that the most effective response is not the
construction of counter heroes and counter villains, not the recruitment of
minions and supporters, but reasoned debate that recognizes nuance, the
mix of interests, and the complexity of motives.

We cannot thank Robert enough for this succinct warning about the dangers of public characters. Let us end by addressing the three questions he raises. First, he agrees with us that characters are ubiquitous and influential in a variety of political, social, and artistic realms. How and why they are so effective is the primary topic of this book.

But he questions whether they are inevitable, at least in political arenas. As long as people talk to one another, recruit allies, endeavor to grab attention, offer moral vocabularies and visions, and endorse one course of action over others—and this is the stuff of politics—we suspect they will use public characters to do all these things. Our minds need shortcuts, mnemonic aids, and feelings to operate effectively, perhaps at all. For the three of us it is hard to imagine political discourses that lack any reference to individuals who embody what is admirable or despicable, who represent means that are weak or strong, courses of action that are passive or forceful. Political arguments lacking human characters and examples would look like the algorithms of a computer. Such approaches have had their proponents, but they have never been popular or genuinely attempted. It is hard to imagine what this "administration of things," a world without politics, would be based on: consensual values? utilitarian pleasures and pains?

If nothing else, "reasoned debate" may not be the best response to real villains. Writing during World War II, Ernst Cassirer worried about liberals' ability to understand and counter myths. "The political leaders of Weimar . . . completely failed to understand the character and the strength of the new weapon used against them. In their sober, empirical, 'matter of fact' way of thinking they had no eye for the dangerous explosive force contained in political myths."[3]

Whether the impossibility of avoiding characters is a good or a bad thing—Robert's third complaint—is more difficult to answer. Any tool can be put to good or to bad purposes, just as a hammer can be used in building a house or bashing in a skull. (This is different from a tool's effectiveness: we can disapprove of Trump's purpose in characterizing Mexicans as criminals, but acknowledge his ability to create or at least grasp such stereotypes.)

In Robert's view, the simplifications of characters are always bad for politics (although fine for films and pro wrestling). We agree that they are usually simplifications, a streamlining of meanings and feelings, but these may have their uses. They are satisfying to individual audience members: we thrill to Dr. King's speech and to his example; we love to hate Vladimir Putin; we enjoy laughing at *Saturday Night Live* renditions of Trump. Robert is right: these individual motivations do not necessarily add up to a healthy political debate. But they may help draw people into political action who would not otherwise be involved; even Trump has given voice to rural Americans who have felt excluded and disrespected.

In the end, our disagreement with Robert may boil down to the *inevitability* of harm when we deploy characters. They may entail some cognitive simplifications, as all symbols do, but their tight link to emotions helps motivate actions. Victims may arouse compassionate aid, heroes may encourage someone to vote and volunteer, villains may inspire the kind of moral outrage that stimulates good action as well as bad. Characters may inspire bad actions—the destruction of villains, the dehumanization of victims and minions, the granting of unhealthy authority to heroes—but also good ones. If they attract new players, adding new voices to public debate, that enriches it. If new groups are allowed to play powerful, active, good roles, that broadens democracy. Instead of following the long iconoclast tradition and condemning characters as a whole, we find it more useful to judge particular cases for their impact on human cooperation, capabilities, and compassion.

Robert downplays the contemplative use of characters. We think about them when we are forced to think about our own lives, seeking guidance. Around historical figures form many stories, many aspects and angles, many relationships that help us with our own complicated worlds. Endless biographies of George Washington or Abraham Lincoln do not make them less heroic—although biographers can try to debunk heroes too—but we learn new things about them that enrich our understanding not just of them but of the human world more generally: epidictic rhetoric.

This long book has shown that public characters are not so simple after all. There are many sources of strength, often at odds with each other, and often appealing to different audiences. Moralities also clash, complicating the question of who is a villain, who a hero; who is a minion, and who a victim. Character workers often try to simplify their creations, but they do not always succeed. Audiences remake characters according to their own complicated views and feelings. Public characters can be the beginning of feeling and thinking processes, not the end of them.

Whether public characters are deployed in beneficial or harmful ways, and there are plenty of cases of each, *understanding* those characters and the motivations behind them can only help us all. Deconstructing them may allow us to reject the distorted uses of characters and embrace the positive ones. If public characters are inevitable, we had *better* figure out ways to make them beneficial.

APPENDIX | Unsettling Humor

> In a world where everything is ridiculous, nothing can be ridiculed. You cannot unmask a mask.
>
> *—G. K. Chesterton*

ONE OF THE FUNNIEST MOVIES ever made, *Galaxy Quest* (1999), portrays a group of aging actors who cannot escape their roles in a 1970s low-budget television series with a cult following (*Star Trek*, in essence). They spend their days signing autographs at conventions and opening new stores at shopping malls ("by Grabthar's hammer, what a savings!" spits a contemptuous Alan Rickman). A naïve but technically advanced civilization from far, far away has seen rerun broadcasts of these heroes, ever triumphant, and invites them to help defeat a leathery green villain and his minions. Their own moral simplicity (perfect victims) has led to disastrous tactical results.

As only humor could show, these terrified actors—transported to outer space—grow into genuine heroes in large part because of the adulation and expectations of the adoring Thermians. Captain Quincy Taggart (a perfectly cast Tim Allen, playing actor Jason Nesmith) launches them on impossible missions that of course succeed. At one point he and Gwen DeMarco (Sigourney Weaver) must shut down a nuclear reactor programmed to blow up their ship. "Well Jason, *I* don't know how to shut down a nuclear reactor, and unless you took some Learning Annex course I don't know about, I'm pretty sure *you* don't know how to shut down a nuclear reactor!" And yet of course they do, with two tense seconds to spare.

Alan Rickman plays former Shakespearean Alexander Dane, who had been a Spock-like character in the series. In one scene he (with his own doting sidekick) saves dozens of Thermians from suffocation. The victims exclaim, "He has saved us!" But Dane is not the central hero of the story, and the chant immediately becomes "Captain Taggart has saved us!" Dane's expression changes from proud triumph to crestfallen exasperation, another occasion for his ongoing complaint that Jason stole Alexander's best lines, a pointed reminder that individual heroes, the leaders, are often credited for successful collective endeavors. One theme of the movie is the captain's final recognition that they are a unified team. "What kind of a captain would I be without my crew?" is midpoint along this arc: Nesmith is still the hero even as he needs his crew, but they are not yet equals. By the end, they are.

Only a fictional parody could lay bare the precise mechanisms by which public characters are created, laughing at them even while using them for the film's emotional impact. By the end we are no longer laughing at actors playing heroes; we are cheering them on as heroes.

Humor disrupts and unsettles. It surprises us with hidden meanings, prying open tiny cracks in our common sense, undermining how we understand the world. It inspires wonder and terror. To laugh is one of the greatest human pleasures, so we take the risks that humor poses to our worldviews and pieties in order to experience its convulsions. We forgive the clowns and satirists, sometimes even when they turn their wit against us (but we don't *always* forgive them). Humor picks apart the strands of meaning with which we build our worlds, including those that make up public character tropes. The observant comedian notices a glance or gesture that is a bit off, an incongruous name, a hesitation or false note in a performance. She pounces on these holes in our carefully defended realities. Parodies and satires point at the essential elements of characters, more accurately than cumbersome sociological analyses do. They can teach us a lot.[1]

Despite and because of its dangers, humor is one of the supreme tools of rhetoric. This is not merely because of the immediate pleasure it offers audiences. The right joke, hitting a carefully constructed character at its weak joint, can bring the whole edifice crashing down through an irreversible gestalt shift. A candidate switches from being a serious, heroic figure into the butt of jokes and caricatures. A snarling villain becomes a ridiculous minion. A joke that hits its target is the most efficient form of character work, whether visual or verbal, because it forever changes its audience's perceptions. A scandal can destroy a character's moral reputation, but a joke can devastate the moral *or* the strength dimension, quickly repositioning a public character.

This is similar to the ways that Aristotle and others have described epidictic rhetoric: aimed at general moral intuitions rather than at concrete outcomes such as votes or judicial decisions.[2] Aristotle, who also said that wit is educated insolence, reminds us that all epidictic rhetoric constructs not one but two characters: the orator as well as the person the orator is describing. In many cases, a character claim tells us *more* about the person making it. A particularly nasty jibe or joke rubs off on the subject as well as the object, as we saw: Chris Christie's attack on Marco Rubio as robotic crippled Rubio's presidential campaign in 2016, but it also destroyed Christie's own.

Comedy can be aimed not only at particular characters but at the entire system of characters. Because heroes and villains no longer have divine power, only its echoes, we are better prepared to view them with irony, ridicule, and other forms of distance. Audiences have always acknowledged these kinds of complexities, but they have many more media to reinforce that intricacy in the modern world. We are more aware that characters are fleeting, fragile, and tentative. Clowns have always been a part of character work, ready to poke fun at inflated reputations, but an ironic view of character has taken greater hold in the modern world, bringing doubts to the entire character scheme. The moral and the strength dimensions are both challenged. No one is all *that* good, no one is all *that* strong.

Humor's ability to bring the whole system of cultural meanings tumbling down is why we have (partly) segregated it here in a (mostly) safe appendix, including and excluding it from our discussions at the same time. We've allowed it a modest role in the main text, mostly in the form of a few qualifications here and there. We've deferred its full destabilizing force until now, when most readers have left us.

One distinction that runs through our discussion is that between *buffoons* and *satirists*. Buffoons such as fools and jesters are out for a laugh by any means, while satirists have a sharp moral ambition in their humor. Buffoons have no ambition to be political players, and no concern for their dignity. Satirists frequently attack others for their own strategic purposes. Satirists often try to advance themselves by demeaning others, in contrast to fools who expose the fragile plight of all humans.

Jesters

The first reference to a court jester dates to more than four thousand years ago, in Egypt of the Sixth Dynasty, and jesters have appeared in courtly settings around the world ever since. Perhaps emerging out of traveling troupes of actor-comedians, their purpose was to entertain, combining their trademark humor with doggerel and limericks, dancing, bawdy songs, juggling, slapstick, mime, and anything else to get a laugh. But their jokes could be quite pointed, because powerful monarchs, surrounded by sycophants, sometimes wish to hear—or at least can tolerate—the truth. Some fools were simple-minded, meant to be laughed *at* more than *with*, especially in the cruel courts of medieval Europe. But in most settings, the jesters were expected to give sharp advice and especially warn of missteps.

Unlike other courtiers, the fool had no wealth of his own that might give him some power: he was not eligible for more heroic or villainous roles. Dwarfs and hunchbacks were famously recruited as jesters, and not only because their appearance was callously amusing. Their deformities may have given them an alternative, perhaps jaundiced, view of regular human affairs. They were ineligible to play more powerful roles. Tyrion Lannister in *Game of Thrones* is no jester, but his diminutive stature made him the smartest—and funniest—character in the Seven Kingdoms.

At first glance the fool's wit would seem a kind of power. It could disrupt the order of things, place the powerful in a ridiculous position, uncover hidden nepotism and injustice, and at an extreme disrupt the plans of the rich and strong. But the fool's wit never gave him any benefit. He accumulated no land or wealth from it, and depended entirely on the favor of the monarch (which was frequently removed after a joke went too far: more than one jester was executed).

Jesters could not be powerful, but they were not exactly victims either. They might be beaten or mistreated, especially by those they mocked, but they seem to have had a foolhardy capacity to rebound from bad treatment. Their high activity levels made them more like survivors than passive victims. One commentator speaks of "the clown's irrepressible resistance to punishment, the vitality of an eternal victim who can never truly be overcome, disciplined, or confined." He accepts his weakness, but is not dispirited by it. "The beatings merely underscore his basic immunity and capacity to survive, even as they contribute to the violent reordering and revitalization that the clown engenders."[3] Pain and even death do not necessarily make clowns into victims.

Beatrice Otto, who has written a charming history of the court jester across many times and cultures, especially China's courts, observes an early modern shift in European attitudes toward fools (a broader category than jesters). In medieval times, fools were both God's simplest children and the Devil's own sinners: the best and the worst. Death was often portrayed as a fool, mocking worldly ambitions. With his *Praise of Folly* (1515), Erasmus used folly to purvey considerable humanist wisdom, so that "with the Renaissance some of the ambivalence toward the fool dissolved and judgment came down on his side." Otto notes, "A fool could also be anyone who did not conform to a particular set of norms—a category not limited to medieval notions, having existed in some totalitarian state psychiatric wards."[4]

Fools do anything for a laugh, carefully observing the flow of social life for cracks to exploit. They will mock themselves, others, and the social order itself. Comedy is always on the edge of going too far, of shocking people rather than amusing them, and it frequently goes over that edge. Rabelais gave us a great fictional portrait of the clown in Panurge: "Irreverent, libertine, self-indulgent, witty, clever, roguish, he is the fool as court jester, the fool as companion, the fool as goad to the wise and challenge to the virtuous, the fool as critic of the world."[5]

The fool's mockery has always appealed to humanists like Erasmus, in whose eyes we are all fools who deserve basic human sympathy. At the dawn of the modern age, Erasmus used irony to challenge the religious certitudes that were soon to ravage Europe, creating comic figures who even mocked their own mockery and thus took some of the moral sting out of comedy. His embrace of rhetoric, as opposed to the more logical theological disputation that had driven heresy trials, was part of this tolerance.[6]

Tricksters

The common mythical figure of the trickster also challenges accepted categories. This character, almost inevitably male, is nonetheless a boundary-crosser, according to Lewis Hyde, transcending and undermining distinctions such as "right and wrong, sacred and profane, clean and dirty, male and female, young and old, living and dead." He is not found in settled places, but on the road between them. This includes the path between heaven and earth, and if that boundary is supposed to be impassable, then the "trickster travels not as a messenger but as a thief, the one who steals from the gods the good things that humans need if they are to survive in this world," such as fire and agriculture. Through their very disruptions, they create culture.[7]

Hyde suggests why tricksters contain something of the hero, bringing fire and other good things to humans, and something of the villain, lying, cheating, and making trouble. Monotheism pits God against the Devil, with clear heroes of good against the proponents of evil. But the trickster is amoral, not immoral. "He embodies and enacts that large portion of our experience where good and evil are hopelessly intertwined," a complex experience that monotheism tends to downplay. Tricksters are common in the more intricate moral universe of polytheism, says Hyde.[8] If the trickster blurs the moral dimension, he also challenges the strength dimension, as he gets his way through weapons of the weak, not through trials of traditional male strength. Fairy tales are filled with characters who cleverly deceive others.

Wendy Griswold, on the other hand, links the Trickster and the Devil by pointing out that, despite centuries of Hebrew and Christian efforts, the Devil never became a figure of complete evil but remained "a bit of a wag," playing harmless tricks on people when he was not capturing their souls. The Devil and the Trickster, she says, are both "smart, energetic, lying, quick to take advantage of an opportunity."[9] Not exactly a villain, indeed not quite a public character at all.

Griswold scrutinizes the characters of late medieval and Jacobean drama, in particular tracing a line from the Vice character in morality and mystery plays to the new Gallant figure. Vice was minion to the Devil's villain, often portrayed as the Devil's apprentice or son, and usually more appealing and entertaining than the old man. Vice played both clown types, the buffoon and the satirist (Griswold uses these terms). He "appealed directly to the audience during the play, commenting on the action, soliciting their approval as well as their contributions, forcing their participation in the temptation being enacted." Vice was "less dignified, less powerful, wittier, and more inventive" than the Devil. The Gallant continued this tradition: always scheming, living off his wits, typically initiating the action, resorting to disguises and obscenities, and relying on cunning to take advantage of richer or stronger players. In morality plays Vice and the Devil were ultimately defeated, whereas in the emerging market society of four hundred years ago the Gallant's economic ambitions were often realized. He frequently became a respected member of society.[10]

Myths about the trickster usually begin with him wandering about aimlessly, something Americans celebrate today—being on the road—but which betokened insanity to most ancient peoples: another sign of the trickster's liminal status. He has "broken all his ties with man and society."[11] Like many clowns from literature, the trickster is inordinately concerned with feeding his belly and his lust, basic human concerns but hardly elevated pursuits. And like other clowns, the trickster has little shame, about his body or about the niceties of social life. He says things no one else will. A clown's shocking comments can unravel the little lies that keep a political order together, including its characters, or they can help reform that order.

Clowning Around

Clowns are hard to place in our character table. Some are malevolent, divided between feckless minions (with high-pitched, squeaking giggles) and more aggressive villains (with deeper, slower bursts of laughter, more mocking and sarcastic than mirthful). Others are well intentioned, aiming only to amuse others, and so they are in the same box as victims. And many clowns *are* victims, of pratfalls and of their own efforts to make others laugh; many present themselves as a hapless "everyman" victimized by life itself. But even if we can find several distinct places for them in the character table, they probably don't belong there at all because they are not typically epidictic products: no one in politics does character work to create a clown. The closest we see is the intentional making of ridiculous minions.

Most clowns are neither good nor bad: they are not earnest enough on the one hand, not threatening enough on the other. Funny heroes have been rare in history. Most are recent inventions, part of the prevailing tendency to downgrade heroes into normal folk rather than divine creations. Most villains, as well, are too serious to act the clown, Batman's nemesis the Joker notwithstanding. The Batman comics embrace a contemporary worldview that sees villains as less strong and so can allow them some humor. But of course, the Joker is not all that funny; Batman gets better comedic lines. (Neither villain nor hero takes his role very seriously.)[12]

As we suggested, clowns can deploy humor in a way that unsettles the character work that other players undertake. Donald Trump has a gift for pithy character assassination: Lyin' Ted Cruz; Little Rubio, Pocahontas, Little Rocket Man, Leakin' James Comey, Cryin' Chuck Schumer, and of course, fake news. A mocking epithet can stick fast, especially if it is funny or seems to get at a character truth. Heroes and villains are not as strong as they pretend. Victims are not so innocent, heroes not so good, and villains perhaps not so bad. Clowns can articulate a skeptical stance toward the very idea of characterization, whether by ridiculing the pretensions of strong or moral characters, or by showing that characterizations are only thin veneers over complex realities. Clowns show us the hazards of a naïve view toward the characters we encounter, and instead offer an ironic, irreverent, or simply silly view of the same players.

Heroism and victimhood themselves become ridiculous, hardly worth fighting for. Threats from particular villains become part of the existential human condition, which we can laugh at but not change. This deeper mockery, which does not take itself seriously enough to be called critique, unravels not only character work, but much of the motivation for doing politics. We lapse into cynicism, irony, fatalism, and black humor.

Sociologists Ronald Jacobs and Philip Smith see a narrative genre of Irony, as opposed to Romance, that helps to recognize difference and support tolerance in civil society. They suggest that these two genres have been institutionalized in different roles. The bard tells epic stories and legends that "link the social to the sacred sources of social order." They do not say this, but bards celebrate heroes. In contrast, "the jester's unpredictability embodies the disorder and contingency of the periphery, and his masks and tricks threaten stable categories and taken-for-granted knowledge." Satirical jesters offer wisdom as well as laughs. The medieval jester served much the same role as intellectuals today, they suggest.[13] Complexities and qualifications undermine the essentialism of most character work.

Humor is always dangerous. A sense of humor can undermine a character's moral weight and sometimes its image of strength. Victims are not supposed to joke about their plight, because this would lighten their burden. Heroes are not supposed to joke, because this might indicate that they are not taking their protective tasks seriously enough.

As a regular carrier of information, humor is a key tool for building characters. Jokes transform those who tell them and those they are told about. By making a cruel or snide comment, victims can regain some aura of agency at the expense of others, like prostitutes who tell each other anecdotes about their clients (sometimes in coded language right in front of the clients).[14] Jokes are a standard weapon of the weak, making gross inequities easier to bear. Yet even that small bit of power undermines a victim's moral standing.

Mockery of the pretensions of major political players who present themselves as heroes probably always exists, but most of the time it is hidden from sight. James Scott has described these kinds of jokes, gossip, and alternative views as "hidden transcripts" that make up part of the weapons of the weak. Those in nondemocratic political systems, who are subject to severe repression and surveillance, must resort to surreptitious forms of resistance, which can be denied when necessary. What the weak say about the strong (and sometimes about each other) is frequently intended to undermine the careful pretensions to strength and goodness that leaders claim.[15]

There is a robust (although not very entertaining) literature on political jokes, especially the humor of the former Soviet empire. Most of the jokes focus on the ineptitude of the autocrats and the broad absurdities of life under their rule, undermining the cheery narratives of national progress that the propagandists create. But even as such jokes ridicule the powerful, they often encourage a fatalistic resignation: what can we do except make cynical jokes?[16]

In political regimes that claim to be democratic, such jests can be broadcast more widely, although with varying degrees of freedom. In civil society, journalists and intellectuals can play something of the role of jesters in their critiques of accepted knowledge, as Jacobs and Smith indicate. In a very modern twist, serious newspapers and television newscasters report jokes from *Saturday Night Live* and late-night comedians.

Jokes are not always weapons of the weak; they can demonstrate how tough, clever, or cruel the joker is, through the power of words. Donald Trump creates an aura of strength by belittling his rivals. Humor can also have the opposite effect, in self-mockery that makes the teller appear less competent or powerful, more victim than perpetrator. (Some stand-up comics are self-deprecating, others are aggressive and angry, complaining about politicians or mocking their own audiences: very few manage to combine the two characters.)

Most human societies have recognized that some of the deepest truths can only be presented as paradoxes or jokes, and one of those truths is the folly of human endeavor. The most ambitious projects of both heroes and villains eventually turn to dust and ruin, like the legs of Ozymandias protruding from the sand. Certain roles have emerged for those able to pierce the falsities of courtly life or even everyday experience, allowing them to tell uncomfortable truths. Aristophanes, at the very birth of oratory, poked fun at it. In *The Clouds* he placed Socrates at the head of his academy, The Thoughtery, where inferior arguments win out over superior arguments through the tricks of rhetoric. The thinkers who are heroes to many turn out to be mischievous deceivers.

The clown tradition mocks the idea of a political player with a unified agenda, the claim of a public character to be exactly what she seems.[17] Collective identities are necessary for politics, but fraudulent as claims about reality. As *necessary fictions*, they are ripe for satire and critique.[18] Most political players dislike clowns because they don't like to be mocked by them. The earnest New Left detested the Hippies and Yippies, whom they considered apolitical clowns. But many groups have self-consciously adopted the label of clown as a deeper critique of a political system, as we saw in chapter 10.

We met the clown armies there, but plenty of other self-consciously humorous groups mock the essentialism of characters. In 2001 a group called Billionaires for Bush performed satiric street theater insulting the president's wealthy supporters. Laughter at the Lenin Shipyard in 1980 punctured the inflated reputations for strength that the Polish Communists had long sustained, helping create Solidarity. Authorities can look even more ridiculous when they try to suppress humor, like the Spanish judge who in 2016 jailed a puppet (or the protestor inside it) for carrying a banner, "Gora Alka-ETA," long live Alka-ETA, or Al-Qaeda-ETA. This sly reference to the government's tendency to blame all terrorism on the ETA ran into Spain's not-so-funny—yet ridiculous—gag law.[19]

In public discourse clowns can raise issues that many audiences find threatening. The pronounced American reversal in public attitudes toward gays and lesbians, from a prevalent homophobia to extensive acceptance, advanced greatly in 1990s television. Comedian Ellen DeGeneres, starring in her own sitcom (1994–1998), teased audiences with allusions to her sexual orientation for several seasons before finally coming out. A few rightwing watchdog groups protested, and ABC's parent, the Disney Company, decided to end the series, even though the coming-out episode was the most watched show of the entire series (it included Oprah Winfrey as Ellen's therapist). Don't feel sorry for Ellen: NBC picked up the *Ellen DeGeneres Show* in 2003, and it is still on the air.

Another comedian, Rosie O'Donnell, also titillated audiences with oblique jokes about her sexuality, but came out publicly only two months before *The Rosie O'Donnell Show* ended (1996–2002). Ellen and Rosie shared a humor style that was extremely nice as well as extremely funny, and both have had active careers since their pathbreaking shows. Then, from 1998 to 2006, NBC's *Will and Grace* featured not one but two gay men among the four central characters. Like *Ellen*, the show was funny, winning sixteen Emmy awards. Humor helped mainstream audiences entertain ideas before they explicitly accepted them.

In the end it is difficult and unsatisfying to distinguish between laughing at clowns and laughing with them, because they challenge the very categories that allow us to do either one. Humor is not easily contained or directed, and always threatens to get out of control. This layer of complexity, a reminder of the provisional nature of all character work, is a good caveat with which to end.

Because in the end the fool is us, the audience. A long comic tradition features a simple character who observes the madness around him, is often the victim of it, and sometimes comments on it: Goha or Everyman. In many tales he starts off as a put-upon victim, but manages to triumph in the final act, sometimes just by surviving. We can only hope.

NOTES

Introduction

1. Gary Alan Fine, *Difficult Reputations* (University of Chicago Press, 2001), 2. Also see Robert S. Jansen, "Resurrection and Appropriation: Reputational Trajectories, Memory Work, and the Political Use of Historical Figures," *American Journal of Sociology* 112 (2007):953–1007.

2. Alasdair MacIntyre, *After Virtue* (Notre Dame University Press, 1981), 29, 28. MacIntyre has difficulty seeing the emotional impact of characters, since his animus is directed against emotivism, in which morality is merely the expression of each person's own feelings. In his view emotions are inner, subjective feelings detached from immediate social context—a view we reject. On the difference between social roles, specific to institutions, and public characters, related to fundamental values, see George Arditi, "Role as a Cultural Concept," *Theory and Society* 16 (1993):565–591, who blames the slippage between the two concepts on Talcott Parsons, who "tried to tie the person to the most general levels of social organization" (573); for Parsons each role reflected society's basic moral values.

3. We would use the feminine for the third-person indefinite singular pronoun, except that this might be confusing in the many cases in which different characters interact with each other in our sentences. So most of the time we use the feminine for heroes and victims (partly because we often discuss how victims become heroes), the masculine for villains (why not?), and the plural for minions. The highly gendered nature of public characters is a challenge, in that the strong pair (heroes and villains) have traditionally been masculine, the good and weak characters (victims) feminine. But that is changing in the modern world. As authors we face our own rhetorical hero-victim dilemma (strong versus good?) in describing women.

4. Stéphane Latté distinguishes categorical and circumstantial victims in "Les 'Victimes': La Formation d'une Catégorie Sociale Improbable et ses Usages dans L'Action Collective," doctoral thesis, Ecole des Hautes Etudes en Sciences Sociales, Paris, 2008.

5. Aidan McGarry and James M. Jasper, eds., *The Identity Dilemma* (Temple University Press, 2015) plays out the idea that all collective identities are necessary fictions: necessary for mobilizing people to do politics, fictional in that the identities distort many individuals' feelings. Identities carry with them a number of benefits, costs, and risks. Character work carries many parallel dilemmas. When applied to groups, character work is a strand in the group's collective identity, bringing both advantages and disadvantages.

6. Philip M. Taylor, *Munitions of the Mind*, 3rd edn. (Manchester University Press, 2003).

7. On social movements, see Jasper, Michael P. Young, and Elke Zuern, "Character Work in Social Movements," *Theory and Society* 47 (2018):113–131. On trauma, Jeffrey C. Alexander, Ron Eyerman, Bernard Giesen, Neil J. Smelser, and Pyotr Sztompka, *Cultural Trauma and Collective Identity* (University of California Press, 2004); Didier Fassin and Richard Rechtman, *L'Empire du Traumatisme* (Flammarion, 2007), translated as *The Empire of Trauma* (Princeton University Press, 2009); Jeffrey Alexander, *Trauma* (Polity, 2012).

8. Intellectuals pose the powerful-allies dilemma for many movements: Walter Nicholls and Justus Uitermark, "Giving Voice," in James M. Jasper and Jan Willem Duyvendak, eds., *Players and Arenas* (Amsterdam University Press, 2015).

9. Susan Keith, "Forgetting the Last Big War," *American Behavioral Scientist* 56 (2012):204–222.

10. Hubert L. Dreyfus, "Heidegger on the Connection between Nihilism, Art, Technology, and Politics," in Charles Guignon, ed., *The Cambridge Companion to Heidegger* (Cambridge University Press, 1993), 298.

11. Charles Taylor, in *Sources of the Self* (Harvard University Press, 1989), traces the modern interiority of the self back to Christian thinkers such as Augustine.

12. A note on terms. Characters come in many forms, far beyond the basic public characters that we highlight. Any fictional protagonist is a character, even if she's not a hero, villain, victim, or minion. We use the word in both ways, and we trust that the context will make the difference clear. "Character" is also used to connote "moral fiber" in common language, although that is rarely of interest in this book.

13. Jane Tompkins, *West of Everything: The Inner Life of Westerns* (Oxford University Press, 1992), 39.

Chapter 1

1. As befits a play largely about an illegitimate son, *King John* contains marvelous language about personal and national identity, indeed language that creates such identities. See G. R. Hibbard, "From Dialectical Rhetoric to Metaphorical Thinking: *King John*," in *The Making of Shakespeare's Dramatic Poetry* (University of Toronto Press, 1981); and Barbara Hodgdon, "Fashioning Obedience," in *The End Crowns All* (Princeton University Press, 2014).

2. Scholars disagree about when *King John* was written: either 1590, merely two years after the Spanish Armada, or 1595–96. It may also have been first composed in the former year, then rewritten extensively in the latter years, as Harold Bloom believes (*Shakespeare: The Invention of the Human* [Penguin Putnam, 1998], 51).

3. Julia R. Dobrow and Calvin L. Gidney, "The Good, the Bad, and the Foreign: The Use of Dialect in Children's Animated Television," *Annals* 557 (1998):105–119.

4. Will Wright, *Sixguns and Society: A Structural Study of the Western* (University of California Press, 1975), 49–59.

5. Gérard Genette, *Figures of Literary Discourse* (Columbia University Press, 1982), 140. Classical forensic rhetoric had a specific place for a "narrative," namely the presentation of the basic facts of a case.

6. Perhaps the most thorough catalogue of the techniques that help a narrative "make sense" and appear to be a natural sequence is *S/Z* (Editions du Seuil, 1976), Roland Barthes' astounding book-length analysis of a "realist" story by Balzac.

7. In his *Poetics* Aristotle's dubious hierarchy of decreasing importance was plot, character, diction, thought, and finally song and spectacle.

8. Vladímir Propp, *Morphology of the Folktale*, 2nd edn. (University of Texas Press, 1928/1968), 21.

9. In the gendered world of Disney, princesses retain many passive, weak aspects, but they have been joined by fairies, led by Tinker Bell, with magical powers. Even the princesses are tougher and spunkier than they used to be.

10. Algirdas Julien Greimas, *Sémantique Structurale* (Larousse, 1966), and *Du Sens* (Seuil, 1970). Claude Bremond at least envisioned characters as initiators of functions rather than the other way around, in *La Logique du Récit* (Seuil, 1973), but he too remained a structuralist, deriving the universe of actions from an analysis of social roles, much as Pierre Bourdieu attributed habitus to structural positions. Although he does not discuss narrative, Martin Jay traces the "denigration of vision" in French structuralism and poststructuralism; the promotion of words over images supports the privileging of narrative over character: *Downcast Eyes* (University of California Press, 1993).

11. Cesare Segre, *Structures and Time: Narration, Poetry, Models* (University of Chicago Press, 1979), 34.

12. Deidre Shauna Lynch, *The Economy of Character: Novels, Market Culture, and the Business of Inner Meaning* (University of Chicago Press, 1998), 16. Lynch restores the third part of rhetorical analysis, the audience, to theories of character that had focused too much on the intent of the creator or on the message itself (the other two parts). History, to the structuralists, was no more than "capitalism" or "the subject," categories too gross to capture the historical changes and contexts that Lynch addresses.

13. Seymour Chatman, *Story and Discourse: Narrative Structure in Fiction and Film* (Cornell University Press, 1978), 126.

14. Percy Lubbock, *The Craft of Fiction* (Viking Press, 1957), 7.

15. Francesca Polletta, Monica Trigoso, Britni Adams, and Amanda Ebner, "The Limits of Plot," *American Journal of Cultural Sociology* 1 (2013):289–320.

16. E. M. Forster, *Aspects of the Novel* (E. Arnold, 1927).

17. James Wood, *How Fiction Works* (Farrar, Straus and Giroux, 2008), 128.

18. Robert Alter, *The Pleasures of Reading in an Ideological Age* (Simon and Schuster, 1989), 57–58, 51.

19. Tzvetan Todorov, *The Poetics of Prose* (University of Minnesota Press, 1977).

20. Not all character "development" is open-ended or complex: Christian spiritual narratives of seekers lay down a rigid path that must be followed toward enlightenment. In such cases "[d]evelopment is really a moral motif which functions much like a mythic

pattern or any traditional story line as a factor which limits the extent to which character can be explored for its own sake." Robert Scholes, James Phelan, and Robert Kellogg, *The Nature of Narrative*, rev. edn. (Oxford University Press, 2006), 169. Such narratives tend to be allegorical.

21. Wayne C. Booth, *The Rhetoric of Fiction* 2nd edn. (University of Chicago Press, 1983), 129, 131. Even Booth barely touches on character. In a much-reproduced treatise, Georges Polti catalogued plots and emphasized the emotions the audience was supposed to feel for each: *Les Trente-Six Situations Dramatiques* (Mercure de France, 1896). In a much-cited article on civil rights narratives, Francesca Polletta observes that the "dramatis personae" of these stories "expressed a set of appropriate emotions." From this she concludes that "narrative made 'real' the movement in a way that non-narrative 'facts' could not." See "'It Was Like A Fever . . .': Narrative and Identity in Social Protest," *Social Problems* 45 (1998), 148.

22. Freddie Blassie with Keith Elliot Greenberg, *Listen, You Pencil Neck Geeks* (Gallery Books, 2004).

23. Francesca Polletta et al., "The Sociology of Storytelling," *Annual Review of Sociology* 37 (2011), 110.

24. Stuart Hall called these three parts the "encoding," the code, and the "decoding" of messages, translating into semiotic jargon what had been pretty straightforward in rhetoric theory: "Encoding/Decoding," in Stuart Hall, Dorothy Hobson, Andrew Lowe, and Paul Willis, eds., *Culture, Media, Language* (Methuen, 1980).

25. Talmudic debate styles may have influenced the extremely adversarial style of Israeli politics: Shoshana Blum-Kulka, Menahem Blondheim, and Gonen Hacohen, "Traditions of Dispute: From Negotiations of Talmudic Texts to the Arena of Political Discourse in the Media," *Journal of Pragmatics* 34 (2001):1569–1594.

26. The traditional argument that only a good man can be a good orator conflates two definitions of good: morally good in the one case, technically expert in the latter. For a recent discussion see Michael S. Kochin, *Five Chapters on Rhetoric* (Pennsylvania State University Press, 2009), chap. 1.

27. This is not the place for a review of the sociology of scientific facts or the sociology of knowledge, but for one influential—and extremely rhetorical—study see Bruno Latour and Steve Woolgar, *Laboratory Life* (Sage, 1979). A more general demonstration that constructionism need not be subjectivism is Richard J. Bernstein, *Beyond Objectivism and Relativism* (University of Pennsylvania Press, 1983).

28. For a more general approach to arenas and audiences (or players), see Jasper, *Getting Your Way* (University of Chicago Press, 2006) and the introduction to James M. Jasper and Jan Willem Duyvendak, eds., *Players and Arenas* (Amsterdam University Press, 2015).

29. For a catalogue of emotions in social life: Jasper, *The Emotions of Protest* (University of Chicago Press, 2018).

30. Nicole Loraux, *L'Invention d'Athènes: Histoire de l'Oraison Funèbre dans la "Cité Classique"* (Editions de l'Ecole des Hautes Etudes en Sciences Sociales, 1981).

31. Wayne C. Booth, *The Rhetoric of Rhetoric* (Blackwell, 2004), 17.

32. Thucydides, *The Peloponnesian War* (Random House, 1951), 108. Over time, epidictic became more and more associated with literary displays, as did the study of rhetoric more generally. But recently a number of scholars have resurrected its use in

shaping political common sense and moral values. Celeste Michelle Condit emphasizes its ability to shape a sense of community in "The Functions of Epideictic: The Boston Massacre Orations as Exemplar," *Communication Quarterly* 33 (1985):284–299. Dale L. Sullivan makes a similar argument in "The Ethos of Epideictic Encounter," *Philosophy & Rhetoric* 26 (1993):113–133. Christine Oravec finds in Aristotle more than a form of entertainment, but also a moral, educational function in "'Observation' in Aristotle's Theory of Epideictic," *Philosophy & Rhetoric* 9 (1976):162–174.

33. Quintilian, *The Orator's Education*, Volume 1 (Harvard University Press, 2001), 291. On Congress, see Francesca Polletta, *It Was Like a Fever* (University of Chicago Press, 2006), 141–165.

34. See Jasper, *Getting Your Way*, on these three main families of strategy.

35. On the character work that social movements perform, see our article, "Character Work in Social Movements," and Charles Tilly's discussion of WUNC displays in *Contentious Performances* (Cambridge University Press, 2008)

36. Wendy Christensen and Myra Marx Ferree, studying the debates about whether the United States should invade Iraq, found that opinion pieces that carried out character work (containing ad hominem remarks, in their operationalization) gave fewer reasons behind the opinions. The authors assume that character work is not part of logical argumentation, reflecting longstanding suspicion about rhetoric. See their "Cowboy of the World? Gender Discourse and the Iraq War Debate," *Qualitative Sociology* 31 (2008):287–306.

37. Stephen F. Ostertag and David G. Ortiz, "The Battle over Meaning: Digitally Mediated Processes of Cultural Trauma and Repair in the Wake of Hurricane Katrina," *American Journal of Cultural Sociology* 1 (2013):186–220.

38. On theatrical anxiety see Jonas Barish, *The Anti-Theatrical Prejudice* (University of California Press, 1981). We'll examine image anxieties in chapter 2.

39. Jeffrey C. Alexander, *Performance and Power* (Polity Press, 2011); Jeffrey C. Alexander, Bernhard Giesen, and Jason L. Mast, eds., *Social Performance* (Cambridge University Press, 2006). In his own dramaturgical theory, Kenneth Burke used agent, act, agency, scene, and purpose to address questions of who, what, when, where, and why.

40. Alexander, *Performance and Power*, 24.

41. Jeffrey C. Alexander, *The Civil Sphere* (Oxford University Press, 2006), 57–58. He includes one other dimension of civil relations, critical versus deferential, that does not obviously align with heroes and villains.

42. Jeffrey C. Alexander, *The Performance of Politics* (Oxford University Press, 2010), 64, 67, 64.

43. Jean-Christophe Agnew, in a study of Tudor and Stuart England, stresses emerging markets as a source of anxieties over personal and social identities, forcing people to question "the nature of social identity, intentionality, accountability, transparency, and reciprocity in commodity transactions—the who, what, when, where, and why of exchange," *Worlds Apart: The Market and the Theater in Anglo-American Thought, 1550–1750* (Cambridge University Press, 1986), 9.

44. On Shakespeare's medieval influences, see Ruth Morse, Helen Cooper, and Peter Holland, eds., *Medieval Shakespeare* (Cambridge University Press, 2013). Robert Weimann sees the Bastard as a combination of Vice's bucolic humor and a modern humanistic hero's moral valor: "Mingling Vice and 'Worthiness' in *King John*,"

Shakespeare Studies 27 (1999):109–133. On the Bastard as a Garcio, Karen Oberer, *The Arc of Character: Medieval Stock Types in Shakespeare's English History Plays* (McGill University, 2011).

45. John Rudlin, *Commedia dell'Arte: An Actor's Handbook* (Routledge, 1994), 130. For visual images, see M. A. Katritzky, *The Art of Commedia* (Editions Rodopi, 2006).

46. Philip Smith, *Why War?* (University of Chicago Press, 2005), 21.

47. Molly Andrews, *Shaping History: Narratives of Political Change* (Cambridge University Press, 2007), 179.

48. Monika Fludernik, *Towards a "Natural" Narratology* (Routledge, 1996), 183.

Chapter 2

1. Jonathan I. Israel, *The Dutch Republic* (Oxford University Press, 1995), 256.

2. The three faiths share suspicion of idolatry, expressed in the biblical command-ment, "Thou shalt not make unto thyself any graven image, nor the likeness of anything that is in heaven above, or in the earth below, or that is in the water under the earth." Christians use images to instruct, to remember, and to inspire, but instruction and inspi-ration have often collided, with divine (and emotional) inspiration crowding out instruc-tion. As art historian Michael Baxandall puts it, "Idolatry was a standing preoccupation of theology: it was fully realized that simple people could easily confuse the image of di-vinity or sanctity with divinity or sanctity itself, and worship it: *Painting and Experience in Fifteenth Century Italy* (Oxford University Press, 1972), 42.

3. Juan de Zumárraga, quoted in Enrique Krauze, *Mexico, Biography of Power* (Harper-Collins, 1997), 34.

4. Especially Stuart Ewen, *All-Consuming Images* (Basic Books, 1988). In *PR!* (Basic Books, 1996), he excoriates AT&T for shifting its advertising "toward a more pictorial and impressionistic notion of persuasion . . . designed to evoke an essentially psychological response . . . [and to] trigger feelings above thought" (195–196). Not only images but all of psychology becomes suspect, the opposite of real thought. But the most notorious Marxist critique of the visual, the book that launched a thousand study groups, is Guy Debord's *The Society of the Spectacle* (Zone Books, 1967/1994): "the most ab-stract of the senses, and the most readily deceived, sight is naturally the most readily adaptable to present-day society's generalized abstraction" (p. 17).

5. Alain Besançon, *L'Image Interdite* (Arthème Fayard, 1994). *The Anti-Theatrical Prejudice* (University of California Press, 1981) that Jonas Barish recounts since Plato is also related to a suspicion of images as superficial and artificial. Jack Goody extends this line of analysis to relics and even fictional writing in *Representations and Contradictions: Ambivalence towards Images, Theatre, Fiction, Relics and Sexuality* (Blackwell, 1997). On the subtleties and vicissitudes of Muslim iconoclasm, especially reactions to the flood of images from the West in recent centuries, see Gilbert Beaugé and Jean-François Clément, eds., *L'image dans le Monde Arabe* (Editions CNRS, 1995). To be sure, many instances of iconoclasm are merely efforts by one group to clear the way for images that support its own beliefs and regime: a fear of opposed images, not of all images.

6. Richard Turner, *La Renaissance à Florence* (Flammarion, 2008), 165. Although we concentrate here on Florence's hero tropes, it and other Italian towns also had stylized

ways to portray villains through *immagini infamanti*: murals of criminals and political opponents hanging upside down by one foot. These were used in place of trials for evildoers who had fled justice.

7. Chandra Mukerji, *Territorial Ambitions and the Gardens of Versailles* (Cambridge University Press, 1997), 319: "France and the king were manufactured together on the battlefield, in the world of fashion, in scholarly debates between Ancients and Moderns, and in the Observatory where the problem of locating France cartographically was discussed. This whole material approach to power was more than a matter of propaganda. It was a political strategy with multiple sites and myriad local consequences."

8. Lynn Hunt, *Politics, Culture, and Class in the French Revolution* (University of California Press, 1984), 104. Parisian crowds contained more women than the revolutionary leaders thought proper. "Crowd theorists" such as Gustav Le Bon have often considered mobs to be feminine in their supposed emotionality and suggestibility. Lenin launched a similar program of sculptural heroes (along with many, many posters) after the Russian revolution: Victoria E. Bonnell, *Iconography of Power* (University of California Press, 1997).

9. E. H. Gombrich, *Art and Illusion: A Study in the Psychology of Pictorial Representation* (Princeton University Press, 1960), 349.

10. The Counter-Reformation involved one of the great explosions of art and architecture in history, with painters such as Titian, Rubens, Bernini, and hundreds of others vying to fill the new Baroque churches with their masterpieces: a colossal piece of character work on behalf of the popes and the Catholic Church.

11. Sir Joshua Reynolds, *Discourses on Art* (Yale University Press, 1797/1975), 61.

12. In the nineteenth century, Honoré Daumier's tiny satirical busts of the public figures of his day would seem to be an exception to the rule that only heroes are worthy of sculpture. The giant noses, sleepy eyes, and improbable hairstyles of these characters are anything but heroic. Only inches tall, they were meant to amuse, not glorify. But it turns out that most of these were not final epidictic products. The series from the 1830s known as the "Celebrities of the Juste Milieu" were meant to be models for Daumier's own lithographs in two satirical monthly magazines, where the purpose was mocking amusement, not glorification.

13. Lynch, *The Economy of Character*, 28, 10.

14. Afaf Lutfi Al-Sayyid Marsot, "The Cartoon in Egypt," *Comparative Studies in Society and History* 13 (1971), 2.

15. Examples from Nancy Macdonald, *The Subculture* (Palgrave, 2001), who observes that most of the names "communicate notions of strength, power and control" (198). Most analyses of graffiti are, like this one, about the internal dynamics of the subculture rather than about their impact on external audiences. For a more political take, see Guillaume Marche, "Expressivism and Resistance: Graffiti as an Infrapolitical Form of Protest against the War on Terror," *Revue Française d'Etudes Américaines* 131 (2012):78–96.

16. Lushly illustrated histories of the poster include John Barnicoat, *Posters* (Thames and Hudson, 1972), Max Gallo, *The Poster in History* (W. W. Norton, 1974), and Jeffrey T. Schnapp, *Revolutionary Tides* (Skira, 2005).

17. Erving Goffman, *Gender Advertisements* (Harper Colophon, 1979).

18. Goffman, *Gender Advertisements*, 7.

19. Goffman, *Gender Advertisements*, 7.

20. Goffman, *Gender Advertisements*, 48–51.

21. Goffman, *Gender Advertisements*, 29, 5.

22. Goffman, *Gender Advertisements*, 45, 46.

23. Goffman, *Gender Advertisements*, 57.

24. Jonathan H. Turner, "Toward a General Sociological Theory of Emotions," *Journal for the Theory of Social Behaviour* 29 (1999), 138. One need not accept his evolutionary theory or his claim that the visual is primary in order to recognize that the visual is not given the attention it deserves. Amusingly, in a good recent book of cultural sociology that tries to analyze visual meaning, out of the sixteen contributions, three contain a single image, one chapter presents eight images, and the rest have none at all: Jeffrey C. Alexander, Dominik Bartmanski, and Bernhard Giesen, eds., *Iconic Power: Materiality and Meaning in Social Life* (Palgrave Macmillan, 2012). The ubiquity of PowerPoint should be changing academic attitudes toward the visual, although far too many PowerPoint slides merely present words!

25. Cynthia Hahn, *Portrayed on the Heart: Narrative Effect in Pictorial Lives of Saints from the Tenth through the Thirteenth Centuries* (University of California Press, 2001), 95.

26. T. V. Reed examines a number of these in *The Art of Protest* (University of Minnesota Press, 2005), although he follows scholarly fashion by extracting the ideas from his many media rather than looking at how the media convey their messages visually. At least he does provide 18 images.

27. Rens Vliegenthart, "The Professionalization of Political Communication? A Longitudinal Analysis of Dutch Election Campaign Posters," *American Behavioral Scientist* 56 (2012):135–150.

28. For a complicating view of what animals symbolize, based on Jungian psychology and including a long discussion of serpents, see Barbara Hannah, *The Archetypal Symbolism of Animals* (Chiron Publications, 2006).

29. William Ian Miller, *The Mystery of Courage* (Harvard University Press, 2000), 185, 186. Fat men, he also notes, are morally suspect because we imagine that they place their gluttony above moral ends. Except when they are also tall, and thereby become "big" men, capable of moral heroics that short fat men apparently are not (189).

30. J. Anthony Lukas, *Big Trouble* (Simon and Schuster, 1997), 221. "Yet there was something in the heft of those meaty shoulders, in the fierce blaze of that single eye," comments Lukas, "that made him seem to loom over mere mortals." Most heroes do.

31. Anne-Marie Lecoq, "The Symbolism of the State," in Pierre Nora, *Rethinking France: Les Lieux de Mémoire* (University of Chicago Press, 2001), 255.

32. Quoted in James M. Jasper and Dorothy Nelkin, *The Animal Rights Crusade* (Free Press, 1992), 72.

33. Stephen Rogers Peck, *Atlas of Facial Expression* (Oxford University Press, 1987). On emotions in politics see Jasper, *The Emotions of Protest*.

34. Theodore D. Kemper, *A Social Interactional Theory of Emotions* (Wiley, 1978).

35. Ennio Morricone and Sergio Miceli, *Composing for the Cinema* (Scarecrow Press, 2013), 78, 102.

36. Alfred Brendel, *Musical Thoughts and Afterthoughts* (Princeton, 1976), 83.

37. Quoted in Roger Manvell and John Huntley, *The Technique of Film Music* (Hastings House, 1975), 90. Books on film music tend to ignore the construction of characters in favor of larger structural issues of composition or production techniques.

38. François-Xavier Yvart catalogues the emotional impacts of various combinations of mode, tempo, pitch, rhythm, harmony, and volume: cited in Johanna Siméant and Christophe Traïni, *Bodies in Protest* (Amsterdam University Press, 2016), 106.

39. Jeff Rona, discussing the music he composed for *White Squall* in *The Reel World*, 2nd edn. (Hal Leonard Books, 2009), 22. See Annabel J. Cohen, "Music as a Source of Emotion in Film," in Patrik N. Juslin and John A. Sloboda, eds., *Handbook of Music and Emotion* (Oxford University Press, 2001). The handbook is a good introduction to the literature on music's unique ability to engage our emotions.

40. Sonny Kompanek, *From Score to Screen* (Schirmer, 2004), 58.

41. Hanns Eisler, *Composing for the Films* (Oxford University Press, 1947), 24. Eisler's book is mostly a brief for using twelve-tone and other modernist music in movies. A collaborator of Brecht's, he was expelled from the U.S. in 1948 and lived until 1962 in East Berlin.

42. Eisler, *Composing*, 24.

Chapter 3

1. Richard E. Nisbett and Timothy D. Wilson, "The Halo Effect: Evidence for Unconscious Alteration of Judgments," *Journal of Personality and Social Psychology* 35 (1977):250–256.

2. Daniel T. Gilbert, "Ordinary Personology," in Daniel T. Gilbert, Susan T. Fiske, and Gardner Lindzey, eds., *The Handbook of Social Psychology*, 4th edn. (McGraw-Hill, 1998), 89. This is an amusing review essay, upon which we rely heavily in this section.

3. Solomon E. Asch, "Effects of Group Pressure on the Modification and Distortion of Judgments," in Harold Guetzkow, ed., *Groups, Leadership, and Men* (Carnegie Press, 1951).

4. Solomon E. Asch, "Forming Impressions of Personality," *Journal of Abnormal and Social Psychology* 41 (1946), 284. It is a sign of how far cognitive psychology has advanced, in a healthy Gestalt shift, that abnormal and social psychology are no longer lumped together.

5. Fritz Heider, *The Psychology of Interpersonal Relations* (Wiley, 1958), 53.

6. We look for covariance of variables, to be precise: Harold H. Kelley, "Attribution Theory in Social Psychology," in David Levine, ed., *Nebraska Symposium on Motivation* 15 (1967):192–238.

7. On the training, discipline, and competence that keep wildland firefighters alive, see Matthew Desmond, *On the Fireline* (University of Chicago Press, 2009).

8. Lee Ross dubbed this the fundamental attribution error, but in our view there is no reason to rank-order cognitive biases, or to insist on a clear distinction between correct and incorrect modes of thinking: Lee Ross, "The Intuitive Psychologist and His Shortcomings: Distortions in the Attribution Process," in Leonard Berkowitz, ed., *Advances in Experimental Social Psychology* 10 (Academic Press, 1977):173–220. Research shows that more individualistic cultures like that of the United States encourage

more of this attribution effect: Michael W. Morris and Kaiping Peng, "Culture and Cause: American and Chinese Attributions for Social and Physical Events," *Journal of Personality and Social Psychology* 67 (1994):949–971.

9. E. Tory Higgins, William S. Rholes, and Carl R. Jones. "Category Accessibility and Impression Formation," *Journal of Experimental Social Psychology* 13 (1977):141–154.

10. Janine Willis and Alexander Todorov, "First Impressions: Making Up Your Mind After a 100-ms Exposure to a Face," *Psychological Science* 17 (2006):592–598.

11. For example Jerry S. Wiggins, "A Psychological Taxonomy of Trait Descriptive Terms: The Interpersonal Domain," *Journal of Personality and Social Psychology* 27 (1979):395–412.

12. Gilbert, "Ordinary Personology," 109.

13. Gilbert, again, summarizes the kinds of biases people make in their thinking, including their thinking about others ("Ordinary Personology," pp. 120–127). One is *idealism*: we have pre-existing ideas about what we are going to see, and we tend to see what we expect. Another is *egotism*: we often see what we want to see, an effect that is closely related to idealism. Learning is not neutral, but guided by our own values and desires. *Realism* is a third bias: the lack of awareness of our other biases and hence an inability to compensate for them. *Circumstantialism* is Gilbert's name for a fourth bias: we use whatever information comes to mind quickly and easily, ignoring information that might be better but is harder to retrieve. We may be drawing inferences from the wrong information. All these biases lead us to resist new information if it does not fit our current views.

14. Phil Rosenzweig, *The Halo Effect . . . and the Eight Other Business Delusions that Deceive Managers* (Free Press, 2007); also Rakesh Khurana, *Searching for a Corporate Savior* (Princeton University Press, 2002). We will examine this elevation of CEOs further in chapter 4.

15. Daniel T. Gilbert, Brett W. Pelham, and Douglas S. Krull, "On Cognitive Busyness: When Person Perceivers Meet Persons Perceived," *Journal of Personality and Social Psychology* 54 (1988):733–740. Also see Norman H. Anderson and Arthur J. Farkas, "New Light on Order Effects in Attitude Change," *Journal of Personality and Social Psychology* (1973):88–93.

16. Alexander Todorov, Anesu N. Mandisodza, Amir Goren, and Crystal C. Hall, "Inferences of Competence from Faces Predict Election Outcomes," *Science* 308 (2005):1623–1626. Also Nikolaas N. Oosterhof and Alexander Todorov, "The Functional Basis of Face Evaluation," *Proceedings of the National Academy of Sciences* 105 (2008):11087–11092; Janine Willis and Alexander Todorov, "First Impressions," *Psychological Science* 17 (2006):592–598; and Chappell Lawson, Gabriel S. Lenz, Andy Baker, and Michael Myers, "Looking Like a Winner," *World Politics* 62 (2010):561–593.

17. Todorov et al., "Inferences of Competence," 1625.

18. Betsy Leondar-Wright, *Missing Class* (Cornell University Press, 2014). On influential aspects of appearance beyond faces, see Michael L. Spezio, Laura Loesch, Frédéric Gosselin, Kyle Mattes, and R. Michael Alvarez, "Thin-Slice Decisions Do Not Need Faces to Be Predictive of Election Outcomes," *Political Psychology* 33 (2012):331–341.

19. Stuart and Elizabeth Ewen, *Channels of Desire: Mass Images and the Shaping of American Consciousness* (McGraw-Hill, 1982), 112, 246. A wave of research in the 1970s, especially in Britain, showed how working-class subcultures reworked the meanings of clothing to assert their identities, like the safety pins favored by many

punks: Dick Hebdige, *Subculture* (New Accents, 1979). In many cases the young men (much more studied than the young women) saw themselves as heroic because they were active, taking speed instead of the pot—and the passive lethargy—they thought middle-class youths favored.

20. Susan T. Fiske, *Envy Up, Scorn Down: How Status Divides Us* (Russell Sage Foundation, 2011), 130.

21. Fiske, *Envy Up*, 135.

22. Fiske, *Envy Up*, 134–135.

23. Fiske, *Envy Up*, 49–50. Also Lamont, *The Dignity of Working Men* (Harvard University Press, 2000).

24. Michael W. Kraus, Paul K. Piff, Rodolfo Mendoza-Denton, Michelle L. Rheinschmidt, and Dacher Keltner, "Social Class, Solipsism, and Contextualism: How the Rich Are Different from the Poor," *Psychological Review* 119 (2012):546–572.

25. James M. Jasper and Jane Poulsen, "Fighting Back: Vulnerabilities, Blunders, and Countermobilization by the Targets in Three Animal Rights Campaigns," *Sociological Forum* 8 (1993):639–657.

26. There would seem to be a parallel case in which virtuous acts are convincing when the actor hid them and they only came to light later by accident. But audiences may still suspect the whole revelation was stage-managed all along.

27. Amy J. C. Cuddy, "Just Because I'm Nice, Don't Assume I'm Dumb," *Harvard Business Review* 87 (2009):24.

28. Diego Gambetta, *Codes of the Underworld: How Criminals Communicate* (Princeton University Press, 2009), 40.

29. Gambetta, *Codes*, 42.

30. Gambetta, *Codes*, 82. Marek Kaminski found tests of toughness to be highly ritualized in Polish prisons: "Games Prisoners Play: Allocation of Social Roles in a Social Institution," *Rationality and Society* 15 (2003):188–217.

31. Michel Foucault finds the same distinction between worthy and unworthy poor at the end of the seventeenth century. The good and the evil poor were confined in the same places, the former in order to help them and the latter in order to punish them; whether or not they were grateful for their incarceration proved if they were worthy or unworthy! *History of Madness* (Routledge, 1961/2006), 60.

32. David O. Sears, "Political Behavior," in Gardner Lindzey and Elliot Aronson, eds., *Handbook of Social Psychology* (Addison-Wesley, 1969); Donald R. Kinder and David O. Sears, "Prejudice and Politics: Symbolic Racism versus Racial Threats to the Good Life," *Journal of Personality and Social Psychology* 40 (1981):414–431; and David O. Sears, C. P. Hensler, and L. K. Speer, "Whites' Opposition to 'Busing': Self-Interest or Symbolic Politics," *American Political Science Review* 73 (1979):369–384. For more on the interactions among short-, medium-, and long-term emotions see Jasper, *The Emotions of Protest*.

33. David O. Sears, "Symbolic Racism," in Phyllis A. Katz and Dalmas A. Taylor, eds., *Eliminating Racism* (Plenum Press, 1988).

34. David O. Sears and Jack Citrin, *Tax Revolt*, enlarged edn. (Harvard University Press, 1985), 169.

35. Selina Todd, *The People* (John Murray, 2014), 79, 94. For political purposes Todd conflates the poor or unemployed and the working class, but they often are subject to opposed character work, especially on the moral dimension.

36. World Health Organization, "Gender and Women's Mental Health": http://www.who.int/mental_health/prevention/genderwomen/en/.

37. Larissa Z. Tiedens, "Anger and Advancement versus Sadness and Subjugation," *Journal of Personality and Social Psychology* 80 (2001):86–94.

38. Stephanie A. Shields, *Speaking from the Heart: Gender and the Social Meaning of Emotion* (Cambridge University Press, 2002); also Leah R. Warner and Stephanie A. Shields, "The Perception of Crying in Women and Men," in Ursula Hess and Pierre Philippot, eds., *Group Dynamics and Emotional Expression* (Cambridge University Press, 2007).

39. Wendy M. Christensen and Myra Marx Ferree, "Cowboy of the World? Gender Discourse and the Iraq War Debate," *Qualitative Sociology* 31 (2008), 301.

40. Michael A. Messner, Max A. Greenberg, and Tal Peretz, *Some Men: Feminist Allies and the Movement to End Violence against Women* (Oxford University Press, 2015).

41. Actors are brand names who must be concerned with their public character. Comments Michael B. Jordan on the heroic roles he prefers, "I want people to see me win. I want to be the leading man": Aisha Harris, "More Than a Movie Star," *New York Times*, 27 November, 2018.

42. Charles E. Osgood, George J. Suci, and Percy H. Tannenbaum, *The Measurement of Meaning* (University of Illinois Press, 1957), 325. They applied factor analysis to a number of scales of traits. Those that loaded heavily on *evaluation* were: good-bad, beautiful-ugly, sweet-sour, clean-dirty, tasty-distasteful, valuable-worthless, kind-cruel, pleasant-unpleasant, sweet-bitter, happy-sad, sacred-profane, nice-awful, fragrant-foul, honest-dishonest, and fair-unfair. Those that loaded heavily on *potency* included: large-small, strong-weak, heavy-light, and thick-thin. A number of scales, including notably brave-cowardly, weight heavily on both factors. Finally, scales that loaded distinctively on *activity* were fast-slow, active-passive, hot-cold, sharp-dull, and angular-rounded (pp. 36–38). For a later summary of dozens of studies on EPA conducted around the world, see Charles E. Osgood, William H. May, and Murray S. Miron, *Cross-Cultural Universals of Affective Meaning* (University of Illinois Press, 1975).

43. Osgood, Suci, and Tannenbaum, Measurement, 109.

44. For a direct comparison of Fiske's "stereotype content model" with affect control theory, see Kimberly B. Rogers, Tobias Schröder, and Wolfgang Scholl, "The Affective Structure of Stereotype Content: Behavior and Emotion in Intergroup Context," *Social Psychology Quarterly* 76 (2013):125–150.

45. High points in the tradition include Lynn Smith-Lovin, "Behavior Settings and Impressions Formed from Social Scenarios," *Social Psychology Quarterly* 42 (1979):31–43; David R. Heise, *Understanding Events* (Cambridge University Press, 1979) and *Expressive Order* (Springer, 2007); and Neil J. MacKinnon and David R. Heise, *Self, Identity, and Social Institutions* (Palgrave, 2010). For more on the relationship between character theory and ACT see Kelly Bergstrand and James M. Jasper, "Villains, Victims, and Heroes in Character Theory and Affective Control Theory," *Social Psychology Quarterly* 81 (2018):228–247.

46. Most ACT studies find that the word "victim" is coded as slightly negative morally, the only exception to our expected characterizations. We suspect that victims are frequently seen as too passive, so that respondents judge them poorly for not doing more to help themselves. In addition, the word victim encompasses more roles than the political

tropes that we are examining, not all of which may be so admirable. We examine immoral victims in chapter 8.

47. Osgood, Suci, and Tannenbaum, *Measurement*, 108. Also 121.

48. Commentators often talk about this potential compassion fatigue, especially among care givers. But empirical studies have not always found it in the general public: Bruce G. Link, Sharon Schwartz, Robert Moore, Jo Phelan, Elmer Struening, Ann Stueve, and Mary Ellen Colten, "Public Knowledge, Attitudes, and Beliefs about Homeless People: Evidence for Compassion Fatigue?" *American Journal of Community Psychology* 23 (1995):533–555.

49. George E. Marcus, *The Sentimental Citizen* (Pennsylvania State University Press, 2002); George E. Marcus, W. Russell Neuman, and Michael MacKuen, *Affective Intelligence and Political Judgment* (University of Chicago Press, 2000).

50. Lory Britt and David Heise, "From Shame to Pride in Identity Politics," in Sheldon Stryker, Timothy J. Owens, and Robert W. White, eds., *Self, Identity, and Social Movements* (University of Minnesota Press, 2000).

51. Jasper, Young, and Zuern, "Character Work in Social Movements."

52. Linda E. Francis, "Ideology and Interpersonal Emotion Management: Redefining Identity in Two Support Groups," *Social Psychology Quarterly* 60 (1997):153–171.

53. Christopher Wetzel, "Envisioning Land Seizure: Diachronic Representations of the Occupation of Alcatraz Island," *American Behavioral Scientist* 56 (2012):151–171.

54. Neil J. MacKinnon and David R. Heise, *Self, Identity, and Social Institutions* (Palgrave, 2010), suggest (p. 50), "the 'Red Power' political movement so enhanced the identity of Indian in the United States that the population of self-identified native Americans grew from about half a million in 1960 to close to two million in 1990."

55. Now that we have all three dimensions of character in place, we can note that they are compatible with the "big five" personality traits acknowledged in most theories of personality. Two of these seem to have a lot to do with strength or weakness: *conscientiousness* (efficiency, precision, diligence) and *emotional stability* (self-confidence, optimism, calmness). Heroes, in particular, are calm and confident, because of their strength. One of the big five seems related to morality, namely *agreeableness*, which includes sincerity, loyalty, generosity, and cordiality. The final two dimensions seem to capture activity levels: *extraversion* (consisting of energy, dynamism, and activity) and *openness to experience* (creativity and innovation). Public characters are made from the same stuff as our personal traits. Dan P. McAdams criticizes the big five as fairly external traits, observable by others, which in fact makes them perfect for describing the visual and narrative construction of characters: "What Do We Know When We Know a Person?" *Journal of Personality* 63 (1995):365–396.

56. Gregory M. Walton and Mahzarin B. Banaji, "Being What You Say: The Effect of Essentialist Linguistic Labels on Preferences," *Social Cognition* 22 (2004):1913; Andrea Carnaghi, Anne Maass, Sara Gresta, Mauro Bianchi, Mara Cadinu, and Luciano Arcuri, "Nomina Sunt Omina: On the Inductive Potential of Nouns and Adjectives in Person Perception," *Journal of Personality and Social Psychology* 94 (2008):839–859; Sylvie Graf, Michal Bilewicz, Eerika Finell, and Daniel Geschke, "Nouns Cut Slices: Effects of Linguistic Forms on Intergroup Bias," *Journal of Language and Social Psychology* 32 (2013):62–83. The stability that nouns promise may link them to conservative politics: Aleksandra Cichocka, Michal Bilewicz, John T. Jost, Natasza Marrouch, and

Marta Witkowska, "On the Grammar of Politics—or Why Conservatives Prefer Nouns," *Political Psychology* 37 (2016):799–815. As a result they may also favor public characters in their rhetoric.

Chapter 4

1. Orrin E. Klapp, *Heroes, Villains, and Fools* (Prentice-Hall, 1962), 17. He relied on a Chicago-school image of "types" or social roles that does not clearly distinguish between the epidictic construction of the individual—her symbolic reputation in the eyes of others—and the individual's own goals, habits, and identities.

2. William J. Goode, *The Celebration of Heroes* (University of California Press, 1978). Patricia A. Taylor applied Goode's system to communist Yugoslavia, where she found that a different kind of elite nonetheless created heroes to reproduce the social structure from which they benefited: "The Celebration of Heroes under Communism," *American Sociological Review* 52 (1987):143–154.

3. Jack Katz, "Essences as Moral Identities: Verifiability and Responsibility in Imputations of Deviance and Charisma," *American Journal of Sociology* 80 (1975):1369–1390.

4. The language of players and arenas is developed in James M. Jasper and Jan Willem Duyvendak, eds., *Players and Arenas* (Amsterdam University Press, 2015) and Duyvendak and Jasper, eds., *Breaking Down the State* (Amsterdam University Press, 2015).

5. William Roy could be describing character work when he notes, "institutions shape the taken-for-granted categories that reify repeated social practices into 'things' like money, markets, corporations, and institutions themselves": *Socializing Capital* (Princeton University Press, 1997), 140.

6. Lucy Riall, *Garibaldi: Invention of a Hero* (Yale University Press, 2007), 46.

7. Zuern and Jasper, "Heroes and Victims in Postcolonial Nation-Building: The Case of Namibia," forthcoming.

8. Delphine Gardey documents the Bourbon Palace as the collection of physical and social apparatuses that enable but also constrain the French National Assembly in *Le Linge du Palais-Bourbon: Corps, Matérialité et Genre du Politique à l'Ère Démocratique* (Editions Le Bord de l'eau, 2015). For a recent summary of the vast literature on heritage, especially the constant contestation over it, see Rodney Harrison, *Heritage* (Routledge, 2013). On heritage movements as strategic players see Tod Jones, Ali Mozaffari, and James M. Jasper, "Heritage Contests: What Can We Learn from Social Movements?" *Heritage and Society* 10 (2017):1–25.

9. Barry Schwartz, *Abraham Lincoln in the Post-Heroic Era* (University of Chicago Press, 2008), 187, 188.

10. Robin Wagner-Pacifici and Barry Schwartz, "The Vietnam Veterans Memorial: Commemorating a Difficult Past," *American Journal of Sociology* 97 (1991), 395. As always, one side's hero can be the other's villain, as Gary Alan Fine shows with John Brown in *Difficult Reputations*, chap. 3.

11. Riall, *Garibaldi*, 61, 64.

12. Quoted in Sean McMahon, *Rebel Ireland* (Mercier, 1999), 30–31. A number of the Risorgimento campaigns in Italy were just as hopeless, pursued primarily to arouse attention and sympathy. Mazzini realized this even if Garibaldi did not.

13. Even in Homi Bhabha's edited volume, *Nation and Narration*, only the chapter on Latin American fictions actually engages the work of heroes: Doris Sommer, "Irresistible Romance: the Foundational Fictions of Latin America," in *Nation and Narration*, ed. Homi Bhabha (Routledge, 1990).

14. Helke Rausch, "The Nation as a Community Born of War? Symbolic Strategies and Popular Reception of Public Statues in Late Nineteenth-Century Western European Capitals," *European Review of History* 14 (2007):73–101.

15. Richard Eichenberg, "Victory Has Many Friends: US Public Opinion and the Use of Military Force, 1981–2005," *International Security* 30 (2005), 165.

16. Kristen Hoganson, *Fighting for American Manhood* (Yale University Press, 1998), 11.

17. Hoganson, *Fighting*, 17.

18. George L. Mosse, *Fallen Soldiers* (Oxford University Press, 1990), 27, 26. The film *A Few Good Men* (directed by Rob Reiner, 1992) formulates this tension between heroism and normalcy.

19. Cindy Kam and Donald Kinder, "Terror and Ethnocentrism: Foundations of American Support for the War on Terrorism," *The Journal of Politics* 69 (2007), 321.

20. Kam and Kinder, "Terror," 335–336.

21. Christina Simko, *The Politics of Consolation* (Oxford University Press, 2015), viii.

22. Kam and Kinder, "Terror," 337.

23. Fifty years ago Orrin Klapp offered a typology of such encounters, but he conflated stage settings with the strategic outcomes: *Symbolic Leaders* (Aldine, 1964), chap. 3. No public encounter can be entirely scripted in advance, but there is a wide variation in how much advance preparation there is and in what effects it has.

24. Fine, *Difficult Reputations.*

25. Gary Alan Fine, *Sticky Reputations* (Routledge, 2012), xiii; also "Reputational Entrepreneurs and the Memory of Incompetence," *American Journal of Sociology* 101 (1996):1159–1193.

26. Charles Horton Cooley, *Human Nature and the Social Order* (Scribner's, 1902), 308.

27. Fine, *Sticky Reputations*, 170, 171.

28. Joel Best, *Threatened Children* (University of Chicago Press, 1990) and *Random Violence* (University of California Press, 1999). If political arenas have an "essential trio" of victim-villain-hero, the field of social problems substitutes an "atrocity triangle" of victim-villain-observer since the main player there is the bystander public: Stanley Cohen, *States of Denial* (Polity, 2001), 14.

29. In his initial article, "The Gospel of Wealth," originally published in 1889 and reprinted in Andrew Carnegie, *The Gospel of Wealth and other Timely Essays* (Harvard University Press, 1962), Carnegie emphasized the philanthropic powers of capitalists. Only in response to criticism did he expand their heroic deeds to the economy as a whole.

30. Roland Marchand, *Creating the Corporate Soul: The Rise of Public Relations and Corporate Imagery in American Big Business* (University of California Press, 1998). We rely on this thorough history here.

31. Gary Alan Fine writes about Ford's reputations among multiple audiences in *Difficult Reputations*, chap. 5.

32. Rakesh Khurana, *Searching for a Corporate Savior* (Princeton University Press, 2002), 71.

33. Mary-Hunter McDonnell and Brayden G. King, "Keeping Up Appearances: Reputational Threat and Impression Management after Social Movement Boycotts," *Administrative Science Quarterly* 58 (2013):387–419. Protestors also target the financial strength of corporations as well as their morality: Ion Bogdan Vasi and Brayden G. King, "Social Movements, Risk Perceptions, and Economic Outcomes," *American Sociological Review* 77 (2012):573–596. For an overview, Brayden G. King, "Reputation, Risk, and Anti-Corporate Activism," in Lorenzo Bosi, Marco Giugni, and Katrin Uba, eds., *The Consequences of Social Movements* (Cambridge University Press, 2016).

34. For more details see our article, "Character Work in Social Movements."

35. Clifford Bob, *The Global Right Wing and the Clash of World Politics* (Cambridge University Press, 2012), 17.

36. Bob, *Global Right Wing*, 34.

37. We elaborate on WUNC displays in our article, "Character Work in Social Movements."

38. Nancy C. Whittier, "Emotional Strategies," in Jeff Goodwin, James M. Jasper, and Francesca Polletta, eds., *Passionate Politics: Emotions and Social Movements* (University of Chicago Press, 2001).

39. Francesca Polletta, forthcoming research.

40. Martin Wattenberg, "The Declining Relevance of Candidate Personal Attributes in Presidential Elections," *Presidential Studies Quarterly* 46 (2016), 125.

41. David Holian and Charles Prysby. "Candidate Character Traits in the 2012 Presidential Election," *Presidential Studies Quarterly* 44 (2014), 487.

42. Arlie Hochschild explores this resentment by rural white Americans, their feeling that government policies have passed them over, in *Strangers in Their Own Land* (New Press, 2016).

43. Jane Caputi, "Character Assassinations: Hate Messages in Election 2008 Political Paraphernalia," *Denver University Law Review* 86 (2009), 591, 608.

44. R. I. Moore, *The War on Heresy* (Profile Books, 2012).

45. Neal Feigenson, *Legal Blame* (American Psychological Association, 2000), 89.

46. Stacy Lee Burns and Mark Peyrot, "Tough Love: Nurturing and Coercing Responsibility and Recovery in California Drug Courts," *Social Problems* 50 (2003):416–438.

47. Olga Tsoudis and Lynn Smith-Lovin, "How Bad Was It? The Effects of Victim and Perpetrator Emotion on Responses to Criminal Court Vignettes," *Social Forces* 77 (1998):695–722. The emotions displayed are read as signs of public characters.

48. Cristina Flesher Fominaya and Rosemary Barberet, "Defining the Victims of Terrorism," in Athina Karatogianni, ed., *Violence and War in Culture and the Media* (Routledge, 2012).

49. *The Staircase* (2004, directed by Jean-Xavier de Lestrade), episode 8.

50. Brian Doherty and Graeme Hayes, "Having your Day in Court," *Comparative Political Studies* 47 (2014):3–29.

51. David L. Altheide, *Creating Fear: News and the Construction of Crisis* (Aldine de Gruyter, 2002), 89, 90–91, 92.

52. Barry Glassner, *The Culture of Fear* (Basic Books, 1999), 109.

53. Stanley Cohen, *Folk Devils and Moral Panics* (MacGibbon and Kee, 1972), 9.

54. Lynn Chancer, *High-Profile Crimes: When Legal Cases Become Social Causes* (University of California Press, 2005).

55. Chancer, *High-Profile Crimes*, 11.

56. Jeffrey M. Berry and Sarah Sobieraj, *The Outrage Industry: Political Opinion Media and the New Incivility* (Oxford University Press, 2014), 7, 12.

57. Mahmood Mamdani, "The Politics of Naming: Genocide, Civil War, Insurgency," *London Review of Books* 29 (8 March 2007). He analyzes Nicholas Kristof's columns in *The New York Times*, and the application of "genocide" as "part of a rhetorical arsenal that helps you vilify your adversaries while ensuring impunity for your allies."

58. Joanne B. Freeman, "Slander, Poison, Whispers, and Fame: Jefferson's 'Anas' and Political Gossip in the Early Republic," *Journal of the Early Republic* 15 (1995): 29–30. Also see her *Affairs of Honor: National Politics in the New Republic* (Yale University Press, 2001).

59. Freeman, "Slander," 32.

60. Ari Adut, *On Scandal* (Cambridge University Press, 2008).

61. Harold Garfinkel, "Conditions of Successful Degradation Ceremonies," *American Journal of Sociology* 61 (1956), 421. He observes that such claims accept characterological "essences" that social scientists would reject (p. 422): "While constructions like 'substantially a something' or 'essentially a something' have been banished from the domain of scientific discourse, such constructions have prominent and honored places in the theories of motives, persons, and conduct that are employed in the handling affairs of daily life."

62. Moore, *War on Heresy*.

63. Quoted in Fine, *Sticky Reputations*, 171–172.

64. Gary Alan Fine and Bill Ellis, *The Global Grapevine: Why Rumors of Terrorism, Immigration, and Trade Matter* (Oxford University Press, 2010), 14, 9.

Chapter 5

1. Erin E. Arvedlund, "Lessons from the Madoff Fraud, 10 Years Later," *Barron's*, 10 December 2018.

2. Orrin E. Klapp, *Heroes, Villains, and Fools*, chap. 2.

3. Ewart Lewis, *Medieval Political Ideas* (Routledge and Kegan Paul, 1954), vol. 1, 249.

4. Thomas E. Nelson, Gregory Gwiasda, and Joseph Lyons, "Vilification and Values," *Political Psychology* 32 (2011), 814.

5. Ellen Barry, "Moscow Attacks May Bring a Return of the Iron Fist to the Caucasus," *New York Times*, 31 March 2010.

6. Quoted in Cristina Flesher Fominaya, "The Madrid Bombings and Popular Protest: Misinformation, Counterinformation, Mobilisation and Elections after '11-M'," *Contemporary Social Science* 6 (2011), 292, 295. Also Brian Martin, *Justice Ignited: The Dynamics of Backfire* (Rowman and Littlefield, 2006), who argues that the solidarity of an attacked group, when it demonstrates its morality by sticking to nonviolent tactics, works to condemn the violence of its opponents more clearly through the contrast between violence and nonviolence, or what Jasper refers to as a "moral battery" of positive and negative emotions combined: "Emotions and Social Movements," *Annual Review of Sociology* 37 (2011), 291.

7. Richard Goldstein, "Petaphilia: The Great American Man-Dog Marriage Panic," *The Village Voice*, 23 March 2004.

8. John W. Dower, *War without Mercy* (Random House, 1986), 81, 92, 99. On the difficulties of mobilizing Americans for World War II (the country's only consensus "good war"), see William L. O'Neill, *A Democracy at War* (Harvard University Press, 1993).

9. The vast literature on apocalyptic thinking includes Norman Cohn, *The Pursuit of the Millennium* (Secker and Warburg, 1957); Richard Hofstadter, *The Paranoid Style in American Politics* (Knopf, 1965); Michael Barkun, *Disaster and the Millennium* (Yale University Press, 1974); Robert Fuller, *Naming the Anti-Christ: The History of an American Obsession* (Oxford University Press, 1995); Mary Manjikian, *Apocalypse and Post-Politics* (Lexington Books, 2012); Philip C. Almond, *The Devil* (Cornell University Press, 2014).

10. Diego Gambetta, *Codes of the Underworld: How Criminals Communicate* (Princeton University Press, 2009), 72.

11. Seneca and Lucan are both quoted in Claude Mossé, *Alexander: Destiny and Myth* (The Johns Hopkins University Press, 2004), 175. Roman historians loved to speculate about what would have happened had their armies met Alexander's on the field of battle.

12. Marlies K. Danziger, "Heroic Villains in Eighteenth Century Criticism," *Poetics* 13 (1959), 41. She is summarizing the esthetic theory of Johann Georg Sulzer.

13. Murray Edelman comments, "The distinction between unacceptable and acceptable opponents, or between enemies and adversaries, lies in whether the focus of attention is upon the inherent nature of the antagonist or, instead, upon the tactics an opponent employs": *Constructing the Political Spectacle* (University of Chicago Press, 1988), 67.

14. Donileen R. Loseke analyzes the character work in Bush II's speeches: "Examining Emotion as Discourse: Emotion Codes and Presidential Speeches Justifying War," *Sociological Quarterly* 50 (2009):497–524. The basic public characters are, in her words, symbolic codes, closely attached to emotion codes or ways of feeling about them. Also Maéva Clément, Thomas Lindemann, and Eric Sangar, "The 'Hero-Protector Narrative': Manufacturing Emotional Consent for the Use of Force," *Political Psychology* 38 (2017):991–1008.

15. Don Heinrich Tolzmann, *The German-American Experience* (Humanity Books, 2000); Mark Ellis, "German-Americans in World War I," in Ragnhild Fiebig-von Hase and Ursula Lehmkuhl, eds., *Enemy Images in American History* (Berghahn, 1998). On the extent of German sabotage, see Howard Blum, *Dark Invasion: 1915* (Harper, 2014).

16. Eric L. Muller, *American Inquisition: The Hunt for Japanese American Disloyalty in World War II* (University of North Carolina Press, 2007), 17.

17. Louise Merrick van Patten, "Public Opinion on Japanese Americans," *Far Eastern Survey* 14 (1945), 207.

18. James Jasper, *The Art of Moral Protest* (University of Chicago, 1997), chap. 16.

19. Different cultures have variations on these themes. Nancy Cauthen and James Jasper describe recurrent American clusters of moral panics "around sex for pleasure rather than procreation (loose morals, homosexuality, teenage pregnancies, abortion), another around race and poverty (crack and other drugs, welfare mothers, urban crime and violence), and a third around immigration (the English language, standards in the schools, overpopulation, job and wage competition)." They continue, "Many of these are

anxieties about groups thought unable to support themselves economically. This kind of 'dependency' is an affront to the deep and abiding Protestant belief that individuals make their own lives, are responsible for their own success or failure." See their "Culture, Politics, and Moral Panics," *Sociological Forum* 9 (1994), 496, 502.

20. Grace Yukich, "Constructing the Model Immigrant," *Social Problems* 60 (2013):302–320; Hana E. Brown, "Race, Legality, and the Social Policy Consequences of Anti-Immigration Mobilization," *American Sociological Review* 78 (2013):290–314. The DREAMers raise acute issues of worthy versus unworthy immigrants: Sujatha Fernandez, *Curated Stories* (Oxford University Press, 2017), chaps 4, 5.

21. Jasper, *The Art of Moral Protest*, 355.

22. Jasper, *The Art of Moral Protest*, 352ff.

23. David Fromkin, *A Peace to End All Peace* (Henry Holt, 1989). Doug McAdam, Sidney Tarrow, and Charles Tilly describe a similar outcome in the Kenyan war of independence, as the British, "blind as they were to divisions within Kikuyu society . . . read the sporadic attacks as a coordinated and generalized rebellion." They also assumed the Kenyans were united behind one leader, so that if they captured Kenyatta they could end the rebellion (the opposite happened due to outrage at his imprisonment). See their *Dynamics of Contention* (Cambridge University Press, 2001), 100ff.

24. Phillip Atiba Goff, Jennifer L. Eberhardt, Melissa J. Williams, Matthew Christian Jackson, "Not Yet Human: Implicit Knowledge, Historical Dehumanization, and Contemporary Consequences," *Journal of Personality and Social Psychology* 94 (2008):292–306; Aneeta Rattan and Jennifer L. Eberhardt, "The Role of Social Meaning in Inattentional Blindness: When the Gorillas in Our Midst Do Not Go Unseen," *Journal of Experimental Social Psychology* 46 (2010):1085–1088.

25. Patricia L. Williams, *The Alchemy of Race and Rights* (Harvard University Press, 1991), 219.

26. Fine, *Difficult Reputations*, chap. 2.

27. Lionel Tiger, *The Manufacture of Evil: Ethics, Evolution, and the Industrial System* (Marion Boyars, 1991), 3–4. Literary critic Andrew Delbanco also writes about *The Death of Satan* (Farrar, Straus and Giroux, 1995); yet demagogues continue to mobilize followers by constructing villains, he says.

28. Thomas Szasz, *The Myth of Mental Illness* (Harper, 1961).

29. Quoted in Robert Mann, *Daisy Petals and Mushroom Clouds* (Louisiana State University Press, 2011), 83.

30. Quoted by Mann, *Daisy Petals*, 75.

31. Quoted by Mann, *Daisy Petals*, 31. Another Johnson commercial showed a similar young girl eating an ice cream cone, while a motherly voice warned of the dangers of Strontium 90 due to nuclear testing: Dan Nimmo and James E. Combs, *Subliminal Politics* (Prentice-Hall, 1980), 110.

32. "General Pinochet: Old Alone," *The Economist*, 18 December 2004.

33. "Pataki Strategy to Defuse Embarrassing Situation Fits Pattern," *New York Times*, 4 January 2005.

34. "CIA Whistleblower Jeffrey Sterling Found Guilty on All Counts," RT.com, 26 January 2015.

35. Cyanne E. Loyle and Christian Davenport, "Transitional Injustice," *Journal of Human Rights* 15 (2016):126–149.

36. Quoted in Mark D. Jordan, *Recruiting Young Love: How Christians Talk about Homosexuality* (University of Chicago Press, 2011), 141. The "vicious" gay community responded by taking screwdrivers off the menus in many gay bars, replacing them with Anita Bryants, vodka and apple juice.

37. Jordan, *Recruiting*, 141.

38. Jordan, *Recruiting*, 146.

39. Krista De Castella, Craig McGarty, and Luke Musgrove, "Fear Appeals in Political Rhetoric about Terrorism: An Analysis of Speeches by Australian Prime Minister Howard," *Political Psychology* 30 (2009), 8.

40. Gary Alan Fine, *Difficult Reputations*, 49. The three American soldiers who detained André could have been portrayed as minions, since they were probably planning to rob him. But because they decided to hand him over to their superiors instead, and because Arnold's evil was so great, they were elevated to hero status along with everyone else who was not Arnold. Arnold's large negative number had to be balanced by the positive numbers of many other characters.

41. David S. Reynolds, *John Brown, Abolitionist* (Random House, 2005), 8.

Chapter 6

1. On the Irish, see Richard Ned Lebow, *White Britain and Black Ireland* (Institute for the Study of Human Issues, 1976).

2. Dower, *War without Mercy*, 111.

3. Dower, *War without Mercy*, 116.

4. Memo from Jack Valenti to President Johnson, September 7, 1964, in Mann, *Daisy Petals*, 133–135.

5. Maéva Clément, Thomas Lindemann, and Eric Sangar substitute cowards for minions in an analysis that otherwise parallels ours: "The 'Hero-Protector Narrative': Manufacturing Emotional Consent for the Use of Force," *Political Psychology* 38 (2017):991–1008.

6. Jeffrey C. Alexander, *The Civil Sphere* (Oxford University Press, 2006), 57ff.

7. For more on the dangerous emotionality of mobs see Jasper, *The Emotions of Protest*, appendix 1.

8. Classics include some of the most famous social science ever written: T. W. Adorno et al., *The Authoritarian Personality* (Harper, 1950); David Riesman et al., *The Lonely Crowd* (Yale University Press, 1950); William Kornhauser, *The Politics of Mass Society* (Free Press, 1957); William H. Whyte, *The Organization Man* (Doubleday, 1957); and Stanley Milgram, *Obedience to Authority* (Harper & Row, 1974).

9. Will Wright, *Sixguns and Society*, 75. He discusses *High Noon, Johnny Guitar*, and *Broken Arrow* as examples of the new films. Bystanders can vary or be ambiguous characters on the moral dimension: they are dominated by weakness and passivity, which may or may not lead them to do bad things. Once freed from the dominance of the villain they often become good.

10. Quoted in Reynolds, *John Brown Abolitionist*, 161.

11. Gyanendra Pandey, *The Construction of Communalism in North India* (Oxford University Press, 1990), 27.

12. Pandey, *Construction*, 65.

13. Paul R. Brass, *The Production of Hindu-Muslim Violence in Contemporary India* (University of Washington Press, 2003), shows how riots are produced by "conversion specialists" skilled at turning insignificant incidents into large-scale communal violence. It is not just historians who construct essentialist narratives, but political players themselves, in this case especially Hindu nationalists. For a Putnamian view that active civic associations can prevent this kind of communal violence by creating Muslim-Hindu ties, see Ashutosh Varshney, *Ethnic Conflict and Civic Life: Hindus and Muslims in India* (Oxford University Press, 2002).

14. Chapters 22 and 21, respectively.

15. Sherill Stroschein, *Ethnic Struggle, Coexistence, and Democratization in Eastern Europe* (Cambridge University Press, 2012), 238.

16. M. Tullius Cicero, *Pro Sexto Roscio Amerino Oratio* (Forgotten Books, 2012), par. XLVI, page 51.

17. Peter Maas, "The Way of the Commandos," *New York Times Magazine*, 1 May 2005, 40. The Al Iraqiya network that aired the series was established by the U.S. Department Defense, which had an obvious stake in ridiculing terrorists.

18. Daniel Byman and Christine Fair, "The Case for Calling Them Nitwits," *The Atlantic*, July/August 2010, 106–108.

19. Benny Morris, *Righteous Victims* (Random House, 1999), 13.

20. Iris Murdoch, *Under the Net* (Penguin, 1954/1960), 207.

21. Guy Lesser, "War Crime and Punishment," *Harper's Magazine*, January 2004, 39.

22. In fact in his legal case, Eichmann's lawyer did not generally use the excuse of following orders, even in the sentencing phase, but rather an "acts of state" defense on the grounds that acts of sovereignty are outside the legal realm: Hannah Arendt, *Eichmann in Jerusalem*, rev. edn. (Penguin, 1965), 93. As part of the Nazi state, Eichmann remained more villain than minion.

23. In the courts martial after the notorious My Lai massacre of 1968, Lieutenant William Calley Jr. was convicted despite his minion defense, while the captain whose orders he claimed to be following was not. However, Calley's original sentence of life in prison was gradually reduced to three and one-half years of house arrest at Fort Benning.

24. Bettina Stangneth, *Eichmann Before Jerusalem* (Knopf, 2014).

25. Peter Novick, *The Holocaust in American Life* (Mariner Books, 2000), 134.

26. Hannah Arendt, "Thinking and Moral Considerations," *Social Research* 38 (1971), 417.

27. Christopher R. Browning, *Ordinary Men* (HarperCollins, 1992), 184–185.

28. Arne Johan Vetlesen, *Evil and Human Agency* (Cambridge University Press, 2005), 137.

29. Primo Levi, *The Drowned and the Saved* (Simon and Schuster, 1988), 59, 53.

30. Justice Minister Michael Masutha quoted in *The Guardian*, 30 January 2015.

31. Pumla Gobodo-Madikizela, *A Human Being Died that Night: A South African Story of Forgiveness* (Mariner Books 2004).

Chapter 7

1. Walter A. McDougall, *Promised Land, Crusader State: The American Encounter with the World since 1776* (Houghton Mifflin, 1997).

2. Joseph Campbell, *The Hero with a Thousand Faces* (Princeton University Press, 1949), 30, 315–316; also Federico Navarette Linares and Guilhem Oliver, eds., *El Héroe entre el Mito y la Historia* (UNAM, 2000).

3. Campbell, *Hero*, 319.

4. Campbell, *Hero*, 319.

5. On the tension between uniformed and non-uniformed victims, see Cristina Flesher Fominaya and Rosemary Barberet, "Defining the Victims of Terrorism: Competing Frames around Victim Compensation and Commemoration post-9/11 New York City and 3/11 Madrid," in Athina Karatzogianni, ed., *Violence and War in Culture and the Media* (Routledge, 2012), 118, 123. They recognize the hero-victim dilemma.

6. Klapp, *Symbolic Leaders*, 78, 80.

7. Klapp, *Symbolic Leaders*, 218.

8. Jane Tompkins, *West of Everything* (Oxford University Press, 1992), 12.

9. Robert Filmer, *Patriarcha* (1680), known today primarily because of John Locke's attacks on it in his *Two Treatises of Government* (1689).

10. Edward C. Banfield coined the term amoral familism to explain poverty in Southern Italy: there was no room for a common good beyond the family; *The Moral Basis of a Backward Society* (Free Press, 1958).

11. Valerie Sperling, *Sex, Politics, and Putin* (Oxford University Press, 2015), 44.

12. Matthew Arnold, reviewing Grant's memoirs, complained that Grant "is not to the English imagination the hero of the American Civil War; the hero is Lee." "General Grant," *Murray's Magazine* 1 (1886). A generation later W. E. B. Du Bois, at the height of the KKK and the Southern effort to exonerate their ancestors, wrote, "What Lee did in 1861, other Lees are doing in 1928. They lack the moral courage to stand up for justice to the Negro because of the overwhelming public opinion of their social environment." Physically heroic, but immoral. *The Crisis*, March 1928, v.35, n. 3. Grant's own memoirs were an effort to present himself as a blunt, laconic, Western-style hero, in contrast to both Northeastern intriguers and Southern apologists for slavery. See Ron Chernow, *Grant* (Penguin, 2017).

13. Quoted in Anthony DiMaggio, *When Media Goes to War* (Monthly Review Press, 2009), 101. He observes that Americans believed their forces were preventing catastrophe, while Iraqis believed the opposite.

14. Jeffrey D. Tatum, "Compassion on Trial: Movement Narrative in a Court Conflict over Physician-Assisted Suicide," in Joseph E. Davis, ed., *Stories of Change* (State University of New York Press, 2002), 189. Kevorkian became a martyr, and his prosecutor therefore became the villain, an impersonal bureaucrat persecuting the good doctor (p. 193).

15. Don Herzog, *Cunning* (Princeton University Press, 2006), 8, 7. Also Jasper, *Getting Your Way*, 99.

16. Philip Tetlock finds that experts' own narrow focus leads them to make worse predictions than broad thinkers who can draw on diverse traditions of thought: *Expert Political Judgment* (Princeton University Press, 2006).

17. Gary Alan Fine, *Sticky Reputations*, 152.

18. Fine, *Sticky Reputations*, 154.

19. Fine, *Sticky Reputations*, xx.

20. Gordon S. Wood, *Empire of Liberty* (Oxford University Press, 2009), 730. Wood is actually quoting an English children's book, "True Heroism," but he observes that it was popular in the U.S. and fit the emerging commercial celebration of inventors such as Eli Whitney and Robert Fulton.

21. Jean-Marie Apostolides, *Héroïsme et Victimisation: Une Historie de la Sensibilité* (Editions du CERF, 2011), especially 20ff.

22. Josef Früchtl, *The Impertinent Self* (Stanford University Press, 2009), 54, 55.

23. Robert Hughes, *Rome* (Random House, 2011), 12.

24. Propp, *Morphology of the Folktale*, 53.

25. Jeffrey C. Alexander, "Heroes, Presidents, and Politics," *Contexts* 9 (2010), 18. In *The Performance of Politics* (Oxford University Press, 2010), he gets at the threatening nature of strength: "The military can be a noble field of prowess, and from ancient Athens right up until today the civil sphere's survival has, in critical historic moments, depended upon battlefield success. However, military prowess depends on violence and promotes primal hatred, actions and values that are antithetical to the civil behavior and the more universal forms of incorporation that define democratic life" (p. 77).

26. *Saturday Night Live* brilliantly ridiculed McCain's confusion in a skit about an Obama-McCain debate, in which McCain wandered aimlessly around the stage. Clowns can have devastating epidictic effects by commenting on moral dramas without themselves being characters in them.

27. Orrin Klapp, *Symbolic Leaders* (Aldine, 1964), 228, 230.

28. Stephanie A. Shields, *Speaking from the Heart* (Cambridge University Press, 2002).

29. Brian W. Dippie, *Custer's Last Stand: The Anatomy of an American Myth* (University of Nebraska Press, 1976), 10, 4.

30. Max Weber, *Economy and Society* (University of California Press, 1978), 1, 241–243.

31. Quoted in Jonathan Rieder, *The Word of the Lord Is Upon Me* (Harvard University Press, 2008), 149.

32. Michel Foucault, *The Courage of Truth: Lectures at the Collège de France 1983–1984* (Picador, 2011), 15.

33. In the lectures collected in *The Government of Self and Others* and *The Courage of Truth*.

34. George Orwell, *The Road to Wigan Pier* (CreateSpace, 2014), 99.

35. Damien de Blic and Cyril Lemieux, "The Scandal as Test," *Politix* 71 (2005), 22.

36. William Ian Miller, *The Mystery of Courage* (Harvard University Press, 2000), 214.

37. Quoted in Miller, *Mystery*, 215.

38. Thomas de Zengotita, "The Romance of Empire," *Harper's* (July 2003), 32.

39. Memo from Horace Busby to Bill Moyers, 29 July1964, in Mann, *Daisy Petals*, 123.

40. Memo from Fred Dutton to Bill Moyers, 26 September 1964, in Mann, *Daisy Petals*, 146–148.

41. Daniel Kahneman, *Thinking, Fast and Slow* (Farrar, Straus and Giroux, 2011), 256.

42. Kahneman, *Thinking*, 256, 263.

43. Jasper, *Getting Your Way*, 112.

44. C. Fred Alford, *Whistleblowers: Broken Lives and Organizational Power* (Cornell University Press, 2001), 34.

45. Alford, *Whistleblowers*, 60.

46. Ivan Morris, *The Nobility of Failure: Tragic Heroes in the History of Japan* (Farrar, Straus, and Giroux, 1970), 183. He is speaking here of Ōshio Heihachirō's 1837 uprising to protest widespread famine, a romantic failure that inspired novelist Yukio Mishima in 1970 to attempt to trigger a military coup. He took his own life when it failed.

47. Morris, *Nobility*, 285.

48. Michel Foucault, "What Is an Author?" in Foucault, *Language, Counter-Memory, Practice* (Cornell University Press, 1977), 115. Writing, he observes (p. 117) has become a form of sacrifice, even of life itself: this is true of most heroic acts.

49. David B. Morris, *The Culture of Pain* (University of California Press, 1991), 54.

50. R. Tyson Smith, "Pain in the Act: The Meanings of Pain among Professional Wrestlers," *Qualitative Sociology* 31 (2008), 141. In addition to heroic stoicism, he finds pain to connote authenticity to audiences, but also to build solidarity among wrestlers at the same time that it reinforces the pecking order among them.

51. Jonas Barish, *The Anti-Theatrical Prejudice* (University of California Press, 1981), 186.

52. Yael Zerubavel, *Recovered Roots* (University of Chicago Press, 1995), 160.

53. Randall Collins, *Violence* (Princeton University Press, 2008), 383.

54. Heroes can resolve the dirty-hands dilemma by justifying their own violence as a form of vengeance against villains who deserve punishment. Talal Asad observes of suicide bombers, "To save the nation (or to found its state) in confronting a dangerous enemy, it may be necessary to act without being bound by ordinary moral constraints": *On Suicide Bombing* (Columbia University Press, 2007), 63.

55. Kristen Monroe, *The Hand of Compassion* (Princeton University Press, 2004). See Michael Walzer's portrait of early Protestants in *The Revolution of the Saints* (Harvard University Press, 1982).

56. Antipathy toward protestors can denigrate their psychological makeup, denying them any heroic strength or even good intentions. In an intellectual tradition popular in the mid-twentieth century, protestors were ineffectual because they were merely working out their own internal psychological issues, resolving Oedipal complexes or searching for satisfying identities.

57. Craig D. Parks and Asako B. Stone, "The Desire to Expel Unselfish Members from the Group," *Journal of Personality and Social Psychology* 99 (2010):303–310.

58. Wright, *Sixguns and Society*, 57

59. Jane Tompkins, "Fighting Words: Unlearning to Write the Critical Essay," *Georgia Review* 42 (1988), 586, 587.

60. Joanne Esch, "Legitimizing the 'War on Terror': Political Myth in Official-Level Rhetoric," *Political Psychology* 31 (2010), 377.

61. De Blic and Lemieux, "The Scandal as Test."

62. Yael Zerubavel, *Recovered Roots*, 19–20.

63. Thomas Olesen, "Global Political Iconography: The Making of Nelson Mandela," *American Journal of Cultural Sociology* 3 (2015), 51.

Chapter 8

1. Psychologist Jonathan Haidt, reporting his research on how people make moral judgments, was surprised how often his subjects invented victims in order to justify their moral intuitions, even though he "had written the stories carefully to remove all conceivable harm to other people." His respondents found it difficult to condemn actions morally in the absence of victims. *The Righteous Mind* (Pantheon, 2012), 24.

2. Francesca Polletta, *It Was Like a Fever*, chap 5.; Nancy Whittier, "Emotional Strategies," in Goodwin, Jasper, and Polletta, eds., *Passionate Politics.*

3. Martha Nussbaum, *Women and Human Development: The Capabilities Approach* (Cambridge University Press, 2000).

4. Leslie A. Zebrowitz, Judith A. Hall, Nora A. Murphy, and Gillian Rhodes, "Looking Smart and Looking Good: Facial Cues to Intelligence and their Origins," *Personality and Social Psychology Bulletin* 28 (2002):238–249; Andrea L. Sparko and Leslie A. Zebrowitz, "Moderating Effects of Facial Expression and Movement on the Babyface Stereotype," *Journal of Nonverbal Behavior* 35 (2011):243–257.

5. Jack Katz analyzes crying in *How Emotions Work* (University of Chicago Press, 1999), especially as a vocabulary of nonlinguistic communication.

6. Emmanuel Levinas, "Useless Suffering," in Robert Bernasconi and David Wood, eds., *The Provocation of Levinas* (Routledge, 1988), 158.

7. Hollywood movies (*Blood Diamond, The Last King of Scotland, The Constant Gardener*) often play this role of witness to the suffering of victims, isolating them from the viewer in various ways that make them appear more passive, less capable of organizing in their own defense.

8. Arne Johan Vetlesen, *Evil and Human Agency: Understanding Collective Evildoing* (Cambridge University Press, 2005), 204.

9. Vetlesen, *Evil*, 218.

10. Vetlesen, *Evil*, 137.

11. Susan Sontag, *Regarding the Pain of Others* (Farrar, Straus and Giroux, 2003), 12.

12. Franz Fanon, *The Wretched of the Earth* (Grove Press, 2004), 51.

13. Sontag, *Regarding the Pain of Others*, 40.

14. Sontag, *Regarding the Pain of Others*, 42.

15. Sontag, *Regarding the Pain of Others*, 44, 45.

16. Sontag, *Regarding the Pain of Others*, 58.

17. Sontag, *Regarding the Pain of Others*, 117, 118.

18. Susan Sontag, *On Photography* (Farrar, Straus and Giroux, 1977).

19. Sontag, *Regarding the Pain of Others*, 111.

20. Philippe Ariès, *Centuries of Childhood: A Social History of Family Life* (Random House, 1962), 129. He also points (p. 360) to the emerging practice that, in the absence of a priest, the youngest child should say grace before a meal—a custom which survives today in many Christian families. The older tradition had been that any young boy might do it, but now the idea emerged that the youngest child was the purest, closest to God, able to officiate at this central family ritual. A critic of Ariès, Shulamith Shahar, *Childhood in the Middle Ages* (Routledge, 1990), 18, 101, suggests that children had been seen as innocent and pure in medieval Europe as well, in a debate that does not affect our argument.

21. Taken by itself as a word outside any social context, "victim" tends to be rated as slightly immoral in affect-control surveys, perhaps because there are so many types of victims, both good and bad. In the rhetorical settings that interest us, good victims are more useful. See Bergstrand and Jasper, "Villains, Victims, and Heroes"

22. Sujatha Fernandez, *Mobilizing Stories* (Oxford University Press, 2017), 86.

23. A case at Yale University in 2018 used all the old tricks: Vivian Wang and Cheryl Weinstock, "Yale Student Found Not Guilty in Rape Trial," *New York Times*, 7 March 2018.

24. Paul Hoggett, *Politics, Identity, and Emotion* (Paradigm, 2009), 164.

25. Ron Eyerman, *The Cultural Sociology of Political Assassination* (Palgrave Macmillan, 2011), 31.

26. Robert D. Benford and Scott Hunt, "Dramaturgy and Social Movements," *Sociological Inquiry* 62 (1992), 40. Also see William A. Gamson, *Talking Politics* (Cambridge University Press, 1992) and James M. Jasper, "Constructing Indignation: Anger Dynamics in Protest Movements," *Emotion Review* 6 (2014):202–207. We address the construction of public characters in movements in "Character Work in Social Movements."

27. Hugh Gusterson, *Drone: Remote Control Warfare* (MIT Press, 2016).

28. Robert D. Hare, *Without Conscience: The Disturbing World of the Psychopaths among Us* (Simon and Schuster, 1993), 43. In his analysis of a murderer's confession, Jack Katz also notices the man's efforts to cast himself as a victim, in *How Emotions Work*, 280.

29. In her study of Ohio Revco's massive Medicaid fraud, Diane Vaughan observed that Revco found a number of reasons for blaming the state's welfare department, which it said was not processing legitimate claims in a timely way: *Controlling Unlawful Organizational Behavior* (University of Chicago Press, 1983).

30. Alexander and Marguerite Mitscherlich, *The Inability to Mourn* (Grove Press, 1984), 64, also see 15. Daniel Goldhagen created a furor by puncturing this comfortable epidictic effort to assign all blame to Hitler and his tiny circle: *Hitler's Willing Executioners* (Knopf, 1996).

31. Martha Minow, *Between Vengeance and Forgiveness* (Beacon Press, 1998).

32. Philip Gourevitch, *We Wish To Inform You that Tomorrow We Will Be Killed with Our Families* (Farrar, Straus and Giroux, 1998).

33. Marie Beatrice Umutesi, *Surviving the Slaughter: The Ordeal of a Rwandan Refugee in Zaire* (University of Wisconsin Press, 2004); Rene Lemarchand, *The Dynamics of Violence in Central Africa* (University of Pennsylvania Press, 2009).

34. Jack Katz, *How Emotions Work*, chap. 1.

35. The importance of imposing a beginning and end on the infinite flow of events—"emplotment"—was one of the key insights of narrative theory: Hayden White, *Metahistory* (Johns Hopkins University Press, 1973); Edward W. Said, *Beginnings* (Johns Hopkins University Press, 1975).

36. Luca Andrighetto, Silvia Mari, Chiara Volpato, and Burin Behluli, "Reducing Competitive Victimhood in Kosovo: The Role of Extended Contact and Common Ingroup Identity," *Political Psychology* 33 (2012):513–529.

37. Erving Goffman, "On Cooling the Mark Out," *Psychiatry* 15 (November 1952), 455.

38. Alyson Cole, *The Cult of True Victimhood* (Stanford University Press, 2007), 6. The focus of backlash politics may be on efforts to redress that supposed victimhood through efforts like affirmative action, when there is no real victimhood in the first place: Arlie Hochschild, *Strangers in Their Own Land*.

39. Candace Clark, *Misery and Company: Sympathy in Everyday Life* (University of Chicago Press, 1997), 13, 256, 257.

Chapter 9

1. Lori A. Allen, "The Polyvalent Politics of Martyr Commemorations in the Palestinian *Intifada*," *History and Memory* 18 (2006), 117.

2. Quoted in Laleh Khalili, *Heroes and Martyrs of Palestine* (Cambridge University Press, 2007), 103. We rely on her analysis of *sumud* here (pp. 99–103), along with Sophie Richter-Devroe, "Palestinian Women's Everyday Resistance," *Journal of International Women's Studies* 12 (2011):32–46; and Anna Johansson and Stellan Vinthagen, "Dimensions of Everyday Resistance," *Journal of Political Power* 10 (2015):109–139.

3. Mahmoud Darwish, *Journal of an Ordinary Grief* (Archipelago Books, 2010), 76.

4. Paul R. Brass, "Victims, Heroes or Martyrs? Partition and the Problem of Memorialization in Contemporary Sikh History," *Sikh Formations* 2 (2006), 19.

5. Mark Juergensmeyer, *Terror in the Mind of God*, 3rd edn. (University of California Press, 2003), 162. Religious narratives tend to emphasize heroes and villains: "When a struggle becomes sacralized, incidents that might previously have been considered minor skirmishes or slight differences of understanding are elevated to monumental proportions" (p. 166).

6. Apostolides, *Héroïsme et Victimisation*, 65.

7. Apostolides, *Héroïsme et Victimisation*, 62, 23. We could write a volume on the Catholic church's character work through the ages. Those who established new Catholic institutions are favorite candidates for canonization, and their stories reinforce and spread the orders they found.

8. Gerald Vizenor, *Manifest Manners: Narratives on Postindian Survivance* (University of Nebraska Press, 1999).

9. William Ian Miller, *The Mystery of Courage* (Harvard University Press, 2000), 118, 119.

10. Mary Beth Rose, *Gender and Heroism in Early Modern English Literature* (University of Chicago Press, 2001), xv.

11. Campbell, *Hero with a Thousand Faces*, 37.

12. Two works on the concept of resistance are Jocelyn A. Hollander and Rachel L. Einwohner, "Conceptualizing Resistance," *Sociological Forum* 19 (2004):533–554; and Stellan Vinthagen and Anna Johansson, "'Everyday Resistance': Exploration of a Concept and its Theories," *Resistance Studies* 1 (2013):1–46.

13. Quoted in Sujatha Fernandes, *Curated Stories* (Oxford University Press, 2017), 65.

14. Robert D. Benford, "Controlling Narratives and Narratives as Control within Social Movements," in Joseph E. Davis, ed., *Stories of Change: Narrative and Social Movements* (State University of New York Press, 2002), 58. In this book about narratives, we find plenty of heroes, victims, and villains who make those narratives appealing.

15. Randall Collins, *Interaction Ritual Chains* (Princeton University Press, 2004), 132.

16. Jennifer Lois, *Heroic Efforts: The Emotional Culture of Search and Rescue Volunteers* (NYU Press, 2003), 144.

17. Lois, *Heroic Efforts*, 144.

18. Max Plowman, quoted in Miller, *Mystery of Courage*, 190. Similarly, rescuing the fallen—often seen in World War I as a form of malingering—has gained prominence in modern battle, which offers "less opportunity for individual heroic acts in the old style," due to the remoteness of the enemy (Miller, *Mystery of Courage*, 123). More U.S. Congressional Medals of Honor are given for rescuing comrades than for killing the enemy.

19. Nancy Whittier, "Emotional Strategies: The Collective Reconstruction and Display of Oppositional Emotions in the Movement against Child Sexual Abuse," in Goodwin, Jasper, and Polletta, eds., *Passionate Politics*, 233. Her argument is elaborated in *The Politics of Child Sexual Abuse* (Oxford University Press, 2009).

20. Whittier, "Emotional Strategies," 238.

21. Whittier, "Oppositional Emotions," 244.

22. Quoted in Whittier, "Emotional Strategies," 240.

23. Whittier, "Emotional Strategies," 244.

24. John J. Mearsheimer and Stephen M. Walt, *The Israel Lobby and U.S. Foreign Policy* (Farrar, Straus and Giroux, 2007), 81, 83. They also demonstrate the assiduous efforts to demonize the Palestinians, especially Yasser Arafat.

25. Jocelyn A. Hollander, "Vulnerability and Dangerousness: The Construction of Gender through Conversation about Violence," *Gender and Society* 15 (2001), 87. It might alternatively have been titled, "the construction of victims through conversation about gender." Also see Hollander, "Resisting Vulnerability: The Social Reconstruction of Gender in Interaction," *Social Problems* 49 (2002):474–496; and Hille Koskela, "'Bold Walk and Breakings': Women's Spatial Confidence versus Fear of Violence," *Gender, Place and Culture* 4 (1997):301–320. There is also a large literature on rape victims such as P. A. Frazier, "Victim Attributions and Post-Rape Trauma," *Journal of Personality and Social Psychology* 59 (1990):298–304; and Patricia Yancey Martin, *Rape Work: Victims, Gender, and Emotions in Organization and Community Context* (Routledge, 2005).

26. Jocelyn Viterna, *Women in War* (Oxford University Press, 2013). Miranda Alison similarly suggests that the use of women in the Israeli army implies that the nation's situation is urgent and moral: *Women and Political Violence* (Routledge, 2009), 116.

27. Marguerite Guzman Bouvard, *Revolutionizing Motherhood* (SR Books, 1994/2004), 8.

28. Guzman Bouvard, *Revolutionizing Motherhood*, 79.

29. Peter Popham, *The Lady and the Peacock* (The Experiment Press, 2012); Hans-Bernd Zöllner, *The Beast and the Beauty* (Regiospectra, 2012).

30. Roger Cohen, "This Is Not a Morality Tale," *New York Times*, 26 November 2017.

31. Phil Brown and Faith T. Ferguson, "'Making a Big Stink': Women's Work, Women's Relationships, and Toxic Waste Activism," *Gender & Society* 9 (1995), 162.

32. Ilena Rodriguez, *Women, Guerillas and Love: Understanding War in Central America* (University of Minnesota Press, 1996).

Chapter 10

1. Robert Nisbet, *Prejudices* (Harvard University Press, 1982), 152–158.

2. Ronald N. Jacobs, "The Problem with Tragic Narratives," *Qualitative Sociology* 24 (2001), 229, 238.

3. George L. Mosse, *Fallen Soldiers* (Oxford University Press, 1990), especially chapter 5, "The Cult of the Fallen Soldier."

4. Christina Simko, *The Politics of Consolation* (Oxford University Press, 2015), 202. Tragic narratives, she argues, are a way to deal with trauma and move forward despite moral complexities.

5. Barry Schwartz, *Abraham Lincoln in the Post-Heroic Era* (University of Chicago Press, 2008), 6.

6. Zeno Franco and Philip Zimbardo, "The Banality of Heroism," *Greater Good*, Fall–Winter (2006–2007), 34.

7. Schwartz, *Abraham Lincoln*, 189.

8. Akiko Hashimoto, *The Long Defeat* (Oxford University Press, 2015), 17.

9. Deborah A. Stone, "Causal Stories and the Formation of Policy Agendas," *Political Science Quarterly* 104 (1989):281–300.

10. Didier Fassin and Richard Rechtman, *The Empire of Trauma* (Princeton University Press, 2009). Other works of what has been dubbed "victimology" include Kristin Bumiller, *Civil Rights Society: The Social Construction of Victims* (Johns Hopkins University Press, 1988); Pascal Bruckner, *La Tentation de l'Innocence* (Grasset, 1995); Guillaume Erner, *La Société des Victimes* (La Découverte, 2006); and Gilles William Goldnadel, *Les Martyrocrates: Dérives et Impostures de l'Ideologie Victimaire* (Plon, 2004).

11. Jeffrey C. Alexander, "Toward a Theory of Cultural Trauma," in Alexander et al., *Cultural Trauma and Collective Identity* (University of California Press, 2004), 27, 22.

12. Ewa Bogalska-Martin, ed., *Victimes du Présent, Victimes du Passé: Vers la Sociologie des Victimes* (L'Harmattan, 2004), 11.

13. Neil Ferguson, Mark Burgess, and Ian Hollywood, "Who Are the Victims? Victimhood Experiences in Postagreement Northern Ireland," *Political Psychology* 31 (2010), 875.

14. Fassin and Rechtman, *The Empire of Trauma*, chap. 4; and Allan Horwitz, *PTSD* (Johns Hopkins University Press, 2018).

15. Stéphane Latté, "Les 'Victimes': La Formation d'une Catégorie Sociale Improbable et ses Usages dan l'Action Collective," doctoral thesis, Ecole des Hautes Etudes en Sciences Sociales, Paris, 2008.

16. Daniel Cefaï, *Pourquoi se Mobilise-t-on?* (La Découverte, 2007), 133.

17. Nan Goodman, *Shifting the Blame* (Routledge, 2000), 161. She also describes a pre-industrial sense of blame, in which one's superiors in a social hierarchy are responsible for what happens to a person, whether or not they were negligent in helping to cause an accident or other harm. Because of their strength, characters are fused into the social ladder.

18. Quoted in Christina Simko, "Rhetorics of Suffering: September 11 Commemorations as Theodicy," *American Sociological Review* 77 (2012), 887. Simko describes character work behind heroes, villains, and victims, but in her theoretical elaboration these disappear in favor of narrative genres.

19. Philip Kennicott, "The 9/11 Memorial Museum Doesn't Just Display Artifacts, It Ritualizes Grief on a Loop," *Washington Post*, 7 June 2014.

20. Simko, "Rhetorics of Suffering," 889.

21. Annemarie Goldstein Jutel, *Putting a Name to It: Diagnosis in Contemporary Society* (Johns Hopkins University Press, 2011), 3.

22. Michel Foucault, *Abnormal: Lectures at the Collège de France 1974–1975* (Picador, 2003), 19–21.

23. Michel Foucault, *History of Madness* (Routledge, 2006), 96.

24. Stanley Cohen, *Folk Devils and Moral Panics* (MacGibbon and Kee, 1972), 9–10.

25. Michel Foucault, *Abnormal*, 119.

26. Foucault, *Abnormal*, 35.

27. Nicola Beisel, *Imperiled Innocents* (Princeton University Press, 1997).

28. Michael P. Young, *Bearing Witness against Sin* (University of Chicago Press, 2007).

29. Julian McAllister Groves, "Animal Rights and the Politics of Emotion," in Goodwin, Jasper, and Polletta, eds., *Passionate Politics*, 215, 217. Also Groves, *Hearts and Minds* (Temple University Press, 1997).

30. Hilary J. Ramsden, "Clowns, Buffoons and the Killing Laugh," *European Journal of Humour Research* 3 (2015):145–163; Paul Routledge, "Sensuous Solidarities," *Antipode* 44 (2012):428–452.

31. Lisa Wedeen, *Ambiguities of Domination: Politics, Rhetoric, and Symbols in Contemporary Syria* (University of Chicago Press, 1999), 24.

32. "The Song Dynasty," *The Economist*, 12–18 March 2016.

33. Hochschild, *Strangers in Their Own Land*, 224.

34. Simko, *The Politics of Consolation*, 203.

Conclusion

1. ACT UP meeting, Cooper Union, 16 September 1991. Fieldnotes by JMJ.

2. Kathleen Hall Jamieson, *Eloquence in an Electronic Age* (Oxford University Press, 1988). Political advertising, whose history she traces, can distort the facts, and her solution is for the news media to check and correct them: *Packaging the Presidency* (Oxford University Press, 1996). She then traces the breakdown of the news media in Jamieson and Joseph N. Cappella, *Echo Chamber* (Oxford University Press, 2008).

3. Ernst Cassirer, "Judaism and the Modern Political Myths," in *Symbol, Myth and Culture* (Yale University Press, 1979), 236.

Appendix

1. Murray S. Davis, *What's So Funny?* (University of Chicago Press, 1993), observes, "Sociologists can use the way humor deconstructs the social world to comprehend more precisely how people have constructed it" (314). Peter L. Berger adopts the same approach in *Redeeming Laughter* (de Gruyter, 1997), possibly the least funny book about humor not written in German.

2. Michael Apter describes humor as a paratelic mode, in contrast to telic modes aimed at goals: "A Structural Phenomenology of Play," in John H. Kerr and Michael J. Apter, eds., *Adult Play* (Swets and Zeitlinger, 1991). But this is too narrow; humor often has the goal of character assassination. Charles Gruner goes to the opposite extreme to view all humor as an effort to assert our superiority over others: *The Game of Humor: A Comprehensive Theory of Why We Laugh* (Transaction, 2000); also Michael Billig, *Laughter and Ridicule* (Sage, 2005). Michael Andrew Phillips-Anderson distinguishes rhetorical humor, intended to change the beliefs of audiences, from other types in "A Theory of Rhetorical Humor in American Political Discourse," Ph.D. thesis, University of Maryland, 2007; also Quentin Skinner, "Political Rhetoric and the Role of Ridicule," in Kari Palonen, Tuija Pulkkinen, and José Maria Rosales, eds., *The Ashgate Research Companion to the Politics of Democratization in Europe* (Ashgate, 2008).

3. David Shulman, *The King and the Clown in South Indian Myth and Poetry* (Princeton University Press, 1985), 204.

4. Beatrice K. Otto, *Fools Are Everywhere: The Court Jester around the World* (University of Chicago Press, 2001), 32. A China scholar, she was delighted to find that the court jester is "very much a universal character, more or less interchangeable regardless of the time or culture in which he happens to cavort—the same techniques, the same functions, the same license" (xvi).

5. Walter Kaiser, *Praisers of Folly: Erasmus, Rabelais, Shakespeare* (Harvard University Press, 1963), 126.

6. Walter Kaiser remarks that "The Praise of Folly" is better translated as "Folly's Praise of Folly," in other words as undermining its own comic pretensions: *Praisers of Folly*, 36.

7. Lewis Hyde, *Trickster Makes This World* (Farrar, Straus and Giroux, 1998), 7, 6. He suggests that tricksters are almost always male because in their societies men were inevitably the players, those active or strong enough to matter.

8. Hyde, *Trickster*, 10.

9. Wendy Griswold, "The Devil's Techniques," *American Sociological Review* 48 (1983), 670. She attributes the long character campaign that went into making the Devil so evil to the Jews' time in exile, when they were influenced by Zoroastrian dualism.

10. Griswold, "Devil's Techniques," 671.

11. Paul Radin, *The Trickster* (Schocken, 1972), 133, speaking of Winnebago trickster myths.

12. Batman's powers come from his wealth and the technologies it buys; the Joker was transformed by an industrial accident: neither has supernatural powers.

13. Ronald N. Jacobs and Philip Smith, "Romance, Irony, and Solidarity," *Sociological Theory* 15 (1997), 75. On the parallel between jesters and intellectuals, they cite a nineteenth-century work by Dr. [John] Doran, *The History of Court Fools* (Haskell, 1966/1858).

14. Teela Sanders, "Controllable Laughter: Managing Sex Work through Humour," *Sociology* 38 (2004):273–291. From a broadly social perspective, sociologists frame prostitutes as victims, but in their interactions with clients they are "professionals" in charge.

15. James C. Scott, *Domination and the Arts of Resistance* (Yale, 1990). The weak can also speak to the strong through humor: Sean Zwagerman, *Wit's End: Women's Humor as Rhetorical and Performative Strategy* (University of Pittsburgh Press, 2010).

16. David M. Bozzini, "The Catch-22 of Resistance: Jokes and the Political Imagination of Eritrean Conscripts," *Africa Today* 60 (2013):38–64.

17. Wolfgang Zucker contrasts the disintegrated character of the clown with the hyperintegrated self of hero tropes: "The Clown as the Lord of Disorder," in Conrad Hyers, ed., *Holy Laughter* (Seabury Press, 1969).

18. On collective identities as necessary fictions see Aidan McGarry and James M. Jasper, eds., *The Identity Dilemma* (Temple University Press, 2015).

19. Two recent works on humor and protest: Janjira Sombatpoonsiri, *Humor and Nonviolent Struggle in Serbia* (Syracuse University Press, 2015), and Altug Yalcintas, ed., *Creativity and Humour in Occupy Movements* (Palgrave Macmillan, 2015).

INDEX

For the benefit of digital users, indexed terms that span two pages (e.g., 52–53) may, on occasion, appear on only one of those pages.

benefactor (character type), 193
betrayal, 146
binary codes, 19–20, 21–22, 34–35
Black Panthers, 204
blame, 113, 140, 144–46, 156, 203, 204,
    207–9, 238, 242
bodies, 198
Bouazizi, Mohamed, 215, 218
bravery, 165, 169, 172–73, 179, 180
British Empire, 154
Brown, John, 146–47
buffoons, 261
Bush, George W., 84, 101–2, 103–4,
    111–12, 134–35, 184–85, 191, 201,
    242, 246–47
business leaders, 75

capabilities, 197
capitalism, 107–9, 190
caricature, 5, 47, 50, 51
Carnegie, Andrew, 107
Carter, Jimmy, 150–51
Ceaușescu, Nicolae, 248
CEOs, 108–9
Chancer, Lynn, 116
character work, 169; reflexive effects, 5–
    6; tradeoffs of, 9
characters, categorical, 5;
    changing understanding of, 87;
    circumstantial, 5; definition of, 2;
    inevitability of, 255–56; inferred,
    22–23, 42–43, 72, 73–75; main
    types of, 3–4; minor, 4; national, 31;
    "round" and "flat", 23–24, 25–26,
    49–50, 116
charisma, 180–81
children, 197, 202, 209, 245
Cicero, 31, 156–57
cities, 136
civilization, 19
Clandestine Insurgent Rebel Clown
    Army, 246–47
class, socio-economic, 76, 80, 136, 168,
    244. See also status
Clinton, Hillary, 62–63, 66, 112,
    125, 180

clothing, 76–77
clowns, 151, 182, 246–47, 260, 262–66
coercion, 32–33, 133, 140
cognitive biases, 184–85
collective memory, 45, 98–99, 105–6,
    206, 237–38
comedy, 38, 154. See also humor; irony
comic books, 167, 253–54
commemoration, 234, 242
compassion, 199, 201–2, 209, 249
compassion fatigue, 201
competence, 77–78, 86, 175
confidence, 173, 183–85, 189
conformity, 160–61
consequences -unintended, 238
conspiracy theories, 127–28, 131, 156
containment, 140
contempt, 90–91, 150
context, historical, 65–66
conversion, 134
Cooper, Anderson, 85
corporations, 107–9, 143. See also
    institutions, as character workers
courage, 218–19
cowboys. See Western films and novels
criminals, 79–80
crying, 197–98. See also emotion:
    display of
Cuddy, Amy, 78, 79, 80
culture, 251–52
Custer, George, 180

danger society, 242
dangerous spaces, 136
David (Old Testament figure), 43–45, 46
de Kock, Eugene, 162
death, 166, 187–88, 213, 241
DeGeneres, Ellen, 85, 266
degradation ceremonies, 117–18
dehumanization, 137–38
demagoguery, 153
democracy, 34–35
demonization, 125, 129–31, 137–38;
    backfiring, 130
depression, 83
Despicable Me (film), 148

developmental psychology, 80–81
Devil, the, 141, 262
disgust, 77
dishonesty, 127
donor (character role), 21, 166, 181,
    192, 193
Dower, John, 130–31, 150
drama, 36–37; characters in, 17–18;
    medieval, 262; traditional, 24–25

Edison, Thomas, 175–76
Egypt (ancient), 261
Eichmann, Adolph, 159–60, 162.
    |See also Arendt, Hannah;
    Holocaust; Nazis
El Salvador, 227–28
emotion, 8, 25, 27, 30, 41, 65, 66–
    67, 83–84; and mobilization, 225;
    aroused by characters, 87–89, 251–
    52; characteristic and structural, 88;
    displays of, 180, 197–98, 245–46;
    effect of character work on, 7; of
    victimhood and heroism, 224
empathy, 112
endurance, 90, 227–31, 240; heroes of,
    214, 218–20
enemies, 134–36
energy, emotional, 222
envy, 77, 79
EPA (evaluation, potency, activity) space,
    85–86, 88
epidictic, 30–31, 45–46, 156–57;
    political, 32–33
epithets, 35
Erdoğan, Recep Tayyip, 248
ethnocentrism, 103
evil, 138–39, 140–41
example, heroes of, 216
expectations, 86–88, 118–19. See also
    audience
experts, 174–75
extremism, 129

faces, 74, 75–76
fascism, 177, 234–35, 249
fear, 173–74, 179

feminism, 230–31
fiction, 96
film, 148, 166, 174, 193–94, 232–33, 260.
    See also Western movies and novels
Fine, Gary Alan, 2, 105–6, 118, 119,
    146, 175
Fiske, Susan, 77–78, 79, 86
flooding out, 58
folk devils, 244
Ford, Henry, 108
foreigners, 136, 137
Forster, E. M., 23–24, 27
Foucault, Michel, 181, 187, 221, 243,
    244, 245
framing, 206. See also strategy:
    rhetorical
France, 240–41
French Revolution, 46, 99

Galaxy Quest (film), 259
Game of Thrones, 71, 261
Gandhi, Mahatma, 221
Garibaldi, Giuseppe, 94–95,
    96–97, 99–100
Gates, Bill, 193
gender, 11–12, 46, 56, 57–58, 62–63, 66,
    82–85, 92, 112, 153, 156–57, 197, 213,
    214, 218–19, 227–30, 239, 240, 246;
    and war, 102–3
generosity, 189
genocide, 206–7, 229. See also Holocaust
Gestalt psychology, 73
gods, 182–83
Goffman, Erving, 56–58, 83, 92–93, 208
Goldwater, Barry, 111–12, 141–42, 151
goodness, 175. See also morality
gossip, 116–17; political, 116–17, 118
government. See institutions
Goya, Francisco, 199–200
graffiti, 52–53
Grant, Ulysses S., 171
gratitude, 168–69
greed, 208
Greeks, ancient, 10–11, 28, 33, 98, 99,
    152, 169, 181, 216. See also Aristotle;
    Hercules

loyalty, 176
Lucretia, 216–17, 218
Luther, Martin, 189

Machiavelli, Niccolò, 173
Madoff, Bernie, 5, 123–25
Mandela, Nelson, 194, 219–20, 233
Marcos, Ferdinand, 65, 177
martyrdom, 166, 168–69, 185–188, 213, 214–17, 218, 221
Marxism, 168
McCain, John, 35, 164–65, 179
meaning -and suffering, 200
meaning, 40–41
media, 114–16
medicalization, 241, 243–44, 245
mental illness, 141, 225–26
Milosevic, Slobodan, 159
minion (definition), 148
minion defense, 159–61, 162, 183
minions (movie characters), 148
mobilization, 9–10, 12, 89
mobs, 151–53, 154–56
moral panics, 115, 139, 244–45
morale, 223
morality, 3, 29, 31, 38–39, 41, 59, 74, 77, 78–79, 81–83, 85–86, 92, 133–34, 141, 169–70, 188, 243–44, 263; collapsed, 161
music, 66–69
Mussolini, Benito, 46, 177
myth, epic, folktale, 8

narrative, 20
nation-building, 176–77
nationalism, 12, 97, 98–99, 100–1, 155, 177, 187–88, 201–2, 234–36, 237, 248–49. *See also* fascism
Nazis, 159–61, 189, 205–6. *See also* Holocaust; World War II
negligence, 241–42
news media, 136
Nietzsche, Friedrich, 216
nonviolence, 221. *See also* strategy
normality, 6–7, 221–22, 243–44, 245
norms, social, 95
nostalgia, 136–37

O'Donnell, Rosie, 266
Obama, Barack, 35, 82, 83–84, 112, 125, 127, 169, 173, 179, 180, 242, 249
obedience, 176
optimism, 184–85
orator, 30–31, 119, 260. *See also* rhetoric; rhetorical strategy
Orban, Viktor, 233, 248
ordinary personology, 72

outrage, 116, 205. *See also* anger
outsider status, 19
pain, 199
painting, 47–49. *See also* art; imagery; Italian renaissance
Palestinians, 158, 213–14
passivity, 11–12, 57, 198, 202, 203, 207, 219, 227. *See also* activity level; initiative; weakness
Pearl Harbor, 130–31, 158, 172, 191. *See also* World War II
performance, 33–34
persuasion, 29–30, 32–33, 95–96, 133, 219
photography, 201
pity, 90–91, 110, 205
plot, 24
police, 65–66
politics, 27, 60, 84–85, 87, 106, 129, 237, 252; American, 209, 226; American compared to European, 143–44; as site of corruption, 143; electoral, 75–76, 81, 85–86, 111–12, 125, 150–51, 154, 164–65, 179, 183–84, 190; of victimhood, 208; rejection of, 250
pollution (moral), 188
posters, 53–54
posture, 57–58, 63, 65
power, 3, 12, 45–46, 58, 60, 63, 84–85, 128–29, 161; military, 176–77, 183–88, 188, 261, 263–65; social, 33–34. *See also* activity level; competence; status; strength
powerlessness, 198
predispositions, 80–81
pride, 77
priming, 74

problem of theodicy, 182–83
propaganda, 7, 40, 50, 101, 102–3.
    See also strategy: rhetorical
prophets, 180–82
Propp, Vladímir, 21, 166, 178, 181
protestors, 84–85, 91, 106, 109–10,
    111, 114
psychology, 25, 50, 141. *See also* Gestalt
    psychology
public relations, 31–32
Putin, Vladimir, 65, 82, 129–30, 248

race, 82
racism, 112, 139–40, 149
radical-flank effect, 140
Ramses II, 45
rape, 204, 227–28
rationality, 41, 246; of victims, 202–3
Reagan, Ronald, 24–25, 27, 65,
    150–51, 170
reasoned debate, 255–56
reconciliation, 162
religion, 40–41, 42–43, 47, 59, 65–66,
    129, 131, 143–44, 154–55, 166–67,
    168, 202, 216, 217–18, 221, 229,
    233–34, 249–50
reparations, 206–7
reputation, 2, 79–80, 132–34; content
    and scope of, 104; contested, 106–
    7; fragility of, 78–79, 87; impact
    of, 106; mediated, 105–6;
    political, 98; scope of, 104–5;
    symbolic, 105
resilience, 185
resistance, 199, 204, 214, 261, 265;
    emotions of, 224; gendered, 227–29;
    heroes of, 220–21; violent, 213, 227–28
responsibility, 113, 239
retaliation, 162, 190–91
rhetoric, 28–30, 95–96. *See also* audience;
    orator
rhetorical anxiety, 33, 57, 152,
    173–74, 252–53
ridicule, 150–51, 156–57, 246–47
risk, 92, 192, 215–16, 238, 242

Rome, 42, 45, 46, 47–48, 216–17, 252.
    See also Cicero
Roosevelt, Franklin D., 86, 191
rumor, 118–19
Rwanda, 144, 206–8

sacrifice, 165, 236–37
sages, 192
sainthood, 216, 217–18
satirists, 261
scandal, 117, 118
scapegoats, 162
Schwartz, Barry, 98–99, 236
sculpture, 41–45, 177; defaced, 46;
    democratic, 46. *See also* imagery
secrecy, 127
self-control, 140
self-righteousness, 189
selfishness, 142–43
sexual orientation, 85
Shakespeare, William, 17–18, 36, 72, 107,
    127, 138, 203
shame, 198
Sikhs, 215–16
sincerity, 172
sinners, 245
size, 62–63, 150–51
sleeping giants, 89, 101, 134–35, 136,
    165–66, 190–91
Snow, Jon, 71–72
Snowden, Edward, 106–7
social movements, 89, 109–10, 197, 205,
    221–22, 223, 224–25, 237
Sontag, Susan, 141, 199–201
South Africa, apartheid-era, 162
Spade, Sam, 188
Spiderman, 171
St. George, 42–43
Star Wars (films), 166, 193
state role in defining victims, 240–41
status, 79, 150. *See also* class, socio-
    economic; power
stereotypes, 207
stock characters, 35–39.
    See also drama

storytelling, 27

strategy, 137–38, 179–80, 184–85, 206, 251–52; rhetorical, 157–58, 161–62, 163, 209–10, 224–25

strength, 25–26, 37–38, 44–45, 49, 52–53, 56, 59, 74, 80, 81–82, 89–90, 112, 132–34, 138–39, 161, 169, 170, 173–74, 175, 184, 188, 190, 197, 215, 219, 260, 262; combining multiple sources of, 177; moral, 216; physical, 178

structuralism, 21, 24, 34

subordination, 57

suffering, 198; represented, 199–201; structural, 204

suicide, 218

superheroes, 167

supporters, 193

survivor (as role), 214

technology -victims of, 195

television, 200–1, 224

terrorism, 129–30, 140, 145–46, 157, 158, 216

Thomas, Clarence, 209

Tompkins, Jane, 11, 170, 190–91

trade unions, 241

tradeoffs, 7

tragic narratives, 234

trauma, 238–39, 240

trials; legal, 204, 240

tricksters, 262

Trump, Donald, 27, 111–12, 125, 127, 164–65, 169, 170, 227, 233, 249, 252–53, 264–65

Trumpeldor, Yosef, 187–88

trust, 77, 84–85

truth commissions, 162

uncertainty about character, 6

underdogs, 226–27

values, social, 95

Vetlesen, Arne Johan, 161, 198

victimhood, 9; accepted, 213; national, 100–1; "evil", 204

victims, 58, 90–91, 110, 111, 115; categorical and circumstantial, 208–9; compensated, 113–14; necessity of, 195; secondary, 239–40; villainless, 238–39

video, 54–55

Vietnam War, 200–1, 220–21

villain-minion dilemma, 157–58, 161–62

villains, 21, 34, 89, 110; active, 127; as "crazy", 141–42; claiming victimhood, 205–6; constructed, 126–27; greatest of, 138; in children's literature, 26–27; irrational, 139; national, 101; self-identified, 127, 131–34; strengths of, 126, 131–34; typology of, 128; utility of, 147; with heroic potential, 134

violence, 176–77, 199, 217–18. *See also* resistance; strength

visual communication, 59–66. *See also* film; imagery; sculpture; television

vocal cues, 66

war, 101–4, 125, 134–36, 176, 205, 234–35

war photography, 200–1

warmth, 77–78, 86

Washington, George, 146, 171, 220–21

Western movies and novels, 19–20, 84, 153, 169, 170, 185, 189–91, 232–33

whistleblowers, 185–86

women's movement, 197

World War I, 54, 135, 223, 234

World War II, 10, 130–31, 135, 150, 160–61, 174, 186, 191, 192, 237–38

wrestling, 7, 25–26, 37–38

Xi Jinping, 248